£14 95

JOHN WILKES

For Lisa

John Wilkes
The Lives of a Libertine

JOHN SAINSBURY

ASHGATE

Published by
Ashgate Publishing Limited
Gower House
Croft Road
Aldershot
Hampshire GU11 3HR
England

Ashgate Publishing Company
Suite 420
101 Cherry Street
Burlington, VT 05401-4405
USA

01252 331 551

Ashgate website: http://www.ashgate.com

British Library Cataloguing in Publication Data
Sainsbury, John
 John Wilkes: the lives of a libertine
 1.Wilkes, John, 1727–1797 2.Radicals – Great Britain –
 Biography 3.Great Britain – Politics and government – 1760–1789
 941'.073'092

Library of Congress Cataloging-in-Publication Data
Sainsbury, John, 1946–
 John Wilkes: the lives of a libertine / John Sainsbury.
  p. cm.
 Includes bibliographical references (p.) and index.
 ISBN 0-7546-5626-8 (alk. paper)
 1. Wilkes, John, 1727–1797. 2. Politicians – Great Britain –
Biography. 3. Whig Party (Great Britain) – History – 18th century. 4.
Great Britain – Politics and government – 1760–1789. 5. Libertinism –
Great Britain – History – 18th century. I. Title.

 DA512.W6S35 2006
 941.07'3092–dc22

2005029879

ISBN 0 7546 5626 8

Typeset in Palatino by Pat FitzGerald, West Sussex

Printed and bound in Great Britain by MPG Books, Bodmin, Cornwall

Contents

List of Illustrations

Foreword

by Tony Banks, Lord Stratford

Professor Sainsbury's biography of John Wilkes steers a careful and steady course between admirers and assailants. However, I am an unapologetic admirer since for me, in eighteenth-century politics, three names stand out above all others: Pitt the Younger, Charles James Fox and John Wilkes.

Pitt was the most successful politician of the trio but it is Fox and Wilkes who catch the imagination. Both shared many similarities, particularly in the notoriety of their private lives. Both were hugely popular and radical within the context of their own time and were viewed with great suspicion by much of the political establishment of the day, whom they alternately courted and confronted. Both were political giants of the century but ultimately it is John Wilkes who has proved the more historically significant.

As John Sainsbury points out, in his day Wilkes was a radical, rabble-rousing, duel fighting, political adventurer described by George III as 'that devil Wilkes'. He spent most of his life in debt and some of it in prison or exile. Despite all this, or maybe because of it, he became one of the most celebrated politicians of that remarkable century. I suppose it was the sheer dynamism of Wilkes and his willingness to live dangerously which makes him such a fascinating character to this day and meriting regular re-evaluation.

Whatever his failings Wilkes remains a major figure in British political history. He was involved in campaigns that secured the right of duly elected MPs to take their seats and established the reporting of Parliamentary debates in the press. He was one of the founders of the mass radical movement in Britain which led to the 1832 Reform Act and beyond. He was an early advocate of shorter Parliaments, franchise extension and the accountability of MPs. He was also a fierce supporter of the American struggle for independence reflected to this day in Wilkes place-names in the USA.

In his personal life Wilkes really did live dangerously, and no modern scandal involving sexual peccadilloes of MPs can begin to compare. It is difficult at such distance to make any useful comparison between the public's moral perception of politicians in the eighteenth and twenty-first centuries but Wilkes got away with personal behaviour which would destroy any modern politician.

Wilkes's political influence owed much to his popularity amongst those largely denied the vote, or 'the mob' as others preferred to describe them. It was Wilkes's ability and readiness to articulate those early stirrings of political emancipation which has ensured his place in history. Whilst I was a Member of the House of Commons I regularly tabled a motion around 17 October each year to commemorate Wilkes's birthday calling on the House to echo the cry of 'Wilkes and Liberty'. It was always well supported. Perhaps there are still those who believe him to be more villain than hero, but for me the description on his coffin – 'A Friend of Liberty' – remains a fitting epitaph to his political contribution to modern democracy.

Acknowledgements

I am indebted in my research to the archivists, librarians, and curators at the many institutions where Wilkes-related materials are to be found. In particular, I thank the helpful staffs of the Guildhall Library, London, and the William L. Clements Library, University of Michigan.

I acknowledge with gratitude the following, who have granted me permission to quote from manuscripts in their possession: the Earl of Malmesbury and the Hampshire Record Office; the William L. Clements Library; the Beinecke Rare Book and Manuscript Library, Yale University; the American Philosophical Society; the Princeton University Library; and the Derbyshire Record Office.

Research for the book was supported by funding from the Social Sciences and Humanities Research Council of Canada. My home institution, Brock University, has also helped with research money and remission from teaching duties. Chapter 6 is a revised version of my article 'John Wilkes, Debt, and Patriotism', *Journal of British Studies*, 34 (1995): 165–95. The section entitled 'The Field of Honour' in chapter 2 is based on my paper '"Cool courage should always mark me": John Wilkes and Duelling', *Journal of the Canadian Historical Association*, new series, 7 (1997): 19–33.

I thank all those who have helped bring this book to fruition through their encouragement, hospitality, critical insights, and sundry other contributions. Many thanks to Donna Andrew, Nigel Aston, Leah Bradshaw, Michael Driedger, Craig Hanyan, Mungo Henderson, Andrea McKenzie, Jane McLeod, Carol Merriam, Alice Prochaska, Frank Prochaska, Nick Rogers, Linda Sainsbury, Elizabeth Sauer, and Joanne Wright. Above all, I thank Lisa, my wife, for cheerfully accommodating my fascination with Wilkes over many years. She would have had cause to echo King George III in muttering epithets about 'that devil Wilkes'. But instead she has engaged with the project in a variety of crucially important ways. This book is dedicated to her with love and admiration.

Finally, I wish to pay special tribute to the late Tony Banks, Lord Stratford, whose irreverent wit matched that of Wilkes himself. Despite dissenting from some of my judgements on Wilkes, Tony supported my work with generosity and enthusiasm. His Foreword to this book was completed just a week before he suffered the stroke that took his life.

List of Abbreviations

[Almon] *History of Late Minority*: [Almon, John] *The History of the Late Minority, Exhibiting the Conduct, Principles, and Views of the Party, during the years 1762, 1763, 1764, and 1765.* Third Impression, London, 1765; reprinted with some additions in 1766 [John Wilkes's copy with his extensive marginalia].

Bleackley, *Wilkes*: Horace Bleackley, *The Life of John Wilkes* (London, 1917).

Boswell Collection: Boswell Collection, General Collection, Beinecke Rare Book and Manuscript Library, Yale University.

Boswell, *Italy*: *Boswell on the Grand Tour: Italy, Corsica, and France, 1765–1766*, ed. Frank Brady and Frederick A. Pottle (London and Toronto, 1955).

BL Add. MSS: British Library, Additional Manuscripts.

Burke Correspondence: *The Correspondence of Edmund Burke*, ed. Thomas W. Copeland *et al.*, 10 vols (Cambridge and Chicago, 1958–78).

Controversial Letters: *The Controversial Letters of John Wilkes, Esq. The Rev. John Horne, and their Principal Adherents* (London, 1771).

English Liberty: *English Liberty: Being a Collection of Interesting Tracts from the Year 1762 to 1769,* 2 vols, continuous pagination (London, 1769) [with manuscript supplement, Guildhall MS 3332].

Grenville Papers: *The Grenville Papers: Being the Correspondence of Richard Grenville, Earl Temple, K.G., and the Right Hon. George Grenville, Their Friends and Contemporaries*, ed. William J. Smith, 4 vols (London, 1852–53).

Letters between Grafton etc. and Wilkes:	*Letters between the Duke of Grafton, the Earls of Halifax, Egremont, Chatham, Temple, and Talbot, Baron Bottetourt, Right Hon. Henry Bilson Legge, Right Hon. Sir John Cust, Bart. Mr. Charles Churchill, Monsieur Voltaire, the Abbé Winckelman, etc. etc. and John Wilkes, Esq. With Explanatory Notes* (London, 1769).
ODNB:	*Oxford Dictionary of National Biography* (Oxford, 2004).
Osborn Collection:	James Marshall and Marie-Louise Osborn Collection, Beinecke Rare Book and Manuscript Library, Yale University.
Thomas, *Wilkes*:	Peter D.G. Thomas, *John Wilkes: A Friend to Liberty* (Oxford and New York, 1996).
Walpole Correspondence:	*The Yale Edition of the Correspondence of Horace Walpole*, ed. W.S. Lewis *et al.*, 48 vols (New Haven, 1937–83).
Wilkes and Potter, ed. Cash:	John Wilkes and Thomas Potter, *An Essay on Woman: A Reconstruction of a Lost Book with a Historical Essay on the Writing, Printing, and Suppressing of this 'Blasphemous and Obscene' Work*, ed. Arthur H. Cash (New York, 2000).
Wilkes–Churchill:	*The Correspondence of John Wilkes and Charles Churchill*, ed. Edward H. Weatherly (New York, 1954).
Wilkes Correspondence:	*The Correspondence of the Late John Wilkes with his Friends Printed from the Original Manuscripts in Which are Introduced Memoirs of his Life*, ed. John Almon, 5 vols (London, 1805).
[Wilkes] *Letters to Daughter*:	*Letters from the Year 1774 to the Year 1796, of John Wilkes Esq. Addressed to his Daughter, the Late Miss Wilkes*, 4 vols (London, 1804).
Wilkes MSS:	Wilkes MSS, William L. Clements Library, University of Michigan.
Wilkes Speeches:	*Speeches of Mr. Wilkes in the House of Commons*, 3 vols, continuous pagination (London, 1786).
Wilkes Volume:	Volume belonging to John Wilkes with verses by him in print and manuscript. British Library Call No. 1106. ccc. 33.

Introduction

Wilkes in Private and Public

'I go to Mrs Cornely's grand masquerade Monday sevennight, and have made me a blue silk domino, as masquerades are likely to be so much in fashion.' John Wilkes wrote this to Polly, his daughter, on 4 May 1770.[1] Wilkes enjoyed a masquerade and he was correct in thinking that they had become fashionable. In the minds of some of his enemies, though, Wilkes had a yen for disguising his identity that went beyond seeking an innocent divertissement. One of them even spitefully suggested that his famously ugly features – squinting eye, pug nose, twisted jaw, and crooked teeth – were themselves a mask, which he wore to baffle 'the indignant eye of mankind'.[2]

The spirit of this jest was widely echoed. 'It is ... not altogether unpardonable if a writer should err in the portrait of a character so equivocal', concluded one frustrated contemporary.[3] The comment is misleading to the extent that Wilkes did have qualities that were manifest and enduring: optimism in the face of misfortune; a vivacity that, according to his friend James Boswell, was 'incessant and universal';[4] and, most famously, an unshakeable attachment to personal liberty, which lent more continuity to his political conduct than is usually conceded. Yet within this rudimentary framework, one encounters paradox everywhere. Despite his notoriety as a rake, Wilkes won a reputation in some circles as 'one of the politest men of his time'; an alleged blasphemer, he remained attached to his 'mother church'; a would-be aristocrat, he became 'a man of the people'; a spendthrift with an aversion to paying his creditors, he contrived to retain the allegiance of hard-pressed London tradesmen. Wilkes's career persistently confounded William Hogarth's pictorial cautionary tales. Whereas Hogarth's Tom Rakewell was destined for the madhouse, Wilkes's

---

[1]   BL Add. MSS 30879, fol. 138.

[2]   *Auditor*, 8 February 1763, quoted in *A Collection of All the Remarkable and Personal Passages in the Briton, North Briton and Auditor* (London, 1766), p. 65.

[3]   Robert Holloway, *A Letter to John Wilkes, Esq; Sheriff of London and Middlesex* (London, 1771), p. 2.

[4]   Boswell's endorsement on a note from Wilkes (16 April 1779), Boswell Collection, C3093.1.

comparably rakish progress took him to the Mansion House, as Lord Mayor of London.[5]

Faced with such ambiguities, historians have tended to sidestep the problem of Wilkes's personality and conduct, focusing instead on the supposedly larger issues of the movements conducted in his name or in response to his persecutions. Disregarding contemporaries' fascination with the minutiae of his life, and even his appearance, such accounts reduce him to merely the occasion, not in a meaningful sense the source, of campaigns assumed to have separate deep-seated origins.[6] There are a few exceptions, notably some important essays and chapters by John Brewer, in which Wilkes's personality occupies centre stage.[7] But even traditional narrative biographies, following the lead of Horace Bleackley, typically represent the more colourful aspects of his conduct and personality as merely a backdrop to the momentous legal and constitutional issues that he almost accidentally brought to the political foreground. Specifically, his libertinism is accorded significance only to the marginal extent that it inflected the reformist agenda. That approach is evident in the most scholarly biography of Wilkes, whose author, Peter D.G. Thomas – an eminent authority on eighteenth-century Parliamentary politics – offers an authoritative and comprehensive account of the narrowly political implications of his subject's career.[8]

The narrative in Wilkes biographies follows a by-now well-trodden path, apart from some inevitable digression over points of detail and interpretative nuance. I present now a synopsis of them, which is also offered as an introduction to Wilkes's career, especially its political dimension, for those readers who might be unfamiliar with it.

Born in October 1725,[9] the son of a prosperous London distiller, Wilkes was raised as a gentleman and provided by indulgent parents with an education and an estate appropriate to that condition. In early adulthood he exhibited libertine tendencies and political ambition, a combination that at the time was hardly incompatible. A protégé of the Whig faction headed by William Pitt (later Lord Chatham) and Earl Temple – who encouraged his election to Parliament – he would probably have remained in comfortable obscurity had not his political patrons been thrust from office in the palace revolution that followed the accession

---

[5]   William Hogarth, *A Rake's Progress*, 8 plates (1735).

[6]   For instance, Ian R. Christie, *Wilkes, Wyvill and Reform: The Parliamentary Reform Movement in British Politics, 1760–1785* (London and New York, 1962).

[7]   Especially, *Party Ideology and Popular Politics at the Accession of George III* (Cambridge and New York, 1976), ch. 9.

[8]   Bleackley, *Wilkes*; Thomas, *Wilkes*.

[9]   On Wilkes's birthdate, see Bleackley, *Wilkes*, pp. 445–46. Consistent with Bleackley's evidence, Wilkes's age is given as thirty-eight in the announcement, dating from July 1764, of the sale of his Aylesbury house. Hugh Hanley, *The Prebendal, Aylesbury* (Aylesbury, 1986), p. 7.

of George III in 1760. Finding himself in opposition, Wilkes took up his pen with sensational effect, especially in his weekly periodical, *North Briton,* which excoriated the new administration, particularly its leader, John Stuart, the 3rd Earl of Bute, for corruption and for pusillanimity towards France and Spain, Britain's opponents in the Seven Years' War.

His attacks on Bute were scurrilous in the extreme: Wilkes accused him of installing a 'petticoat' government, insinuating that the Scottish nobleman owed his influence to a sexual liaison with the king's mother. When in issue no. 45 of the *North Briton* – published on 23 April 1763 – Wilkes broadened his attack to include the king himself, the wrath of the government, now led by George Grenville, came down on his head. Arrested on the authority of a controversial general warrant issued by the secretaries of state, he was confined in the Tower of London, until the Court of Common Pleas released him on the grounds that his detention had violated his privilege as an MP. By now, his cause was attracting widespread support, especially in London, from those who had grievances of their own against government. 'Wilkes and Liberty' became the new popular cry.

Flushed with his triumph, Wilkes launched legal suits against his persecutors and embarked on new publishing ventures. But the government was plotting its revenge, and on 15 November it made its moves. In the House of Commons, it secured a motion condemning *North Briton,* no. 45, as a 'false, scandalous, and seditious libel' – a clear prelude to Wilkes's prosecution in the courts. Meanwhile, in the House of Lords, Wilkes was being denounced for his complicity in the production of *An Essay on Woman* (a pornographic parody of Alexander Pope's *Essay on Man*), a copy of which the government had obtained by underhand means. To compound his woes, Wilkes was shot in the groin the following day while duelling with a former government minister, whom he had libelled in the *North Briton.* With the House of Commons stripping him of the protections of Parliamentary privilege against criminal prosecution, burdened by debt, and concerned about the welfare of his daughter in Paris, Wilkes decided on a strategic retreat. On Christmas Day, 1763, he crossed the Channel to France; except for two clandestine visits, he would not return to England for another four years.

Wilkes could only observe from a distance as Parliament and the courts continued their legal assault. In January 1764 he was expelled from the House of Commons. The following month, he was tried and convicted in the Court of King's Bench, presided over by Lord Chief Justice Mansfield, for the offences of *North Briton* no. 45 and *An Essay on Woman.* Failing to appear for sentencing, he was later declared an outlaw, stripped of all rights of citizenship, including the right to sue his persecutors in the courts. He could draw little consolation from the Parliamentary challenge to general warrants, since most of its advocates took pains to dissociate themselves from the man who had brought the issue to national attention. Indeed, his apparent neglect by the Whig grandees was as vexing to

Wilkes as his legal plight. Fearful also that popular enthusiasm for 'Wilkes and Liberty' was abating, he bombarded the London press with essays, squibs, and news items, all designed to keep his name and cause in the public eye. This campaign was the precursor to a calculated gamble. In defiance of his outlawry, he returned to England on the eve of Parliamentary elections in 1768, offering himself as a candidate for the City of London. Defeated there, he appealed to the electors of Middlesex, who amid scenes of popular excitement returned him as their MP. They rendered this electoral verdict three more times when the House of Commons, under intense government pressure, repeatedly voted to deny him the seat. When the Commons made the fateful decision of declaring his most recently defeated rival, Colonel Henry Luttrell, the legally elected MP for the county, there was a national outcry that the rights of electors were being violated, a clamour that in more radical circles reanimated the demand for Parliamentary reform. Though many of those who petitioned the crown for redress supported the issue, not the man, Wilkes had by now fully reclaimed his popular following, especially in London. During one incident – dubbed the 'Massacre' of St George's Fields – troops fired their muskets in the vicinity of his supporters, killing seven people, who were swiftly anointed as martyrs in his cause.

Meanwhile, the law was finally catching up with Wilkes even as his popularity was growing. Though a court tossed out his outlawry on a technicality, he was sentenced, in June 1768, to a prison term of twenty-two months for his offences. His incarceration in the King's Bench Prison was a luxurious one, however, and it scarcely put a crimp in either his libertine or political careers. In January 1769, he capitalised on his popularity in the capital by securing election as one of its aldermen. His transformation into a City politician with a national following would shortly win crucial support with the founding of the Society of the Supporters of the Bill of Rights (SSBR), a group pledged to pay his debts and to advance the progressive political agenda that he inspired. Following his release from prison, Wilkes masterminded a scheme that pitted the privileges of the City of London against those of the House of Commons in order to secure the right of printers to publish Parliamentary debates; its successful outcome was perhaps the most tangible gain for the liberty of the subject in Wilkes's entire career.[10] Shortly afterwards, Wilkes's popularity in London was endorsed by his election as sheriff. Three years later, in 1774, he reached the pinnacle of civic office with his election as Lord Mayor. That triumph was followed in short order by his re-election as MP for Middlesex. On this occasion the government, disinclined to face another battle with its old adversary, made no attempt to prevent him from taking his seat. This tacit vindication of the rights of electors would be formalised in 1782, when

---

[10]   This view is persuasively offered in Thomas, *Wilkes*, pp. 125–40.

after repeated demands by Wilkes, the Commons finally voted to expunge from its records the original resolution expelling him from the House. Wilkes would remain an MP until 1790 and a London alderman until his death in 1797.

Wilkes's return to the Commons in December 1774 is generally represented as the high point of his career, after which all else is a long diminuendo, punctuated by a fitful support for religious toleration, the rights of American colonists, Parliamentary reform, and the cause of friends such as Warren Hastings, impeached for abuse of power while Governor-General of Bengal. Consistent with their primary focus on matters political, narrative biographies typically devote more than half their pages to the 12-year period from 1763 to 1774, in a lifespan of more than 70 years; the concentration is even more pronounced in George Rudé's still indispensable study of the sources of Wilkes's support.[11] Wilkes's later description of himself as an 'extinct volcano' is usually taken as justifying especially scant attention to the remaining years of his life. During that time, in Rudé's compelling phrase, Wilkes lived in the 'odour and sanctity of the new Toryism', suggesting to progressive-minded historians that he had entered a period of political senescence, not worthy of serious study.[12]

This barebones account of the manner in which Wilkes has been treated by his previous biographers fails to do justice, of course, to the richness of detail that typically enlivens their descriptions. What makes Wilkes's story so inviting, and compels its periodic retelling, is the way in which his picaresque career intersects promiscuously with matters of high moral and political significance. Predictably, he was dubbed England's Quixote, even as someone more Quixotic than Don Quixote himself.[13] Yet the exotic details of his career, when deployed merely for human interest, can hinder understanding. Wilkes himself is obscured by them, remaining, in John Brewer's phrase, 'a mercurial elusive rake'.[14] To some extent, Brewer's description accurately suggests an irreducible quality of personality: Wilkes took a mischievous, perhaps cynical, pleasure in confounding any straightforward representation of himself as the disinterested advocate of liberty. But it also hints at inadequacies in narrative approaches that give priority to the rush of external events over the claims of the subject. My biography seeks to address this difficulty in two ways.

First, it pays more attention to Wilkes's life outside the narrow timeframe of his political celebrity, and especially to his formative years. Wilkes did not, like Pallas Athene, appear from nowhere into the public realm, fully grown and

---

[11] George Rudé, *Wilkes and Liberty: A Social Study of 1763 to 1774* (Oxford, 1962).

[12] Ibid., p. 192.

[13] *Public Advertiser*, 23 December 1764; Anna Clark, 'The Chevalier d'Eon and Wilkes: Masculinity and Politics in the Eighteenth Century', *Eighteenth-Century Studies*, 32 (1998): 31.

[14] Brewer, *Party Ideology*, p. 21.

ready to do battle with his adversaries. He brought with him a set of attitudes that help to explain conduct that is often casually and reductively dismissed as opportunistic. (Even conceding that Wilkes was an opportunist, the question remains as to what prior experiences he brought to bear on the identification of opportunities for self-gratification and for social and political advancement.) Second, the biography takes a thematic approach instead of a traditionally chronological one, enabling Wilkes to emerge as a subject from the distorting clamour of contingent events. His libertine career is set against the following themes: family, ambition, sex, religion, class, and money. Each chapter adds a layer of Wilkes's life experience to the chapters that precede it. The intention is not to establish six discrete personae, but to illuminate cumulatively different facets of the same personality, the influences that shaped his conduct, and some of the reverberations of his actions. Defining themes in the way I have indicated is perhaps an artificial exercise in the sense that they are far from being mutually exclusive categories, and frequently impinge on each other, but the manner in which they converge or overlap is itself revealing, and together they adumbrate much that is significant in Wilkes's life.

These approaches are deliberately intended to imply more than the customary attention to what might be described as Wilkes's private existence: there is more here on his sex life, for example, than there is on his support for Parliamentary reform. And with the exception of chapter 6 (where I offer a particular view on Wilkes's appeal in a commercial society), there is more about Wilkes himself than about his followers.[15] My emphasis on Wilkes's personal career does not, however, presume a corresponding indifference to his public one. Because, while Wilkes's contemporaries acknowledged a distinction between public and private, they were also continually demonstrating how porous and unstable the line between them actually was. Indeed, the whole concept of a sphere of private intimacy was arguably itself a public construction, justifying 'an unprecedented discussion and unparalleled public exposure of private life'.[16] Here Wilkes was something of an accidental pioneer, according to a leading social theorist, because the focus on his quirks of conduct and character helped 'transform the very meaning of a public realm'.[17] Wilkes's contemporary, Edmund Burke,

---

[15]   For works where the emphasis is on Wilkes's followers, see especially Rudé, and Kathleen Wilson, *The Sense of the People: Politics, Culture and Imperialism in England, 1715–1785* (Cambridge and New York, 1995), chs 4 and 5.

[16]   I quote from John Brewer's appraisal of the seminal work of Jürgen Habermas: 'This, That and the Other: Public, Social and Private in the Seventeenth and Eighteenth Centuries', in *Shifting the Boundaries: Transformation of the Languages of Public and Private in the Eighteenth Century*, ed. Dario Castiglione and Lesley Sharpe (Exeter, 1995), p. 6.

[17]   Richard Sennett, *The Fall of Public Man* (New York and London, 1992), p. 100.

understood what was happening. 'The crowd allways want to draw themselves from abstract connections to personal attachments,' he wrote in 1768, 'and since the fall of Ld. Chatham [William Pitt], there has been no Hero of the Mob but Wilkes.' Later, Burke concluded that Wilkes's 'imprudence' was 'some unusual and eccentrick kind of Wisdom'.[18]

Wilkes himself was acutely conscious of the intersections between public and private, which he sought selectively to exploit. He once referred to himself as 'a private English gentleman, perfectly free and independent', a condition that he held to be 'of the highest dignity'. This should not be read as expressive of a desire for a cloistered retirement; on the contrary, Wilkes was seeking to establish his credentials for a renewed engagement in public life. Significantly, his comment was in a preening account of his conduct during a duel, originally contained in a *private* letter, which in 1767 he made *public* through the medium of the London press on the eve of his return from exile in France.[19]

Wilkes saw it as inevitable and desirable that there should be interest in the private lives of men in the public eye. This is what he wrote in a fragment of autobiography:

> It is the certain fate of all men, who have eminently distinguish'd themselves on the great theatre of the world, that their private actions will likewise become the subjects of enquiry, and the little anecdotes of their lives be eagerly sought after, and nicely scrutiniz'd. This proceeding, tho' it has its' [sic] rise in idle curiosity, may be attended with real benefit, and solid instruction.[20]

The prospect 'of being gratefully remember'd by posterity,' he asserted, 'has been the fairest spur to those worthies of our own country, as well as those of Greece and Rome.'[21] Wilkes argued, though, that there were some limits to legitimate public interest. He rejected, for example, the sexual prurience of the Roman historian Suetonius in favour of the uplifting biographical vignettes of Plutarch. And in his autobiography, he wrote that he would not 'profanely rend the veil of the sanctuary of love, so as to lead to a discovery which might wound the honour, the peace, or the domestick happiness of a single individual' – a pious claim immediately vitiated, however, by his torrid account of his affair with the Italian courtesan, Gertrude Corradini.[22] Elsewhere, Wilkes used sexual revelations to discredit opponents, and he was of the view that homosexuals

---

18 *Burke Correspondence*, vol. 1, p. 349 and vol. 2, p. 490.
19 *St James's Chronicle*, 14–16 May 1767.
20 BL Add. MSS 30865A, fol. 2.
21 Ibid., fol. 4.
22 Ibid., fols 4–6.

should be exposed to public censure.[23] There was, however, one zone of privacy that Wilkes insisted should remain inviolable, especially from the intrusions of state authority, and that was the exercise of private conscience, something clearly distinct from 'private actions'. Reflecting bitterly on his prosecution for *An Essay on Woman*, he insisted that he had the right to engage in private speculation on doctrinal matters.[24] Yet Wilkes was not above impugning the religious motives of enemies and erstwhile friends.

Wilkes's own inconsistencies in defining legitimate areas of inquiry into the private sphere reflect the practical impossibility of constraining an inquisitive public stimulated by the ever-expanding medium of the press. There were scattered voices of protest against the tendency. One essayist asked 'whether any thing tends more to extirpate the Old English Good Humour, than the raking into the Characters of Noblemen and Gentlemen as private Men, and not as Servants of the Public, in which Light the People have a Right to judge of their Conduct'. And he gave credence to his pseudonym, IMPARTIAL, by decrying the personal attacks on both Wilkes and his persecutors.[25] Yet there was a plaintive quality about his appeal, and its even-handedness was exceptional. More typical was the approach of the famous *Junius* who deemed Wilkes's private character irrelevant to the public issues he was promoting, while launching a scathing assault on Wilkes's nemesis, the Duke of Grafton, for his loose sexual morals.[26] Such partiality could, of course, work in the opposite direction, and Wilkes's own private life came under withering scrutiny from his enemies. In 1764, addressing the electors of Aylesbury, his first Parliamentary constituency, he called, not for the suspension of enquiry into his private affairs, but for a recognition that 'true candour always weighs in the same balance faults and virtues', adding, with the voice of experience, that 'the shades in private life are darkened by an enemy, but scarcely seen by a friend'.[27]

The attempt to discredit Wilkes for his private conduct took two connected forms. The first emphasised motive, insisting that Wilkes's self-representation as the public's champion was inauthentic to the point of fraudulence because it was driven by 'sordid private Pique, and from the vilest passions which agitate the human Heart'.[28] (This kind of attack occasionally incorporated contemptuous references to Wilkes's origins, as in this jingle: 'See how the Vulgar rage, like

---

[23]   Anna Clark, *Scandal: The Sexual Politics of the British Constitution* (Princeton, 2004), pp. 44–45.

[24]   'Letter to the Electors of Aylesbury', in *Wilkes Correspondence*, vol. 3, p. 113.

[25]   *Public Advertiser*, 7 December 1763.

[26]   *The Letters of Junius*, ed. John Cannon (Oxford, 1978), pp. 63, 67, 75, 78–80.

[27]   'Letter to the Electors of Aylesbury', *Wilkes Correspondence*, vol. 3, p. 117.

[28]   *A Mirror for the Multitude; or, Wilkes no Patriot* (London, 1769), p. 17.

headstrong fire: / By Gin [the Father's Poison] first undone, / Now with false British Spirit by the Son.'[29]) The second emphasised character, even when its relevance to public conduct was ritualistically denied. The following sally is typical: 'I shall ... pass over his [Wilkes's] *private* character and attend only to his *public*; though I must ... beg leave to urge, that if a man's *private character* is bad, it must proceed from want of *principle,* and it does not require any extraordinary abilities to determine the rectitude of a man's *public* actions, where *principle* is wanting.'[30] Others were less coy in denying any conceivable public merit to a man 'gigantic in Vice, and whose Life and Manners were a Scandal to Society'.[31]

Wilkes and his supporters used a number of strategies to such attacks. One was to emphasise Wilkes's political virtue, his indomitable public spirit, compared to which his sexual offences and moral failings were mere peccadilloes. He was, said one rhymester, 'A lion in a leopard's skin, / His spots without, his heart within.'[32] Another strategy was to concede some youthful folly on his part, while insisting that in response to the public need he had become a reformed character. In 1768, shortly after his return from France, such an apologia, probably composed by Wilkes himself, appeared in the press: 'He [Wilkes] has too long been lulled in the lap of pleasure, but he is now a publick man, and, I trust, his whole soul is devoted to his Country, and the great pursuit of Liberty and the Constitution of England.'[33] A third strategy was to deploy the language of sentiment in his defence. If he erred, it was because he was 'sincere' and 'artless', not, as his enemies would have it, because he was depraved and calculating. Wilkes himself complained that he was victimised because he had 'the openness of a frank nature'.[34] 'Fool that he was,' agreed one of his advocates, 'he could never bring himself to put on the mask of hypocrisy, which ... covers a multitude of sins.'[35]

---

[29]   *St James's Chronicle*, 19–21 February 1765.

[30]   Philo-Patriae, *An Address to the Public Wherein the Conduct of Mr. Wilkes is Candidly and Impartially Considered* (London, 1768), p. 3.

[31]   *Mirror for the Multitude*, p. 24.

[32]   'The Lion in the Toils', by Mr Kenrick, in *Wilkes's Jest Book; or the Merry Patriot* (London, 1770), p. 22. For the contemporary debate over the relative dangers of sexual offences, moral failings, and the loss of public virtue, see Joanna Innes, 'Politics and Morals: The Reformation of Manners Movement in Later Eighteenth-Century England', in *The Transformation of Political Culture: England and Germany in the Late Eighteenth Century*, ed. Eckhart Helmuth (London, 1990), esp. pp. 58–60.

[33]   *Political Register*, 2 (1768): 414–15. See the comment in Wilkes's autobiography: 'He is to be consider'd not always as a patriot, but too frequently as a man of pleasure, who lov'd to sacrifice to the graces, to the nymphs, and to the muses, as well as on every great occasion to the genius of English liberty.' BL Add. MSS 30865A, fol. 6.

[34]   *Controversial Letters*, p. 11.

[35]   *A Letter to the Right Hon. Thomas Harley, Esq; Lord Mayor of the City of London. By an Alderman of London*, 4th edn (London, 1768), p. 19.

The interplay of Wilkes as a public and private man is a major concern of this study. I resist, however, the extreme view that Wilkes's identity was entirely a public construction. Although competing partisan judgements complicate the biographer's task, it is possible to recognise Wilkes as having qualities of character and purpose that preceded or stood apart from the clamour of public debate, even as they often served to incite it. His religious attitudes, for example – examined in detail in chapter 4 – were shaped before he entered the public arena, and he retained them with remarkable consistency throughout his life. Yet even as this biographical study seeks to present Wilkes as someone with an autonomous personality, it offers no magic key that will unlock access to an underlying consistency of conduct. Irresolvable contradictions persist. Wilkes was neither saint nor ideologue, whose behaviours are determined by binding political, religious, or moral imperatives. Nor was he the slavish follower of shifting cultural norms. He was, however, alert – even susceptible – to them, and that is one of the reasons why he is such a fascinating and important subject for study: he provided a mirror upon which many of the cultural and moral uncertainties of the period – especially with respect to family, ambition, sex, religion, class, and money – were reflected. For example, like many of his male contemporaries with pretensions to gentility, he sought to reconcile the twin requirements of manliness and politeness, but it was a difficult undertaking. As Michèle Cohen has pointed out, 'politeness, like all the practices which could secure men's status as gentlemen, simultaneously threatened to compromise their masculinity'.[36] Caught in this dilemma, Wilkes appears on some occasions (depending on circumstance) as an incorrigible rake, and on others as a model of politesse, even 'a man of feeling'; his attempts to reconcile these self-representations often fell disastrously short. He was not unique in displaying such inconsistencies – the project of politeness was far from complete in the eighteenth century even among its self-appointed advocates – but few had their conduct exposed to such unremitting public scrutiny.

Many of Wilkes's attitudes – not just to sex and religion, but also to family, class and money – are evoked by the word libertine (a term applied to him by James Boswell and others). For that reason, and because its discursive associations shaped public debate on Wilkes, I employ the word libertine in the title of this study, and liberally throughout the text.[37] 'Libertine' has complex and shifting

---

[36] 'Manliness, Effeminacy and the French: Gender and the Construction of National Character in Eighteenth-Century England', in *English Masculinities 1600–1800*, ed. Tim Hitchcock and Michèle Cohen (London and New York, 1999), p. 58.

[37] The literature on libertinism is myriad. For this preliminary discussion, I have found the following especially useful: Tiffany Potter, *Honest Sins: Georgian Libertinism and the Plays and Novels of Henry Fielding* (Montreal and Kingston, 1999); Randolph Trumbach, *Sex and the*

meanings, but it serves well precisely for that very reason: not because it magically reconciles the incongruities of Wilkes's behaviour, but because its contrary definitions match their disparities. The issue is not over whether Wilkes was a libertine – few, including Wilkes himself, would have disputed that – but over what kind of libertine he actually was.

At its core, libertinism implies a challenge to conventional religious and sexual constraints, but beyond that it conveys some very different meanings. Sometimes the libertine appears on the historical stage as the model of refined sociability, and sometimes as the anti- or pre-social individual, driven by selfish passions.[38] Abiding images of the latter are that of the hyper-sexualised Lord Rochester pursuing his Priapic career, and then glorifying it in pornographic verse, or that of Lord Wharton mocking the Eucharist by bathing his penis in wine and distributing excrement to an assembled 'congregation'. Wilkes's enemies strove hard to associate him with the rampant misogyny and outrageous blasphemy of these Restoration rakes. Wilkes and his allies, though, had recourse to the more benign types of libertinism that had evolved by the middle of the eighteenth century – ones that had assimilated some aspects of the competing claims of sensibility or sentiment. One version was the aristocratic and Epicurean man of pleasure, a term that Wilkes applied to himself. Lord Chesterfield, who gave the term currency, drew a large distinction between the man of pleasure and the rake. 'There are not in the world two characters more different', he insisted. 'A rake is a composition of all the lowest, most ignoble, degrading and shameful vices.'[39] Many contemporaries were not persuaded that Chesterfield's distinction was a fundamental one, however, suspecting that his man of pleasure was the selfish rake overlain with a polite and socially acceptable veneer. In opposition to this version of the Georgian libertine, with its taint of hypocrisy, was yet another, which found literary expression in Henry Fielding's Tom Jones and Richard Sheridan's Charles Surface. Their conduct, while certainly rakish, was marked by good-heartedness, genuine benevolence, and consideration towards women.[40]

Gender Revolution, vol. 1: *Heterosexuality and the Third Gender in Enlightenment London* (Chicago, 1998), ch. 3; James G. Turner, 'The Properties of Libertinism', in *'Tis Nature's Fault: Unauthorized Sexuality during the Enlightenment*, ed. Robert Purks Maccubbin (Cambridge and New York, 1987), pp. 75–87.

[38] On this distinction, see Elena Russo, 'Sociability, Cartesianism, and Nostalgia in Libertine Discourse', *Eighteenth-Century Studies*, 30 (1997), pp. 383–400. Russo claims that in France the movement in libertinage was from sociability towards its transgression. Arguably, in England, the movement was in the opposite direction.

[39] Quoted in Potter, p. 13.

[40] Wilkes eagerly looked forward to receiving a copy of *Tom Jones*. Wilkes to Thomas Edwards [1749], Wilkes MSS 4, fol. 3.

Was Wilkes the reincarnation of Lord Rochester, a disciple of Lord Chesterfield, or a living version of Tom Jones or Charles Surface? The answer is none of the above, but at different times and on different occasions, he arguably manifested aspects of each of them. The moral ambivalences of libertinism that Wilkes embodied, moreover, help to explain why he acquired a simultaneous reputation as a moral bandit and a moral scourge. In particular, as we shall see, the controversy that erupted over his *Essay on Woman* served to highlight this duality, despite hostile expectations that his exposure as a pornographer would brand him squarely as a reprobate.

Chapter 1
Family

Favourite Son

Libertinism of whatever kind offered a challenge to eighteenth-century reformers of male manners. Suffused with the new culture of sensibility, and usually animated by religious zeal, they saw in the home itself, when properly constituted, a compelling alternative to the disreputable resorts of libertine men, and one in which a proper notion of manhood might be redefined.[1] As a well-known rake, Wilkes was an obvious target for such a campaign, yet at the same time he posed something of a conundrum for it, because, borrowing the language of sensibility, he insisted that he loved the domestic life. Confounding the assumptions of the reformers, he offered the curious spectacle of the domestic libertine. His admission to James Boswell that he 'was not too fond of whole families' qualified his avowed attachment to hearth and home, but far from erased it.[2]

The paradox of Wilkes the domestic libertine does begin to fray, however, once we recognise that, despite the best efforts of the moral reformers, the polarities of libertinism and domesticity were not as sharply etched in the eighteenth century as they subsequently became. As an adult, Wilkes engaged in what is often called the practice of enlightenment, appealing to a reified nature, supported by classical precept, as a guarantee that erotic freedom could be reconciled with domesticity in a way that was orderly, fulfilling, and benign. His association with some of the leading French *philosophes* and their families, who simultaneously offered both progressive ideas and hospitality for Wilkes and his daughter, supported such an outlook. The tenets of practical enlightenment would be eventually overtaken by the success of evangelical Protestantism in imposing a definition on domesticity – one with a heavy stress on monogamy – that cast nineteenth-century libertines

---

[1]   On the home as an antidote to libertinism, see G.J. Barker-Benfield, *The Culture of Sensibility: Sex and Society in Eighteenth-Century Britain* (Chicago, 1992), ch. 2, *passim*; Leonore Davidoff and Catherine Hall, *Family Fortunes: Men and Women of the English Middle Class, 1780–1850* (London and Chicago, 1987); John Tosh, 'The Old Adam and the New Man: Emerging Themes in the History of English Masculinities, 1750–1850', in *English Masculinities, 1600–1800*, ed. Tim Hitchcock and Michèle Cohen (London and New York, 1999), pp. 217–38.

[2]   *Boswell, Italy*, p. 100.

such as Lord Byron beyond the margins of respectable society. In Wilkes's lifetime, however, they retained sufficient vitality to offer an ideological counter to prescriptions derived from religious pietism, not merely a louche transgression of them.[3] How libertinism could be reconciled with domesticity in a practical sense was another matter, however, and Wilkes's concurrent careers as libertine and family man often seemed jarringly incongruous, with enlightened values offering little more than an attenuated gloss over their disparate features.[4]

While the practice of enlightenment refined Wilkes's attitude to family life, its importance should not be exaggerated; his enduring attachment to domesticity was for the most part a product of his early experience. He was the favoured son in a close, loving, and prosperous family. Its wealth was established by his grandfather, Israel Wilkes, who climbed from lowly origins to become a successful gin distiller, first in Southwark, then in Clerkenwell, a 'respectable' suburb just north of the City of London. Here, in the family home in St John's Square, John Wilkes was born and raised. Israel Wilkes deployed the profits from the distillery shrewdly. While grandees were compounding their wealth through speculative development in Westminster, he looked eastward to Spitalfields, the centre of the silk-weaving industry. He acquired there a large section of property memorialised by Wilkes Street, which still runs through the district. Just before John's birth, Israel Wilkes retired from business, and the distillery and house in St John's Square were taken over by his son, Israel Wilkes, Jr, John's father. Like his own father, the younger Israel Wilkes supplemented profits from the distillery through the returns on property investments. In 1730, he purchased tenements in the east-end suburb of Shoreditch for £3,800.[5]

While consolidating the family fortune, Israel Wilkes, Jr, also knew how to enjoy it, in the manner supposedly typical of the son of a self-made man. In a display of conspicuous consumption not lost on his contemporaries, he drove his family around in a splendid six-horse carriage. He entertained lavishly, his

---

[3]   John Sainsbury, 'Wilkes and Libertinism', *Studies in Eighteenth-Century Culture*, 26 (1998): 158–59; Bleackley, *Wilkes*, p. 155; Alan Charles Kors, *D'Holbach's Coterie: An Enlightenment in Paris* (Princeton, 1976), pp. 25–26, 101–02, 109, 113; Davidoff and Hall, *Family Fortunes*, esp. pp. 73–192.

[4]   See Randolph Trumbach's judgement: 'It was not possible in the real world to combine an exclusive male heterosexual desire and a romantic, domesticated sexuality. Wilkes … could manage the one but not the other.' 'Erotic Fantasy and Male Libertinism in Enlightenment England', in *The Invention of Pornography: Obscenity and the Origins of Modernity, 1500–1800*, ed. Lynn Hunt (New York, 1993), p. 282.

[5]   William J. Pinks, *The History of Clerkenwell*, 2nd edn (London, 1882), p. 314; *Survey of London*, gen. eds, F.H.W. Sheppard et al., vol. 27: *Spitalfields and Mile End New Town* (London, 1957), pp. 110–11; 'An Abstract of the Prior Title to Hoxton Square Estate', BRA/437/4, London Metropolitan Archives.

guests including not only fellow businessmen, but also members of the literati, who reportedly had an influence on the young John Wilkes.[6] An anecdote from John's childhood, told to his daughter Polly, suggests that his father combined shrewdness with teasing humour:

'Jack, have you got a purse?' My answer was, 'No sir.' – 'I am sorry for it Jack,' said my father; 'if you had, I should have given you some money to put in it.' I soon got a purse, and in two or three days my father asked me again, 'Jack, have you got a purse?' – 'Yes, sir.' – 'I am glad of it,' said my father; 'if you had not had a purse, I would have given you one.'[7]

According to John's own account, he was the 'favourite' of his father, 'who treated him on every occasion with tenderness and indulgence'.[8] The affection was reciprocated; as an adolescent, Wilkes's expressions of devotion for his parent went beyond the customary filial pieties. Acknowledging 'those marks of his affection I every day receiv'd', he declared that 'there is none I desire so much to approve myself to, as my Papa'.[9] Later, John's relationship with his father developed tensions. Though generous, Israel became alarmed by his son's extravagances. His will contained a hint of reproach: John had already received 'the whole fortune and provision … intended for him'; he could expect no more. Yet the two were never estranged, and John experienced genuine distress at the death of his father in January 1761.[10]

Wilkes's patrimony was important, and not just in the obvious material sense. His commercial origins also had the enduring benefit of helping him to win the loyalty of men with a similar outlook to his father's when, in the 1770s, he went through a transition from aspiring aristocrat to City dignitary. It was in London and its suburbs that he would recover his political career, with the support of the capital's tradesmen and manufacturers. Though he always retained a flamboyant gentleman's persona and often kept an ironic distance from his middle-class supporters, he could read their language and motivations in ways denied to ambitious outsiders.

Even Wilkes's libertinism, while emulative of an aristocratic lifestyle, retained a tincture of his antecedents. Though his extravagances became part of his notoriety,

---

[6]   *Wilkes Correspondence*, vol. 1, p. 3; Pinks, p. 314; [Wilkes] *Letters to Daughter*, vol. 1, pp. 11–12.

[7]   [Wilkes] *Letters to Daughter*, vol. 2, p. 42.

[8]   BL Add. MSS 30865A, fol. 7.

[9]   John Wilkes to his father, 22 January 1744, General Manuscript Collection: Wilkes, Columbia University Library, New York.

[10]   Will of Israel Wilkes, PROB 11 862/40 (microfilm), National Archives, London; Wilkes to John Dell, 31 January 1761, Wilkes MSS 6, fol. 5.

it was not because he lacked a grip on his personal affairs that he indulged in them. Rather they were calculated, deriving from a strong sense of entitlement to an elegant way of life, irrespective of his immediate financial circumstances. He was free with other people's money, following Giacomo Casanova's dictum that if money was going to be squandered anyway, then he should be the one doing the squandering. Unlike Casanova, however, he was not a gambler in his adult years. His father reportedly paid a gambling debt for him in his youth, with the injunction: 'Jack, mind, I do so no more.' After that, Wilkes eschewed gambling, becoming a staunch opponent of what he called 'that most destructive vice'. By resisting the lure of the gaming tables, Wilkes not only escaped a common route to penury and debtors prison, he also avoided a potentially damaging association with what was identified as a quintessential aristocratic failing, one even regarded as a threat to manhood itself. In eighteenth-century England, gambling was gendered as a feminine lure, 'an enchanting witchery' with the potential to overwhelm masculine identity.[11]

Wilkes's father was an amiable and important presence in his son's life, but his mother, Sarah Wilkes, was a more vivid one, especially in matters of religion and moral instruction. She was the daughter of John Heaton, a tanner from the south London district of Bermondsey, whose family had long been on friendly terms with that of Israel Wilkes's in neighbouring Southwark. Her marriage to Israel Wilkes, Jr, was a typical union between the offspring of two well-off families with similar business interests. As part of her dowry, Sarah Wilkes brought with her a valuable addition to the Wilkes property holdings in east London. The families' compatibility was religious as well as economic: Israel Wilkes and John Heaton were members of the same dissenting congregation (though it is not now possible to establish which one).[12]

Sarah Wilkes was not, however, the gloomy sectarian that she is often depicted as. She indulged a passion for secular objects, collecting Dresden china, marble sculptures, bronzes, and pictures on pagan themes. Her will listed six statuettes of Bacchus alone. Despite this taste for pagan art, however, she remained a firm Christian moralist, unflagging in her attempts to curb John's libertine tendencies. She never ceased to regard him as a hero, but his adult career as a *rake*-hero clearly bothered her. His reformation would 'cause a mother's heart to sing for joy', she wrote. She was creative in her campaign, even resorting to drafting a letter, purporting to be from a third party, complaining of the 'criminality and

---

[11]   Giacomo Casanova, *Chevalier de Seingalt, History of My Life*, trans. Willard R. Trask, 12 vols (Baltimore, 1997), vol. 1, pp. 34–35; [Wilkes] *Letters to Daughter*, vol. 2, p. 217, and vol. 4, p. 135. Gillian Russell, '"Faro's Daughters": Female Gamesters, Politics, and the Discourse of Finance in 1790s Britain', *Eighteenth-Century Studies*, 33 (2000): 485.

[12]   Bleackley, *Wilkes*, p. 4; *Wilkes Correspondence*, vol. 1, pp. 2–3.

infamy' of his conduct.[13] Her belief that women, Eve-like, were the initiators of sexual transgression (once she warned a grandson against 'licentious connections with *my own* most dangerous sex', imploring him to be 'firmly guarded against their treacherous wiles'[14]) offered mitigation but not absolution for her son's philandering. Yet despite her consternation at his behaviour, her love for him was unconditional; whatever his flaws, in her eyes he always retained what she called his 'lovely disposition'.[15] She remained fully engaged with his political campaigns, serving at times as his amanuensis: the Wilkes family papers are full of her transcriptions of political material, including squibs, poems, and essays intended for the London press.[16] Just how much of Wilkes's unshakeable confidence was attributable to his mother's constancy is difficult to assess, but their case certainly lends some credence to Sigmund Freud's famous dictum that 'if a man has been his mother's undisputed darling he retains throughout life the triumphant feeling, the confidence in success, which not seldom brings actual success with it'.[17] More to the point here, Wilkes was never obliged to choose between a libertine career and the support of his parental family.

While often seeming the object of a singular devotion from his parents, John Wilkes did have five siblings, three of whom carried distinct marks of failure. Sarah, the eldest, was a reluctant spinster, denied what she called 'the balm of matrimony'. In later life, she became a recluse, living in candlelight behind closed curtains, supposedly a model for Miss Haversham in Charles Dickens's *Great Expectations*.[18] John's older brother, Israel, never enjoyed the benefits, emotional or material, traditionally conferred on the eldest son, because most of them were transferred to John himself. Israel was subject to some casual humiliations as a result. In 1752, when he wanted to marry against his parents' wishes, his mother urged him to consult his younger brother – already married but well advanced on his libertine's progress – for some sober advice.[19] Israel might have redeemed himself by emulating the commercial success of his ancestral namesakes, but he was obliged to admit that he was not cut out for business. 'I have tryed Trade but cannot I am afraid fix my Mind to it', he wrote sheepishly to his father. He spent

---

[13]   Will of Sarah Wilkes, PROB 11, 1074/53, National Archives; Sarah Wilkes to John Wilkes, 23 October 1773, Wilkes MSS 2, fol. 95; draft letter, fol. 115.

[14]   Sarah Wilkes to John de Ponthieu Wilkes, 12 April 1773, Wilkes MSS 2, fol. 108.

[15]   Sarah Wilkes to Matthew Leeson, 9 February 1743, ibid., 1, fol. 8.

[16]   Ibid., fols 32, 41, 53, 55, 56, 62, 71, 92.

[17]   Sigmund Freud, 'A Childhood Recollection from *Dichtung und Wahreit*', *The Standard Edition of the Complete Psychological Works of Sigmund Freud*, ed. James Strachey, 24 vols (repr. London, 1968), vol. 17, p. 156.

[18]   Sarah Wilkes to Sophia Nesbitt, 19 August 1755, Wilkes MSS 2, fol. 34; Louis Kronenberger, *The Extraordinary Mr. Wilkes: His Life and Times* (London and Garden City, 1974), p. 4.

[19]   Wilkes MSS 1, fol. 28.

much of his life in a wandering quest for employment, an odyssey that would end in New York, where he sought John's influence to secure an appointment as a commercial agent.[20] John's younger brother, Heaton, had similar difficulty in establishing his independence. He had the misfortune to take over the family distillery at a time when the gin trade had fallen on hard times; subsequent ventures as a coal merchant and property speculator were unsuccessful; and in 1784 he had to flee temporarily to the continent to avoid debtors prison. For much of his adult life, he was reduced to serving as a dogsbody for John, a function he performed cheerfully, with only occasional spats of fraternal irritation.[21] John's younger sister, Mary, despite her 'brimstone Qualities', was more successful in the marital stakes than her elder sister, marrying three rich husbands in a row. Ann, the youngest child of the family – a person of 'great merit and sweetness of temper', according to John Wilkes – died of smallpox at the age of 14.[22]

The most consequential demonstration of the special regard that John Wilkes's parents felt for him was the attention they paid to his formal education. At the age of nine he accompanied his brothers to a boarding school in Hertford run by John Worsley, a classical scholar and a birch-wielding, Presbyterian schoolmaster of some renown. John Wilkes became his star pupil. When he left the school five years later, Worsley lauded him for his 'generous Sentiments and ... Love of Letters'. 'Go on, Dear youth,' he urged, 'and prosper in your noble pursuits.'[23] Unlike his brothers, Wilkes enjoyed the benefit of a continuing classical education under the tutelage of Matthew Leeson (an elderly friend of his parents and a Presbyterian minister), first in Thame, Oxfordshire, and then in Aylesbury, where he was probably Leeson's only pupil. Wilkes later characterised Leeson as a boring pedant, but he was a dedicated teacher. Thanks to his instruction, Wilkes acquired a facility in Greek as well as a mastery of Latin.[24]

That Wilkes should have acquired this competence testifies not only to his aptitude, but also to the indulgence of his parents. Many middle-class families were sceptical about the benefits of a classical education, seeing it as a potentially dangerous distraction from the practical demands of commerce. It was, however, an essential hallmark of gentlemanly status. 'Latin between 1600 and 1800', writes Anthony Fletcher, 'became firmly installed as the male elite's secret language, a language all of its own, a language that could be displayed as a mark of learning, of superiority, of class and gender difference at the dinner table, on the quarter

---

[20] Ibid., fol. 2; *Wilkes Correspondence*, vol. 5, pp. 148–49.

[21] *Wilkes Correspondence*, vol. 1, p. 4; Wilkes MSS 2, fol. 110; Bleackley, *Wilkes*, pp. 366, 394; *Morning Post*, 18 June 1779.

[22] BL Add. MSS 30869, fol. 98; Bleackley, *Wilkes*, pp. 21, 369.

[23] Bleackley, *Wilkes*, pp. 8, 35; BL Add. MSS 30865A, fol. 7; BL Add. MSS 30867, fol. 4.

[24] BL Add. MSS 30865A, fols 7–8.

sessions bench and in those final bastions of male privilege, the Houses of Lords and Commons.'[25] Wilkes would display it in all those forums, with the exception of the House of Lords. And in later life, it gave him an opportunity for familiar discourse even with opponents like Samuel Johnson and Lord Mansfield.[26] One immediate benefit was to enable the 15-year-old John to flaunt his superior classical knowledge in the face of his less privileged older brother:

> Reading Homer lately I met with the following remarkable passage, as you have read only [Alexander] Pope, novelty will excuse my mentioning it, it is in Iliad. book, 15 v. 280 ..., the litteral Latin translation wou'd be, *omnisbusque in pedes decidit animus,* or in English, their courage fell to their feet; what the opinion of the critics may be on this place, I cannot say, but to me, who am not a little prejudiced, I must confess in favor of Homer, this witticism seems to have a very mean look in an heroick poem, where every thing ought to be grand, noble, and truly sublime, and every thing mean and vulnerable to be excluded; such a turn of wit wou'd have become Hudibras, but in Homer it quite shocks me ...[27]

(Not surprisingly, Israel was slow to respond to John's letters.[28])

The adolescent prig, offended by a scatological reference in Homer, was a short-lived phase, however. Instead, the classics would become an essential component of Wilkes's libertinism, which was not his parents' object in supporting his schooling. (Wilkes often resorted to Latin for salacious correspondence with fellow rakes; one recipient gleefully reported his sister's frustration at being deprived access to this male code.[29]) Although the adult Wilkes admired authors such as Cicero, whose models of virtuous political behaviour yielded one of the presumed benefits of a classical education, he would come to identify with pagan poets such as Catullus, who challenged conventional sexual morality and offered inviting scripts for amorous conduct.[30]

Wilkes's progress as a classicist and as a libertine was advanced by his university experience, another privilege denied to his siblings. His parents' choice

---

[25] Margaret Hunt, *The Middling Sort: Commerce, Gender, and the Family in England, 1680–1780* (Berkeley and Los Angeles, 1996), pp. 62–63; Anthony Fletcher, *Gender, Sex and Subordination in England, 1500–1800* (New Haven and London, 1995), p. 302.

[26] *Wilkes Correspondence*, vol. 4, pp. 218–38; BL Add. MSS 30873, fol. 114; Add. MSS 30874, fol. 92.

[27] 6 March 1741, Wilkes MSS 1, fol. 4. The mention of Pope refers to his loose translation of the *Iliad*.

[28] Wilkes MSS 1, fol. 3.

[29] BL Add. MSS 30880B, fol. 21.

[30] *Wilkes Correspondence*, vol. 4, pp. 218–19; George McCracken, 'John Wilkes, Humanist', *Philological Quarterly*, 4 (1923): 109–34.

John Wilkes

was Leiden University, where he was sent in 1744, attended by Matthew Leeson as his tutor and unofficial (and ineffective) guardian. Associated with the Glorious Revolution and the tradition of Whig dissent, it was a cosmopolitan place, and here Wilkes acquired his fluency in French. On arriving in 1744, he enrolled as a law student, which suggests that he or his father at one time envisaged the law as a possible future career for him. Previously, in November 1742, he had been admitted to Lincoln's Inn of Court, though he never took up residence there. It soon became evident, however, that the pursuit of a vocation was not the primary purpose of his presence at Leiden. His brother Israel advised that the university offered an opportunity for making useful social contacts among the 'English Gentlemen' there, and 'for fixing such generous and virtuous and heroic principles, as will render you useful to the world, and an honour to your friends at least, perhaps to your country & the age you live in'. Despite the pathos of Israel's efforts to exercise the authority expected of an elder brother, this agenda for John's self-improvement, with its combination of pragmatism and idealism, was not entirely risible. John did acquire an abiding notion of himself as a patriot-hero along classical lines; and he took full advantage of the rich opportunities for social and intellectual exchange with peers and with mentors, notably the philosopher Andrew Baxter, who in 1741 had left Scotland to become a tutor to his young countrymen at Utrecht.[31]

Yet Wilkes's own cryptic description suggests an aspect of his student life at odds with the expectations of his family: '[A]lways among women at Leyden. My father gave me as much money as I pleased. Three or four whores; drunk every night. Sore head morning, then read. I'm capable to sit thirty hours over a table to study'. Not surprisingly, his letters home were terse and guarded.[32] His parents were clearly mistaken if they had thought that by sending John to Leiden he would escape the debauchery for which Oxford and Cambridge had become notorious. His experience, on the contrary, seemed to lend support to the fear of xenophobes about the dangers to young Englishmen of a continental education. 'They return full of foreign airs, disgusted with the manners of their

---

[31] Matthew Leeson to Sarah Wilkes, 2 February 1744, Wilkes MSS 1, fol. 10; John Jaques, 'The Life of John Wilkes Esq. with Anecdotes of his Friends and Contemporaries', BL Add. MSS 59680, fol. 18; Alexander Carlyle, *Anecdotes and Characters of the Times*, ed. James Kinsley (London, 1973), pp. 84–88; Arthur H. Cash, 'Wilkes, Baxter, and D'Holbach at Leiden and Utrecht: An Answer to G.S. Rousseau', *The Age of Johnson*, 7 (1996): 397–426; *Records of the Honourable Society of Lincoln's Inn: Admissions*, 2 vols (London, 1896), vol. 1, p. 425; Israel Wilkes to John Wilkes, 26 September 1744, Wilkes MSS 1, fol. 12.

[32] *Boswell, Italy*, pp. 56–77. Wilkes's brother Israel offered a shilling for every letter that John wrote and pleaded that they not be 'on Lilliputian Paper, with a Margin half a foot Wide'. Wilkes MSS 1, fol. 12.

own Country, and import foreign vices', wrote Baxter.[33] (Wilkes himself would later have to contend with the grave charge of Francophilia.) Baxter's diatribe is a typical attribution of vice to foreign corruption; yet it is an odd statement given his vocation as a tutor to Britons abroad. Perhaps he was voicing disappointment at the way in which one of his own pupils had turned out. He would certainly not have had Wilkes in mind, however. Such was Wilkes's gift for self-representation that he always appeared to Baxter as a dedicated student. Nor did Wilkes's parents betray any concern that, at Leiden, their favoured son had begun his transformation, not only into the polished gentleman that they wanted him to become, but also into a gentleman libertine.

Neglectful Husband

When John Wilkes returned to Clerkenwell in July 1746, his parents had already marked out his future path. He was to fill the role of gentleman for which he had been groomed since childhood. The acquisition of the estate required to support this status came at a price, or at least that is the way Wilkes would later characterise his lot. The price was marriage to Mary Mead, an heiress and already a rich woman in her own right. Mary Mead was from a prosperous dissenting family that had long been on friendly terms with the Wilkeses. Sarah Wilkes was especially close to Mary's widowed mother, and the two women worshipped together in the Carter Lane Chapel, Blackfriars, when Mrs Mead resided at her London home in Red Lion Court. Mrs Mead was also the lessee of the Prebendal estate in Aylesbury, which conferred on her the status of the lady of the manor. She had extensive properties at her disposal. One of these, the Parsonage House, she made available to Matthew Leeson when he moved to Aylesbury in 1741, accompanied by John Wilkes. Master and pupil occupied this 'commodious' sanctuary – where John had his own apartment with 'a closet adjoining ... very proper for his study' – at a nominal rent, probably thanks to the influence of Sarah Wilkes. In Aylesbury, John Wilkes would have become acquainted with his future wife, but there is no evidence that at the time of first meeting there was mutual romantic interest. Perhaps the age difference discouraged it; he was sixteen, she was nine years older. Negotiations for the union almost certainly began while John was at Leiden.[34]

The image of Mary Wilkes left to posterity is unflattering, not because she had any reliably documented deficiencies of personality, but because she was eclipsed

[33]   BL Add. MSS 30867, fol. 14.

[34]   Hugh Hanley, *The Prebendal, Aylesbury: A History* (Aylesbury, 1986), pp. 8–9; Matthew Leeson to Sarah Wilkes, 6 May 1741, Wilkes MSS 1, fol. 3; Bleackley, *Wilkes*, pp. 9–10, 15–16.

by a husband who was a colourful self-publicist and who took a dislike to her, effectively casting her into shadow. The most vivid portrayals of the marriage are Wilkes's bitter reflections on it after its collapse in 1756. His wife, he told the diarist James Harris in 1763, 'was a most disagreeable woman, twenty years older than himself, and had the most odious Relations'.[35] He imbued the complaint with self-pity when, 15 years later, he sought sympathy from Maria Stafford, a woman he was pursuing, and who, like Wilkes, had undergone a marital separation:

> In my non-age, to please an indulgent father, I married a woman half as old again as myself of a very large fortune; my own that of a gentleman. It was a sacrifice to Plutus not to Venus … I stumbled at the very threshold of the temple of Hymen … Are such ties at such a time of life binding and are school boys to be dragged to the altar?[36]

If Wilkes had misgivings about the marriage, however, he did not betray them at the time; he was certainly not 'dragged to the altar'. Indeed, there was nothing to indicate trouble ahead, except perhaps the age disparity. It was unusual for middle-class brides to be older than their husbands, though Wilkes's claim that he was 'a schoolboy' at the time of the wedding was a piece of exaggeration, spuriously supported by his insistence that he was two years younger than he actually was. In most respects, the path to the altar was a well-trodden one of a type that usually led to enduring and often affectionate unions. It was not at all like William Hogarth's iconographic *Marriage à la Mode,* a cynical exchange of wealth for status whereby a rich alderman bartered his daughter's hand in marriage to the son of an improvident earl. Outwardly at least, the union of John and Mary replicated the circumstances of the successful marriage of John's own parents. It originated in a desire for closer ties between two families, the Wilkeses and the Meads, who were of similar religious outlook and material standing and already enjoyed friendly relations.

Like most marriages within the prosperous middle class, it was conceived in the first instance as an economic alliance. Yet though the future bride and groom were subject to parental influence, they were spared coercion. The hope and expectation was that courtship would promote a genuine affection. Wilkes himself was far from being a reluctant suitor. In his visits to the Meads – 'this excellent family', he called them – he was assiduous in the role: 'his manners were elegant and polite, and his conversation gay and entertaining'. Despite his later confession to James Boswell that he was by this time an experienced roué, there was no hint of rakishness in his deportment. Otherwise the pious Mrs Mead

---

[35]   Malmesbury MSS 9M73/G730, Hampshire Record Office, Winchester.
[36]   BL Add. MSS 30880B, fol. 71.

would not have been convinced that she had found in Wilkes the ideal son-in-law, whose merits surpassed those of some rival suitors, including a bona fide aristocrat (Lord Bellenden), for her daughter's hand.[37]

It is possible that Wilkes was motivated, as he later claimed, by a desire to gratify the wishes of indulgent parents. In the process, however, he managed to persuade himself that his future wife had desirable qualities beyond a handsome dowry. Despite his subsequent gripes about Mary's family, he was probably also impressed by the fact that her relatives included the celebrated physician, Dr Richard Mead, a potentially influential patron who later sponsored Wilkes's membership of the Royal Society.[38] Wilkes kept his acquaintances informed of the progress of the courtship, and their responses suggest that his praise for Mary Mead was unqualified. Paul Henri Thiry d'Holbach (later Baron d'Holbach), a Leiden friend, wrote:

> I wish that all your desires be crown'd with Success, that a Passion that proves fatal to great many of men be void of sorrow for you, that all the paths of love be spred [sic] over with flowers that you may not address in vain to the Charming Miss M.[39]

He later congratulated his friend on the success of his courtship of his 'Lovely mistress'.[40] From Baxter, the sentiments were less fulsome, but equally wholehearted, as he offered a homily on the benefits of early marriage.[41] The marriage ceremony took place on 23 May 1747, in St John's Church, Clerkenwell, next to the home of Wilkes's parents. If it followed the usual pattern of middle-class weddings, it would have been a sedate affair with only immediate family present. The marriage was legalised by a licence from the diocese of London, which obviated the requirement of having the banns called in church, a practice that publicised weddings in some unwelcome ways – by increasing pressure to invite large numbers of guests and alerting the poor of the neighbourhood to engage in their traditional practice of making a row outside the house of the newlyweds until bribed to go away.[42]

By virtue of the marriage settlement, which bestowed extensive property on the couple, John Wilkes was transformed into a prosperous country squire. His

---

[37]   Wilkes to Sarah Wilkes, 24 August 1746, Wilkes MSS 1, fol. 14; *Wilkes Correspondence*, vol. 1, p. 12; *The Life and Political Writings of John Wilkes, Esq.* (Birmingham, 1769), p. 2.

[38]   *Royal Society, Journal*, vol. 20, p. 36.

[39]   BL Add. MSS 30867, fol. 21.

[40]   Ibid., fols 18–19.

[41]   Ibid., fol. 22.

[42]   Parish Register, St John the Baptist, Clerkenwell, Microfilm X97/244, London Metropolitan Archives; Peter Earle, *The Making of the English Middle Class: Business, Society and Family Life in London, 1660–1730* (London and Berkeley, 1989), p. 179.

father donated real estate with a rental income of £350 per annum and a promise of more to come. From the Meads came rural properties in Buckinghamshire and other counties as far afield as Lincolnshire. In October 1746 Mary had taken over the lease of the Prebendal estate in Aylesbury, and with it the position of lady of the manor, from her mother. After the wedding, the estate was administered by the trustees of the marriage settlement until 1752, when Wilkes persuaded his wife and the trustees to relinquish sole possession to him. For a nominal fee of £37 a year – a sum virtually unchanged since the beginning of the sixteenth century – John Wilkes became lord of the manor in his own right. This status carried with it the usual quasi-feudal mixture of rights and responsibilities. In addition to the use of land and property, the lessee was entitled to tithes of corn, grain, hay and grass; in return he was obliged to supplement the income of the local vicar and to keep the chancel of the parish church in good repair.[43]

The principal residence of the estate was the Prebendal House, which was intended as the summer residence of John and Mary; in the winter months they would join Mrs Mead and her brother, Richard Sherbrooke, in their London home in Red Lion Court. At first, Wilkes adjusted well to this arrangement, and apparently to marriage itself. Shortly after the wedding, Andrew Baxter wrote to Wilkes of his pleasure 'that your marriage has crown'd all your wishes'. The birth of a daughter in August 1750 added, for John at least, a further happy dimension to family life. His sister Sarah wrote ecstatically to her cousin about the joyful ménage at the Prebendal House with the infant baptised as Mary, but known to all as Polly, at its emotional centre.[44]

Wilkes was at heart an urban personality; he never embraced the life of the bucolic squire in all its traditional aspects. Though a keen horseman, he had little enthusiasm for country sports such as hunting and shooting. These were in any case no longer regarded by this time as essential markers of genteel manhood, according to the new canons of civility. (When Wilkes took up hunting in later life, it was as a healthy exercise.)[45] Yet he happily assumed the character of a rural patrician, appreciative of the wonders of nature, especially as enhanced by the hand of man. The role of improving landlord evidently appealed to him.[46] Aristocratic rusticity, after all, was celebrated by some of his favourite classical authors, especially Horace and Virgil, as well as by d'Holbach, who claimed, while

---

[43]   Marriage Settlement [John Wilkes and Mary Mead], 21 May 1747, Duncombe Estate Deeds, D/DU 138, Buckinghamshire Record Office, Aylesbury; Hanley, pp. 8–9, 40–41.

[44]   Baxter to Wilkes, 21 August 1747, BL Add. MSS 30867, fol. 23; Sarah (Sally) Wilkes to Sophy Nesbitt, 27 July 1753, and 3 August 1755, Wilkes MSS 1, fols 31, 33.

[45]   Thomas, *Wilkes*, p. 216; Fletcher, pp. 326–29; [Wilkes] *Letters to Daughter*, vol. 2, pp. 7, 9–11.

[46]   Wilkes to John Dell, 13 April 1758, Osborn Manuscript Files W, Folder 16155, Osborn Collection.

still at Leiden, to 'act pretty well the part of Country Squire'.[47] The landowner and naturalist Thomas Edwards, a family friend and one of the trustees of the marriage settlement, took it upon himself to coax Wilkes into becoming a genuine 'ruris amator'. Edwards was a plausible advocate, a 'wise Nestor' in Wilkes's words.[48] From Turrick, his home in the Vale of Aylesbury, Edwards chided Wilkes for blaspheming 'the divini gloria ruris' when Wilkes complained that nature was dead in the winter. 'Nature dead!' protested Edwards. 'No sir, no more than a sleeping Venus is a dead Venus.'[49] It was the kind of erotic imagery calculated to appeal to Wilkes, who was far from being an unwilling pupil, and who himself rhapsodised to a friend about 'the wonderful verdure of the rich vale of Aylesbury and the fragrance of [his] bean-fields in full blossom'.[50]

Edwards recognised that Wilkes was often caught between the competing tugs of town and country. Wilkes sometimes found it difficult to quit London – 'this charming warm, wicked town', as he called it – but on occasion, 'the infernal din of the sons of riot' caused him to yearn for the tranquillity of Aylesbury, and he sometimes went there over the objections of Mary Wilkes, who preferred to stay in Red Lion Court.[51] At the heart of his provincial idyll were the Prebendal House and its gardens. Not all rakes, of course, were as attached to home and hearth as Wilkes. A vivid portrayal of eighteenth-century domestic ennui can be seen in the second plate of Hogarth's *Marriage à la Mode*, showing the newly married Viscount Squanderfield slumped in a chair after a night of dissipation, utterly dissociated from the extravagantly vulgar home environment in which he almost accidentally finds himself (Fig. 1.1). This image undoubtedly reflected some specific cases, but it signified the opposite of Wilkes's domestic tendencies. His lifestyle can scarcely be described as a dissipated one. After the excesses of his student days, he drank alcohol sparingly, rose early, exercised regularly, and was an advocate of whole-wheat bread.[52]

He was, moreover, fussily attentive to questions of décor and domestic comfort, whenever he had the means and opportunity to be so. The Prebendal House – an unpretentiously stylish building of the Queen Anne period, which can still be seen today – offered inviting possibilities for the exercise of his classical taste. To its

---

47   BL Add. MSS 30867, fol. 18.
48   Edwards to Wilkes, 10 April 1751, BL Add. MSS 30867 fol. 47; Wilkes to Edwards, Wilkes MSS 4, fol. 3.
49   Edwards to Wilkes, 27 November 1747, MSS Bodl. 1011, Bodleian Library, Oxford.
50   Wilkes to Edwards, [1749?], Wilkes MSS 4, fol. 3; *Wilkes Correspondence*, vol. 1, p. 41.
51   Wilkes to Dell, 11 December 1757, Wilkes MSS 6, fol. 18; Wilkes to Edwards, Wilkes MSS 4, fol. 3.
52   See below, p. 89n.30; Wilkes to ?, 20 May 1788, Osborn Manuscript Files W, folder 16123, Osborn Collection; [Wilkes] *Letters to Daughter*, vol. 4, pp. 180–81.

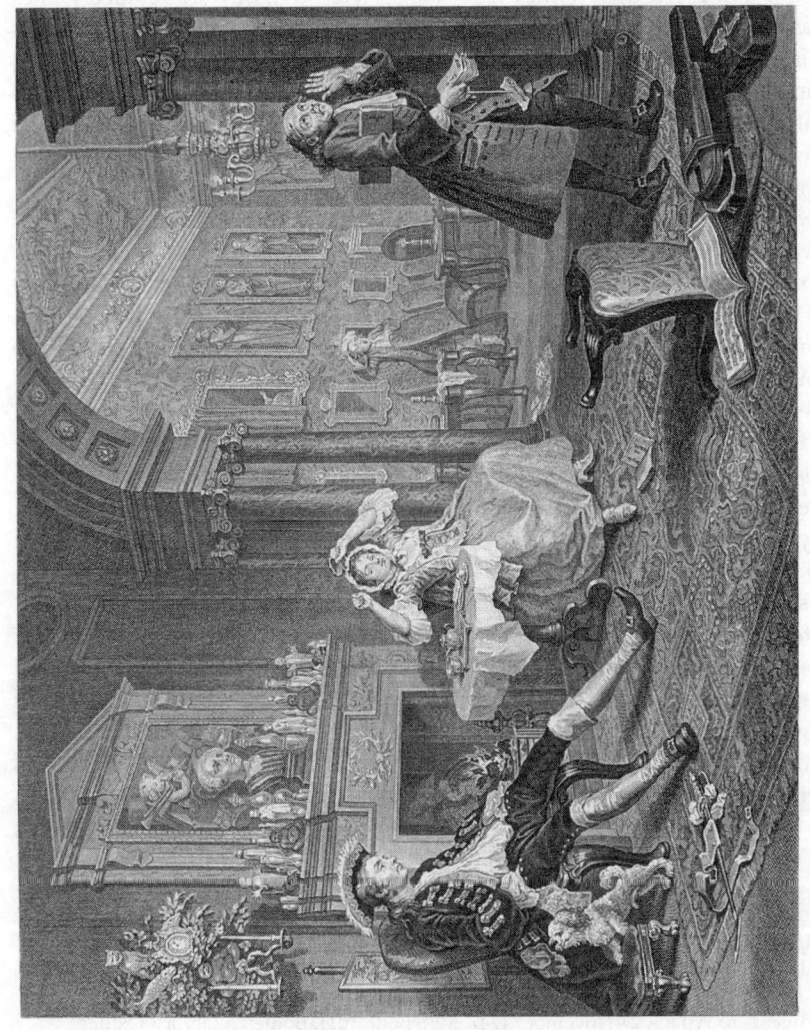

Figure 1.1　William Hogarth, *Marriage à la Mode*. Plate 2. By permission of the Guildhall Library.

main doorway, Wilkes added a painted wooden portico, with Ionic columns and a carved frieze; a side-door was redesigned to match. The windows he likewise refitted in classical style. More practically, he added (or possibly extended) a south wing for the servants' quarters and a brew house, which also served as a washing and ironing room. Behind this new wing, he erected a stable-cum-coach house and an arch that led into the field known as Parson's Fee.[53]

As well as extending the house and renovating its façade, Wilkes transformed its interior. He embellished fireplaces with carved marble, erected an elegant staircase, partially panelled and 'hung all the way with Paper representing Landscapes, Architecture, Trophies'; and made liberal use of the newly fashionable wallpapers – a green embossed paper for the dining room and 'India paper of the Chinese Landscape Pattern' for the drawing room. A well-fitted library was the domestic sanctuary of the gentleman-scholar, and Wilkes converted a ground floor room to this purpose; his extensive collection of classical works was housed behind 'sixteen Brass Wire Doors framed in Mahogany'.[54]

Wilkes lavished attention on his gardens, enlarging them through the acquisition of adjacent properties. He was single-minded in this pursuit. One neighbour (whose land Wilkes admitted coveting 'most inordinately notwithstanding the tenth commandment') held out for over two years before yielding his property, which Wilkes planted as a fruit orchard. Priding himself on 'so much taste', Wilkes devoted particular care to what in the language of the time was known as a 'pleasure garden'. When completed, it featured a lawn, sloping away from the house and bordered by 'a curious serpentining Shrubbery brocaded with Flowers', through which ran 'intricate paths'. The layout was in conformity with the vogue in landscaping, which strove for a 'natural' effect, as distinct from the straight-lined symmetry of the 'polite' gardens of a previous generation.[55]

The garden also contained the classical emblem of 'a rustic Temple' (part of which served as a dovery), as well as a grotto constructed of roots and lined with moss – a sanctuary, imagined a friend, where Wilkes might escape 'glaring noon' and entertain his mind in the 'friendly gloom'.[56] Because, from the early 1750s, Wilkes was so frequently absent from Aylesbury, he was obliged to rely on others to implement and sustain his projects. The death in 1754 of John Smart, his gardener, was a blow, and the garden fell into 'a state of chaos' until Wilkes's friend, Revd John Stephens, the vicar of Aylesbury, came to the rescue, planting trees, among other undertakings, according to Wilkes's detailed instructions.[57]

---

53 Hanley, pp. 14–17; Wilkes to Dell, 19 April 1757, Wilkes MSS 6, fol. 10.
54 Hanley, p. 21; Wilkes to Dell, 23 November 1756, Wilkes MSS 6, fol. 32.
55 Wilkes MSS 6, fols 23, 31; Hanley, pp. 31–32.
56 Hanley, p. 32; BL Add. MSS 30875, fol. 6.
57 Hanley, p. 31; Wilkes to Dell, 7 January 1755, Wilkes MSS 6, fol. 31.

Wilkes's attachment to domesticity should have augured well for his marriage, but in fact it might have contributed to its breakdown. The business of renovation was a male prerogative, but in his close concern for domestic detail – the direction of servants, the prudent laying-in of provisions, the attention to internal décor – Wilkes effectively appropriated those functions from which married gentlewomen typically derived personal fulfilment and social esteem.[58] The situation was different, but equally inimical to marital harmony, in the household of Red Lion Court, which was presided over by the unappealing figure of Wilkes's mother-in-law. Here Wilkes bridled under the piety and austerity of a domestic regime over which he had little control. One visitor remarked on his 'rough manners', and reported how he grumbled over dinner when boiled calf's head was served, complaining that 'there were many ways of dressing a calf's head, but that plain boiled was the very worst'.[59]

As for the effect of sexual incontinence on his marriage, in subsequent defences of his own conduct Wilkes blithely disregarded the implications of his progress as a libertine. The double standard for sexual conduct was so well entrenched in the eighteenth century that Wilkes probably never entertained the thought that his philandering, casually assumed to be a gentleman's prerogative, might endanger his marriage. Nor did his friends. In his letters, Dr John Armstrong routinely juxtaposed salacious references to Wilkes's sexual conquests with polite compliments to Wilkes's wife.[60] Mary Wilkes, for her part, seems to have been a complaisant spouse, who was only disturbed by her husband's rakishness when it intruded on her placid existence in Red Lion Court. The problem evidently was not what Wilkes was doing outside the home, but the disruptions he caused within it. Reportedly, Wilkes introduced into the London house a number of 'juvenile, gay, bacchanalians, of dissolute manners and vulgar language', shocking to 'a lady of sensibility and delicacy'.[61] Yet Mary Wilkes was reluctant to seek refuge outside the capital. Even the life of lady of the manor in Aylesbury did not appeal to her.[62] Shortly after her marriage, according to one report, she was 'very willing' to accompany Wilkes on a jaunt to Bath, but she was dissuaded by her relatives, who represented the town as, in the words of a contemporary journal, 'a licentious place, where

---

[58] Wilkes to John Dell, 28 November 1754, Wilkes MSS 6, fol. 22; Amanda Vickery, *The Gentleman's Daughter: Women's Lives in Georgian England* (New Haven and London, 1998), pp. 127–60.

[59] Mrs Fleming as recalled in Elizabeth Smart Le Noir to Cuthbert Sharp, 22 August 1831, Sharp MS 28, Durham Cathedral Chapter Library, the College, Durham.

[60] BL Add MSS 30880B, fol. 8.

[61] *Wilkes Correspondence*, vol. 1, pp. 17–18.

[62] John Wilkes to Thomas Edwards, 1749, Wilkes MSS 4, fol. 3.

the pretext of drinking the waters was pleaded to countenance every kind of vice and immorality'.[63]

Wilkes's libertinism undermined the marriage, but his determination to enter the House of Commons destroyed it. His wife and her mother did not support his political ambitions, especially as they involved further inroads on the Mead fortune. Wilkes even took away some of Mary's jewels, said one hostile witness, and then tried to return them so she could wear them to an election ball in Aylesbury, where he was canvassing voter support. In a rare display of spirit, Mary Wilkes refused, 'saying she had no further occasion for such ornaments'.[64] When, in September 1756, John Wilkes finally moved out of Red Lion Court and into elegant lodgings in St James's Place, the couple had been estranged for nearly a year, as John became increasingly preoccupied with his political career.[65]

In October 1756, Mary Wilkes launched a suit for separation in London's consistory court. The basis for her action was her husband's 'cruelty', one of only two grounds for legal separation, the other being adultery, which was notoriously difficult for a wife to prove. Wilkes himself initially contested her suit, but then, following a common pattern, both parties moved quickly to avoid expensive and wearisome litigation by agreeing to a private deed of separation. Under the agreement, Wilkes assumed all the property that had been brought to the marriage; in return he promised to pay Mary Wilkes an annuity of £200 for life. He also pledged to honour the terms of the separation and not to 'molest' his wife, or her relatives, once it had taken effect. There were disadvantages for both parties in the arrangement. Despite being separated, legally they remained husband and wife, which meant that neither could remarry without committing bigamy. Unquestionably, though, the terms were more onerous for Mary Wilkes. She had relinquished a considerable estate in return for the prospect of a quiet life at Red Lion Court. And while her husband could continue his libertine career with virtual impunity, anything that smacked of sexual indiscretion on her part (not that such a thing was likely in her case) would have enabled Wilkes to snatch away the pittance she had been granted.[66]

Despite being the apparent beneficiary of the settlement, Wilkes was back to court a year later, seeking the annulment of his separation agreement and the

---

[63]   *Town and Country Magazine* (1769): 360.

[64]   Elizabeth Smart Le Noir to Cuthbert Sharp, 22 August 1831, Sharp MS 28, Durham Cathedral Chapter Library.

[65]   Wilkes to John Dell, 11 September 1756, Osborn Manuscript Files W, folder 16155, Osborn Collection.

[66]   Records of Consistory Court of London, DL/C/554/030–1, London Metropolitan Archives; *Reports of Cases argued and adjudged in the Court of King's Bench, during the Time Lord Mansfield Presided in that Court*, ed. Sir James Burrows, 5 vols (London, 1812), vol. 1, p. 542.

'restitution of conjugal rites'. It was not belated feelings of attachment to his wife that prompted the action. His enemies would later allege that he begrudged Mary her modest entitlement to £200 annually. But Wilkes was probably taking a longer view. He was now deep in debt after his election as an MP for Aylesbury. Mary Wilkes stood to inherit a large fortune from her mother and uncle; only by being at her side could he hope to enjoy a share in those legacies. Whatever motivated his scheme, it was peremptorily quashed by Lord Mansfield in the Court of King's Bench, in the first of Wilkes's encounters with his legal nemesis. In a scolding judgment, Mansfield held that Wilkes was bound by his 'formal renunciation' of any right to 'force her back to live with him'. Any attempt to seize her would constitute a 'breach of the peace' and 'a contempt of the court'.[67] Subsequently, Mary Mead adjusted her will to make sure that her son-in-law would have 'no benefit' from her own death. It declared that her daughter's life interest in her estate was for 'her sole use', and 'free from the control of her husband'. As a precaution against him getting his hands on the family jewels, the will stipulated they were only to be 'lent to her during his life', with the permission of the estate's executors. Wilkes would have to wait until his wife's death in April 1784 before he could enjoy even an indirect benefit from the Mead fortune through his daughter, who was named the 'residuary legatee' in Mary Mead's will. The evident bitterness between husband and wife dissipated a little after Mrs Mead's death in 1769; the two even managed strained compliments about each other. Rumours of reconciliation were false, however, and when Mary Wilkes died in April 1784 her husband's display of mourning merely accorded with polite convention.[68]

Knowledge of John Wilkes's treatment of his wife was not something that could be easily contained in the private sphere once he became a public figure through his authorship of the anti-ministerial *North Briton*. Perhaps the first press reference to it was in the *Auditor*, a government-sponsored periodical set up to counter the *North Briton*, and which sought to pay back in kind some of the personal abuse that Wilkes was heaping on his opponents. In the issue of 23 September 1762, the *Auditor* – deploying the rhetorical device of disavowing *ad hominem* criticism as an opportunity for engaging in it – remarked: 'Of your behavior to a wife, who trusted her person and her fortune to you, I shall not here make mention'. It was difficult to brush aside such innuendo on the grounds that private conduct was irrelevant to public standing, because the former spoke to issues of character and reputation that were relevant to the latter. While a gentleman

---

[67] Records of Consistory Court of London, DL/C/554/094; *Reports of Cases*, ed. Burrows, vol. 1, p. 542.

[68] Bleackley, *Wilkes*, pp. 210–11, 368–69.

was expected to exercise manly authority in his household, vulgar coercion and boorish behaviour were considered marks of ill breeding. And although, in polite circles, adultery was no longer harshly condemned as an offence against God, it was still ranked as an offence against civility.[69] What purported to be attempts to dismiss the relevance of Wilkes's private life often had a distinctly ironic or facetious quality to them. 'Some have railed at your treatment of your wife,' wrote one anonymous pamphleteer, 'but even if their account be true, that can be no impeachment of your public character: Cato of Utica lent his wife to his friend Servilius, yet that never prevented him from being looked upon as a mirrour of patriots.' Wilkes's more committed supporters were often reduced to arguing that their hero was being held to a higher standard of marital conduct than noblemen such as Lord Sandwich.[70]

When Wilkes returned from French exile in 1768, determined to re-enter public life, the allegations that he had mistreated his wife intensified. Having squandered her fortune, 'he had ... treated her in the most barbarous and villainous manner', declared one anti-Wilkite scribe.[71] Such attacks were discomfiting for Wilkes, who penned a rebuttal, purporting to be from a family acquaintance:

I have heard some of his friends remark that she [Mary Wilkes] is perhaps the woman in the world the most unfit for him, and the only one to whom he would not have been even an *uxorious* husband, for he loves a domestic life ... She was certainly a large fortune, but unhappily half as old again as Mr. W. when he married her. I have often dined with them together in town and country. He was admired as an extremely civil and complaisant husband, rather cold, but exactly well-bred, and set an example of polite and obliging behaviour in his family, which many of those who find fault with him, would do well to imitate.[72]

Whether such arguments, skilfully crafted though they were, helped to secure a reputation for civility, good breeding, and politeness is questionable. More certain, however, is that Wilkes's claim to these qualities seemed more in evidence in his relationship with his daughter, which took on many of the features of a companionate marriage so conspicuously absent in his marriage itself.

---

[69] Vickery, p. 217; David M. Turner, *Fashioning Adultery: Gender, Sex and Civility in England, 1660–1740* (Cambridge and New York, 2002), pp. 46–48.

[70] *An Epistle from Col. John Lilburn in the Shades, to John Wilkes, Esq; late a Colonel in the Buckinghamshire Militia* (London, n.d.), pp. 41–42; 'Poets Corner: Jack Wildfire and Jemmy Twitcher', *St James's Chronicle*, 14–17 May 1763.

[71] *A Vindication of the D[uke] of G[rafton]* (London, 1769), p. 30.

[72] *Political Register*, 2 (1768): 416. Wilkes wrote this letter in response to 'A Woman's Man' in *St James's Chronicle*, 19 May 1768. On Wilkes's authorship, see *Wilkes Correspondence*, vol. 1, p. 21.

Sentimental Father

One can glimpse the obvious rancour between John and Mary Wilkes even through the obfuscating formality of the legal records, but it was not, as was so often the case, compounded by friction over child custody and visiting rights. Eighteenth-century law was adamant that a father had full patriarchal authority over his children. But the law's brutal impact was often mitigated in private deeds of separation, which provided an opportunity for mothers to assert the primacy of the maternal bond by pressing for generous access to their children, even practical custody of them. Mary Wilkes, though, seems to have been strangely untouched by the usual emotions of motherhood; she seemed quite willing to yield her daughter to her husband's care, asking only for the right to see her 'occasionally'.[73]

It was John Wilkes who made all the provisions for Polly's education. He took the responsibility seriously. On his library shelves at Aylesbury was *Traité de l'éducation des filles*, originally written – by the French bishop, François de Salignac de la Mothe-Fénélon – for the guidance of an aristocratic couple blessed with eight daughters.[74] Fénélon was insistent that female education was an important matter and that it should begin early. Accordingly, after detailed enquiries of his friend, the novelist Tobias Smollett, Wilkes sent Polly to a school in Chelsea 'where a great number of young ladies of the first fashion in England were educated'.[75] From here, she wrote the first of her many letters to her father; it was in French, in a bold hand, unlike that of her later years, which resembled a compressed version of her father's.[76] Polly was just six years old when she was first sent to the school, suggesting that John Wilkes's decision derived more from a desire that his daughter should become suitably accomplished than from feelings of paternal affection.

Affection was clearly evident, however, when shortly after her arrival at the school she fell dangerously ill with smallpox. She contracted it through inoculation, a controversial procedure that was supposed to prevent the deadly disease or mitigate its effects, but which in some cases produced a full-blown version of it. Wilkes probably authorised the inoculation because his sister Ann had died of the disease a few years previously and more recently a friend's daughter had fallen very ill with smallpox contracted 'in the natural way'. Wilkes would later say, only half in jest, that inoculation was more necessary

---

73   *Wilkes Correspondence*, vol. 1, p. 31.
74   *Sale Catalogues of Libraries of Eminent Persons*, gen. ed. A.N.L. Munby, vol. 8, *Politicians*, ed. Seamus Deane (London, 1973), p. 92.
75   Bleackley, *Wilkes*, p. 47.
76   BL Add. MSS 30879, fol. 1.

than baptism. He was fussily attentive throughout Polly's illness and full of praise for his daughter's spirit. 'Nothing can be conceiv'd more patient and good-humour'd than she has been the whole time', he wrote. He fretted over the possibility that she would be left pockmarked, but, to his relief, he was able to announce that she would not have 'a single scar'. When she was sufficiently recovered, he brought her, attended by a personal maidservant, to Aylesbury, where the two shared a summer holiday together. The whole episode intensified the emotional bond between Wilkes and his 'little angel', while widening the estrangement between husband and wife. During Polly's illness, Mary Wilkes refused to come near her daughter, despite John's entreaties, perhaps because she was fearful of contracting the infection herself. Her apparent lack of maternal instincts stood in contrast to the affectionate concern of John's mother, who was daily at her granddaughter's bedside.[77]

In April 1763, Wilkes took Polly, then 12 years old, to Paris, where he arranged for her to continue her schooling under the tutelage of one Madame Carpentier.[78] On his return to England, before embarking from Calais, he wrote Polly a long and revealing letter; it resonates with affection, but also with an anxious concern that there should be no omission in her finished education:

I wish you directly to enquire of Mr. Neville, who is secretary to the Duke of Bedford, *about the Dancing Master belonging to the Court*. He mention'd him to me, and he is the only man for you to learn of. You may either go to him, or he to come to you, as you find it best. By no means employ any other ... I wish likewise that you wou'd soon get the best musick-master and buy a harpsichord, the best you can.

He encouraged her to master the French language: 'Let me beg of you, my dearest girl, to write to me *in French* and *once every week*.' (He would later encourage her to emulate his own progress in Italian.) His letter concludes with advice on reading:

You have an excellent genius, given you from heaven; and it will be your own pleasure to cultivate it. Read the best books and they will be your pleasure thro' life. Desire Monsieur Carpentier to buy for you *Boileau*, *Racine*, and *Molière* in small volumes, you cannot read them, as well as *Shakespeare*, *Pope*, and *Swift* too often; yet by no means tire yourself. God has given you an excellent understanding, but the best land requires cultivation.[79]

---

[77] Wilkes to Jean-Baptiste Suard, 20 June 1769, Wilkes MSS 3, fol. 23; Wilkes to John Dell, 19, 26 April, and 3, 12 May 1756, ibid. 6, fols 10, 37, 38, 39; Wilkes to Dell, 13 April 1758, Osborn Manuscript Files W, Folder 16155, Osborn Collection.

[78] Bleackley, *Wilkes*, p. 87.

[79] BL Add MSS 30879, fols 8–11.

A year later, himself an exile in Paris and virtually destitute, he wrote: 'My plan for my daughter's education is the greatest expense to me, and that is a point I cannot dispense with'.[80]

Wilkes's concern for Polly's education was probably influenced by the attention that his own parents had paid to his. The regimen he organised for her was similarly strenuous, with appropriate allowance for what he insisted was Polly's fragile constitution.[81] Polly also enjoyed enriching associations with the families of leading *philosophes,* especially that of Claude Adrian Helvetius, becoming an intimate friend of his family. Yet there were significant differences in the respective educations of Wilkes and his daughter, in content and purpose, which in turn reflected conventional assumptions about gender. John's education was designed to advance his status as an independent gentleman; he made no attempt to provide Polly with the rigorous classical education that he had himself received. Polly's education had different goals and hence a different curriculum. 'I would have my dear daughter as much distinguished by every valuable accomplishment, as she is by her goodness and sweetness of temper', Wilkes wrote. Thus equipped, she could better exercise 'the sov'reign art, the art to please'. That revealing phrase is in a poem that Wilkes addressed to his daughter on her seventeenth birthday, in which he lauds her 'softness and sweetest innocence' and 'fair modesty'. The cloying language is that of an exquisite sensibility that idealised female delicacy and equated it with virtue. It was precisely such sentiments, especially the notion that women should be 'taught to please', that Mary Wollstonecraft would roundly condemn at the end of the century.[82]

Wilkes's expectations were duly fulfilled; Polly became a dutiful, affectionate, and accomplished daughter, a young woman equally at ease in polite company, at home and abroad, and at the easel and keyboard. No less an authority than Edmund Burke, called her a 'perfect ... judge both of the French and of the English Language'.[83] A drawing of father and daughter by Louis Carrogis, the duc d'Orléans' resident portraitist, shows the two of them posed in an idealised expression of their relationship. Polly is seated at a table, while John stands over her, one hand on her left shoulder, the other pointing to a musical score.[84] When it came to socializing, Polly, like her father, took delight in that most elegant of

---

[80]   Ibid. 30869, fol. 40.

[81]   *Wilkes Correspondence*, vol. 2, p. 155.

[82]   Wilkes to Polly, 10 March 1765, ibid., vol. 2, p. 142; [Wilkes] *Letters to Daughter,* vol. 1, p. 199; Vickery, p. 93; Mary Wollstonecraft, *A Vindication of the Rights of Woman* [1792] (repr. London, 1992), pp. 106, 110.

[83]   *Burke Correspondence*, vol. 6, p. 205.

[84]   That the portrait is of Polly, not of Gertrude Corradini as had earlier been proposed, is made clear in John Ingamells, *National Portrait Gallery: Mid-Georgian Portraits, 1760–1790* (London, 2004), p. 486.

entertainments, the masquerade, usually dressing, presumably in tribute to him, as 'Liberty'.[85] To John Wilkes, his daughter was always without flaw, except perhaps for her occasional inattention to questions of domestic management, her apparent deficiencies in this area lending credence to a widely held prejudice that an emphasis on the display of accomplishment was incompatible with a young woman's commitment to domestic duties.[86] The image of the adolescent Polly that is left to posterity is rather less appealing than the one witnessed through the eyes of her doting father. Left alone in Paris in the autumn of 1763, she quickly had a falling-out with an exasperated Madame Carpentier, complaining bitterly that she was being deprived of money, clothes (apart from 'two shifts') and earrings.[87] The same petulance was in evidence a year later when she was obliged to return to England – after living for nearly a year in Paris with her outlawed father – when Wilkes quit the French capital to escape his creditors and pursue his Italian mistress. Polly was taken into the family home in St John's Square, now occupied by her uncle, Heaton Wilkes, who promptly sent her personal maid back to Paris, despite Polly's insistence that she could not manage without her *femme de chambre*. 'What can it be to him whether I have a French, Italian, or any other servant', she protested to her father.[88] Predictably, Wilkes's sympathies were all with Polly. 'Heaton is a barbarian', he wrote. 'He has done the most cruel thing in the world by Miss Wilkes, and has held a language to her about me, which is false, insolent, and infamous … I have cried ever since I read her letter.'[89] Nothing aroused Wilkes's fury more than what he considered mistreatment of his daughter.

Compounding Heaton's offence in his brother's mind was his apparent complicity in a scheme to effect a reconciliation between Polly and her mother. Before Polly left Paris, John had instructed her that she could visit her family in Red Lion Court, but under no circumstances was she to spend the night there. Mary Wilkes and her mother, now showing a belated interest in Polly, had other ideas. Their family lawyer advised them that the moment Wilkes became a legal outlaw he lost all rights to his daughter. They were now determined that Polly should come to live with them. Eventually a compromise was struck between the Wilkeses and the Meads, whereby Polly was to spend half the week at St John's Square and the other half at Red Lion Court. Peace was also restored within the

---

[85] Charles Chevenix Trench, *Portrait of a Patriot: A Biography of John Wilkes* (Edinburgh and London, 1962), p. 235.

[86] Ibid., p. 366; Michèle Cohen, *Fashioning Masculinity: National Identity and Language in the Eighteenth Century* (London and New York, 1996), pp. 64–73.

[87] Polly Wilkes to Wilkes, 6 November 1763, Wilkes MSS 1, fol. 52.

[88] BL Add. MSS 30879, fol. 30.

[89] Ibid. 30868, fol. 164.

Wilkes family, where flare-ups were not uncommon but were usually quenched as quickly as they arose. Polly herself became happily reconciled to the arrangement, pampered as she was by her relatives from both sides of her family.[90] The staid Meads indulged her yearning for fashionable society by arranging for friends to take her to plays and balls, even to the pleasure gardens at Ranelagh. 'I always say I liked *France* very well, but to be sure nothing comes up to *Old England*', she reported to her father. Even he acknowledged that Polly was 'on the best terms with her mother's family'. He was probably also affected by the rumour that she would be cut out of her maternal grandmother's will unless the Mead family was propitiated.[91] Yet Wilkes clearly regarded the arrangement for his daughter as a temporary expedient. In May 1766, after a clandestine visit to England, he took Polly back to France with him, where she arrived, he reported, 'as well as can be after four terrible hours [of] seasickness'.[92]

The motives for Wilkes's action were far from straightforward and, like his marriage, they engaged the attention of an inquisitive public. At their core, though, was the essential fact that he was never emotionally reconciled to the loss of Polly's company after their separation in December 1764. 'Ever since Miss Wilkes embark'd, I have had an oppression of spirits I never felt before, not even in the Tower', he wrote.[93] As he continued his travels through France and Italy, he bombarded Polly with letters full of advice, concern, and affection. He wrote from Naples: 'Let us both continue to love one another more than all the world, and that will sweeten every thing, however cross and disagreeable it may appear.' After a visit to Voltaire, he assured her: 'I do not know when I have been so highly entertained; but I know, after all, that I had rather be with my dear girl than the first wits or beauties in the world.'[94] Yet Wilkes himself admitted that there was a mercenary element in his anxious desire to get Polly back by his side. He candidly acknowledged that the legacy Polly stood to inherit on the death of her mother and uncle represented a golden opportunity to restore his own financial independence. But now he calculated that the risks in allowing Polly to stay with the Meads outweighed those in removing her, because they might find her a husband who would supplant Wilkes as a potential beneficiary of the family fortune. 'I therefore found it too dangerous to let my daughter remain with them, and I preferred the encountering with greater difficulties here', he

---

[90] Bleackley, *Wilkes*, pp. 166–68.

[91] John Nesbitt to Wilkes, 2 May 1765, BL Add. MSS 30868, fol. 172; Polly Wilkes to Wilkes, 19 December 1764, BL Add. MSS 30879, fol. 33; Wilkes to Temple, 11 May 1767, *Grenville Papers*, vol. 4, p. 17.

[92] Fitzherbert Papers, 0239M/F8254, Derbyshire Record Office, Matlock.

[93] Wilkes MSS 6, fol. 78.

[94] *Wilkes Correspondence*, vol. 2, pp. 155, 184.

explained.[95] Once he had committed the deed there was no turning back. He told Heaton:

> I cannot risk, in my present condition of outlawry, that Miss Wilkes shou'd come to England for an hour, unless I had security from Red Lion Court for her return, which I think cannot be given to our mutual satisfaction. I have often thought of this but I cou'd never please myself after Jacomb's [the Mead family lawyer] insolent declaration, that I had no rights to her, that I was dead as an outlaw.[96]

The strategy, however, ran the risk of producing the opposite of the desired outcome as Lauchlin Macleane, a friend of Wilkes, pointed out:

> Your Friends are uneasy on Miss Wilkes's account, her grandmother [Mead] is very much chagrined at her going off to France against her Inclination, and there are serious Fears of her cutting her off from the Patrimony she designs her, in favour of another Branch of the Family unless she returns very speedily ... For Godsake weigh the consequences of persisting to make her uneasy. The good soul it seems is terribly afraid that Miss Wilkes will turn Roman Catholick, and She cannot with a safe Conscience leave her money to a Papist.[97]

As it turned out, Macleane's fears were unfounded, but the potential damage to Wilkes's public reputation, if not to his financial prospects, was nonetheless serious. One ostensibly friendly correspondent warned: '[I]t is a certain truth that your carrying Miss Wilkes ... to France was a great stumbling block to many who became your friends on account of your patriotism, and a little cooled the warmth of their zeal for you.' Driving such concerns was the issue of Polly's French education. For Wilkes, such schooling was *sans pareil*, an opportunity for his daughter to achieve the exquisite manners and politesse that he craved on her behalf. The contrary and widespread anti-Gallic view was that a French education was at best unnecessary, because there was nothing Polly could learn in France that she could not learn in England, and at worst dangerous, because her 'tender mind' could become 'infected with the superstition of the country'. The spectre of Catholicism was still liable to produce hysteria and distortion; the false rumour even circulated that Wilkes had sent his daughter to the 'popish seminary' at Douai in northern France.[98]

---

95 BL Add MSS 30868, fol. 40; Wilkes to Temple, 11 May 1767, *Grenville Papers*, vol. 4, p. 17.
96 Wilkes MSS 2, fol. 10.
97 BL Add. MSS 30869, fol. 42.
98 John Woodhouse to Wilkes, 24 June 1766, BL Add. MSS 30869, fols 47–48; *A Letter to the Right Honourable the Earl of T[empl]e: or, the Case of J[oh]n W[ilke]s, Esquire* (London, 1770?), p. 7.

The intimate companionship of Wilkes and his daughter drove an ongoing quest for the ideal domestic setting in which it might find its full expression. For a while, events conspired against them. Wilkes's reunion with Polly in Paris in 1766 had lasted barely eighteenth months before they were obliged to flee their apartment in the Rue des St Pères to evade his creditors. Back in England, Wilkes was at liberty for only three months before being confined in the King's Bench Prison, where he would reside in material (though not familial) comfort for the next two years. Even while a fugitive and prisoner, however, he was intent on coaxing Polly into becoming a proficient domestic partner. From The Hague, en route to England, he advised her to emulate his mother in such important matters as the proper airing of bed linen.[99] Before his incarceration, he installed Polly in a rented house in Prince's Court, Westminster, where she was joined by her faithful *femme de chambre*. His expectation was that Polly, by then aged 18, would learn to manage a household independently of her mother's family. From prison, he counselled domestic prudence: 'I beg my dear girl to buy a house-book, and to set down all expences, beginning from the first of her coming to Prince's-court.'[100]

Wilkes's release from prison in April 1770 finally gave him the opportunity to fulfil his domestic yearnings. On the fly-leaf of his copy of the *Almanach des Muses* for 1770, he wrote: '*Vivons en famille / C'est destin le plus doux / De tous. / Nous serons, ma fille, / Heureux sans sortir chez nous.*'[101] He wasted no time in fashioning the appropriate environment for his family idyll. He did so initially in Polly's absence; with his encouragement, she went off to France to attend the Dauphin's wedding and its accompanying festivities. Meanwhile Wilkes leased a larger house in Prince's Court as their principal residence and engaged carpenters, bricklayers, masons, and painters to make extensive repairs and renovations, all the while imagining Polly's presence there. Two rooms were designated as print-rooms; 'one for you, the other for myself', he explained to her. Her designated role in the refurbishment was to acquire domestic items only obtainable in France, including Sèvres china and two umbrellas, one for his friend and neighbour, Revd Thomas Wilson, and one for her own use, 'as the house at Prince's court is at a little distance from the street'.[102]

Wilkes also rented a furnished cottage in Elysium Row, Fulham (at that time, still on the fringes of the metropolis), for which he purchased glass and china 'in abundance'. There he installed a 'menagerie' of pets – those 'stock symbols

---

[99] *Wilkes Correspondence*, vol. 3, p. 226.
[100] Ibid., p. 286.
[101] Chevenix Trench, p. 271.
[102] *Wilkes Correspondence*, vol. 4, pp. 31, 34, 47, 49.

of pathos' by which a person's ethical sensibility was measured[103] – including a cat ('whose nails ... I shall order to be cut ... for having ... scratched me to-day'), a goldfish, bullfinch, linnet, canary, and 'four exquisitely beautiful Indian perroquets'.[104] He personally tended the cottage's 'little garden (which is a secret)', trimming the rose trees in such a way that their petals would blow around when she returned to his side. In this suburban Arcadia, there was even 'great harmony' among the servants. After Polly's return to England in August, father and daughter were reunited here, before they embarked together on a triumphal tour through the southern counties.[105] In the late 1770s, their affectionate union was captured in Johan Zoffany's portrait, showing John – as Horace Walpole, the celebrated gossip, put it – 'squinting tenderly at his daughter' (Fig. 1.2).[106]

Wilkes's desire for domestic elegance and comfort was an expensive undertaking, and hence a matter of concern for his mother, who tried to persuade Polly to curb her father's spending habits.[107] His extravagance was also an issue that spilled over from the private sphere. While he was in King's Bench Prison, some of his political allies had formed the Society of the Supporters of the Bill of Rights (SSBR) to pay off his debts, so that he could enjoy ease and independence, as well as immunity from any malicious creditors who might seek to perpetuate his incarceration. Confidently expecting ongoing financial support from the society after he left prison, he showed no inclination to curb his expenditure. His attitude irritated some of its members, who felt that he was abusing their generosity and perverting the public purpose of the society for selfish ends. The most vocal of the malcontents, Revd John Horne, an erstwhile ally, took aim in the press at Wilkes's spending: his need for 'expensive accommodation'; sending his daughter to Paris to see the Dauphin's wedding; his liking for claret; keeping six domestics, '*three* of them ... *French*'. By associating a craving for luxury with an unpatriotic hankering for all things French, Horne had contrived a potentially embarrassing polemical weapon, and Wilkes felt its sting. (He never purchased claret, he protested, and he had only two French servants in his family establishment, not three.)[108] Yet much of Horne's attack fell on deaf ears. There was little public criticism of Wilkes's pursuit of domestic comfort, perhaps because, in the political economy of the time, it had become 'a legitimizing motive

---

[103] Colin Campbell, 'Understanding Traditional and Modern Patterns of Consumption in Eighteenth-Century England: A Character-Action Approach', *Consumption and the World of Goods*, ed. John Brewer and Roy Porter (London and New York, 1993), p. 49.

[104] *Wilkes Correspondence*, vol. 4, pp. 44–45, 47, 59.

[105] Ibid., pp. 37–38, 53–54, 77–78.

[106] *Walpole Correspondence*, vol. 33, p. 138.

[107] Wilkes MSS 2, fol. 63.

[108] *Controversial Letters*, pp. 176, 196.

Figure 1.2   Johan Zoffany, *Mary [Polly] Wilkes; John Wilkes*. By permission of
the National Portrait Gallery.

for popular consumption patterns', quite distinguishable from the dangerous pursuit of luxury.[109] Any overt attack on the domestic existence of Wilkes and his daughter would have seemed crass, an offence against sentiment.

By now the relationship between father and daughter was taking on many of the features of the ideal companionate marriage, despite the fact that Wilkes never formally opposed the idea of Polly falling in love and marrying (unless it were to be the Meads controlling the process). Indeed, fleetingly anyway, he appeared to welcome the prospect. On her 18th birthday, he had conveyed the following benediction: 'And may kind Heaven a lover send / Of sense, of honour, and a friend, / Those virtues always to protect, / Those beauties – never to neglect'.[110] Even then, however, the prospect of Polly getting married was diminishing, as she became more and more a surrogate spouse for her father. The shift did not signify the onset of a meaningful egalitarianism; Polly's role was circumscribed, conducted largely according to her father's agenda; she still remained in her own words, his *'obéissante fille'*.[111] Yet her status was always much more than that of the spinster-housekeeper, and it carried the distinct benefit that she enjoyed a psychological and practical ascendancy over the other women who were connected with her father in various ways. No mistress or courtesan was permitted to challenge her role. This became publicly evident following her father's election as Lord Mayor of London in 1774. Polly served as his 'Lady Mayoress' – a role in which her public and private spheres converged – to great, albeit sycophantic, applause. When she presided over the traditional Easter rout (a fashionable civic soirée), one observer enthused that for 'affability, ease, attention and politeness [she] perhaps is superior to most of her sex'. Meanwhile, Marianne Charpillon, Wilkes's current mistress, chafed on the sidelines, dropping futile hints that she would like to be seen next to him during his mayoralty.[112]

Aside from the troubling issue of Polly's Parisian education, Wilkes's treatment of his daughter was, on the whole, an asset to his public image to the extent that it challenged notions that he was the self-absorbed rake that his enemies were anxious to depict him as. Wilkes himself had shown no scruples about putting his devotion to his daughter on public display when it suited his purpose. While imprisoned in the Tower of London for his authorship of issue no. 45 of the *North Briton,* he wrote her an affectionate letter that also appeared in the press a few days later. In it, he stoically and tersely alludes to his persecution, while declaring,

---

[109] John E. Crowley, *The Invention of Comfort: Sensibilities and Design in Early Modern Britain and Early America* (Baltimore, 2000), p. 143.

[110] [Wilkes] *Letters to Daughter,* vol. 1, pp. 201–02.

[111] *Wilkes Correspondence,* vol. 4, p. 96.

[112] William Purdie Treloar, *Wilkes and the City* (London, 1917), pp. 148–49; BL Add. MSS 30880A, fols 63–64.

'the most agreeable News I can hear, will be the Continuance of your Health'. The rest of his letter is full of domestic chit-chat ('the knives you desired are almost finished, and are very elegant') and gossipy enquiries about friends and acquaintances in Paris. The casual reader would scarcely have recognised in this paragon of fatherhood the monster of sedition depicted by his political opponents; and that is surely the reason why Wilkes secured the letter's publication.[113] By the time of his death 34 years later, his reputation as an excellent father had been long since secured, as this tribute in the *European Magazine* makes clear:

> With a variety of mental qualifications, Wilkes was reckoned one of the politest men of his time; and, very much to his credit, this politeness, mixed with a sincere affection, he shewed to his daughter upon all occasions. In all his trials of adversity, in all the bursts of popular applause, he never swerved from his duty; she was the constant object of his attention and paternal regard. Those who knew him most intimately have observed, that the topics of conversation which he introduced in her presence were of the *best* kind, and that he always spoke his *best* upon those occasions. Let this praiseworthy conduct balance many of his defects; and let it be followed as an example by all parents.[114]

The accolade is forceful, but also explicitly circumscribed. Politeness did not dispel his 'defects', but 'balanced' them. And by the time the accolade was pronounced, politeness itself was no longer seen as an unqualified gentlemanly asset, having been recast in moral discourse as appropriate for men in domestic spaces, but as potentially effeminizing outside them.[115] One cannot imagine Wilkes sending that touchstone of sentimental feeling, Goethe's *The Sorrows of Young Werther,* to his male friends as he did to Polly.[116] In her company, Wilkes could even indulge a conceit of himself as a fop, the caricature of the excessively polite gentleman, a creature exposed to mounting abuse in the 1770s. Polly was a willing accomplice. In 1770 he asked that she persuade Baron d'Holbach to purchase for him 'scarlet cloth ... of the finest sort and color ... for a compleat suit of clothes ... likewise the most fashionable gold buttons for the whole'. Perhaps he was wearing the suit that resulted when a young woman at Bath teased him about his *'froc Français du patriote Anglois'*. Reporting her comment to Polly, he called

---

[113] The original letter, dated 1 May 1763 is in BL Add. MSS 30879, fol. 13. It appeared in embellished form in the *Public Advertiser,* 9 May 1763.

[114] *European Magazine,* 33 (1798): 229.

[115] Michèle Cohen, 'Manliness, Effeminacy, and the French: Gender and the Construction of National Character in Eighteenth-Century England', in *English Masculinities 1600–1800,* ed. Tim Hitchcock and Michèle Cohen (London and New York, 1999), pp. 57–61.

[116] [Wilkes] *Letters to Daughter,* vol. 3, p. 59.

himself 'undoubtedly the greatest fop ... or the most perfect *macaronissimo* of the age'.[117] It was the kind of self-deprecating jest that, if performed in the public arena, would have sullied a carefully nurtured reputation for manliness.

The accolade in the *European Magazine* also evaded the connected issue of whether Wilkes was able in any meaningful way to reconcile his sexual libertinism with an attachment to domesticity with Polly at his side. In fact, Wilkes was far from even remotely approaching a seamless integration of domesticity and libertinism until late in life. Polly, for example, would have been unaware that she had a half-brother, John (a 'lively little rogue' in Wilkes's description), born in 1762 to Wilkes's housekeeper, Catherine Smith.[118] Wilkes kept up the pretence that John was his nephew, and when Polly became aware of his existence she invariably referred to him as 'Mr Smith'. In his son's case, Wilkes would go beyond the rake's creed of meeting minimal obligations to bastard offspring, but not to the extent of wholeheartedly including him in his family circle.

During his continental exile, Wilkes was at pains to quarantine his life with Polly from his sexual career. Sometimes he sailed close to the wind, most egregiously when he planned the seduction of Madame Carpentier, the married woman he had entrusted with Polly's care. Wilkes acknowledged that when Polly was with him in Paris, he led a double life, enjoying his daughter's company by day and gratifying 'other passions' by night.[119] When in the spring of 1765, with Polly back in London, he pursued the courtesan Gertrude Corradini to Italy, he concealed the main purpose of this expedition in letters to his daughter, offering only this bland comment that 'I went to pay my compliments to mademoiselle Corradini, and dined every day at her house while I staid at Bologna'.[120] Whether the young Polly could remain entirely innocent of the covert intrigues of her father is questionable, though through her adolescent eyes she likely saw them as romantic. Catching the spirit, she did some intriguing of her own, encouraging a dangerous liaison between her maidservant and Wilkes's valet, Matthew Brown. 'My woman languishes to see you', she wrote to Brown on Christmas Day, 1763.[121]

As Polly matured, Wilkes became less concerned about shielding her from the evidence of his philandering; but even as his double lives converged, he continued to uphold a double standard. Polly exchanged compliments and gifts with Mariannne Charpillon, though it is unlikely that the two ever met.[122]

---

117 BL Add. MSS 30879, fol. 155; [Wilkes] *Letters to Daughter*, vol. 2, p. 85.

118 Wilkes to Humphrey Cotes, 17 February 1764, BL Add. MSS 30868, fol. 40.

119 Ibid. 30880B, fol. 10.

120 *Wilkes Correspondence*, vol. 2, p. 128.

121 BL Add. MSS 30879, fol. 25.

122 Grace E. Thompson, *The Cyprian: The Life of a Covent Garden Lady* (London, 1932), pp. 225–26.

Subsequently, Wilkes made the occasional coy allusion to his amours. 'Good night, dear Polly: just ready to fall into the arms of – sleep', he wrote to her in 1778.[123] He seemed more concerned about protecting her from the bawdy conversation of his male companions than knowledge of his sexual encounters. Once he advised her not to visit him in the King's Bench Prison, because he was expecting the arrival of members of the libertine Beefsteak Club – 'too numerous a company of *he* creatures for you', he explained.[124] Over time, Wilkes and his daughter developed their own risqué (as distinct from bawdy) mode of communication, permissible within the expansive boundaries of eighteenth-century politesse. Given her experiences, it is not surprising that Polly's interest in matters of sex and gender hovered between innocence and prurience, as suggested in her enquiry to the Chevalier d'Eon, the French diplomat whose sexual identity became a matter of rampant public speculation in the early 1770s:

> Miss Wilkes presents her compliments to Monsieur the Chevalier D'Eon, and is very anxious to know if he is really a woman as everyone asserts, or a man. It would be very kind of Monsieur the Chevalier D'Eon to communicate the truth to Miss Wilkes, who entreats, with all her heart, to be informed of it. It would be still more kind of him if he would come and dine with her and her papa, to-day or to-morrow, or, in fact, as soon as he is able to do so.[125]

It is, of course, highly probable that Polly's apparently ingenuous enquiry was in fact prompted by her disingenuous father. Certainly engagement in gossip was a sustaining feature of their relationship. What presents itself as idle chatter can also carry a didactic purpose, and Wilkes deployed it to convey opinions about female merit, defined by the canons of eighteenth-century sensibility. His comparison of the celebrated Linley sisters is a case in point. The elder he judged 'the most modest, pleasing, delicate flower', whereas the younger was 'a mere coquet; no sentiment'. He described another female acquaintance as having 'her share of satirical wit; perhaps too large a one for the softer sex'.[126] Rather in the tones of his late mother, he reported to Polly the case of Jemima – 'whom you thought a modest, pretty girl, and so she certainly was, and unaffected' – who had had to be confined because she had gone 'mad for love' for a neighbour. 'Heaven guard us all from Cupid's bow', he commented solemnly and without a hint of irony.[127] These judgements on ideal womanhood and its deviations

---

[123] [Wilkes] *Letters to Daughter*, vol. 2, p. 80.

[124] *Wilkes Correspondence*, vol. 3, p. 285.

[125] Quoted in J. Buchan Telfer, *The Strange Career of the Chevalier d'Eon de Beaumont* (London, 1885), p. 280.

[126] *Wilkes Correspondence*, vol. 4, pp. 31, 97–98.

[127] [Wilkes] *Letters to Daughter*, vol. 4, pp. 50–51.

– from Wilkes the Sensible Man – stand in marked contrast to those of Wilkes the Rake, to be examined in detail in chapter 3.

Apotheosis of the Domestic Libertine

By the 1780s Wilkes was in a position at least to try to integrate libertinism and domesticity in ways that had not been entirely possible hitherto. Towards that end, his election as Chamberlain of London in 1779 gave him the financial means to maintain several domestic establishments. The death of his mother in 1781 removed the possibility of maternal censure, and that of his wife in 1784 meant that he was now at last free from the lingering criticism of being an exploitative husband. Even before these events, Wilkes had made a startling and ill-fated attempt to reconcile his erotic and domestic careers. What inspired it was his meeting with Maria Stafford in January 1778. Almost from the outset, he sought her as a domestic partner, and in so doing he represented himself as a 'man of feeling'. That was a condition to which even rakes could aspire, as long as they renounced callous conduct, curtailed their excesses, and accepted that conjugal bliss represented the ultimate attainment in relations between the sexes. Hitherto Wilkes's own claims to be a 'man of feeling' had rested precariously on his sentimental attachment to his daughter. Now, for the first and only time, the emotional affect of that father–daughter relationship pervaded one of his amours. 'I have … often sacrificed to beauty, but I never gave my heart except to you', he told Maria Stafford.[128]

Their first meeting was at a dinner party in Bath. Maria Stafford was a married woman recently separated from her husband, and Wilkes was instantly smitten. 'Since that fatal Saturday you have possessed my whole soul', he wrote to her on his return to London in the first of many love-stricken letters. He lamented that destiny had prevented him from becoming 'the guardian, the protector, the – oh rapture! – the possessor of those wondrous beauties and graces', and then sought pardon for his indiscretion on the grounds that 'an effusion of sentiment is a relief to an unhappy mind'. He made it clear that he valued her as a friend as well as a prospective lover. 'You have a soul tuned to friendship and harmony', he told her. 'I wish to merit the title of friend from a Lady so exquisitely amiable'. In the manner of the truly sentimental lover, he displayed an exquisite concern for her health (she was showing troubling symptoms of consumption) and even proposed to bribe her maid and physician to discover the true state of it.[129]

---

[128] *Some Bath Love Letters of John Wilkes, Esq.*, ed. Emmanuel Green (Bath, 1918), p. 20.
[129] BL Add. MSS 30880B, fols 61, 66.

Maria Stafford – a person of intelligence and wit – was not unmoved by Wilkes's bombardment of letters, poetry, gifts, and sympathy, but she was also alarmed at the intensity of his feelings and fearful that if their correspondence were to continue she might become dangerously compromised. She described eloquently her plight as a separated women, dependent on her husband's financial support: 'Death has deprived me of my natural protection and advisors, infidelity of my legal one, therefore the smallest deviation from prudence must inevitably ruin me'. With candour and good sense, she rejected what she saw as the only options available to them if she and Wilkes were to draw closer: a squalid affair ('too horrid even to be hinted at') or 'a sentimental unimpassioned friendship'. Even if Wilkes 'cou'd be spiritualiz'd to that degree', she observed, the world would never give her credit for 'the metamorphose of Mr. W. into a platonist'.[130] Wilkes responded that he indeed sought a 'sentimental friendship' but not an 'unimpassioned' one, and oblivious to her well-grounded fears, he made his move, proposing in lieu of marriage, 'an honourable and indissoluble union for life'. Seeking to dispel her anxiety about losing her independence for a second time, he insisted that she would enjoy 'Wilkes and liberty'. Revealingly, he cited his treatment of Polly as evidence of his good intentions:

> I have an unbounded confidence in what I love. Parental power is still greater than marital. Have I in any point restrained my own daughter, who has passed her whole life with me? I hold it my duty to make her as happy as I can. You would inspire me with that idea in a still tenderer manner.[131]

For several weeks he pressed his case, at times lamenting his involvement in public affairs and evoking a pastoral vision of the life he might have enjoyed with Maria at his side:

> Oh, that I had been born some happy swain
> In humble life, far from ambition's train,
> Where you the partner of my little state
> With all our smiling offspring at the gate
> Blessing my labours, might my coming wait.[132]

In April, he returned to Bath, where he succeeded in contriving a brief tête-à-tête with Maria. Her defences seemed to be on the point of crumbling until a conversation with a female friend stiffened her resolve. The friend had arrived at Stafford's house unexpectedly and spotted a concert ticket and a bouquet that

---

[130] *Bath Love Letters*, pp. 15, 17–18.
[131] 14 March 1778, BL Add. MSS 30880B, fols 71–72.
[132] Ibid., fol. 76.

Wilkes had sent as gifts. Discovering that John Wilkes was the suitor, she urged Stafford to suspend correspondence with such a notorious character. Brought to her senses and now alerted to her 'want of discretion', Maria Stafford complied.[133] Wilkes was distraught, and with the language of sentiment now wearing thin, he chided her for keeping up 'a foolish prudery which the present age is too refined to relish or approve'. He added some bitter reflections on friendships between women: 'The instances of friendship from your sex to ours are frequent and often most noble; to one another rare and trifling'. Even now, Wilkes was reluctant to abandon his pursuit, but fearful of displaying himself as 'a whining lover', his importunities diminished in intensity.[134] Within the year, Maria Stafford was reconciled with her husband, and, in a triumph for politeness over desire, Wilkes – while grumbling privately about Maria's 'puppy of a husband' – was able to accept the transition from would-be lover to family friend, making several visits to the couple's home in Berkshire and providing hospitality and entertainment when they came to London. (Perhaps the fact that Mr Stafford was a political Wilkite made the situation bearable.)[135]

Meanwhile Wilkes was pursuing a different, less impassioned, route to domestic contentment. Just before meeting Maria Stafford for the first time, he had begun an affair with Amelia Arnold, the daughter of a Wiltshire farmer. In October 1778, she gave birth to a girl, Harriet, whom Wilkes openly acknowledged as his own child. He installed mother and daughter at 2 Kensington Gore, a 'snug little house' near fashionable Knightsbridge.[136] There he was a frequent visitor, and the Arnolds would remain his companions for the rest of his life. Wilkes's reconciliation of libertinism and domesticity remained far from complete, however; although a domestic libertine, he never became a truly domesticated one. His interest in London's courtesans seemed unflagging. At the same time as he was setting up his love-nest with Amelia Arnold in Kensington Gore, he was also meeting one Jenny Wade in various *maisons de rendezvous* in Westminster. As late as 1795 he was reported to be involved with a 'female Dulcinea' in Soho.[137] It was declining libido, rather than the competing attractions of family life, that ultimately constrained his sexual career. 'My Sins of *omission* are daily increasing: – my Sins of *Emission* daily diminishing', he reported shortly before his death.[138]

---

[133] *Bath Love Letters*, pp. 34–35.

[134] 9 May 1778, BL Add. MSS 30880B, fol. 90.

[135] Bleackley, *Wilkes*, pp. 353–55; [Wilkes] *Letters to Daughter*, vol. 2, pp. 176–77.

[136] *Wilkes Correspondence*, vol. 5, p. 140; Transcripts for Parish Records of St Mary Abbot's, and press cutting, Kensington and Chelsea Public Library. The house was leased in the name of Amelia Wilkes.

[137] BL Add. MSS 30880A, fols 1–34; *Bon Ton Magazine*, 5 (1795): 275–76.

[138] BL Add. MSS 32568, fol. 24.

Meanwhile, sentimental attachments were compensating for the decline of libidinal ones. Harriet quickly became a favourite. Wilkes described her to Amelia as 'a sweet little girl ... almost as saucy as her Mama'. Sometimes her pertness raised his ire (accustomed as he was to the more docile Polly), but it always proved to be short-lived. Wilkes showered Harriet with gifts and he helped to install a menagerie of pets in the Kensington Gore house. When her pet owl, Peter, died, he consoled her with an epitaph: 'Minerva's bird, poor Peter's dead; / The gravest form, the gravest head; / From glare and noise he chose to go / To quiet in the realms below.' He watched over Harriet's education, instructing her in English grammar and encouraging her to learn French.[139] He took pride in her talent as an artist. 'Did you receive my little Harriet's Hygeia?' he wrote to Polly, in reference to an engraving that Harriet had made from an antique gem.[140] John Almon, the radical publisher and bookseller, reckoned that Harriet matched 'her sister, in every elegant grace that a finished education could give'.[141] Harriet was responsive to her father's attentions; her letters to him are solicitous and full of humour.[142]

Wilkes's attention to Harriet and her mother in no way diminished the central place of Polly in his life. For her part, Polly, totally secure of her place in her father's affections, shared his delight in her much younger half-sister. (In a delicious irony, Polly even willed a substantial portion of the Mead fortune to the daughter of her father's mistress.)[143] Although Wilkes and Polly remained emotionally bound, they were not literally inseparable. Both were inveterate travellers, for reasons of both pleasure and health. By the 1770s, Wilkes was suffering from recurrent fevers (diagnosed as 'marsh ague'), which he sought to combat with sea bathing and 'the centaur exercise of riding and hunting'.[144] Two of his favourite resorts for these purposes were Brighthelmstone (now Brighton) and Eastbourne, both on the Sussex coast. He also continued to visit Bath, though now for medicinal rather than libidinal purposes. After his return from French exile, Wilkes never left his native shores again, but he encouraged Polly to visit France and renew old friendships among its literati and aristocracy; between 1784 and 1789, she made frequent and lengthy visits there. It would not have been fitting for Wilkes, as a patriotic City father, to accompany her, but he took vicarious pleasure in her acceptance in French polite society. The physical separations of Wilkes and Polly were bridged almost daily through their spontaneous recourse

---

139 Chevenix Trench, pp. 366–68; *Wilkes Correspondence*, vol. 5, pp. 140–45.
140 [Wilkes] *Letters to Daughter*, vol. 4, p. 140.
141 *Wilkes Correspondence*, vol. 5, p. 286.
142 BL Add. MSS 30874, fols 53, 55, 108.
143 *Wilkes Correspondence*, vol. 5, p. 109.
144 [Wilkes] *Letters to Daughter*, vol. 2, p. 7.

to 'the familiar letter as intimate conversation'.[145] Through this medium, they remained emotionally in each other's presence, continually enquiring after the health of the other and advising appropriate remedies, sharing the events of the day, discussing the perennial problem of servants, and exchanging chatter about the foibles and follies of acquaintances, friends and family.[146]

Even as he entered old age, Wilkes remained untiring in his domestic enterprises. He busily clipped newspaper advertisements for items of home improvement, including one for the recently patented 'self-acting WATER CLOSET'.[147] In 1791, he gave up his London home in Prince's Court, replacing it with one in the more fashionable locale of Grosvenor Square. Polly was assigned the task of supervising renovation, while her father fretted about health hazards ('Let me entreat you ... my dearest daughter ... to run no risk from the smell of paint, dampness of new furniture, etc.'), commiserated about the disruption ('I truly sympathize with you in your present plague of workmen'), sang the joys of home improvement ('There is not a more surprising or more beautiful metamorphosis than that from laying down a beautiful carpet on a dull floor'), and kept in view the ultimate purpose of the undertaking ('I ... trust that for many, many years, you will enjoy the fruits of your cares and elegant exertions, in that first of domestic enjoyments, a good London house').[148]

Meanwhile, he directed another domestic project, one close to his heart. For many years, he had sought a residence on the Isle of Wight, where he was a frequent visitor. An anonymous poet, writing in 1777, imagined him, 'harassed with Public Life', seeking asylum there 'to meditate the Weal of Human Kind', as visions of the patriot heroes of ancient Rome passed before his eyes.[149] In 1788, after an extensive search, Wilkes leased Sandham Cottage (his 'villakin' he called it) on the downs of Sandown Bay on the south coast of the island (see Fig. 1.3). It commanded a splendid view of the ocean: Its 'magnificence of prospect ... charm[s] the Mind with a display of Nature's Grandeur', rhapsodised one of Wilkes's friends.[150] Painters, carpenters, and stonemasons were put to work to renovate the house; Polly Wilkes's contribution was to recommend a white

---

[145] Bruce Redford, *The Converse of the Pen: Acts of Intimacy in the Eighteenth-Century Familiar Letter* (Chicago, 1986), p. 1.

[146] BL Add. MSS 30879 is a rich cache of letters between Wilkes and his daughter. Many of these from John Wilkes are printed in [Wilkes] *Letters to Daughter*, vols 2, 3, and 4, and between father and daughter in *Wilkes Correspondence*, vol. 2, pp. 22–29, 107–89; vol. 3, pp. 222–33; and vol. 4, pp. 24–171.

[147] BL Add. MSS 30892, fol. 94.

[148] [Wilkes] *Letters to Daughter*, vol. 4, pp. 52, 63, 67, 186.

[149] *Poetical Excursions on the Isle of Wight* (London, 1777), pp. 17–19.

[150] BL Add. MSS 30873, fol. 9.

Figure 1.3   Wikes's Cottage, The Isle of Wight. James Marshall and Marie-Louise Osborn Collection. Courtesy of Beinecke Rare Book and Manuscript Library, Yale University.

marble chimneypiece for the drawing room, like one she had seen in Lord Gower's London residence.[151] Wilkes took special delight in supervising the transformation of the four acres of grounds, barren and windswept as they were. Some of the property he left in its natural state, but he installed curved paths with herbaceous borders running through the bracken heath. One visitor captured an image of Wilkes in rustic mode: 'His dress was perfectly Arcadian; instead of a crook, he walked about his grounds with a hoe, raking up weeds and destroying vipers'.[152] He and his gardeners succeeded in maintaining a flourishing orchard of dwarf apple trees behind the house and an extensive lawn in front of it, dotted with seats and arbours. Beside a flourishing kitchen garden, he installed a fishpond, stocked with carp, perch, and eels. He imported Chinese pigs and fretted about the proper location of the pigsties. He indulged his love of bird life: there were bird-boxes full of corn hanging from the trees, aviaries, several dovecotes, a 'pheasantry', and a 'long gallery' for chickens and other fowl; and he became a dedicated pigeon breeder.[153]

A feature that struck visitors as unusual were two large pavilions for summer use, constructed from a newly available canvas material. One of these he called his 'Tuscan Room'. Here he put his collection of Italian vases and some prints given to him by a neighbour. The other, containing fine furniture and china, was dedicated to his daughter: 'To filial piety' read its inscription. The home was a shrine to friendship and patriotism as well as to family. In its grounds, beneath a grove of weeping willows and cypresses, Wilkes erected a monument to his friend, the poet Charles Churchill, who had died in 1764. It consisted of a Doric column made of oak, supporting 'an antique sepulchral urn of alabaster' given to Wilkes by Johann Winckelmann, the celebrated art historian. On it Wilkes had engraved a Latin tribute to Churchill's wit and patriotism. He kept in the column bottles of fine port wine, a jest that, with its satiric allusion to the Eucharist, his libertine companion would surely have appreciated.[154]

His home on the Isle of Wight became the place of Wilkes's annual retreat from City business – the rural haven of the patriotic citizen, a place where manliness and domesticity could be reconciled. He usually spent enough time there to mark, with romantic lyricism, both the passing of spring and the coming of autumn. He pretended to glory in the not-so-simple fare that failures of supply from

---

[151] Ibid., fol. 148.

[152] *The Life and Times of Frederick Reynolds*, 2 vols (London, 1826), vol. 2, p. 105.

[153] Ibid., pp. 105–06; *European Magazine*, 33 (1798): 151–52, 163–65; Bleackley, *Wilkes*, pp. 380–81; Myers Collection, No. 2421, New York Public Library; BL Add. MSS 30874, fols 134–35.

[154] Bleackley, *Wilkes*, p. 380; *European Magazine*, 33 (1798): 152, 163. Judging by its cost, £349/12s/6d, the monument must have been a considerable structure. BL Add. MSS 30874, fol. 26.

the mainland sometimes necessitated: 'I live in the primitive simplicity of the patriarchal age, on fruits, milk, honey, and a little of the firstlings of the flock, and a trifling morceau de venaison from the field or forest'. From Sandham Cottage he wrote his last letter to Polly: 'The country is in great beauty, the scenery of this cottage in particular, and all in perfect order'.[155] Sometimes he was there alone; sometimes Polly and the Arnolds joined him; there was no embarrassment in the families mingling together in a contented *ménage-à-quâtre*.[156]

Absent, however, from the scenes of family delight at Sandham Cottage, and also from Kensington Gore and Grosvenor Square, was Wilkes's natural son, John Smith. Wilkes had been predictably conscientious in ensuring that his 'nephew' received an education 'fitt for a gentleman', sending him first to Harrow and then to the academy of Monsieur Lauchoix in Paris. In 1774, Wilkes brought him back to London for two years, where he allowed him to be cosseted by Marianne Charpillon. After receiving instruction in horsemanship at the famous Angelo riding school, Smith was packed off to Germany, the intention being that he would enlist in the Hessian cavalry. Instead, in debt, he wound up behind a clerk's desk in Hamburg. Wilkes recalled him to London again, only to have him sent out in 1782 to India, that convenient repository for unwanted relatives, as an ensign in the Bengal Cavalry.[157] From the far-flung reaches of empire, Smith anxiously sought recognition from the family circle. He used the exotic products of Asia as a bait, sending perfume (attar of roses) to his 'cousin' Polly and offering to send her muslin; he begged his 'uncle' to provide letters of recommendation so that he might escape the poverty of a junior officer; he requested a watch and a double-barrelled gun. By 1796, he was reduced to simply pleading for letters, complaining that he had received no replies to those he had sent to Polly and his father 'for some years past'.[158] His elderly mother Catherine Smith (of whose existence John Smith was probably unaware) was also kept at arm's length by Wilkes. 'Exceeding ill, and in the greatest distress', dreaming of her former lover and wishing herself young again, she pleaded for attention and relief. Wilkes obliged with a pittance each quarter until her death in 1795 released him from the obligation.[159] Wilkes was selective as to whom he allowed into the charmed circle of his domestic world; some, like the Smiths, were vulnerable to ruthless exclusion once their existence became a source of annoyance and possibly public embarrassment.

---

[155] [Wilkes] *Letters to Daughter*, vol. 4, pp. 142, 197.

[156] A letter from Harriet to a friend (BL Add. MSS 39781, fol. 54) makes clear that Harriet and her mother stayed at Sandham Cottage with Polly.

[157] Wilkes to Jean-Baptiste Suard, 8 August 1769, Wilkes MSS 4, fol. 11; Bleackley, *Wilkes*, pp. 345, 394; *Wilkes Correspondence*, vol. 5, pp. 117–22.

[158] BL Add. MSS 30873, fols 38–40, 78–79, 80; BL Add. MSS 30874, fols 194–95.

[159] Ibid. 30874, fols 30, 112, 118, 126, 153.

Chapter 2
Ambition

Patrician in the Making

John Wilkes's genius in attracting popular support for his causes should not obscure the fact that it was as a protégé of aristocracy that he first sought to fulfil his social and political ambitions. Even after he became a 'man of the people' and a City politician, he retained a lingering attachment to aristocratic society.

The term aristocracy has a flexible meaning. In its narrowest definition, the British aristocracy meant the peers of the realm – those individuals with the right to sit in the House of Lords. Wilkes's early ambitions were grandiose, but not unlimited: there is no evidence that he aspired to join the exclusive caste of the titled peerage, though he did seek an easy familiarity with its members, access to some of its prerogatives, and a sense of identification with its political power. In its broadest definition, aristocracy included the lesser landed gentry of whom, arguably, Wilkes became a member through a marriage settlement, which in effect made him lord of the manor of Aylesbury and provided him with sufficient income to support that status. Such an enlarged notion of aristocracy is not useful, however, because it obscures some real differences between the minor gentry and those above them on the social scale: the nobility and the 'overgrown gentry' (to borrow a term used by Wilkes himself[1]), who approached the nobility in wealth and social cachet and who in a cultural, if not a legal, sense shared their aristocratic character. The distinction between minor gentry and aristocracy, thus defined, was one of self-perception as well as of economic circumstance. The cultural hallmarks of the former were politeness, civility, and 'good breeding', but their desire to emulate the sumptuous, cosmopolitan elegance of those dubbed the *ton,* or 'the quality', was far from being universal. As Amanda Vickery has pointed out, 'it would be mistaken to see them as simply fawning junior members of a monolithic upper class'.[2] For a man like John Wilkes's father, Israel, the connected world of

---

[1] Wilkes to Jean-Baptiste Suard, 28 August 1769, John Wild Autograph Collection, vol. 38, fol. 106, Princeton University Library.

[2] Amanda Vickery, *The Gentleman's Daughter: Women's Lives in Georgian England* (New Haven and London, 1998), p. 36.

the urban bourgeoisie and minor provincial gentry, especially that substantial part of it with nonconformist connections, was a self-contained one; it was not merely a waiting room for those with larger ambitions. This is not to say that Israel Wilkes did not attempt to enhance his social standing incrementally. Quite probably he adopted Anglicanism more for social reasons than for religious ones. He also indulged in the selective acquisition of some expensive markers of elite status – notably the horse-drawn carriage – but here he was likely revelling in the fruits of his family's self-made prosperity, not engaging in some anxious attempt to define himself as aristocratic through material display.[3]

John did have larger ambitions than his father, but they were far from straightforward. Amanda Vickery has described the minor gentry's ambivalent attitudes towards the aristocracy as encompassing 'fascinated admiration, deferential respect, scandalized horror, amused condescension and lofty disregard'.[4] While this list does not fit precisely the range of Wilkes's responses, it constitutes a useful starting point for teasing them out. He certainly expressed 'fascinated admiration' for Earl Temple, his first (and last) aristocratic patron, and even, against his character, a modicum of 'deferential respect'. Later, having fallen out with his highborn libertine companions, he contrived displays of 'scandalized horror' at their aristocratic decadence, as we shall see in chapter 5. 'Amused condescension and lofty disregard' were also part of his subsequent repertoire of response, but paradoxically these could be defined as aristocratic attitudes simply directed back towards the incumbent aristocracy.

John Wilkes's ambitions were encouraged early by his classical education and by the generosity of his parents in giving him the means to fashion himself as a gentleman. They were advanced at Leiden, where his social aspirations were noted by Alexander Carlyle. Shortly after his arrival at the university, Carlyle met Wilkes while taking a stroll along the Rhine. Wilkes's 'Ugly Countenance … was very Striking', Carlyle recorded. Enquiring of his friend, John Gregory, about this curious person's identity, he was informed that 'he was the Son of a London Distiller or Brewer, who wanted to be a Fine Gentleman and Man of Taste, which he never could be, for God and Nature had been against him'. These early references to Wilkes's facial deformity suggest that it, as much as his class origins, was a social liability that he was continually obliged to overcome until such time as his features, especially his squint, became embedded in the consciousness of his well-wishers as idiosyncratic emblems of liberty and patriotism. Once acquainted with Wilkes, Carlyle found, him to be a 'Sprightly Entertaining Fellow', who 'even then … shew'd Something of Daring Profligacy'. At the same

---

[3]   On the horse-drawn carriage as a marker of affluence, see Vickery, p. 13, and Paul Langford, *Public Life and the Propertied Englishman, 1689–1798* (Oxford and New York, 1991), p. 10.

[4]   Vickery, p. 37.

time, 'he was fond of Learning and passionatly [*sic*] Desirous of being thought Something Extraordinary'. He was also 'very fond of Shining in Conversation'; but here he was outdone by another Leiden student, Charles Townshend, who despite having 'still less Furniture in his Head' than Wilkes, had more engaging manners, 'more Wit and Humour, and a Turn for Mimickry'.[5] As the son of a viscount, Townshend also enjoyed more social advantages; the implication of Carlyle's account is that, by comparison, Wilkes was a *parvenu*, albeit an engaging one, striving for acceptance from the upper crust.

His experiences in the Netherlands in themselves helped to equip him for that undertaking by smoothing away some of the rough edges that Carlyle had detected. There, he enjoyed the acquaintance of a number of young men who were talented or wellborn or both. They included William Dowdeswell – like Charles Townshend a future chancellor of the exchequer – and Mark Akenside, author of the *Pleasures of the Imagination* and already well on his way to becoming one of the leading poets of his generation.[6] Their influence, though, was negligible compared to that of Paul Henri Thiry d'Holbach, whose close friendship with Wilkes is discussed in detail in the next chapter. Of German birth, d'Holbach inherited his fortune and title from a French uncle, becoming one of the luminaries of Parisian intellectual society. Wilkes was a favoured guest at d'Holbach's famous salon, when the two were reunited in the 1760s. Not unusually for a *philosophe*, d'Holbach was a staunch supporter of aristocracy, warning in 1773 against the 'chimera of Democracy', which he feared was becoming 'fashionable' in France. He took pride in the marriage of his daughter into the French nobility.[7] Wilkes and d'Holbach shared similar social attitudes, then, and probably Wilkes found it easier to sustain a friendship with a continental seigneur like d'Holbach than with his English counterparts, for the very reason that it remained unentangled with issues of politics and personal ambition.

For the first few years after his return from Leiden, Wilkes's ambitions remained modest and consistent with his family's expectations for an incremental improvement in its social standing. He settled comfortably into the role of provincial notable to which his status as a local landowner entitled him. Having assumed the lease of the Aylesbury Prebendal estate, he became qualified to sit as a Justice of the Peace on the Buckinghamshire county bench. This was his

---

[5]   Alexander Carlyle, *Anecdotes and Characters of the Times*, ed. James Kinsley (London, 1973), pp. 86–88. When Townshend died suddenly in 1767, Wilkes remarked: 'Poor Charles Townshend! He had the brightest parts of any man I ever knew, but no character.' Wilkes MSS 2, fol. 31.

[6]   Arthur H. Cash, 'Wilkes, Baxter, and D'Holbach at Leiden and Utrecht: An Answer to G.S. Rousseau', in *The Age of Johnson*, 7 (1996): 397–422.

[7]   Alan Charles Kors, *D'Holbach's Coterie: An Enlightenment in Paris* (Princeton, 1976), pp. 150, 322–23.

first, though not his last, opportunity to serve as a magistrate, and he did so conscientiously in a county where most JPs tended to be lax in their duties. He liked to keep close at hand his copy of Richard Burn's *Justice of the Peace and the Law Officer*, the standard guidebook for the eighteenth-century magistrate. 'The grave Justice, my brother ... writes nothing but warrants for noisy, quarrelsome fellows, and his worship is as solemn all the morning as a City alderman, and as upright I assure you as a candle in a socket', his sister Sarah reported.[8] The work might have been tedious, but Wilkes would have been aware that 'reputation and prestige' were its traditional rewards.[9] Also serving as a turnpike trustee and feoffee of the local grammar school, Wilkes clearly relished being at the centre of a web of local dignitaries, solid citizens of the kind who throughout his career would draw a veil over his vices and lend him friendship and support. In Aylesbury, John Dell, in particular, became a trusted ally and confidante; Wilkes called him 'Old Steady'. A farmer and brewer, he served in a variety of parish offices, including Parish Constable and Overseer of the Poor. His industry and intimate knowledge of the local scene would make him the ideal political agent when Wilkes sought to become an MP for the borough.[10]

Although Wilkes did not enter civic affairs in London until after his return from exile in 1768, he had for some time been involved in the capital's associational life. His engagement was not simply with libertine clubs, but also with 'respectable' organisations – scientific, philanthropic, and artistic. They included the Royal Society, which he joined in 1749 after paying twenty guineas in lieu of a learned presentation, and the governing body of the London Foundling Hospital, to which he was elected in 1758. The following year, he took the lead in establishing the hospital's Aylesbury branch, serving as its first treasurer. Though his stewardship was later blighted by financial scandal, he took his responsibilities seriously, planning for the reception of one hundred orphaned children. Through his connection with the Foundling Hospital, Wilkes also became involved in the institutional patronage of British artists. The hospital itself functioned as an informal art gallery, because, following the lead of William Hogarth, several

---

8   Wilkes to John Dell, 8 April 1756, Osborn Manuscript Files W, Folder 16113, Osborn Collection; Sarah (Sally) Wilkes to Sophy Nesbitt, 3 August 1755, Wilkes MSS 1, fol. 33.

9   Anthony Fletcher, *Gender, Sex and Subordination in England, 1500–1800* (New Haven and London, 1995) p. 145. Wilkes's experience is consistent with the generalisation that 'when they secured land, middling-class estate owners also inherited the obligations and authority of gentry paternalism', often becoming 'fervent keepers of the flame of paternal ideology'. Richard Price, *British Society, 1680–1880: Dynamism, Containment and Change* (Cambridge and New York, 1999), p. 303.

10   George Rudé, *Wilkes and Liberty: A Social Study of 1763 to 1774* (Oxford, 1962), pp. 217–40; Wilkes MSS 6, fol. 65; Alan Dell, 'A Political Agent at Work in Eighteenth-Century Aylesbury', *Records of Buckinghamshire*, 30 (1988): 117–22.

painters and engravers, including Joshua Reynolds and Thomas Gainsborough, donated their works to it. Here, in November 1759, Wilkes presided over a meeting of artists that led, in 1760, to the first free exhibition of contemporary British art. It took place in a building in the Strand owned by an organisation of 'gentlemen improvers' known as the Society for the Encouragement of Arts, Manufactures, and Commerce.[11] This attempt to break the monopoly in artistic patronage exercised by wealthy grandees – with an unpatriotic predilection for continental artists – arguably prefigured in aesthetics what Wilkes and his supporters would later strive for in politics. At this stage in his career, however, Wilkes was using his civic and associational activity to seek access to traditional privilege, not to contest or undermine it. And at the Buckinghamshire Quarter Sessions, the Royal Society, and the boardroom of the London Foundling Hospital – an institution that enjoyed noble patronage – he rubbed shoulders with those who could support his ambitions.

A few years after his arrival in Aylesbury, he was clearly seeking to expand his social horizons. The influence of Thomas Potter – neighbour, fellow libertine, and a colleague on the Foundling Hospital board – was crucial here. A person of means and influence, Potter was master of the Ridgmont estate in Bedfordshire (which lies adjacent to Wilkes's Buckinghamshire) and an MP. Accused of initiating Wilkes into vice, Potter can also be credited (or blamed) for fuelling his friend's social and political ambitions. Wilkes began his political career as a protégé of aristocracy, thanks in large part to Potter's connections. Through him, Wilkes was introduced in 1753 to the Grenvilles, the powerful political faction grouped around Lord Temple and his brothers George, Henry, and James, all of whom had served the national government in various capacities, or would do so in the near future.[12] The party included the charismatic politician William Pitt the Elder who, though coming to the end of his long ministerial tenure as paymaster-general, stood on the eve of his political greatness. Pitt was a cousin of the Grenvilles and, in November 1754, the family connection became even closer when he married their sister, Hester. The Grenville faction was one of a number of proprietary parties that collectively constituted the Whigs, but it retained a self-conscious identity that set it apart from Old Corps Whigs like

---

[11] *Royal Society, Journal*, vol. 20, pp. 36, 96; R.H. Nichols and F.A. Wray, *The History of the Foundling Hospital* (London, 1935), pp. 299–300, 366, 369; Wilkes MSS 6, fols. 51, 54; William T. Whiteley, *Artists and their Friends in England, 1700–1799*, 2 vols (New York and London, 1968), vol. 1, pp. 163–66; Jonathan G.W. Conlin, 'High Art and Low Politics: A New Perspective on John Wilkes', *Huntington Library Quarterly*, 64 (2001): 361; John Brewer, *The Pleasures of the Imagination: English Culture in the Eighteenth Century* (London and New York, 1997), p. 232.

[12] John Beckett, *The Rise and Fall of the Grenvilles: Dukes of Buckingham and Chandos, 1710 to 1921* (Manchester, 1994), pp. 41–42.

the Duke of Newcastle. Some of its adherents, including Temple and Pitt, had been initiated into politics in the 1730s under the patronage of Temple's uncle, Viscount Cobham. They were known as 'Cobham's cubs' or the 'boy patriots', and they won their spurs as dissident Whigs, vocal in their opposition to the allegedly pusillanimous policies of Sir Robert Walpole.[13] Twenty years later, their self-image as the guardians of patriotism would be renewed by the circumstances of the Seven Years' War.

Wilkes was attracted by the culture of the Grenvilles, as much as by their politics. Away from London, their principal gathering place was Stowe, Temple's palatial, neo-classical residence in Buckinghamshire. He had taken it over from Viscount Cobham in 1749, and he spared no expense in completing his uncle's transformation of the estate into a lofty expression of patrician authority and refined libertine culture.[14] Wilkes was full of admiration for the effect. 'At *Stowe*,' he wrote, '*antient* and *modern* Virtue are enshrined with grateful Magnificence. Not only *Good Taste*, but *Patriotism*, are conspicuous in this delightful Paradise, the favourite Abode of the *Virtues, Graces,* and *Muses*'; elsewhere, he described it as an 'earthly elizium' (*sic*).[15] Its extensive grounds included temples to Roman patriotism as well as one to Venus, suggestive of the multifaceted contribution of antiquity to the self-definition of the eighteenth-century aristocracy.[16] It was the gardens at Stowe that probably inspired Wilkes to undertake the transformation of his own garden at Aylesbury.[17]

Temple – who according to one dazzled visitor enjoyed 'all the elegance of a real nobleman, and the ease of a private gentleman'[18] – was for Wilkes the epitome of aristocratic merit. Wilkes seemed blind to the flaws that others saw in him: a restless ambition, an unseemly appetite for political skulduggery, and a vanity that caused him to attribute to his own worth the lustre that he enjoyed from his association with William Pitt.[19] 'I am in part the political work of your hands', Wilkes once told his patron. He wanted Polly to model herself on Lady Temple, whose character he also venerated.[20] For his part, Lord Temple was

---

[13]   Ibid., pp. 14–15.

[14]   Ibid., p. 47.

[15]   *St James's Chronicle*, 2–4 June 1763; 'The Temple of the Muses', in *Wilkes Volume*.

[16]   On the erotic imagery at Stowe, see James G. Turner, 'The Sexual Politics of Landscape. Images of Venus in Eighteenth-Century English Poetry and Landscape Gardening', *Studies in Eighteenth-Century Culture*, 11 (1982): 345–47.

[17]   Hugh Hanley, *The Prebendal, Aylesbury: A History* (Aylesbury, 1986), p. 31.

[18]   *Grenville Papers*, vol. 3, p. 89.

[19]   *Memoirs of the Marquis of Rockingham and his Contemporaries*, ed. George Thomas, Earl of Albemarle, 2 vols (London, 1852), vol. 1, pp. 65–66; Beckett, pp. 32–60; Peter D.G. Thomas, *George III: King and Politicians, 1760–1770* (Manchester, 2002), p. 47.

[20]   BL Add. MSS 42085, fol. 22; Wilkes to Heaton Wilkes, 4 December 1764, Wilkes MSS 1, fol. 81.

pleased with his sprightly young client, and eager to indulge his libertinism. In one letter, written in October 1754, Temple thanks Wilkes for his hospitality at Aylesbury and says that he will 'drink to the pious memory of the delightful moments I have passed in your wicked company'. The theme is continued in subsequent letters in which Temple refers to Wilkes as 'my good, though wicked friend' and a 'gallant gay Lothario'.[21]

Temple can hardly be described as a libertine himself (he enjoyed a monogamous and companionate union with Lady Temple, whom he referred to as 'my little woman'[22]), except to the extent that libertinism was itself an ingredient, and not merely the spice, of the aristocratic culture that he exemplified. His indulgence of Wilkes's philandering was one aspect of that; another was his fashionable scepticism towards Christian doctrine. He discreetly encouraged Wilkes in the mockery of Sir George Lyttleton (later known as the 'good' Lord Lyttleton), another cousin and erstwhile member of his political faction, who had displayed an unfashionable piety by writing an essay on the conversion of St Paul.[23]

William Pitt shared many of Temple's attitudes. He took a special joy in his association with Thomas Potter, whom he described as 'one of the best friends I have in the world'.[24] The two spent a lot of time together at Bath (where Pitt went seeking relief from his chronic gout), and their friendship surely predisposed Pitt to look with favour on Wilkes. In October 1754, Potter wrote to Wilkes: 'At Dinner yesterday we read over yr Parody. He [Pitt] bid me tell you that he found with great concern you was as wicked & agreable as ever.'[25] I discuss in the Appendix whether or not this allusion was to *An Essay on Woman* or to one of Wilkes's other obscene parodies. But either way, Potter's comment suggests that Pitt revelled in bawdiness and in poking fun at religion. There was, however, a warning sign that Wilkes failed to heed: whatever his conduct in private, Pitt's public persona was one of gravity and austerity. And he would not take kindly to anything or anyone that tainted that image.

But that cloud had not yet appeared on the horizon. The reception that Wilkes received from his high-born friends must have persuaded him that his libertinism was neither a liability, nor merely an irrelevance, but a positive asset in his quest for political advancement and social acceptance. It contrived to be both an assertion of personal freedom and a dimension of his allegiance to a code of aristocratic values, best described as the honour principle, which served to

---

[21] *Grenville Papers*, vol. 1, pp. 126, 406, 489.

[22] Ibid., p. 406.

[23] Ibid., vol. 4, p. 126. Wilkes's mocking poem on Lyttleton is in *Wilkes Volume*.

[24] *Correspondence of William Pitt, Earl of Chatham*, ed. William Stanhope Taylor and John Henry Pringle, 4 vols (London, 1834–40), vol. 1, p. 173.

[25] BL Add. MSS 30867, fol. 103.

perpetuate a sense of group identity. These values imposed a set of obligations requiring Stoic acceptance, including the need to defend one's honour in a duel if the occasion demanded. At the same time, the code sanctioned a studied disregard for, or liberty from, the legal and moral burdens that lesser mortals were obliged to endure – responsibility for debt to tradesmen, for example, as well as the religiously endorsed constraints of conventional sexual morality. As *Junius* wryly noted, Wilkes believed that 'there are few excesses, in which an English gentleman may not be permitted to indulge'.[26] Wilkes liked to describe himself as a 'man of honour' and he conducted himself accordingly.[27] Perhaps he did so with greater sense of urgency because he lacked the tangible assets – powerful family connections, massive wealth, a public school education – that smoothed the path of many of those he sought to emulate. Wilkes's adherence to the honour code lent a sense of purpose and continuity to his otherwise picaresque career, but the appeal to honour was increasingly criticised as subversive of religious principle, or as a mask for vice.[28] So, like the libertinism with which it was connected, it would prove to be a combination of asset and liability when he sought approval for his actions from a wider public.

Wilkes's connection with the Grenvilles was one of reciprocal benefits. In return for the patronage of this Parliamentary faction, he was able to deliver local influence in a county that it regarded as its regional bailiwick. Moreover, his pen could be, and in time was, deployed for writing spirited political polemic, not just obscene parodies for the titillation of jaded aristocratic palates. For Wilkes, a fruit of his connection with the Grenvilles was his appointment as High Sheriff of Buckinghamshire for 1754. This, the most prestigious of his local offices and 'an initiation rite for new landowners', was a reward for garnering support for what would prove to be Potter's successful bid to become an MP for Aylesbury in the Parliamentary elections of the same year. It was Potter who made the recommendation for Wilkes's appointment to Lord Temple, with George Grenville acting as the intermediary.[29] Seventeen years later, Wilkes assumed an equivalent responsibility for the administration of justice in London and Middlesex. Serving as sheriff in two separate jurisdictions was in itself an unusual distinction; it took on irony in Wilkes's case because in between he was both an outlaw and

---

[26] *The Letters of Junius*, ed. John Cannon (Oxford, 1978), p. 163.

[27] *Wilkes Correspondence*, vol. 2, p. 36.

[28] [John Brown] *Thoughts on Civil Liberty, and Licentiousness and Faction* (Newcastle Upon Tyne, 1765), p. 31; [Mary Davys] *The Accomplished Rake: or the Modern Fine Gentleman* (London, 1756), p. 44.

[29] Potter to Grenville, 11 January 1754, *Grenville Papers*, vol. 1, p. 102. Wilkes's work on Potter's behalf in Aylesbury is documented in Wilkes MSS 6, fols 18, 20. The characterisation of the Buckinghamshire sheriff's office is from Langford, *Public Life*, p. 409.

a convicted felon. In 1754, though, these remarkable shifts of fortune were still below the horizon. Wilkes's appointment as Buckinghamshire's sheriff seemed like just one more step in a steady progress towards the fulfilment of his social and political ambitions. When appointed, Wilkes wrote to John Dell: 'You see I declare myself throughout a friend to liberty, and will act up to it'.[30] The comment was not an early avowal of political radicalism; rather, Wilkes was spouting the conventional abstractions of the Whig politician that he wanted to become.

For this to happen, his election to the House of Commons was a sine qua non. Eliding any distinction between social and political ambition, Lord Chesterfield had famously advised his son: 'You must first make a figure there if you would make a figure in the country.'[31] As a landed gentleman, at least in his own eyes, Wilkes presumably felt it was natural to seek membership in what was still 'pre-eminently a legislature of landowners'; by so doing, he could place a seal on his social pretensions.[32] His path to the Commons would prove to be littered with obstacles, however; they included the objections of his in-laws and of his father, whose ambitions for his son stopped short of wishing to see him enter Parliament. At first, Wilkes considered joining Potter as a candidate for Aylesbury in the 1754 election, but he withdrew in favour of John Willes, the son of a lord chief justice, whom he had earlier promised to support.[33] (The two were friends of a sort; at least Willes thought so. No libertine himself, he paid Wilkes the honour of seeking his expert advice on courting a woman of whom he was 'dotingly fond'.[34]) Potter then explored the possibility of Wilkes's candidature for Bristol, but the scheme was aborted when the Whig magnates intervened to dispatch Wilkes to try his luck at Berwick, adjacent to the Scottish border. The Duke of Newcastle, the new head of the ministry, supported the undertaking, and Temple and George Grenville urged it on their protégé. Wilkes eagerly complied. Some of his statements during the course of the campaign enabled him to characterise himself retrospectively as a model of virtuous independence, but he was clearly the candidate of the ruling Whig oligarchy, carrying in his pocket a letter of recommendation from George Grenville, then one of the lords of the treasury.[35] Despite enjoying government support and spending freely in the campaign, Wilkes was out-polled by John Delaval, himself a wit and a rake, whose family was well established in the area and, more to the point, well-known for its generosity to voters. Wilkes cried

---

[30] Wilkes MSS 6, fol. 4.

[31] Quoted in Lewis Namier, *The Structure of Politics at the Accession of George III*, 2nd edn (London and New York, 1957), p. 1.

[32] Langford, *Public Life*, pp. 288, 294.

[33] *Wilkes Correspondence*, vol. 1, p. 24; Thomas, *Wilkes*, p. 5.

[34] BL Add. MSS 30867, fol. 44.

[35] Thomas, *Wilkes*, pp. 5–6; *Wilkes Correspondence*, vol. 1, pp. 23–27.

foul. Claiming that Delaval had resorted to bribery, he launched a suit in the House of Commons, contesting the validity of the election. The case dragged on for nearly two years until Wilkes, who had been initially confident of success, finally withdrew his petition.[36]

During the course of his suit, an incident occurred that supported his reputation as a man jealous of his gentlemanly honour, and quick to defend it. Wilkes had retained a Scottish attorney, Alexander Campbell, to plead his case in the House of Commons. Just before it was due to be heard, Campbell withdrew his services, but refused to return his retaining fee of fifty guineas. When Wilkes protested, Campbell responded that the law was available to him. 'I have brought my Advocate with me,' Wilkes retorted, laying his hand on his sword, 'therefore, draw; for before I quit this room, I will have my money or satisfaction.' Campbell paid up without further quibble.[37] Like many of the anecdotes assiduously circulated by Wilkes's admirers, the story is plausible but unverifiable. Its significance lies in its contribution to the crafting of Wilkes's manly persona and as an example of the creativity of his publicists in identifying redemptive features in otherwise dire situations.

As his chances in Berwick evaporated, Wilkes again turned his attention to Aylesbury, preparing to declare his candidacy on the basis of rumours that Willes was about to obtain a government position, which would have required him to re-contest his seat. Any allegiance that Wilkes felt towards Willes was now severed. 'I am determined to oppose him,' Wilkes wrote to Dell on 24 November 1755, 'and will attack him with the utmost spirit in every way, particularly the true Aylesbury way of *palmistry*'; 'Sir Thomas Guinea' was to be his key weapon.[38] Wilkes seemed to take a special glee in his willingness to resort to the kind of bribery he had so piously and publicly eschewed at Berwick; revelling in his own hypocrisy was always, in his mind, a repudiation of it. As it transpired, however, Willes did not receive a government post, and the rumour of his resignation turned out to be as erroneous as the reports in May 1756 of Potter's impending demise, which prompted Wilkes to begin a premature campaign to succeed him. In fact, Wilkes was obliged to wait until the summer of 1757, when 'a reshuffle ensued, engineered by Potter and paid for by Wilkes'.[39] William Pitt resigned as MP for the pocket borough of Okehampton in favour of Bath, his adopted home; Okehampton thus became available to Potter, which left Aylesbury vacant for Wilkes, who spared no expense in securing the prize. ('[I] will give two guineas

---

[36]   Thomas, *Wilkes*, p. 6; Bleackley, *Wilkes*, pp. 32–35

[37]   *Wilkes's Jest Book; or the Merry Patriot* (London, 1770), pp. 8–9.

[38]   Wilkes MSS 6, fol. 27.

[39]   Lewis Namier and John Brooke, *The History of Parliament: The House of Commons, 1754–1790*, 3 vols (London and New York, 1964), vol. 3, p. 311.

per man, with the promise of whatever more any one else offers', he had told Dell. 'If you think two guineas not enough, I will offer 3, or even 5, to be secure.')[40] The gratifying reception of his political mentors probably made the financial sacrifice seem worthwhile. Pitt looked forward to Wilkes 'displaying more generally to the world those great and shining talents to which your friends have the pleasure to be so well acquainted'. But Wilkes soon learned that access to the most powerful minister of his generation did not automatically bring favours in its wake. Pitt made a show of keeping a lofty distance from issues of patronage. When Wilkes approached him to seek a contract for a brother, Pitt responded with a quip – 'Be assur'd, I should be extremely glad to promote your desires (always meaning your virtuous ones)' – while informing Wilkes that the matter was out of his hands.[41]

Wilkes entered a political world shaken by the impact of the Seven Years' War with France. Pitt and his allies had been dismissed from the ministry in November 1755, the Duke of Newcastle having turned to Henry Fox, an able but famously corrupt politician, to buttress his support in the House of Commons. Wilkes was far from being depressed by this turn of events. 'Our friends … will all fall to rise higher', he predicted accurately.[42] In the meantime, they constituted themselves as a patriotic opposition to the Newcastle-Fox ministry, which seemed incapable of effective management of the war effort. Armed conflict had actually begun in North America in 1754, but war was not officially declared until 17 May 1756, when the French extended hostilities to Europe by launching an invasion of Minorca, then a British possession. A naval squadron, commanded by Admiral John Byng, was dispatched to beat off the French attack, but it failed in its mission and the British garrison surrendered on 29 June. The island's loss was both a strategic setback and a blow to national pride, which to a large extent was constructed around a belief in the invincibility of the Royal Navy. 'The single loss of Minorca drove the people of England almost to madness', Wilkes later recalled.[43] Byng quickly became the scapegoat for the disaster. Angry mobs throughout the country burned or hanged him in effigy, an ominous portent to his court-martial and execution in March the following year.[44]

The Minorca fiasco was not simply a crisis and humiliation for the Newcastle administration, but arguably for the whole notion of aristocratic government.

---

[40] Wilkes MSS 6, fol. 14.

[41] BL Add. MSS 30877, fols 5, 14.

[42] Wilkes MSS 6, fol. 26.

[43] Wilkes to Arthur Lee, 9 November 1777, Richard Henry Lee Papers, American Philosophical Society, Philadelphia.

[44] Jeremy Black, *Pitt the Elder* (Cambridge and New York, 1992), pp. 118–20, 132, 136–38; Kathleen Wilson, *The Sense of the People: Politics, Culture and Imperialism in England, 1715–1785* (Cambridge and New York, 1995), pp. 178–85.

After all, one of the most basic purposes of aristocratic privilege was that its recipients constituted a virile warrior caste, ready to provide unflinching military and civil leadership when the security of the state was threatened. Even before Minorca, there were mounting expressions of alarm that the manly qualities required to preserve national vigour were being sapped by the insidious inroads of effeminacy among the ruling class. This gendering of political discourse, discussed further in the next chapter, was connected to the xenophobic assumption that the insidious source of effeminizing influence was France, Britain's 'natural' and virtually constant enemy. Capitulation to French manners and fashion, then, was nothing less then a kind of cultural treason to which the English aristocracy seemed peculiarly susceptible. It is noteworthy that the effigies of Byng – the son of a viscount – were clothed in the manner of a fop, signifying his 'identification with aristocratic, frenchified counsels'.[45]

This assault on aristocratic government anticipated in some ways the character of the Wilkite insurgency of the late 1760s and early 1770s, but in the early years of the Seven Years' War, Wilkes himself endorsed only a circumscribed version of it: namely that Britain's disastrous performance at the outset of the war was the fault of the Newcastle administration in particular, not of the aristocracy in general. Wilkes even expressed some initial sympathy for 'Poor Bing' (*sic*), and in October 1756 he clung to a belief that public sentiment was shifting in Byng's favour.[46] His party's attitude was driven by politics; pinning all responsibility on Byng obscured what it saw as the larger culpability of the Newcastle administration in making inadequate preparations for war. To press home the point, the Grenville faction encouraged constituency meetings at which electors drew up instructions to their MPs to demand a parliamentary inquiry into the Minorca disaster. Wilkes was active in the Buckinghamshire and Bedfordshire meetings of August 1756, as Thomas Potter took pains to report to William Pitt:

> Wilkes declares that my tongue is as glib as ever. He has been the occasion of trying it. The Example which the Grand Jury of Bucks have set to the other counties you may see in Saturday's Evening Posts. Wilkes who is likewise a Bedfordshire squire came to our Assizes flushed with Victory. He excited my ambition to imitate him.[47]

This early display of Wilkes's skill as an organiser of political opposition 'out of doors' was short lived, because in October 1756 Pitt and supporters were back in office. In June 1757, the ministry was again reconstituted under the

---

45   Wilson, *Sense of the People*, pp. 185–89.
46   Wilkes MSS 4, fol. 4.
47   Chatham Papers, PRO 30/8/53, fol. 49, National Archives.

joint leadership of Pitt, whose assignment was to secure a military victory, and Newcastle, whose principal job was to manage Parliament. Wilkes entered the House of Commons shortly afterwards and revelled in his association with the political faction most ardent and single-minded in the prosecution of the war. In October 1757, he dubbed Pitt and his followers 'the holy Theban band' after the ancient Greek fraternity who stood apart from the degenerate oligarchs and saved their country from Spartan aggression. (Wilkes chose to overlook the inconvenient circumstance that the original Theban band was as notorious for its homosexuality as it was renowned for its courage.) They alone could 'avert the impending ruin' that now included the possibility of a French invasion. Wilkes was joining the chorus of those who blamed Britain's calamitous performance in the first phase of the war on a failure of leadership by effete and Frenchified aristocrats. But though he supported Pitt's attempt to reach out to the City of London, Wilkes was still far from embracing anti-aristocratic politics. His message was that the patriotic qualities of an aristocratic warrior caste were alive and well among the Pitt circle, while subject to corruption elsewhere. Wilkes forgot his earlier support for Admiral Byng, claiming that he always knew Byng was a congenital coward.[48]

Wilkes seized the opportunity to affirm his martial ardour in an active way by accepting a commission, first as a captain, then as lieutenant-colonel, in the Buckinghamshire militia, which was embodied in 1759 with Sir Francis Dashwood as its colonel. His military service also helped to secure his genteel status. (As one cynical pamphleteer put it: 'Cock-eyed Jack considers himself a gentleman; for he was once a soldier in the Buckinghamshire militia.'[49]) The militia was established by Parliamentary Act in 1757, legislation that Pitt strongly supported. A trained home-defence force released regular troops to fight overseas, and, in symbolic terms, an armed citizenry was a potent expression of militant patriotism. Wilkes himself had signed the Bedfordshire petition urging adoption. The Act, though, was an elite measure, and one that aroused a lot of popular resentment. Many of those balloted into service, and unable to pay for a substitute, saw it as an imposition, especially as it was widely regarded as a device to impress them into service abroad. The Act provoked scattered riots, which had to be suppressed by regular troops. As Horace Walpole sardonically noted: 'The standing army was employed to impose upon the people a constitutional force.' Plebeian opposition was shared for different reasons by some of the Whig gentry who had long been fearful of reviving a militia force led in many counties by Tory gentlemen

---

[48] Wilkes to George Grenville, 22 October 1757, Wilkes MSS 4, fol. 6; Louis Crompton, '"An Army of Lovers": The Sacred Band of Thebes', *History Today*, 44 (November 1994): 23–29; Wilkes to Jean-Baptiste Suard, 27 October 1766, Wilkes MSS 4, fol. 10.

[49] *The Bow-Street Opera … Written on the Plan of the Beggar's Opera* (London, 1776), p. 14.

with an unnerving enthusiasm for the task. The Grenvilles did not share these fears. As lord-lieutenant of the county, Temple assumed nominal command of the Buckinghamshire militia and was attentive to its performance. Wilkes was conscientious in the task of raising, equipping, and drilling an often-truculent bunch of amateur soldiers in ways that won sincere commendations from his superiors (though Temple could not resist a tiresome double-entendre about Wilkes's '*active* service'). There were also some powerful symbolic benefits to be had. The image of the warrior citizen, resplendent in army uniform, obviously appealed to Wilkes; he would continue to sport a military-style scarlet coat long after he had been dismissed from service. The costume became a kind of sartorial rebuttal to those who sought to brand Wilkes a dandy because of his suspicious liking for French fashion.[50]

As the tide of war began to turn in Britain's favour in 1758, Wilkes basked in his identification with the Whig faction credited with this revival of national fortune. Three glimpses of him in that year reveal different facets of the young patrician in the making. The first is his appearance at a governors' meeting of the London Foundling Hospital to whose board he had just been elected. This institution was patriotic as well as philanthropic in purpose, because the 'preservation of deserted children' was a moral cause that could potentially yield extra manpower for an expanding empire.[51] An observer recorded:

> The celebrated Mr. Wilks [*sic*] was elected a Governor when very young and attending on a Court Day in a gay and rather fantastic dress attended by a couple of dogs he sat much observed altho no-one knew his name … The Court was engaged in a knotty discussion and could not arrive at an issue when Mr Wilks rising said 'I see no difficulty in the matter before you – forget all the arguments which have been used – the question is this "Are the benefits of this Charity to be limitted to Children exposed and deserted, that is left naked on Salisbury Plain or a dunghill." I maintain that a Mother dying from want with her infant at her breast is an exposed and deserted case, and that her child is exposed and deserted too – Are we living under the dispensations of Christianity and yet cripple our Notions of Charity.'

---

[50] Ian Beckett, 'Wilkes and the Militia, 1759 1763', *Army Quarterly and Defence Journal*, 112 (1982): 173–77; J.R. Western, *The English Militia in the Eighteenth Century: the Story of a Political Issue, 1660–1802* (London, 1965), pp. 127–61; Wilson, *Sense of the People*, pp. 188, 196; Wilkes to Francis Dashwood, 13 October 1759, MS D.D. Dashwood (Bucks) B 8/1/4, Bodleian Library; Horace Walpole, *Memoirs of King George II*, ed. John Brooke, 3 vols (New Haven and London, 1985), vol. 2, pp. 271–72; Temple to Wilkes, 20 June 1760, BL Add. MSS 30877, fol. 16; Langford, *Public Life*, p. 297.

[51] Ruth Perry, 'Colonizing the Breast: Sexuality and Maternity in Eighteenth-Century England', *Journal of the History of Sexuality*, 2 (1991): 204–34; Donna T. Andrew, *Philanthropy and Police: London Charity in the Eighteenth Century* (Princeton, 1989), pp. 57–65, 98–102.

Then, turning to Hogarth's picture of Moses and Pharaoh's Daughter, 'if so,' continued he, 'let us fall back upon ancient times and take a lesson from the heathen maid.'[52]

The image is that of noblesse oblige refined by sentiment. Here is Wilkes as a stylishly urbane yet good-hearted young gentleman, the accompanying dogs suggestive of a carefully staged rusticity.

A second glimpse of Wilkes at this time shows him in a different, less flattering light, that of the flinty Aylesbury magistrate, nagging John Dell in April 1758 to address the 'growing evil of the poor'. 'Unless something effectual is done,' he wrote, 'it bids fair to ruin you and most other parishes in England.' He urged that a solution be obtained in the 'cheapest manner', whereby 'the poor wou'd not be supported in idleness, as they now are'.[53] His tone is consistent with his invariably disparaging attitude towards the Aylesbury electors. Soliciting support from them was no more than a distasteful necessity. 'I ... shou'd laugh, when the rabble had got my money, to have the wretches come to ask favours of me', he commented during his first (and abortive) campaign in the borough.[54]

The third glimpse is from his visit to Scotland in the autumn of 1758. In private correspondence, he was already essaying some unflattering comments about Scotland – especially its inhabitants' alleged inattention to hygiene – but for the most part his tour confirmed him in his high opinion of the country and its people. He did not at this time regard Scotland as a land of famine. The high point of his itinerary was a visit to Inveraray, the estate of the Duke of Argyll, the premier Scottish peer. Argyll received him warmly, and Wilkes claimed that he quickly became a 'favourite of his Grace'. (His account of the visit to James Boswell, many years later, elicited this strangled couplet: 'Has not your lively humour oft made smile / The state-fix'd features of the wise Argyle.') Wilkes's description of the duke's castle and its prospect verged on the romantic: 'The mountains are stupendous, and their tops are generally cover'd with clouds and vapours. A river runs thro' his garden, in which are four cascades, and very pleasant walks thro' the woods. It is really a most grand place, and cultivated much beyond what an Englishman can have an idea of.'[55]

---

[52]   Quoted in V.E. Lloyd Hart, *John Wilkes and the Foundling Hospital at Aylesbury, 1759–1768* (Aylesbury, 1979), pp. 32–33.

[53]   Wilkes MSS 6, fol. 43. Wilkes was keenly interested in the process of appointing Overseers of the Poor, who were nominated by local vestries for confirmation by the JPs. He wanted 'clever fellows' in that position. Wilkes to John Dell, 8 April 1758, Osborn Manuscript Files W, Osborn Collection.

[54]   Wilkes to John Dell, 1 December 1755, Wilkes MSS 6, fol. 48.

[55]   Joel J. Gold, 'The Unlikely Visitor: John Wilkes in the Highlands', *Notes and Queries*, 224 (1979): 43; Boswell Collection, M287.

The image that these glimpses provide is complex, contradictory even, but by no means untypical of an aspiring patrician. The convoluted manner in which the English landed classes contrived to be at once paternalistic and familiar towards their social inferiors, and yet contemptuous and fearful of them, was a subject of puzzled comment, especially from foreign observers.[56] Less complicated at this stage of his career was Wilkes's 'fascinated admiration' for aristocracy, including its members north of the Tweed, which meant that he distanced himself from the anti-Scottish sentiment that lingered after the Jacobite rebellion of 1745. Aspersions on the basis of nationality, after all, were unbecoming for an officer and a gentleman.[57] It would take the political storms of the 1760s to transform Wilkes, ostensibly at least, into a friend of the (English) people and the hammer of the Scots.

Whig Champion

George III's accession to the throne on 25 October 1760 marked a modest challenge to the existing political order, but one with profound implications for Wilkes's prospects. Encouraged by Lord Bute, George's chief adviser and former tutor, the new king moved to promote national unity by relaxing the proscription of the Tories – there were few remaining – and reintegrating them into public life. The notion of non-party government had potential patriotic appeal, and Pitt himself had courted Tory support. But the king's well-meaning gesture annoyed the 'old Whigs', especially the Duke of Newcastle, who had been around long enough to remember that distant time when the Tories were a genuine threat to Whig hegemony. Wilkes, though, saw no immediate threat to his personal ambition. He played the courtier's role, caught up in the excitement surrounding the king's marriage to Princess Charlotte. 'I kissed the Queen's fair hand', he reported to Dell, and he busied himself in securing tickets for Dell and other Aylesbury friends to attend the coronation that followed the royal wedding.[58]

Wilkes's preoccupation was to secure a seat in the new Parliament, elections for which had to be held within six months of the start of the new reign. The experience heightened his contempt for the Aylesbury electors. He wrote to Dell: 'I have reason both to despise the baseness of the vulgar, and their astonishing fickleness; but I am a philosopher, and I will sooner sell my estate among such wretches, and represent better men, worse I cannot, than be trampled upon.'[59]

---

[56]   Langford, *Public Life*, pp. 274–75.

[57]   Wilson, *Sense of the People*, p. 169; 'Friendly Advice to a Young Officer with Respect to Duelling', *Public Advertiser*, 24 September 1763.

[58]   Wilkes MSS 6, fols 72, 73.

[59]   Ibid., fol. 68.

But with no other seat available to him, he was obliged to submit again to the importunities of his constituents, who were notoriously shameless in their demands on their representatives. After his election, while expressing his 'gratitude towards the independents', he lashed out at the 'lower sort' and contrived an appropriate response for their 'insolence':

> I ... have given ... orders ... [he wrote to Dell] to keep away from the house and gardens all the rabble at A[ylesbury]. If any of the better sort choose at any time to walk in the gardens, the gardener shall attend them ... and then I shall get rid of the numbers of women, children, dogs &c. You wou'd stare at the number of little thefts they make. I mean the lower sort; the best flowers &c. &c.[60]

Wilkes's antipathy to 'the rabble' was exacerbated by the fact that the election left him more deeply in debt than ever. With the election of 1761 looming, Wilkes desperately needed an additional and reliable source of income. So like many distressed gentlemen before and since, he sought financial relief in the form of a government place. Had he been successful, he would not only have supplemented his income, but also enhanced his social standing. He had glimpsed an opening in the autumn of 1760, when Sir James Porter, the British ambassador in Constantinople, requested a recall. Perhaps relishing the possibility of emulating the oriental adventures of some of his libertine associates, Wilkes applied to be Porter's successor. He would later insist that his application had been obstructed by Lord Bute, who became a secretary of state in March 1761, but in truth it was his own friends who had thwarted him. Lord Temple and William Pitt had eyed the position as an ideal one for Temple's brother, Henry Grenville, who was duly appointed to it.[61] With that matter still impending, Wilkes, on 27 February 1761, applied directly to Pitt for a position on the Board of Trade, requesting that the appointment be timed 'between ... parliaments' in order to avoid the 'very disagreeable circumstances' of a by-election at Aylesbury, which appointment to a government post would otherwise have required. In his letter, Wilkes adopted an approach that sought to reconcile clientage with the merit principle. He appealed to Pitt as his 'patron and friend', while asserting his suitability for government service: 'The small share of talents I have from nature are such as fit me ... for active life; and ... I should be entirely devoted to the scene of business I was engaged in.'[62]

Wilkes was sufficiently in touch with the times to appreciate that a position like that of Lord of Trade was no longer available as a sinecure. He was, however,

---

[60] Ibid., fols 68, 71.

[61] *Wilkes Correspondence*, vol. 1, p. 58.

[62] *Correspondence of William Pitt, Earl of Chatham*, vol. 2, pp. 93–95.

overreaching in his ambitions. As yet an undistinguished political novice, he lacked the experience and reputation usually required for a significant ministerial or diplomatic post, and he was without the family connections that might have compensated for these deficits. Yet his sense of entitlement never deserted him. In the summer of 1761, preliminary peace negotiations were proceeding with France, and the assumption was that these would ratify Britain's military conquest of French Canada. Wilkes conceived the notion of becoming the first civilian governor of this vast territory, without ever having set foot in North America. In lieu of appropriate military or administrative experience, he proclaimed his Whig principles: '[H]is ambition was ... to have reconciled the new subjects to the English; and to have shewn the French the advantages of the mild rule of laws, over that of lawless power and despotism.' John Almon claimed, presumably on the basis of Wilkes's own testimony, that 'had the negotiations taken a favourable turn, and peace been the consequence, he [Wilkes] would have been appointed ... for both lord Temple and Mr. Pitt gave him the most flattering assurances'.[63] Their assurances, if indeed ever offered, would shortly be of no avail. Peace negotiations collapsed, and, in October 1761, Pitt and Temple quit the ministry, now dominated by Lord Bute, when it refused to accept Pitt's demand for a pre-emptive strike against Spain, whose government was planning to join forces with France.

The resignation of his friends meant that Wilkes's career was set to follow a radically different course. Disregarding Temple's advice to 'sail with the new current', he went from being a supporter of government to its most virulent scourge. Just what his motives were soon became a raging issue. In September 1762, he told the future historian, Edward Gibbon, then a fellow militia officer, that 'in this time of public dissension he was resolved to make his fortune'. The comment is open to different constructions, the most pejorative of which is that he had not abandoned his quest for a place, but that he was simply adopting a new approach to getting one, the tactic being to raise such a storm that the Bute government would feel obliged to buy him off. Richard Rigby, a minor office holder and occasional boon companion of Wilkes, gave credence to this view, regaling colleagues with a story of how Wilkes proposed a deal to the new ministry: he would abandon opposition in return for appointment as governor of Canada. In a private letter, Wilkes came close to conceding the truth of this report, while in public he represented himself as high-mindedly resisting the efforts of the ministry to corrupt him. (A cartoon, entitled 'Kaw Jack, have Canada or to the Tower', showed a satanic Lord Bute trying to bribe Wilkes, while Lord Temple exclaims *O! Liberty O! my country* (Fig. 2.1).) All the while Wilkes was seeking to

---

[63]   *Wilkes Correspondence*, vol. 1, pp. 59–60.

Figure 2.1   Artist unknown. *Kaw Jack, have Canada or to the Tower* (1763).
Etching and engraving. Courtesy of the Lewis Walpole Library,
Yale University

enhance his stature among opposition Whig statesmen so that he might enjoy
their favour when they returned to power.[64]

The question of his motive is a complicated one, because Wilkes always
combined an unwavering belief in his own political rectitude with an eye for the
main chance. What is clear, though, is that Wilkes's attachment to aristocracy was
unshaken by the triumph of Lord Bute. If anything, it was enhanced. Certainly,
in practical terms, Wilkes proved to be more effective as an advocate for the
disgruntled Whig aristocracy than he had been as a loyal servant of the Pitt
administration. It would take him a while to find his role. That it was not as a

    [64] *Grenville Papers*, vol. 1, p. 479; Edward Gibbon, *Memoirs of My Life and Writings*, ed. A.O.J.
Cockshut and Stephen Constantine (Keele, 1994), p. 136; Thomas, *Wilkes*, p. 12; *North Briton*,
31, 1 January 1763; Wilkes to Humphrey Cotes, 17 February 1764, BL Add. MSS 30868, fol. 40.

Parliamentary orator soon became evident. Though Pitt's departure from office prompted Wilkes to emerge from his virtual anonymity in the House of Commons, his speeches in support of Pitt and his policies cruelly exposed Wilkes's limitations as a speaker. 'He spoke coldly and insipidly, though with impertinence', Horace Walpole recorded; 'his manner was poor, and his countenance horrid'. The diarist's judgement was typically waspish, but nobody seemed inclined to offer a more positive one. At a time, though, when Parliamentary speeches were still largely cloistered events, they had only limited implications for public reputation. Perhaps recognizing his own inadequacies, Wilkes became contemptuous of the devices of Parliamentary oratory. After his relations with Pitt soured, he condemned his former idol for his 'theatrical manner'; Pitt's 'speeches could not be read', because they relied on 'bold, glowing words' at the expense of 'sound reasoning' and 'accuracy of expression'. Later, Wilkes jibed that Edmund Burke's 'wild Irish eloquence' was nourished on 'potatoes and whiskey'.[65] If it is true, as his enemies claimed, that Wilkes was a demagogue, he became one while disdaining the conventional instruments of demagoguery.

It would be as a writer, not a speaker, that Wilkes came to public notice, despite the fact that his early ventures into print were anonymous. How that anonymity was stripped away, and how Wilkes responded in his inimitable way to his exposure, are at the heart of the story of his emergence from obscure party hack to national celebrity. The privacy of his study became the spawning ground for some highly publicised performances in courtrooms and on the hustings. In the 1750s his literary efforts were mainly confined to libertine *jeux d'esprit*, including *An Essay on Woman* (intended for private viewing only) and a satirical swipe at Samuel Johnson that appeared in the *Public Advertiser*. But by 1761 he was publishing political essays in the *St James's Chronicle*, followed by a pamphlet that quickly captured public attention: *Observations on the Papers Relative to the Rupture with Spain*, an unabashed paean to William Pitt, published on 9 May 1762. He also contributed to the *Monitor*, an opposition journal managed by Arthur Beardmore, Lord Temple's 'man of business'.[66] It was, though, his essays in the *North Briton*, the weekly periodical that he launched on his own initiative on 5 June 1762, with Charles Churchill as his collaborator, that brought him the most notoriety.[67]

---

[65]   Horace Walpole, *Memoirs of the Reign of King George the Third*, ed. G.F. Russell Barker, 4 vols (London, 1894) vol. 1, p. 142; *Political Register*, 5 (1769): 107; F.P. Lock, *Edmund Burke*, vol. 1 (1730–1784) (Oxford and New York, 1998), p. 516.

[66]   Wilkes MSS 1, fol. 32; Bleackley, *Wilkes*, pp. 38, 62–63; Thomas, *Wilkes*, pp. 18–19.

[67]   Deciding which issues of *North Briton* Wilkes and Churchill respectively wrote is a challenge. The most systematic attempt to assign authorship is in George Nobbe, *The North Briton: A Study in Political Propaganda* (New York, 1939). His main sources are the correspondence between Wilkes and Churchill in BL Add. MSS 30878 (subsequently published) and the material that the government seized from Wilkes: Guildhall MSS 214/1, Guildhall Library. Nobbe disregarded,

John Almon offered this explanation for Wilkes's success with the *North Briton*: 'His stile was masterly and elegant, his wit and satire truly classical, always exceeding keen, and very seldom gross, which operated incredibly upon the minds of the people. His facts were *always* genuine, and incontrovertible; which gave the paper a character of veracity.'[68] Charles James Fox, who was far from being a friendly witness (Wilkes attacked his father Henry Fox mercilessly), also spoke 'in very high terms' of Wilkes's style, adding that he 'supposed that writing was a very agreable Enjoyment to those in the habit of it'.[69] Fox recognised Wilkes's easy facility as a writer, but his comment tends perhaps to obscure the studied craft by which Wilkes identified a potential readership and responded accordingly. What made his achievement all the more remarkable was that he was not appealing to a single constituency. 'Some Papers should be to the General, others to the Mob', he explained to the *North Briton's* publisher. Hence 'there cannot be too great Variety'.[70] Most of the issues of the *North Briton* had the trappings – classical allusions, Latin tags and so on – customary in writings for the social elite, but Wilkes was also intent on reaching a wider readership, especially among the literate 'middling sort' of London. The essential ingredient was 'personal satire'. 'No political paper, tho' writ in the most masterly manner, wou'd be relished by the public, unless well-season'd with personal satire', Wilkes wrote. And while he attributed this insight to Lord Temple, he was clearly speaking for himself.[71] Later, writing to a French friend, he extended the culinary metaphor:

---

however, evidence provided by Thomas Frye, a friend of Wilkes and President of St John's College, Oxford, whose annotated copy of the *North Briton*, now in the British Library, assigns authorship (including co-authorship) for the first twenty-two issues. Frye's evidence generally supports Nobbe's conclusions, though there are discrepancies. Neil Schaeffer's careful re-examination of the evidence ('Charles Churchill's Political Journalism', *Eighteenth-Century Studies*, 9 [1976]: 406–28) credits Churchill with exclusive responsibility for nine issues, compared to the five credited to him by Nobbe. My assessment of the primary material (including the internal evidence of comparative style) and the secondary interpretations of it, suggest the following: Wilkes wrote issues 1–6, 9, 11–12, 14–16, 20, 23–25, 28–41, 43–45; Churchill wrote issues 7–8, 10, 18, 21, 27, 42. No. 17 (on Hogarth and the militia) was probably a collaborative effort. No. 13 is a garbled version of a seventeenth-century diatribe against the Scots, to which Wilkes added a short introduction. No. 19 is a letter from William Temple. Nos. 22 and 26 consist mainly of verses by Robert Lloyd, prefaced by Churchill's comments. Absolute judgements are difficult given the fine line between extensive editing and co-authorship.

[68]   [Almon] *History of Late Minority*, p. 78.

[69]   *The Journal of the Rev. William Bagshaw Stevens*, ed. Georgina Galbraith (Oxford, 1965), p. 14.

[70]   Wilkes to George Kearsley, 29 August 1769, in Adrian Hamilton, *The Infamous Essay on Woman; or John Wilkes Seated between Vice and Virtue* (London, 1972), p. 53; BL Add. MSS 22132, fol. 32.

[71]   [Almon] *History of Late Minority*, Wilkes's marginalia, p. 401.

Pray remember that in this country our mustard is ten times stronger than yours, our onions ten times ranker than those of Portugal, else an English palate finds both the mustard and the onions quite insipid. The taste of the nation must be consulted. Be so good to apply this to the works of the manufacture of the press. Delicacy is not the thing. Strength and force are requisite ... For my part I endeavour to forget all the excellent lessons of true taste.[72]

While reaching out to the people, however, Wilkes had by no means abandoned his attachment to aristocracy. He was still a long way from seeking to promote a radical political movement, independent of elite control. On the contrary, the *North Briton* became the staunchest public advocate for the Whig magnates and those of their followers pushed aside by Lord Bute. Wilkes's support for Temple and Pitt was predictable enough, but he now went beyond narrow partisanship to pay tribute to the mandarins of Old Corps Whiggery. He showered praise on the most senior Whig statesman, the Duke of Newcastle – hitherto an object of his scorn – who left the ministry in May 1762 over its reluctance to continue the subsidy to Prussia, Britain's wartime ally.[73] Soon afterwards, the Duke of Devonshire, whose great-grandfather was one of the 'Immortal Eight' who in 1688 invited William of Orange to assume the English throne, was unceremoniously dismissed as lord chamberlain and scratched from the Privy Council list; he, too, was hailed by Wilkes in a manner that anticipated Edmund Burke's fulsome depictions of aristocratic merit:

The *Duke* ... descended from a family, whose actions have done honour to their rank, well known for constitutional principles, untainted with base considerations of interest, a stranger to factious zeal, of acknowledged understanding, integrity and moderation, was to every true lover of his country, a rock on which he might with confidence repose his trust, and justice might declare that he would never take part in any action which was contrary to the interest of his country, or give the sanction of his name to countenance a corrupt administration.[74]

Wilkes's praise for the Whig grandees did not go unappreciated at the time. After being lauded in the *North Briton*, the Duke of Newcastle wrote to a young relative, Lord Middleton, who was evidently an acquaintance of Wilkes's: 'I am sure, you will take care, not to discourage Mr Wilkes; if your lordship should, in discourse, have occasion to mention my name, I beg, you would make my

---

72 Wilkes MSS 3, fol. 26.
73 *North Briton*, 6, 10 July 1762; and 8, 24 July 1762.
74 Ibid., 23, 6 November 1762.

best compliments to him.'[75] As for the Duke of Devonshire, Wilkes claimed that he '*soon* warmly espous'd the *North Briton* ... [and] tho' the least heated of the party, came to Lord Temple upon the report of Mr. Wilkes's accepting the government of Canada, and declar'd if he went to America, the opposition wou'd be undone, for Wilkes was the life and soul of it'. Such enthusiasm would abate in the storm that followed Wilkes's arrest for the publication of issue no. 45 of the *North Briton*, but Wilkes had grounds for believing that he was winning influential friends outside the Temple faction. His determination, though, to champion 'the common cause of the opposition' might have cost him some support from his political patrons. When the *North Briton* first appeared, Pitt, haughtily and rather hypocritically, declared that he was 'very warmly against all kinds of political writing, as productive of great mischief'. Temple meanwhile blew hot and cold; Wilkes claimed that Temple was piqued at the *North Briton's* defence of Henry Bilson Legge, who was dismissed as chancellor of the exchequer in March 1761, the first ministerial victim of the new regime. Temple's attitude, Wilkes reflected, was typical of the leaders of opposition: '... they were all secret enemies to each other, and the sacrifice of one seem'd to forward the views of the rest'.[76] But this was a retrospective judgement: in the pages of the *North Briton* the source of political malaise was clearly located, not in the incorrigible factionalism of the Whig grandees, but in the malign influence of Lord Bute.

The *North Briton's* attack on Bute, continuing one that Wilkes had launched in the *Monitor*, was thoroughgoing, encompassing not only Bute's policies, but his nationality and personality as well. Bute was not, however, reviled as a typical representative of aristocratic government; rather, his credentials as a bona fide aristocrat were themselves brought into question, especially through comparison with those of the Whig aristocrats he was displacing. He 'has no *hereditary* right to a seat in parliament ... no, he is chosen by the *opulent* and *independent* nobility of Scotland ...' sneered Wilkes in *North Briton* no. 2. Wilkes also made common cause with the satirical caricaturists who mocked Bute's pretensions in securing for himself the most prestigious of royal accolades, the Order of the Garter. (His strictures must have gratified Lord Temple, whose unremitting campaign for the honour so irritated George II that he reportedly hurled the garter at Temple when he was finally installed in May 1760.)[77] Bute was a '*mushroom* minister' who scorned a defining responsibility of the true nobleman, which was to provide disinterested service and council to his monarch in the manner of the Duke of

---

75   25 January 1763, BL Add. MSS 32946, fol. 206.

76   [Almon] *History of Late Minority*, Wilkes's marginalia, pp. 335, 399, 405, 407.

77   *North Briton*, 2, 12 June 1762; Beckett, p. 44.

Newcastle, and instead had insinuated himself as that most odious of creatures, the 'favourite' or 'overmighty subject'. In this capacity, Wilkes insisted, Bute was brazenly diverting patronage from legitimate public uses to support sycophantic hack-writers and a horde of hungry Scottish place seekers, including many with Jacobite connections.[78]

The means whereby Bute achieved power, according to Wilkes, was as squalid as the manner in which he deployed it. Wilkes repeated the calumny, widely circulated in satirical prints and broadsides, that Bute's influence at court derived from his sexual conquest of the king's mother, the Dowager Princess of Wales. Wilkes's own scepticism about the truth of the charge did not constrain him from giving it audacious expression in *North Briton* no. 5, where he compared Bute to Roger Mortimer, the Earl of March (*c.* 1287–1330) who in Edward III's minority 'was indebted for the enormity of his power to a criminal correspondence with the *Queen Mother*'.[79] Together they had conspired to thwart victory over the Scots for their own selfish purposes. The historical analogy pointed to a solution: Edward III, the scales having fallen from his eyes, secured Mortimer's execution at Tyburn. George III was urged likewise to 'crush the aspiring wretch who mounts to power by ... ignoble means'. The comparison of Bute and Mortimer was one that Wilkes found irresistible. He returned to it in March 1763 in a satirical dedication to Bute of Ben Johnson's play, *The Fall of Mortimer*. 'The ... Prince was held in the most absolute slavery by his Mother and her Minister, the first Nobles of England were excluded from the King's Councils, and the Minion disposed of all places of profit and trust', he gravely recorded. While denying with heavy irony that such a situation pertained at the present day, he lamented the fate of those – Pitt and Earl Temple; the Dukes of Newcastle and Devonshire; the Marquis of Rockingham and the Earl of Hardwicke; and 'the two spirited, young Nobles, who stand so high in fame and virtue ... the Dukes of Grafton and Portland' – who, thanks to Bute, now enjoyed 'only the empty applause of their country', not 'the smiles of [their] Sovreign'.[80]

The charge against Bute was not that of sexual licence per se, but rather that of sexual exploitation to gratify selfish ends in ways that threatened the integrity of the body politic. Wilkes evoked the horrors of venereal disease, punning that Bute had infected the Princess Dowager with 'a reigning disorder'.[81] Clearly,

---

[78]   *North Briton*, 37, 12 February 1763; and 4, 26 June 1762.

[79]   When asked if he believed the tale, Wilkes replied, 'Not I, by G--, but it will make an excellent *North Briton*'. *Memoirs of Brass Crosby, Esq. Alderman of the City of London and Lord Mayor, 1770–1771* (London, 1829), p. 38 note.

[80]   *The Fall of Mortimer: An Historical Play dedicated to the Right Honourable John, Earl of Bute* (London, 1763), pp. ii, ix–x.

[81]   Anna Clark, *Scandal: The Sexual Politics of the British Constitution* (Princeton, 2004), p. 24.

Wilkes had latched on to a potent rhetorical weapon, one that would realise its fullest potential across the English Channel with the vilification of the French royal family, in particular Marie Antoinette, at the onset of the French Revolution. By so doing, Wilkes was establishing a synergetic link with 'the *argot plastique* of the streets, the common language of crowd ritual, woodcut broadsides and cheap ballads'. These plebeian media hilariously represented Bute as 'the boot', a multifarious emblem suggestive, among other things, of sexual virility, especially when placed aside 'the petticoat', the invariable symbol for the Princess Dowager.[82] Essaying appropriate punishments for Wilkes's enemies, one of his libertine friends, Revd Evan Lloyd, half-jokingly suggested that castration would be the appropriate one for Bute, 'that nobly Suffering the Martyrdom of his Manhood, he might give the Nation a Proof that England is not the Isle of Cyprus or Paphos, and that Venus is not to govern us'.[83] The corollary of Bute's ascendancy was George III's pathetic dependency: when he went through London on his way to visit his mother, the crowd asked if he were going to suck.[84]

From Wilkes's perspective, Bute's brutish and alien carnality, deployed as it was for selfish ends, had nothing in common with the aristocratic libertinism, mandated by nature, to which Wilkes subscribed. (Poor Bute was denied aristocratic status even in his alleged vices, which made the attack on him only a partial precedent for the broader attack on aristocratic vice, explored in chapter 5.) And just as Bute was not an authentic aristocrat, he was certainly not a Whig, in Wilkes's view. Nor were those who abandoned longstanding allegiances to support him. Like Bute himself, apostate Whigs were freely branded as Tories.[85] Thus Wilkes was able to raise the spectre of an insurgent Toryism despite the fact that by this time scarcely anyone in public life avowed himself a Tory. Out of the 'tessellated pavement' that in Edmund Burke's acute perspective constituted the political nation,[86] Wilkes somehow discerned stark polarities of Whig and Tory engaged in a renewed 'rage of party'. Those who had allegedly abandoned Whig allegiances included George Grenville, who remained in government as a secretary of state, before succeeding Bute at the head of the ministry. Wilkes deliberately closed the distinction between Grenville's desertion of party and

---

[82]   Diana Donald, *The Age of Caricature: Satirical Prints in the Reign of George III* (New Haven and London, 1996), p. 50.

[83]   E. Alfred Jones, ed., 'Two Welsh Correspondents of John Wilkes', *Y Cymmrodor*, 29: p. 123.

[84]   Clark, *Scandal*, p. 24.

[85]   'It became increasingly common amongst those who opposed the king's ministers to call an apostate whig a tory.' John Brewer, *Party Ideology and Popular Politics at the Accession of George III* (Cambridge and New York, 1976) p. 50.

[86]   Ibid., p. 44.

desertion of his aristocratic family. In a satirical appropriation of Bute's voice, he pronounced Grenville's defection as 'the first-fruits of our labours among the great families of the English nobility'.[87] Wilkes's contempt for Grenville was matched by his abuse of Henry Fox, the notoriously avaricious Paymaster of the Forces. Fox was Bute's principal ally in the House of Commons until his shameless pursuit of a peerage was finally gratified in April 1763.[88] In his attack on Fox, Wilkes even resorted to associating physiognomy with moral deficiency, a crude form of abuse to which, given his distinctive features, he was especially vulnerable himself. Fox's appearance, Wilkes suggested, betrayed 'a dark, crafty inhabitant within'; his 'most unfortunate scowl' indicated that 'much deceit and treachery lurked in a black, malignant heart'.[89] The only member of the administration whom the *North Briton* felt had retained both his honour and his Whig credentials was Charles Townshend, Wilkes's Leiden acquaintance, who stayed in Bute's government until December 1762 as secretary at war. Townshend, 'of a noble *whig* family, ever steadily attached to the *cause of liberty*, and to *revolution principles*', was redeemed partly because he was adjudged to have had 'no share of ministerial confidence'.[90]

Wilkes's lionisation of the Whig nobility, in which true Whigs and authentic aristocrats became almost indistinguishable, was unqualified; yet its fawning quality suggested trouble ahead. Such praise could hardly be sustained unless returned in kind. Moreover, by lauding some branches of the nobility while vilifying others, Wilkes was beginning to edge towards the endorsement of a merit principle that was inimical to the hereditary principle upon which noble entitlement ultimately rested. The notion that aristocratic privilege was conditional on virtuous service to the state was more robustly asserted by Charles Churchill, who shared few of Wilkes's social ambitions even after he achieved fame and a modest fortune for his satirical verse. He remained, at least in his public persona, the eternal outsider, gazing with jaundiced eye on the foibles and conceits of the rich and eminent. Neither city merchant nor '*lordling* proud' was safe from his pen. Claiming the satirist's immunity from any obligation of social deference, he asked rhetorically: 'What's in the name of *Lord*, that we should fear / To bring their vices to the public ear?' When Wilkes's enemies sought to eject him from polite society, Churchill's wrath at 'titled upstarts' proceeded apace.[91]

The extent to which members of the Whig aristocracy would reciprocate Wilkes's valorisation of them would be tested in the political storm that followed

---

87 *North Briton*, 6, 10 July 1762.

88 Fox's ennoblement came a little too late for Wilkes to address it in the *North Briton*.

89 *North Briton*, 36, 5 February 1763.

90 Ibid., 20, 16 October 1762.

91 *The Poetical Works of Charles Churchill*, ed. Douglas Grant (Oxford, 1956), pp. 57, 251, 284.

the publication of *North Briton* no. 45. That issue was prompted by two events: Bute's resignation from the ministry on 8 April 1763, and the King's Speech at the end of the Parliamentary session, lauding the treaty that marked the official end of war with France. Predictably (though wrongly), Wilkes claimed that Bute's retirement was a ruse, and that he had simply reverted to his former position as the secret power behind the throne, while still diverting 'every preferment' to 'the creatures of the Scottish faction'. Allegedly, the 'triple-headed, Cerebrean administration' of George Grenville (Bute's ostensible successor) and the secretaries of state, Lord Halifax and Lord Egremont, was the façade of Bute's continuing authority in 'motley form'. There was nothing remarkable in the level of abuse that Wilkes directed at Bute and his alleged tools in this issue; what set *North Briton* no. 45 apart was that Wilkes's targets now included the king himself. His attack on George III's association with the peace treaty was an oblique one. 'Every friend of his country must lament that a prince of so great and amiable qualities, whom England truly reveres, can be brought to give the sanction of his sacred name to the most odious measures, and to the most unjustifiable, public declarations, from a throne ever renowned for truth, honour, and unsullied virtue', Wilkes wrote, adding: 'I wish as much as any man in the kingdom to see *the honour of the crown* maintained in a manner truly becoming *Royalty*. I lament to see it sunk even to prostitution.' Though Wilkes insisted that George III was merely the mouthpiece for the measures of his ministers, most observers assumed that Wilkes was being ironic and that he was seeking to implicate the king himself in a craven capitulation to French interests.

Even if Wilkes's disclaimers were to be taken seriously, they were insulting in a different way, because they suggested that the king was the pathetic dupe of manipulative advisers. Just what construction George III himself placed on Wilkes's allusions is unclear, but it is certain that he was provoked beyond endurance, and he promptly insisted that his ministers proceed with the prosecution of Wilkes. In short order, he was arrested on the basis of a controversial general warrant – which described *North Briton* no. 45 as 'seditious and treasonable' – and brought before the secretaries of state, who ordered him to close confinement in the Tower of London. Meanwhile, government agents ransacked his house, seizing what they considered to be incriminating documents. Subsequently, in highly publicised appearances in the Court of Common Pleas, Wilkes laced into his 'cruel and implacable enemies' on behalf, not only of himself, but also of all freeborn Englishmen, 'the middling and inferior class of people' as well as 'peers and gentlemen'. As Lord Chief Justice Pratt discharged him from imprisonment on the grounds of Parliamentary privilege, the rafters of Westminster Hall rang with the new plebeian cry, 'Wilkes and Liberty'.[92]

---

[92] Thomas, *Wilkes*, pp. 27–31; Bleackley, *Wilkes*, pp. 91–109; *Annual Register* (1763): 109.

Wilkes would become adept at eliciting such popular displays. His immediate concern, however, was to uphold his dignity as a gentleman, which his arrest so rudely challenged, while seeking active endorsement from the Whig aristocracy. To the extent that he was now reaching out to a wider public, it was as an injured gentleman, not an insurgent radical, that he wished to be regarded. Writing to Polly during his incarceration – the letter would soon be widely published – he insisted that he had 'done nothing unworthy of a man of honour'; yet his sword, that essential symbol of manly gentility, had been taken from him, and his papers 'stolen by ruffians'.[93] His tactic was to turn the tables on his persecutors, by representing them as boors unworthy of their privileged status. His principal target was Lord Egremont. When Wilkes was brought before the two secretaries of state, Egremont had treated him with a studied contempt; a week later he instructed that Wilkes be stripped of his cherished commission in the Buckinghamshire militia. At the hearing, Wilkes 'wounded the stately pride of Lord Egremont' by requesting to be confined in the same apartment in the Tower where Egremont's Jacobite father, Sir William Windham, had once been held on a charge of treason.[94] Later, Wilkes accused Egremont and Halifax of resorting to 'Billingsgate language' when they refused his demand to have his seized papers restored to him.[95] Wilkes apparently felt himself so abused by Egremont – 'the Right Honourable Rascal', he called him – that he claimed to have intended the ultimate recourse of the aggrieved gentleman, the satisfaction of a duel, as soon as Egremont retired from office.[96]

For Wilkes, vilifying his opponents proved to be a simpler task than rallying those he looked to as his political allies. From the time of his arrest, there was disarray in the ranks of the Whig aristocracy about the appropriate response to his persecution. Some highborn friends remained loyal. Lord Temple lent unqualified support, attempting (unsuccessfully) to visit Wilkes in the Tower and offering to stand bail for him. Temple urged solidarity on Newcastle. 'Lord Temple is very full of taking the strongest part; and wants us all to go to see Mr. Wilkes in the Tower', Newcastle recorded.[97] Some of the younger Whig peers responded eagerly to Temple's call. They included Lord Middleton, Lord Villiers (a friend of the Duke of Grafton) and the Duke of Bolton, who like Temple sought access to Wilkes in the Tower, with Bolton joining Temple in agreeing to stand bail for him. Newcastle was under pressure from the Whig cadets to seize what they identified as a golden opportunity for a display of opposition unity. Middleton

---

[93] *Public Advertiser*, 9 May 1763.
[94] *Memoirs of the Marquis of Rockingham*, vol. 1, p. 4.
[95] *Wilkes Correspondence*, vol. 1, p. 128.
[96] *Wilkes–Churchill*, p. 63.
[97] BL Add. MSS 32948, fol. 202.

urged him to show Wilkes 'that we will not abandon him unconvicted to the fury of an insolent minister'.[98] George Onslow, Newcastle's nephew, was convinced that the popular demonstrations that followed Wilkes's discharge were evidence 'that the genius of this Country is Whiggism & that the People will never be satisfied but in the reestablishment of the old system under which this Country has of late year Years flourished under this Family'.[99] The clear implication was that the Whig grandees should place themselves at the head of this groundswell of popular disaffection.

Wilkes remained buoyed by this response throughout the summer of 1763. On 14 June he wrote to Polly: 'Every thing in England goes on as I wish it. Lord Temple and all our friends continue well, and honour me with their applause. I am a greater favourite here than I ought in modesty to say.'[100] He pressed home his legal victory by launching legal actions against his persecutors, while supporting those printers, publishers, and booksellers who were also victims of the government's wrath. With a sense of invulnerability to further legal action, he set up a printing press in his own house; his projects included a handsome, bound edition of the *North Briton* – undertaken despite Temple's strenuous objections – as well as a limited edition of the ill-fated *Essay on Woman*. (After the journeymen printers had completed their work, he reportedly fired them without paying them full wages, suggesting that he was still not the champion of the common man in an economic sense.) In late July, he took a pause from his publishing ventures to visit Polly in Paris. Returning to London in September 'in great spirits', he declared himself 'devoted to the service of the opposition', ready once again to take up his pen on its behalf.[101]

Wilkes was blissfully unaware that the political ground was already shifting beneath his feet. In a different era, the Duke of Newcastle might have been tempted by the appeal of his younger friends to construe the popular excitement aroused by Wilkes as a Whig crusade. Newcastle famously claimed to love a mob, and forty years earlier he had led one in defence of the Hanoverian accession.[102] But now, after some customary dithering, he was more disposed to heed the cautionary words of the Whig mandarins of his own generation, especially those of Lord Hardwicke, a zealot for law and order and a former lord chancellor, whose son, Charles Yorke, was attorney-general and hence deeply implicated in Wilkes's

---

[98]   Ibid., fol. 209.

[99]   Ibid., fol. 235.

[100] BL Add. MSS 30879, fol. 18.

[101] George Onslow to Newcastle, 29 September 1763, BL Add. MSS 32951, fols 220–21; Thomas, *Wilkes*, p. 35.

[102] Ian Gilmour, *Riot, Risings and Revolution: Governance and Violence in Eighteenth-Century England* (London, 1993), p. 70.

prosecution. Hardwicke counselled Newcastle not to be 'possess'd & warm'd by the Discourse of the zealous young Gentlemen' who were urging support for Wilkes. In Hardwicke's view, Wilkes's 'libel' was 'not only unjustifiable but inexcusable'. Far from being encouraged by the appearance of a mob shouting Whig slogans, Hardwicke was terrified by it. He brushed aside Wilkes's conceits about his patrician status by associating him, presciently if hysterically, with incendiary City politicians like Arthur Beardmore. 'These are fellows, who would have hanged your Grace & me a few years ago, & would do so still had they the power', Hardwicke warned his friend.[103] Whether or not Newcastle was moved by the spectre of class warfare, he had concluded by early June, as loyal addresses flooded in from around the country, that Wilkes's 'very indiscrete, & perhaps very indecent' publication had undermined the opposition by creating the 'false imputation' that it was implicated in 'attacking the person of the King, his Honor, & Dignity'.[104] In ways that Wilkes was slow to understand, the Old Corps Whigs, while alert to any attempts to augment royal power, realised that their privileged standing in the nation's hierarchy was ultimately underpinned by an efficient monarchy.

The Field of Honour

Around the time that Wilkes was attacking the honour of the king and his ministers, he was defending his own on the duelling ground. Perversely, one way of trying to get others to recognise your claim to an elevated social status was by duelling with those whom you wished to emulate. The duel's code of honour defined and supported aristocratic culture in a number of ways. It elaborated standards of conduct from which the masses were excluded; it implied a privileged exemption from the full rigour of the criminal law; and it mandated displays of gracious courage, which were the essential hallmark of a virile ruling caste. The corollary of the duel's function as a display of aristocratic *virtù* was that it could counter charges of aristocratic foppishness and effeminacy. Men might redeem their reputations by displaying grace and courage on the duelling ground even when, as in the case of Lord George Sackville, they had been accused of sodomy and cowardice.[105]

---

[103] BL Add. MSS 32949, fol. 57.
[104] Ibid., fol. 21.
[105] V.G. Kiernan, *The Duel in European History: Honour and the Reign of Aristocracy* (Oxford, 1998); Clark, *Scandal*, p. 33; James Kelly, *That Damn'd Thing Called Honour: Duelling in Ireland, 1570–1860* (Cork, 1995), pp. 104–05.

Wilkes himself fought two duels, while coming perilously close to fighting a third. In many respects, he was a politicised prototype of those middle-class 'dandelions on the field of honour' whose quest for glory and social status actually produced a surge in the popularity of duelling – in defiance of the mounting opposition to it – before its abrupt end in the 1840s. Typically, these later duellists came from a commercial background, deriving from military commissions an anxious claim to gentility that they sought to strengthen by engaging in affairs of honour with the high and mighty.[106] Yet there were dangers to reputation in engaging in duels, as well as possible benefits. Increasingly, the practice and the honour principle upon which it was based were denounced as a libertine anachronism in 'a new vision of society based on reasonableness, Christianity and commerce'.[107] Potentially most damaging to Wilkes was the characterisation of the duellist as a man unable to control his anger, a behavioural trait at odds with new requirements of genteel manhood.[108] That objection could be at least partially mitigated in the eyes of the public, however, as long as the duellist displayed coolness in combat and politeness towards his opponent. Hence Wilkes and his supporters were at considerable pains to make sure that his conduct on the field of honour was represented in the best possible light.

Wilkes was not only a militia officer when he fought his first duel; he was still also engaged with the *North Briton*. This circumstance was relevant in a couple of ways. It was the content of the periodical that provoked his duels in the first place, and engaging in them yielded an opportunity to shake off the social odium that often attached itself to press scribes. Although Wilkes always liked to regard himself as an enlightened citizen of the republic of letters, such a volatile social category was susceptible to a less flattering redefinition as Grub Street hack. His first duel was fought on 5 October 1762 with William, Earl Talbot, lord steward of the royal household. The issue of contention was a passage in *North Briton* no. 12, in which Wilkes ridiculed Talbot, a follower of Lord Bute, for an embarrassing display at George III's coronation the previous year. On that occasion, Talbot had attempted a show of horsemanship that involved backing his mount from the royal presence without exposing its rump to the king. The equestrian manoeuvre had gone comically awry. In defiance of its rider, Talbot's horse had turned around and projected its backside towards His Majesty, maintaining this

---

[106] Antony E. Simpson, 'Dandelions on the Field of Honor: Dueling, the Middle Classes, and the Law in Nineteenth-Century England', *Criminal Justice History*, 9 (1988): 99–155.

[107] Donna T. Andrew, 'The Code of Honour and its Critics: The Opposition to Duelling in England, 1700–1850', *Social History*, 5 (1980): 411.

[108] Elizabeth Foyster, 'Boys will be Boys? Manhood and Aggression, 1660–1800', in *English Masculinities, 1660–1800*, ed. Tim Hitchcock and Michèle Cohen (London and New York, 1999), pp. 151–66.

disrespectful posture to the undisguised mirth of the spectators. Talbot deemed himself 'publickly affronted' at Wilkes's facetious reminder of his 'dexterity', and demanded that Wilkes either avow or deny his authorship of the offending piece. This Wilkes refused to do, contesting Talbot's right 'to catechise [him] about an anonymous paper', though from the first Wilkes declared that, 'as a gentleman', he was 'ready to give [Talbot] any other satisfaction'.[109]

The two engaged in a blustering exchange of letters over the next couple of weeks until the terms of the duel were finally settled between their respective seconds. The appointed venue was Bagshot in Surrey, a relatively isolated spot where points of honour could be settled without judicial interference. During the drawn-out preliminaries to the contest, Wilkes combined an attitude of teasing insouciance with a punctilious regard for the courtesies and protocols of the honour code. Consistent with the libertine ambience that often surrounded eighteenth-century duels, Wilkes mentioned on his arrival at the Red Lion Inn in Bagshot that he had come directly from a rakish gathering at Medmenham Abbey, 'where the jovial monks of St. Francis had kept [him] up till four in the morning'. He asked for a postponement of the engagement to the following day on the grounds that public opinion would turn against Talbot if it were suspected that he had fought a man who was assumed to be still drunk from the revelries of the previous night. Talbot, however, 'in an agony of passion', demanded more immediate satisfaction. According to Wilkes, Talbot shocked the seconds by blurting out, in an obvious violation of the honour code, 'If you kill me, I hope you will be hanged'.[110]

During the course of their heated exchange, Wilkes ventured a position that would over time become a settled conviction, that of the essential equality of gentlemen. While expressing appropriate deference for Talbot's noble status, Wilkes described himself as 'a private English gentleman, perfectly free and independent', a condition that he held to be 'of the highest dignity'. He conceded that Talbot was his 'superior in rank, fortune, and abilities', but his 'equal only in honour, courage, and liberty'. 'God had given me a firmness and spirit, equal to his lordship's or any man's', he continued. 'Cool courage should always mark me'.[111] In comparing his own sangfroid to Talbot's passionate anger, he was making clear who had the larger claim to gentility.

The duel eventually took place under moonlight in a garden some distance from the Red Lion Inn. Talbot supplied the weapons (large horse pistols). Wilkes

---

[109] *Letters between Grafton etc. and Wilkes*, pp. 8, 11. Wilkes's description of the affair was confirmed in essentials by Edmund Burke, whose source was one of Talbot's seconds. *Burke Correspondence*, vol. 1, pp. 149–51.

[110] *Letters between Grafton etc. and Wilkes*, pp. 22–23, 28.

[111] Ibid., pp. 24–26.

chipped in with a flask of powder and a bag of bullets. As the preparations were being made, Talbot vented what one of his seconds described as 'a Torrent of Billingsgate' against his opponent, which Wilkes ignored. Facing each other at a distance of about eight yards, the combatants discharged their pistols. Both missed. With honour now satisfied on both sides, Wilkes walked up to Talbot and avowed himself the author of the offending paper. Then followed the effusions of male bonding that typically punctuated non-fatal encounters. 'His lordship paid me the highest encomiums on my courage,' Wilkes reported, 'and said that he would declare everywhere that I was the noblest fellow God had ever made.' After further declarations of friendship, the parties returned to the inn where they shared a bottle of claret 'with great good humour and much laugh'.[112]

By obliging Talbot to recognise his courage and nobility, Wilkes enjoyed the gratification of securing some validation of his social pretensions from a peer of the realm, but Talbot's generosity was fleeting, the product perhaps of post-combat euphoria and alcohol. After the duel, Wilkes wrote a long and self-congratulatory account of the affair to Lord Temple in a letter that, when made public five years later, would rekindle much of the acrimony of the original encounter. But the good opinion of Talbot, a political adversary, was in any event only of passing interest to Wilkes; he was playing to a wider audience, which, with his habitual optimism, he imagined to be responsive. ('I am surfeited with caresses', he reported to Churchill, and, lending credence to the suspicions of moral reformers that when duels occurred debauchery was never far behind, boasted that his martial exploits had enhanced his sexual allure.[113]) Certainly, Temple's response was reassuring. 'Firmness, coolness, and a manly politeness, make up the whole of this transaction on your part', he wrote to Wilkes, the day after the duel.[114] Apart from Temple's predictable reaction, however, Wilkes's display of 'cool courage' failed to elicit accolades from members of the Whig aristocracy. And the public response, to the extent that there was one, appeared to be sceptical rather than laudatory. Some of Wilkes's contemporaries clearly found something inherently comical in contests initiated by a scribbling pen, and this was no exception.[115] A satirical print shows Wilkes brandishing an inkhorn at Talbot, who is protecting himself with a pot lid, a reference to his sinecure as royal steward (Fig. 2.2). A damaging extension to this kind of response was the suggestion that the Wilkes–Talbot duel was actually a fake, stage-managed by its participants to enhance their respective reputations. The charge was implied

---

[112] Ibid., pp. 30–32; *Burke Correspondence*, vol. 1, p. 150.
[113] *Wilkes–Churchill*, p. 19.
[114] *Grenville Papers*, vol. 1, p. 478.
[115] 'A Speech of Falstaff', *St James's Chronicle*, 9–12 October 1762; *Town and Country Magazine* (1770): 157.

Figure 2.2   Artist unknown. Etching with engraving. Courtesy of the Lewis
Walpole Library, Yale University.

in a satirical broadside poem, which included a picture of Wilkes and Talbot
shaking hands while firing their pistols in the air.[116]

The duel did nothing to enhance Wilkes's public reputation because, at the time
it was fought, he had virtually no public reputation to enhance. That would change
sensationally a few months later with the events that followed Wilkes's arrest for
North Briton no. 45. As a part of his campaign to represent himself as a valiant
gentleman, he published in the newspapers his exchange of letters with Lord Talbot
and Talbot's seconds. The successes of Wilkite propaganda are undeniable, yet there
were definite risks in attempting to fashion a reputation around a manly adherence
to the aristocratic code of honour. Reputations so constructed were inherently
fragile; they could be deconstructed in their turn if not vigorously defended against
challenge, especially a literal challenge from an aggrieved opponent. And this was
precisely the situation that Wilkes encountered in August 1763 while visiting Paris.

---

116   B[agsho]t H[eat]h: or, *The Modern Duel* (1762).

Making his way to Notre Dame, he was confronted by one Captain John Forbes, a Scotsman with a commission in the French army. Recognizing Wilkes's distinctive features from William Hogarth's celebrated cartoon, Forbes upbraided Wilkes for his attacks in the *North Briton* on Forbes's fellow countrymen and demanded instant satisfaction in a duel. What ensued was an elaborate display of verbal jousting in which each party sought to defend his honour as a gentleman while denying the same to his would-be opponent.[117]

According to his own account, Wilkes averted an immediate conflict by declaring that 'a squabble on the streets was both unbecoming a gentleman, and an outrage to the laws of the country'. He did, however, enable Forbes to pursue the matter by informing the Scotsman where he lodged. Having failed to find Wilkes at home the same day, Forbes arrived at Wilkes's apartment at six o'clock the following morning, still demanding satisfaction. Wilkes deftly stalled the renewed demand; but the issue of whether he was motivated by a punctilious regard for the protocols of the *code duello* or by a cowardly desire to evade a legitimate challenge became a matter of heated debate in the London press. He followed his usual practice of refusing to avow authorship of anonymous writings, insisted that designated seconds would have to arrange the terms of any duel, and refused in any event to fight until such time as he had settled a 'previous account' with Lord Egremont.[118] Unfortunately for Wilkes, there was no corroborative evidence that he had issued a challenge to Egremont, or contemplated doing so. Suspicion would linger that Wilkes had spontaneously concocted the story of a prior engagement with Egremont in order to avoid one with Forbes. Forbes himself, according to one published version, sarcastically asked Wilkes 'if he came to Paris to fight Lord Egremont'.[119]

At another interview the same day, Forbes again demanded immediate satisfaction and Wilkes again demurred, questioning Forbes's motives and gentlemanly status. 'His proceeding had more the air of an assassin than that of a gentleman', Wilkes remarked.[120] According to another report (which panicky Wilkite scribes strenuously repudiated as an 'absolute Fiction'), Forbes responded in kind by threatening to give Wilkes 'a hundred strokes of a stick, as he deserved no more to be used like a gentleman, but as [an] eternal rascal and scoundrel'.[121]

---

[117] Linda Colley, *Britons: Forging the Nation, 1707–1837* (New Haven and London, 1992), pp. 105–06; Bleackley, *Wilkes*, pp. 122–23. Wilkes's version of his encounter with Forbes (widely circulated in the newspapers) survives in manuscript: Guildhall MS 14176, Guildhall Library.

[118] Guildhall MS 14176.

[119] *Public Advertiser*, 20 September 1763.

[120] Guildhall MS 14176.

[121] *Public Advertiser*, 20 September 1763, and 29 September 1763.

That afternoon the possibility of a duel temporarily receded through the intervention of the French authorities, which at this time were zealous in preventing arranged duels. Wilkes gave his word before the marshals of France that he would keep the peace, and Forbes prudently went into hiding before escaping to England. (Wilkes's enemies, and even some of his friends, assumed that it was none other than Wilkes himself who had invoked the intervention of the authorities as a means of shielding himself from Forbes.)[122] There matters would presumably have rested had not Lord Egremont died unexpectedly a few days later. Wilkes managed an eloquent display of frustration at being deprived of the opportunity to engage his highborn oppressor on the field of honour. 'What a scoundrell [sic] trick Lord Egremont play'd me', he wrote to Charles Churchill. 'I had form'd a fond wish to send him to the Devil, but he is gone without my passport'.[123] More ominously, the death of Egremont removed the main obstacle to an engagement with Forbes.

Forbes, a professional soldier bent on revenge, could be expected to wield pistol or sword with more skill and determination than Lord Talbot. And the likelihood of a deadly encounter raised genuine anxiety among Wilkes's friends back in England. Offering a less martial interpretation of the traditional honour principle, they urged him to pull back from the brink. Charles Churchill observed that, in France, Wilkes appeared to 'live in Romance', not 'under the direction of ... well-temper'd, cool, distinguishing Reason'. 'Your Country Demands your Life', he declared, and he urged Wilkes not to sacrifice it to 'false principles of Honour', assuring him that his duel with Talbot had already secured his reputation for 'valour'.[124] Wilkes himself, though – with a clearer sense of the public mood than Churchill – recognised that a reputation for honourable conduct required periodic renewal, and that a refusal to fight Forbes might consign him to the status of a cowardly and disreputable scribbler. Probably influencing his decision was his receipt of unflattering press reports from London, one of which declared that 'Mr. Wilkes had scandalously declined fighting the Scot, for which poltron [sic] Behaviour no Gentleman will now keep him Company'.[125] Facing up to the challenge (albeit belatedly) would not only redeem his honour but also enhance it, according to Wilkes, who now dubbed himself 'the guardian and protector of English liberty'.[126]

---

[122] Bleackley, *Wilkes*, p. 124; *Wilkes–Churchill*, p. 66. An anonymous account favourable to Wilkes, received by the Duke of Newcastle, reported that Wilkes 'very judiciously, wrote immediately to the Lieutenant de Police' after Forbes had threatened him. BL Add. MSS 32950, fol. 197.

[123] *Wilkes–Churchill*, p. 63.

[124] Ibid., pp. 66–69.

[125] *St James's Chronicle*, 25–27 August 1763. Wilkes read this letter: Wilkes MSS 1, fol. 51.

[126] Wilkes MSS 1, fol. 51.

Precluded from an engagement in France, Wilkes sent word through Forbes's seconds that he would meet his challenger at Menin, in Austrian Flanders, on 21 September. In the meantime, however, Forbes was still in London, preparing to disembark for Lisbon in order to take up a commission in the Portuguese army. Either he had experienced a change of heart about duelling with Wilkes or, more likely, word of the proposed rendezvous never reached him. The affair thus ended with Wilkes waiting at the duelling ground for an opponent who never arrived.

Wilkes, then, with typical adroitness, had contrived an outcome that could be construed as redounding to his advantage, but troubling questions lingered about his conduct, and his eventual agreement to fight did not entirely undo the damage to his manly persona. One persistent critic claimed that Wilkes only went to Menin when he knew that Forbes was incommunicado in London, and that 'the moment he hears that Forbes has left England he resolutely runs over to attack him'.[127] Even newspaper essays in his support struck a defensive note, conceding his initial prevarications, while pushing the charge that Forbes was a hired assassin. 'Is Mr. Wilkes Gladiatour [*sic*] to his Party?' asked one rhetorically. 'Is he a common Prize-Fighter, obliged to enter the Lists with every Jacobite Scot, every Creature of the Scots, that hopes to make his Fortune by killing him?'[128] Another gave Wilkes credit for behaving 'prudently' (a word rarely applied to his conduct) in the face of Forbes's initial challenge and, with an interesting twist on gender, attributed his caution to 'a true masculine Understanding'.[129] Putting on a brave face, Wilkes himself claimed that his 'artless story' of the whole affair had 'put down' the hostile 'scribblers', though he was plainly rattled by their allegations of ignoble 'meanness and cowardice'.[130] On his return to England, he anxiously relayed his side of the story to the leaders of the Whig opposition.[131]

Wilkes would not have to wait long for an opportunity to remove the blot on his reputation. In *North Briton* nos 37 and 40 he had launched a virulent attack on Samuel Martin, MP, a former secretary to the treasury, denouncing him as a despicable tool of Lord Bute and as 'the most treacherous, base, selfish, mean, abject, low-lived and dirty fellow, that ever *wriggled* himself into a secretaryship'. Martin's long-delayed response was delivered in the House of Commons on 15 November 1763. Glaring directly at Wilkes, he declaimed that 'a man capable of writing in that manner, without putting his name to it and thereby stabbing another in the dark, is a cowardly rascal, a villain and

---

127 DEMOCRITUS, *Public Advertiser*, 30 September 1763.
128 C.D., *St James's Chronicle*, 3–5 November 1763.
129 'A Stranger to Mr. Wilkes, but a Lover of Justice, my King and my Country', ibid.
130 *Grenville Papers*, vol. 2, pp. 131–32.
131 BL Add. MSS 32951, fols 220–21.

a scoundrel'.[132] Wilkes at first coolly ignored the studied provocation, but in the small hours of the following morning, he wrote to Martin, acknowledging himself to be the author of the insult in the *North Briton*; Martin, in return, demanded immediate satisfaction. A duel was the predictable outcome, but this one was unusual in that the rage was mutual, and pre-empted the traditional proprieties required by the *code duello*. It was fought in London's Hyde Park within hours of the combatants' letters of challenge. No seconds were present. It ended with Wilkes writhing on the ground, a ball from Martin's second pistol-shot lodged in his groin.[133] (It could have been worse: two of Wilkes's waistcoat buttons diverted the bullet from vital organs; inevitably the buttons became treasured patriotic memorabilia.[134]) Despite the irregularities of the duel itself, in its sequel both men conducted themselves according to the honour code. Martin offered assistance to his erstwhile opponent; Wilkes called on him to make his escape, declaring him a man of honour. The following day, he returned Martin's compromising letter of challenge, and the two would later exchange pleasantries in France.[135]

Although, in a formal sense, honour was now satisfied between the contestants, the duel's circumstances and implications resonated loudly, unlike the muted response to the Wilkes–Talbot contest. The House of Commons was thrown into a state of 'agitation' when news arrived that Martin had shot Wilkes.[136] Elsewhere, partisanship was rife. James Porter, the man whom Wilkes had sought to replace as ambassador in Constantinople, declared Martin a hero and saw the duel's outcome as one of virtue triumphant.[137] There is no evidence that it enhanced Wilkes's standing with the Whig aristocracy, but in the larger public arena it helped to dispel the doubts about his courage arising from his vacillations in the face of the challenge from Captain Forbes. 'That WILKES will fight, the *Scots* deny; / But MARTIN finds the *Scots* can lie', declared one jingle.[138] And while Wilkes (as daily bulletins announced his medical condition) was being compared with other martyred heroes in the Whig pantheon, Martin was subject to unflattering scrutiny. He was accused

---

[132] Bleackley, *Wilkes*, p. 132.

[133] Martin left a detailed description of the duel. BL Add. MSS 41354, fols 75–85. It differs in some details but not in substance from other accounts. Wilkes gave a terse account of the duel and his subsequent surgery in a letter to Polly. BL Add. MSS 30879, fol. 20.

[134] The buttons were preserved by one of Wilkes's friends in a silver box with an inscription praising Wilkes's 'Public Virtue'. *English Liberty*, p. 168.

[135] Bleackley, *Wilkes*, pp. 136–37; Martin to Wilkes, BL Add. MSS 41354, fol. 11.

[136] Malmesbury MSS 9M73/G712.

[137] Osborn Shelves C 127, letter 6, Osborn Collection.

[138] *St James's Chronicle*, 17–19 November 1763.

of tardiness in returning the letter that Wilkes had written on the morning of the duel. More damagingly, there were allegations that he had spent several months engaged in target practice before demanding satisfaction for Wilkes's insults; Wilkes himself made sure that this story was widely circulated.[139] If true, the charge against Martin constituted a serious breach of the honour code, because the pistol duel was intended as a ritualised display of courage under fire, not as an opportunity to kill or maim one's opponent. Martin's intentions, and retrospectively those of Forbes, appeared even more suspect, when in early December Alexander Dun, a Scottish lieutenant in the marines, threatened to kill Wilkes and subsequently managed to gain entry to his house carrying a knife. Dun was obviously deranged, but his actions were quickly construed as part of a continuing Scottish or government-sponsored conspiracy to assassinate Wilkes.[140]

Charles Churchill's poem *The Duellist,* published in January 1764, repeated the charge that Martin was a trained killer, and offered the most developed and nightmarish expression of Wilkite fears. In it, Churchill identified three powerful conspirators bent on securing Wilkes's death: William Warburton, the Bishop of Gloucester; Sir Fletcher Norton, the solicitor-general; and Lord Sandwich, deemed capable of any atrocity in the wake of the *Essay on Woman* affair. Together, they sought 'to work the bane / Of one firm Patriot [Wilkes], whose heart tied / To Honour, all their pow'r defied'. In Churchill's schema, Wilkes, through his steady adherence to the honour principle, had transcended his ambition to emulate aristocracy; he now embodied the aristocratic virtues, which some members of the nobility itself, most notoriously Lord Sandwich, had betrayed or abandoned. Elsewhere, Churchill expressed the fear that 'the damn'd Aristocracy is gaining ground in this country', a proposition that Wilkes would probably have rejected at the time, but to which, for reasons that we shall be examining in chapter 5, he would later give credence.[141]

---

[139] Ibid., 17–19 December 1763, and 10–13 December 1763; Walpole, *Memoirs of George III*, vol. 1, pp. 252–53; DEMOCRITUS, *London Evening Post*, 29 November–1 December 1763; Wilkes to Humphrey Cotes, 10 December 1764, *Wilkes Correspondence*, vol. 2, p. 99.

[140] Bleackley, *Wilkes*, pp. 140–41; POLITICAL INTELLIGENCE EXTRAORDINARY, *Public Advertiser*, 16 January 1764.

[141] *Poetical Works of Charles Churchill*, pp. 261–89; Churchill to Wilkes [February, 1763?], *Wilkes–Churchill*, p. 44.

Chapter 3

Sex

The Company of Rakes

Concurrently with his political career, Wilkes pursued an active sexual one that he balanced, often precariously, with his domestic existence. Wilkes himself would characterise his sexual libertinism as a refined response to erotic, or benignly 'natural', imperatives, but sexual attitudes and conduct, given the intricacy of everything that moulds them, are rarely that simple, and Wilkes's case was no exception. Of matching complexity were the responses to Wilkes's sexual activity and persona as reports of these – both factual and fictitious – leaked from the private realm to fuel the hectic debate over his qualities as a public man. The demands of public life would in turn modify his sexual conduct, or at least the way that he and his allies sought to represent it.

Wilkes's sexual libertinism was mediated through social conditioning, achieving a durable pattern in early adulthood through association with fellow libertines. There had been some false starts. At the age of sixteen, Wilkes addressed one Polly Williams of Aylesbury in the following love-stricken verses:

> Hither, dear Polly, turn your eyes,
> Those lively, sparkling fires,
> One glance where your adorer lies,
> Is all my heart desires.
>
> You kill me now with cold disdain,
> When thus you turn away,
> Oh! grant me but to speak my pain,
> And give a moment's stay.
>
> While I with rapture fondly gaze,
> And every charm explore,
> Struck with your beauty's pow'rful blaze,
> Your mercy I implore.
>
> From that dear breast I seek relief,
> Which gave the fatal dart,

And trust alone to sooth my grief,
To Polly's generous heart.

Fair nymph, now bid your suppliant rise,
That snowy hand extend,
And from the lightning of your eyes
Let beaming smiles defend [descend?]

Forgive the excess of youth and fire,
Let love my pardon gain;
Love blew the tempest of desire,
And swell'd each throbbing vein.

But if with you I may not live,
And mercy you deny,
At least your wrongs, fair saint, forgive,
And cast a pitying eye.

Ah! let me view that beauteous face,
Join those sweet lips to mine,
Indulge me this last dear embrace,
Content I'll life resign.[1]

In its highly charged association of sentiment and eroticism, the performance was perhaps appropriate to his age. Wilkes would not betray himself as a solitary, swooning lover again, until his unusual pursuit of Maria Stafford 35 years later. In between, Wilkes defined himself as 'a man of pleasure',[2] a term suggestive of an Epicurean detachment from the pitfalls of emotional or sentimental engagement.

As an adolescent and beyond, Wilkes would have been confronted with competing messages over the ways in which erotic expression could be reconciled with a sense of true manhood. Sexual prowess remained a marker for masculinity, especially among the aristocracy, whose licence Wilkes sought to emulate. But there were countervailing pressures, especially from within the middle-class circles in which Wilkes was raised. There, young men were generally encouraged to restrain their sexual impulses until they reached the safe harbour of marriage, and masculinity was redefined with an emphasis on control and constraint. By extension, the undisciplined gratification of sexual appetite, especially if continued beyond the passing phase of youth, smacked of aristocratic vice, and its perpetrators were

---

[1] Wilkes MSS 3, fol. 1. Polly Williams was the sister of an Aylesbury friend. BL Add. MSS 30867, fols 5, 6.

[2] BL Add. MSS 30865A, fol. 6.

condemned accordingly. Families played a central role in seeking to enforce moral norms, and Wilkes's mother was especially active in this regard, as we have seen. But in the real world, of course, peers are usually more persuasive than parents in sexual matters. As Wilkes reached adulthood, he sought out the company of libertines, and his attitudes and conduct were influenced accordingly.

Whether Wilkes's peer group at Leiden consisted of sexual libertines is questionable, but he was for the first time effectively free from the control of his parents, and among likeminded young men in a fairly permissive environment. He later boasted to James Boswell of persistent whore-mongering there.[3] According to G.S. Rousseau, however, Wilkes's avowal of rebellious heterosexual conduct does not tell the whole story of his incipient libertinism. Rousseau asserts 'that although he became primarily heterosexual in his maturity, Wilkes seems to have been bisexual or homosexual at this time'. The refusal of biographers to recognise this 'chapter' in Wilkes's life, Rousseau charges, carries 'overtones of intentional neglect if not outright homophobia'.[4] Rousseau has certainly performed a service in challenging casual assumptions about Wilkes's sexual career, but the evidence upon which his challenge is based is less persuasive than he claims.

The focus of Rousseau's inquiry is a 'club' of expatriate students, located in the boarding house of Madam Vander Tasse on the Long Bridge. Five British students lodged there, including Alexander Carlyle; Wilkes lived in another boarding house close by. 'In the Evenings', Carlyle recalled, 'about a Dozen of us met at one anothers Rooms in Turn 3 Times a Week and Drank Coffee and Smoak'd tobacco, and Chatted about politicks, and Drank Claret, and supped on Bukkam (Dutch Red Herrings) and Eggs and Sallad, and never Sate later than 12 a clock'.[5] No suggestion of transgressive sexuality here, but Rousseau claims that it is clearly apparent in the letters between the 'club's' members and their acquaintances, especially the letters from Andrew Baxter and Paul Henri d'Holbach to Wilkes.[6] The following letter by Baxter is central to Rousseau's case:

I think as much upon you as you do upon me. I believe a good deal more. It is my serious Business to think of you. In short never man was thought so

---

[3] *Boswell, Italy*, pp. 56–57.

[4] G.S. Rousseau, '"In the House of Madam Vander Tasse, on the Long Bridge": A Homosocial University Club in Early Modern Europe', in *The Pursuit of Sodomy: Male Homosexuality in Renaissance and Enlightenment Europe*, ed. Kent Gerard and Gert Hekma (New York and London, 1989), pp. 313, 321. For a critique of Rousseau's essay, see Arthur H. Cash, 'Wilkes, Baxter, and D'Holbach at Leiden and Utrecht: An Answer to G.S. Rousseau', *The Age of Johnson*, 7 (1996): 397–426.

[5] Alexander Carlyle, *Anecdotes and Characters of the Times*, ed. James Kinsley (London, 1973), p. 86.

[6] Rousseau, 'In the House of Madam Vander Tasse', p. 315.

much upon by another, I dare say: tho' a woman perhaps may. This is all a Riddle – No 'tis literal. It is my greatest endeavour to make you think, with as much Wit and Sprightliness, with as much Solidity and good Sense as you deserve, at least as I am able. You are the Hero of my Dialogue. I would do Justice to your character. If I succeed in that, I am not so diffident of the rest. If I do not succeed I shall burn my papers, which is the next best thing I can do. Do not tell me then of your thinking so much upon me. I think more upon you, without leting [sic] you know it, till now you have wrested my secret from me.[7]

Rousseau sees a scarcely veiled eroticism here: it is a 'love letter', 'surcharged with libidinal thrusts', one of many declarations of 'erotic devotion from an older married man to a young magnetic man'.[8] Rousseau misconstrues the letter's overt intention, however. It is clearly in response to one from Wilkes in which he claims to be thinking more of Baxter than Baxter does of him. The 'secret' that Wilkes has 'wrested' from Baxter is not that his love for Wilkes is the same as a man's for a woman. It is that Wilkes is the central character in the philosophical dialogue he is writing. Hence it is Baxter's 'serious business' to think about Wilkes. None of this is to deny the evident signs of something resembling an infatuation on Baxter's part, perhaps even a sexual excitement. Certainly his attachment is early evidence of Wilkes's famous ability to 'talk away his face'. 'If Friendship were to appear in a human shape, it would take John Wilks [sic] agreeable form', Baxter wrote in another letter, in which he speaks of his 'passionate love' for Wilkes.[9] Rousseau's claim that Baxter sent numerous love letters is overstated, however. So is his description of Baxter on his deathbed, clutching a copy of the book inspired by Wilkes, his last thoughts with his beloved protégé. Baxter's letter, which purportedly supports this picture, was written in fact a year before he died; it is prosaic in tone and practical in purpose. 'It is my first desire to serve the Interests of Virtue and Religion, if I am able; and my second ardent wish to testify my Respects to Mr. Wilkes', he wrote. The reference is to his new dialogue, to be dedicated to Wilkes, and for which Wilkes was seeking publication in London on Baxter's behalf.[10]

Despite its exaggerations and distortions, Rousseau's reconstruction of Baxter's emotional and sexual state is not inherently implausible. Yet he is stretching the evidence beyond the breaking point when he refers to 'Wilkes's homoerotic affair with Baxter'.[11] Even if one concedes that Wilkes was the object of homosexual

---

[7]　Baxter to Wilkes, 23 June 1745, BL Add. MSS 30867, fol. 8.

[8]　Rousseau, 'In the House of Madam Vander Tasse', pp. 313, 315.

[9]　BL Add. MSS 30867, fol. 10.

[10]　Ibid., 10 April 1749, fol. 37.

[11]　Rousseau, 'In the House of Madam Vander Tasse', p. 321.

desire, it cannot be assumed that this desire was reciprocated. Certainly one has to recognise that discipleship frequently has a complex emotional content, often infused, as in ancient Greece, with eroticism, but there is no evidence that Wilkes regarded Baxter as anything other than an inspiring teacher and mentor to whom he paid grateful honour and respect. After Baxter's death in 1750, Wilkes published one of Baxter's letters to him; he later reprinted it in collections of materials relating to his persecutions in the 1760s.[12] By this time, Wilkes had declared himself the enemy of sodomites, so it is unlikely that he would have drawn attention to anything in his past even remotely suggestive of a homosexual connection.

D'Holbach, according to Rousseau, shared Baxter's alleged sexual infatuation with Wilkes; indeed 'it must have been evident to Wilkes that Baxter and d'Holbach were competing for his intimate friendship'.[13] The principal evidence for d'Holbach's feelings is a letter that he wrote to Wilkes shortly after the latter's return to England in the summer of 1746. The letter, in fractured English, expresses grief at their separation. Stoic philosophy is no consolation, because 'nature was still stronger and the philosopher was forced to yield to the friend, even now I feel the wound is not cur'd'. He indulges in a waking dream 'to sooth the sorrow of absence':

> I think to be at Alesbury [*sic*]! there I see my Dear Wilkes! What a Flurry of Passions! Joy! fear of a second parting! what charming tears! what sincere Kisses – but time flows and the end of this Love is now as unwelcome to me, as would be to another to be awaken'd in the middle of a Dream wherein he is going to enjoy a beautiful mistress; the enchantment ceases, the delightfull images vanish, and nothing is left to me but friendship, which is of all my possessions the fairest, and the surest.[14]

A subsequent letter from d'Holbach is similar in tone. It describes himself and William Dowdeswell, another Leiden student, making 'sincere libations' to their absent friend 'with burgundy and Champaigne'.[15] A third letter is a paean to friendship itself: 'Such are [its] Charms ... every event is shar'd and nothing not even the greatest intervals are able to interrupt the happy harmony of truly united minds'.[16]

If nothing else, d'Holbach's letters speak to the latitude of expression still available to gentlemen avowing friendship even during a period when

---

[12] *A Letter from Mr. Baxter, Author of an Enquiry into the Nature of the Human Soul, and of Matho, to John Wilkes Esq.* (1753); *English Liberty*, pp. 349–52.

[13] Rousseau, 'In the House of Madam Vander Tasse', p. 326.

[14] 9 August 1746, BL Add. MSS 30867, fol. 14.

[15] 3 December 1746, ibid., fol. 18.

[16] Ibid., fol. 20.

sodomitical behaviour was increasingly condemned. According to Raymond Stephanson, public discourse actually encouraged men to envisage their friendships with other men in ways that paralleled their experience of affection for female lovers; d'Holbach's letters were clearly written in this idiom.[17] So, in a less florid vein, were some of Wilkes's own letters to his friend Charles Churchill. The unabashed eroticism of d'Holbach's letters does not preclude the possibility of sexual desire, but, given this background, neither does it confirm it. As for Wilkes, he certainly cherished his friendship with d'Holbach, but evidence that he reciprocated homoerotic desire is non-existent, unless one simply assumes that he responded to d'Holbach in kind.[18]

Back in England after university, Wilkes entered marriage and the company of libertines in quick succession. In London, the pious household in Red Lion Court was conveniently close to the assorted venues of sexual commerce in Covent Garden. Wilkes certainly patronised them, while eschewing the exhibitionism of the kind associated with previous generations of the area's denizens, most notoriously the 'Mohocks', a bunch of young upper-class hooligans who, at the beginning of the eighteenth century, seemed bent on turning Covent Garden into an outdoor theatre of sexual cruelty.[19] Whatever species of libertinism can be attributed to Wilkes, that of 'roaring lad' was never one of them. He was usually, though not invariably, cautious and discreet in pursuit of sexual gratification. Unlike the more reckless James Boswell, he did not resort to streetwalkers, and, unusually for a rake of the period, he seems never to have contracted a venereal disease, perhaps because he used condoms.[20] His sexual adventures were rarely spontaneous. They involved occasional 'intrigues' with married women and liaisons with courtesans that were typically preceded by negotiations, often lengthy, with the courtesans themselves or with their pimps and bawds. Sometimes friends and allies offered their services in arranging trysts.[21]

---

[17] George E. Haggerty, *Men in Love: Masculinity and Sexuality in the Eighteenth Century* (New York, 1999), *passim*; Raymond Stephanson, '"Epicœne Friendship": Understanding Male Friendship in the Early Eighteenth Century, with Some Speculations about Pope', *The Eighteenth Century: Theory and Interpretations*, 38 (1997): 159.

[18] I have found only one letter from Wilkes to d'Holbach (BL Add. MSS 30872, fol. 144), but the warmth of Wilkes's longstanding friendship is evident from other sources, for instance [Wilkes] *Letters to Daughter*, vol. 3, pp. 160–61, 250, 297.

[19] Daniel Statt, 'The Case of the Mohocks: Rake Violence in Augustan London', *Social History*, 20 (1995): 179–99.

[20] Some condoms in an envelope were among the goods taken by government agents from Wilkes's house in April 1763. *Copies taken from the Records of the Court of King's Bench, at Westminster* (London, 1763), p. 63 note (a).

[21] BL Add. MSS 30880B, fols 1–34; *Radical Adventurer: The Diaries of Robert Morris*, ed. J.E. Ross (Bath, 1971), pp. 11–12.

The ancillaries to Wilkes's libertine practices promised discretion and an ambience matching their client's tastes. A keeper of a bawdy house employed the classical idiom, promising Wilkes 'privacy and quietness' in her 'humble habitation', which she proposed 'to dedicate as a private Temple for a few select Votaries to Venus'.[22] In promoting one of his 'young ladies', the pimp Badini flattered his client as a man of the scientific enlightenment:

[She] is an amazing philosopher. She understands the proprieties of movement or motion better than Aristotle and Descartes, or even Locke – As you know that it is impossible to be eminent in philosophy without being very deep in mathematics, she is also a profound mathematician, and can describe such particular, surprising figures, as would puzzle not only Mr. D'Alembert, but all the *Members* of any Academy – Natural and experimental philosophy however is the thing, in which her best parts lie – She will shew you her *Vacuum* ... and if you will but try to put in it a sprightly {cock/bird} you'll soon feel it expiring to your great satisfaction: she will bring it back to life presently through the power of her *Machina Electrica*, which if she does but wheel about as usual, that wonderful phenomenon will strike your senses more than it ever did.[23]

Though he was circumspect, Wilkes's sexual libertinism was far from being a solitary or secret enterprise, whose only witnesses were prostitutes and their agents. Had it been so, he would have risked incurring the unflattering epithet of 'sneaking lecher'. For Wilkes and his fellow rakes, sex was a social activity. In their correspondence, they eagerly reported their sexual exploits and recommended women for their physical attributes and expertise. (Across the Channel, the young Marquis de Sade would offend aristocratic society not because of the nature of his debauches, but because he engaged in them in isolation from his social peers.[24]) Indeed, whoring itself often appears as the essential pretext for a larger enterprise: wittily licentious exchanges between libertine companions, extending to the collaborative production of pornography.

Prominent among Wilkes's early rake friends were two medical doctors, Thomas Brewster and John Armstrong. Both were half a generation older than Wilkes and each had a literary bent. Each contributed to the idiom in which Wilkes's libertine career was enacted. Not unusually for a physician, Brewster was also a classical scholar, praised for his English translation of the obscure satires of the Roman

---

[22] Mrs M. Watson to Wilkes, BL Add. MSS 30880B, fol. 25.

[23] Ibid., fol. 24 ('cock' and 'bird' are both original, one above the other within brackets). Wilkes availed himself of Badini's services. BL Add. MSS 30873, fol. 12.

[24] Francine du Plessix Gray, *At Home with the Marquis de Sade: A Life* (London and New York, 1998), p. 67.

writer Persius. He practised medicine in Bath, where Wilkes became a frequent visitor, joining the annual throng of migrants who made the town England's most fashionable spa resort. With its commercial bustle, genteel entertainments, and unceasing chatter about politics and scandal, Bath was, for many Londoners, a home away from home, 'the continuation of Oxford Street', in the words of one historian.[25] The town would retain its allure for Wilkes throughout most of his life. Not the least of its attractions was the opportunity it afforded those with an uncertain claim to gentility to rub shoulders with 'the quality'. Careful adherence to the rules of etiquette, established by arbiters of fashion such as Richard 'Beau' Nash, had the effect of blurring distinctions that applied in more established social milieus. The injunctions of politesse did not prohibit sexual intrigues there, as long as these were conducted with appropriate decorum. Bath was in fact notorious as a hotbed of amorous adventures. That Wilkes engaged in them during his visits is evident from Brewster's correspondence with him.[26] In one letter, Brewster chided his friend for his 'spirit of infidelity',[27] a phrase that intentionally conflated two sides of libertinism, sexual licence that extended to adultery, and freedom from the constraints of doctrinal orthodoxy. The censure was, of course, playfully ironic; Brewster was offering a tribute, as one rake to another.

John Armstrong was a Scot who practised his profession in London, where he became Wilkes's family doctor. At the time that Wilkes became acquainted with him, he was a physician to the Duke's Hospital for disabled soldiers, in London. Later, during the Seven Years' War, he was appointed as physician to the army in Germany, perhaps through Wilkes's influence. Armstrong's involvement in public service was by default, not by vocational design. According to his own dyspeptic explanation, his aspiration to become a fashionable physician like Brewster (whom he admired) was thwarted by his unwillingness or inability to flatter, scheme, and dissemble. It did not help his notoriously sour mood that, as a graduate of a Scottish university, he had never received a licence to practice medicine in London from the College of Physicians; his engagement in his profession was therefore technically illegal. Compounding his sense of alienation was the Scots-baiting that swept the capital in the wake of the '45 Jacobite rebellion; it perhaps affected him all the more because he was a loyal supporter of the Hanoverian throne.[28]

---

[25]   Alfred Goodwin, rev. Sarah Brown, 'Brewster, Thomas (b. 1705),' *ODNB*; Paul Langford, *A Polite and Commercial People: England 1727–1783* (Oxford and New York, 1989), p. 106.

[26]   BL Add. MSS 30867, fols 49, 51–52, 55–56.

[27]   Ibid., fol. 53.

[28]   William J. Maloney, *George and John Armstrong of Castleton: Two Eighteenth-Century Medical Pioneers* (Edinburgh and London, 1954), pp. 13, 26–30, 34, 85; James Sambrook, 'Armstrong, John (1708/9–1779)', *ODNB*.

The fact that Armstrong stood towards the margins of polite society was certainly no barrier to his friendship with Wilkes. Nor at this time was his Scottish ancestry. Although Wilkes was a committed social climber, he retained some feelings of fellowship with outsiders – especially denizens of Grub Street – perhaps because of a prescient sense that one day he would find himself in a like condition. Armstrong had qualities, moreover, that engaged Wilkes's sympathies in a number of disparate ways. As a man of letters, a poet and essayist, he possessed a lively, satirical style of a kind that Wilkes himself aspired to. And though never a modish physician, Armstrong was a competent and dedicated one, especially attentive to the well-being of Wilkes and his daughter.[29] The author of *The Art of Preserving Health* – a lifestyle manual in verse – Armstrong also prescribed a healthy regimen specifically for Wilkes in a curious poem entitled *A Day*.[30]

Above all, Armstrong engaged with relish in the kind of bawdy exchanges that defined libertinism as a collective enterprise. His interest extended to an apparently precise knowledge of the length of Wilkes's penis (nine inches) and that of his fellow libertines. He represented himself as a rake past his prime, whose role was to urge his younger friends, in the manner of Lord Rochester's 'Disabled Debauchee', to emulate his past heroic adventures. 'For between you and me it is not altogether with me now as it was in times past when the candle of the Lord of Lampsacus [*i.e.* Priapus] burns night and day, so that I could almost

---

[29]   Bleackley, *Wilkes*, pp. 23, 73.

[30]   Like Armstrong's private letters to Wilkes, the work is fawning in tone, a response that Wilkes often elicited from admirers, and which was often a signal of future rifts. *A Day* advocates simple fare ('one plain Dish'); processed meats are to be avoided at all costs ('beware of Brawn – be sure, beware!'). Armstrong is suspicious of claret and champagne, believing they should only be imbibed after dinner. Port, 'that black poison', was to drink as brawn was to solid food, and its consumption was to be avoided at all costs. One's regimen must follow nature's diurnal and seasonal rhythms. Study was best undertaken in early morning, not at night by candlelight. Exercise was essential: 'Rush out, enjoy the Fields and the Fresh Air; / Ride, walk, or drive, the Weather foul or fair.' The best time for such activity was after breakfast, except in the 'torrid months' when it should replace early morning study. As a guide to Wilkes's quotidian habits, *A Day* must be approached with caution. It was a work of prescription, not description, and Armstrong knew from experience that doctors' prescriptions were apt to be ignored. Wilkes's diet was certainly less Spartan than that recommended by Armstrong. Though an advocate of the virtues of whole-wheat bread, he also enjoyed game meats and wine, though rarely to excess in his later years. Yet we can glean, or confirm, some elements of Wilkes's daily routine from the poem. 'You study early', said Armstrong approvingly. And his comment about Wilkes's propensity for taking vigorous walks far and wide through the streets of London (a habit he would continue into old age) matches evidence from other sources. [John Armstrong] *A Day: An Epistle to John Wilkes, of Aylesbury, Esq.* (London, 1761), pp. 4–7, 10, 13–15.

have wrote a lusty roundelay by it in the darkest night', he confessed to Wilkes. And while bemoaning his current sexual inadequacies, he praised his friend's virility: 'It mortifies me that I can't at present enjoy a little of the Cuntry [*sic*] sports along with you, tho' in some shape it is better that it happens not to be in my power, for Priapus knows I should make a poor dangling Figure in Company with such a vigorous and mighty Cunter as the Nimrod of Bucks.' From active rake, he had settled for the role of keen voyeur: 'Come tell me a thousand gallant Stories of your conquests up and down the land', he pleaded.[31]

Armstrong's sexual prurience was matched by that of Thomas Potter, who became Wilkes's closest libertine friend in the 1750s. Armstrong and Potter were very different, though, in conduct and social background. Unlike Armstrong's, Potter's libertinism was marked by nocturnal decadence and physical dissipation. When Wilkes first met him in 1751, he was already suffering from the chronic digestive afflictions, aggravated by painful bouts of venereal and other urethral diseases, which would lead to his death in 1759 at the age of forty-one. His father was the late John Potter, a clergyman who had reached the pinnacle of ecclesiastical preferment with his appointment as Archbishop of Canterbury. Thomas, though the younger son, had inherited his father's large fortune. It was not a case of virtue rewarded. His elder brother emulated his father as an earnest and able clergyman, but he had married a serving-maid, an offence sufficiently grave to cause John Potter to disinherit him. Thomas Potter was a bundle of contradictions. Though his manner became increasingly cynical, he also possessed charm and showed occasional flashes of a social conscience. Like Wilkes, he was a governor of the Foundling Hospital and in 1751 he helped to launch a Parliamentary crusade against the destructive consequences of gin consumption. Horace Walpole once described him as a 'young man of the greatest good nature' and admired his oratorical skills, although he qualified his praise by remarking that Potter 'effaced impressions as fast as he made them'.[32]

Not long after Wilkes and Potter first became acquainted, Potter declared: 'The highest [pleasure] that can be afforded me next to the Company of a Woman is that of my dear Wilkes.' He withheld no confidences from his friend, even keeping him informed of the state of his erections. And as part of the customary process of bonding between libertines, Potter and Wilkes treated their sexual partners as a shared commodity. When Potter learnt that Wilkes was visiting Tunbridge in Kent, he wrote: 'Should you meet there a Goddess under the vulgar appellation of Miss Betty Spooner, offer Incense to her for my Sake, but be cautious of doing it

---

[31]   BL Add. MSS 30880B, fols 5, 8.

[32]   Wilkes and Potter, ed. Cash, pp. 14–16; Horace Walpole, *Memoirs of King George II*, ed. John Brooke, 3 vols (New Haven and London, 1985), vol. 1, pp. 47–49; vol. 2, p. 95.

in my Name lest the Divinity be displeased at me. You will find in her Liveliness and Lechery.'[33]

Potter liked to chaff Wilkes for leading him astray: 'You … have done every thing in your power to ruin and destroy [my health] by strong soups, filthy clarets rakish hours & bad example. Avaunt Satan with all thy temptations.'[34] The comment was disingenuous; Potter was a practised rake well before Wilkes came on the scene, with a wide erotic repertoire. Indeed, he is often blamed for having a corrupting influence on Wilkes, a view originating in John Almon's comment that Potter, as 'an early vicious acquaintance', was 'the ruin of Mr. Wilkes, who was not a bad man early, or naturally. But Potter poisoned his morals'.[35] This opinion needs to be understood in the context of continuing attempts to represent Wilkes as the artless dupe of older, more experienced, rakes; but, stripped of the special pleading, it cannot be entirely discounted. Consider Potter's appeal to Wilkes to abandon hearth and home – and tedious provincial friends – in Aylesbury in favour of the fleshpots of Bath:

> If you have either Religion or morality, if you have but a Pretence to one single social Virtue, if you preferr [sic] young Women & Whores to old Women & Wives, if you prefer the Toying away Hours with little Sattin Back to the Evening Conferences of your Mother in Law, if the charms of the muses are better than the Whiffs of Tobacco from Mr Stevens [vicar of Aylesbury], if the sprightly Notes of the Fiddle are preferable to the squawking of your Brat, if Life & Spirit & Wit & Humour & gaiety but above all if the heavenly inspired Passion called Lust have not deserted you & left you a Prey to Dullness & Imbecility hasten to Town that you may take a Place in my Post Chaise for Bath next Thursday morning whither I am hurrying from the Wisdom of Drs & Midwifes the loathsome bawdy of the Nurses the solemn & hideous lullabies of my mother in law & the odious yell of a young Female yahoo that thrust herself into the World yesterday.[36]

Wilkes was responsive to such appeals. He was, however, resistant to the thoroughgoing contempt of domestic life in which they were couched. Given this discrepancy in attitude, it is tempting to classify Wilkes and Potter as distinct types of libertine, with Potter as an atavistic representative of the Restoration brand – impulsive, misogynistic, and resistant to sentiment – and Wilkes as a standard-bearer of the Georgian rake's putative evolution into the good-hearted man, displaying a sociability that narrowed gender difference. However, while

---

[33] Wilkes and Potter, ed. Cash, p. 17; Potter to Wilkes, 15 January 1753, BL Add. MSS 30880B, fol. 1, and 23 July 1752, Add. MSS 30867, fol. 62.

[34] BL Add MSS 30880B, fol. 1.

[35] *Wilkes Correspondence*, vol. 1, pp. 18–19.

[36] 19 October 1752, BL Add. MSS 30867, fol. 65.

some evident differences between Wilkes and Potter need to be acknowledged, they should not be overstated; there was compatibility between the two, evidenced by their collaboration on *An Essay on Woman,* their infamous parody of Alexander Pope's *Essay on Man.* As I shall suggest in more detail below, the peer-driven culture of the company of rakes was frequently at odds with the competing social obligations of politeness and sentiment.

Around the time of Potter's death, that company now included Charles Churchill. Wilkes and Churchill probably became acquainted in 1759 when Churchill was still an impoverished London curate, married with three children. Two years later Churchill achieved overnight fame and fortune with his publication of *The Rosciad,* a satirical debunking of the pretensions of London's leading actors. Following that literary triumph, Churchill shed the drabness of clerical garb, becoming a striking presence in libertine circles in his new costume of blue coat with metal buttons, gold-laced hat, and ruffles. Other successes quickly followed, including *Night,* a defence and celebration of the nocturnal, rakish lifestyle. In it, Churchill pointedly mocked 'the sage DOCTOR [Armstrong]' and those 'scraps of antient learning' that had deluded him into avowing 'the fatal consequences of midnight air'. The swipe probably contributed to the sundering of relations between Wilkes and Armstrong, and hints at some jostling for ascendancy beneath the apparent bonhomie of libertine friendships.[37]

Through Churchill, Wilkes became acquainted with the circle known as the Nonsense Club, a dining club of literary wits, all former pupils of Westminster School. James Boswell called them the 'London Geniuses'. The fellowship included Bonnell Thornton, a writer and newspaper proprietor, George Colman, a dramatist and theatre manager, and Robert Lloyd, a poet. Each of these men, like Churchill, contributed their talents to Wilkes's political causes.[38] But it was with Churchill that Wilkes achieved a special bond, which found its most important expression in their collaboration on the *North Briton.* Their friendship – an intense one until it was cut short by Churchill's sudden death in November 1764 – was to some extent based on complementary differences. Wilkes's libertinism was associated with social acceptance and the possibility of political advancement; Churchill's was part of the personality of the Bohemian outsider, the antithesis and scourge of respectability. Whereas Wilkes gave Churchill some access to

---

[37] George Nobbe, *The North Briton: A Study in Political Propaganda* (New York, 1939), pp. 54–60; *The Poetical Works of Charles Churchill,* ed. Douglas Grant (Oxford, 1956) p. 52.

[38] Lance Bertelsen, *The Nonsense Club: Literature and Popular Culture, 1749–1764* (Oxford and New York, 1986), pp. 91–131, 161–209; Wallace Cable Brown, *Charles Churchill: Poet, Rake, and Rebel* (New York, 1968), pp. 162–63; two communications from Wilkes to H.S. Woodfall, Osborn Manuscript Files W, folder 16122, Osborn Collection.

his influential friends, Churchill, in his poetry, gave heroic meaning to Wilkes's disconnection from the political establishment.[39]

There were also some divergences in their sexual careers, but ones that ultimately served to strengthen the bond between them rather than loosen it. Like Potter, Churchill was frequently incapacitated by gonorrhoea, describing its ravages in his typically mordant style. Wilkes was sometimes flippant in response, but always sympathetic. When Churchill, at the height of his fame, shocked polite opinion by running off with a fifteen-year-old girl, Wilkes expressed alarm, initially even annoyance, but never moral disapproval. His concern was primarily with Churchill's safety in the light of threats to his life from the girl's family, although he was also aggravated that Churchill had allowed himself to be distracted from the task of political advocacy in the *North Briton*.[40] 'When you can so nobly assist us in our great parts, ought you to run away to sport in dalliance?' Wilkes chided. Churchill was unrepentant. He made light of the jeopardy in which he had placed himself, avowing a reckless hedonism: 'My Life I hold for purposes of pleasure; those forbid, it is not worth my care.' It was not a credo that the relatively more cautious Wilkes ever fully embraced, but Churchill acutely recognised that 'to deserve the name of Friend, which You honour me with, I will rather seek danger than shun it'.[41] This was a dimension of what Wilkes saw as Churchill's 'manly genius',[42] tempered in himself, perhaps, by his social and political ambition.

In any event, differences between Wilkes and Churchill were always marginal to the common ground they shared. The polar stars of love and honour guided both, said Wilkes, while pondering the priorities of pursuing a woman or fighting a duel.[43] The two friends habitually mixed business and pleasure. In one of his letters to Churchill about the *North Briton*, Wilkes included the following invitation: 'I shall return in less than an hour – If you wait you will kiss the *lips* – if you will dine you will kiss the sweetest *bubbies* of this hemisphere.'[44] From Paris, first as a visitor then as an exile, Wilkes plied Churchill with accounts of the city's sensual delights. It was when Churchill was on his way to join him in

---

[39]   Through Wilkes, Churchill joined the libertine circle at Medmenham and also became acquainted with the Duke of Grafton. As well as 'The Duellist', a number of Churchill's poems celebrate Wilkes, including 'An Epistle to William Hogarth'. *Poetical Works of Charles Churchill*, pp. 211–43.

[40]   Joseph M. Beatty, 'Mrs. Montagu, Churchill, and Miss Cheere', *Modern Languages Notes*, 41 (1926): 384–86; Brown, pp. 172–83.

[41]   *Wilkes – Churchill*, pp. 74, 75.

[42]   BL Add. MSS 30865B, fol. 20.

[43]   Ibid. 30878, fol. 36.

[44]   *Wilkes–Churchill*, p. 33.

them that he died in his friend's arms, shortly after arriving at Boulogne, leaving Wilkes grief-stricken and temporarily inconsolable.[45]

What do the exchanges between Wilkes and his rake companions tell us about the character of the libertine enterprise in the middle and late decades of the eighteenth century? At its ideological core was the insistence that their sexual libertinism was mandated by a deified nature, whose ends were always benign and decorous, a central tenet of enlightened thought. By extension, natural sex was a healthy activity; it renewed the mind. Wilkes claimed he was able to write his best *North Briton* while in bed with the London prostitute, Betsy Green.[46] The libertine's creed was proclaimed in John Armstrong's sex-manual in blank verse, *The Œconomy of Love* (published anonymously in 1736): 'What Nature bids / Is good, is wise; and faultless we obey.'[47] Hence for Wilkes, 'lust' was 'a noble passion', for Potter 'a heavenly inspired' one. Begging off a meeting with a friend, Wilkes explained that 'the *great* goddess of my idolatry, for I am a polytheist, has summoned me to her altar at six, and she expects two or three ejaculations from me at least'.[48] Similar language pervades Wilkes and Potter's *Essay on Woman*, where copulation is enjoined as a religious duty: ' ... fuck the Cunt at hand, and God adore. / What future Fucks he gives not thee to know, / But gives that Cunt to be thy Blessing now.'[49] Here the penis becomes a phallic plant, subject to nature's whims.[50] Yet Wilkes was also insistent that the man of pleasure was a man of reason and control who did not capitulate passively to nature's imperatives. Instead he engaged with them in order that his pleasure might be maximised; in the process, mere copulation becomes refined sensuality. Hence the *Essay on Woman* counsels against the unmanly embarrassment of premature ejaculation: 'Observe how Nature works, and if it rise / Too quick and rapid, check it ere it flies; / Spend when we must, but keep it while we can: / Thus Godlike will be deem'd the Ways of Man.'[51] Wilkes continued the injunction in his parody, 'The Dying Lover to his Prick',

---

[45]   Ibid., pp. 64–65, 83; Wilkes to Humphrey Cotes, 19 November 1764, BL Add. MSS 30868, fol. 144.

[46]   *Boswell, Italy*, p. 58 note 3.

[47]   Quoted in Geoffrey Ashe, *The Hell-Fire Clubs: A History of Anti-Morality*, rev. edn (Stroud, 2000), p. 75.

[48]   *Boswell, Italy*, p. 59; BL Add. MSS 30880B, fol. 7.

[49]   Wilkes and Potter, ed. Cash, p. 113.

[50]   'The vegetation of Pego is most astonishing ... It will shoot forth most amazingly, quite on a sudden, especially in a *Hot-bed*, and as suddenly shrink back.' Wilkes and Potter, ed. Cash, p. 99. Paul-Gabriel Boucé comments that the *Essay* makes 'the most complete assimilation of the penis with a phallic plant'. 'Chthonic and Pelagic Metaphorization in Eighteenth-Century English Erotica', in *'Tis Nature's Fault: Unauthorized Sexuality during the Enlightenment* (Cambridge and New York, 1987), ed. Robert Purks Maccubbin, p. 213.

[51]   Wilkes and Potter, ed. Cash, p. 101.

which as he rather gratuitously explained 'was written to check the mad Career of some precipitate young Steeds, and to teach them not to run the earthly Race so furiously as to lose half the Rapture of the Course'.[52] Here, in Karen Harvey's words, the erotic text 'served to buttress the reader's self-control, to confirm men's learning and wit, promising to titillate and to tease, rather than to provoke them into careless, disruptive, de-masculinizing sexual abandon'.[53]

If nature prescribed, it also proscribed. Anything that stood outside its mandate was by definition 'unnatural', and liable to denunciation. In the public discourse of the libertines, this included anal intercourse between a man and a woman, which John Armstrong condemned as a 'foreign vice': 'And man with woman (monstrous to relate!) / Leaving the natural road themselves debase / With deeds unseemly, and dishonour foul. / Britons, for shame! be male and female still.'[54] Yet eighteenth-century libertinism still retained an element of transgression or illicitness, which meant that in private Wilkes and his friends bragged of committing 'unnatural' sexual acts that they condemned in public. Armstrong testified to Wilkes that 'tho' I have frequently put it [the 'candle'] under a Bushel the tight smooth Socket was always my choice'. The boast, with its witty scriptural allusion, appealed to Wilkes so much that in a letter to a friend he plagiarised it verbatim, offering it as an account of his own experience, suggesting that what really counted in libertine culture was not so much the sexual act as the titillating discourse it engendered.[55]

For Potter, sexual transgression extended to bestiality. He claimed to know of a woman who had been 'rogered by a monkey', and he boasted of enjoying sexual intercourse with a cow. 'I glory in what I have done', he told Wilkes. There were, after all, precedents from antiquity that by extension should have conferred on him the status of a 'demigod'. 'What was the Foundation of the History of Jupiter and Io', Potter claimed, 'but some Heathen Priest who in a fit of Lust had stuck it into a cow & being surprised in the very Act had taught the multitude to revere him as a transformed deity'.[56] While Wilkes was always alert to classical models for firing the sexual imagination, it is unlikely that he sought to emulate his friend in this particular way. Yet he was never shocked by Potter's outrageous claims; it was all part of the male bonding experience.

---

[52] Ibid., p. 123.

[53] '"The Majesty of the Masculine-Form": Multiplicity and Male Bodies in Eighteenth-Century Erotica', in *English Masculinities, 1660–1800,* ed. Tim Hitchcock and Michèle Cohen (London and New York, 1999) p. 214.

[54] Quoted in Ashe, p. 77.

[55] BL Add. MSS 30880B, fol. 5. The biblical reference is to the Sermon on the Mount (Matthew 5: 15: 'Neither do men light a candle, and put it under a bushel, but on a candlestick'). Wilkes's plagiarised letter is to [Evan?] Lloyd, BL Add. MSS 30880B, fol. 7.

[56] BL Add. MSS 30880B, fol. 3.

The latitude that the libertines still demanded in sexual conduct perhaps helps to explain why they invested so much loathing in the one act they considered taboo: sodomy, defined in the eighteenth century as sexual acts between men or between men and boys. What marked the sodomite, active or passive, was not merely sexual transgression, but sexual transgression of a kind that disordered gender distinctions, thereby debasing manhood, which the libertines were determined to uphold. With the body of a man, but utterly effeminised, the sodomite constituted a despicable anomaly, a third gender.[57] The attack on sodomy, once largely confined to Christian moralists such as John Wilkes's mother, was joined with relish by libertines, who now appeared as militants for nature's claim. This represented a shift in the character of English libertinage. During the Restoration, libertines such as Lord Rochester could casually confuse the erotic attractions of women and boys (and their respective orifices) without compromising their manhood. Their attitude, James Turner suggests, should remind us that 'sodomy still [at the Restoration] enjoyed its Renaissance association with aristocracy'.[58] To the extent that this connection survived into the eighteenth century, it had taken on wholly negative connotations; its alleged practitioners had become a besieged and despised group, far removed from the arrogant exhibitionism of Rochester and his circle. Wilkes and his libertine friends were shrill in their verbal attack. The *Essay on Woman* is littered with disparaging references to alleged homosexuals. Its most prominent target was Lord George Sackville (later Lord George Germain), whom Wilkes accused of being the catamite of George Stone, Archbishop of Armagh. Wilkes's satirical depiction of Sackville as *Intrepidi Herois* (intrepid hero) connects sexual deviance with a reputation for unmanliness: Sackville had been accused of cowardly conduct at the Battle on Minden in 1759.[59] Later, in 1772, Wilkes joined other City notables in expressing outrage at George III's last-minute pardon of Captain Robert Jones, a flamboyant habitué of masques, who had been sentenced to hang for the crime of sodomy upon a thirteen-year-old boy. In joining this campaign, Wilkes was placing himself on the side of London mobs, whose sport it was to pelt convicted sodomites in the pillory, while distancing himself from *philosophe* friends like Helvetius who were cautiously mooting toleration for sexual deviance.[60]

---

[57]   Randolph Trumbach, 'Sex, Gender, and Sexual Identity in Modern Culture: Male Sodomy and Female Prostitution in Enlightenment London', *Journal of the History of Sexuality*, 2 (1991): 186–203.

[58]   *Libertines and Radicals in Early Modern London: Sexuality, Politics and Literary Culture, 1630–1685* (Cambridge, 2002), p. 226.

[59]   Wilkes and Potter, ed. Cash, p. 85.

[60]   Anna Clark, *Scandal: The Sexual Politics of the British Constitution* (Princeton, 2004) pp. 31–33, 44–45; Rictor Norton, *Mother Clap's Molly House: The Gay Subculture in England, 1700–1830* (London, 1992), pp. 170–71.

The most sustained literary assault on sodomy was Charles Churchill's poem *The Times,* published in September 1764. In it Churchill paints a lurid picture of corrupted metropolitan society in which the advance of sodomy was leading to the abandonment of 'Woman, the pride and happiness of Man'.[61] Wilkes praised the poem as Churchill's best, surpassing the work of Juvenal, who had attacked homosexuality in his *Ninth Satire.*[62] In his observations on sexual deviance in Italy, Wilkes would seek to match Churchill's perfervid rhetoric. Here is his judgement on the modern Romans: 'One enormous vice has been transmitted down to them in all its pristine vigour. Every virtue has been lost. The most deprav'd appetite, to which I allude, formerly shar'd the man with the most natural of all our passions. In the holy city it swallows up all the rest.' 'Cou'd a Promethean fire animate the Venus of Medicis,' he continued, 'she might walk in all security from Turin to Naples. So far from a rudeness being offer'd to her she wou'd be treated with the most cruel neglect.' He claimed that her fate would have been different in the ancient world, his cynosure for manly conduct; then 'the whole orbis Romanus wou'd rise in arms, and a million of drawn weapons wou'd dispute the glorious prize'.[63] Ironically, while in Rome, Wilkes established a friendship with Johann Winckelmann, the historian of classical art, whose own celebration of manly friendship included active pederasty. Yet what redeemed Winckelmann in Wilkes's eyes was that he had 'a heart glowing with the love of liberty', and he was undoubtedly flattered that Wincklemann saw in him a reincarnation of the type of republican virtue sublimely represented in classical statuary.[64]

In condemning the sodomite, the third gender, Wilkes and Churchill were also staking out an attitude to women, one in which 'cruel neglect' of the sex represented the greatest offence. But, within the converse of the broad parameter of 'cruel neglect' to women, what constituted appropriate attention? Wilkes insisted that his own conduct with women was invariably marked by politeness, and he was severe on decadent rakes, whom he alleged breached propriety and decorum in their relations with the opposite sex.[65] At times, he seemed to be broaching a kind of sexual egalitarianism, in which women were respected as equal partners in erotic encounters, or in the manner in which they inhabited the libertine imagination in erotica and pornography. Against the charge that *An Essay on Woman* was 'calculated to depreciate the Sex', Wilkes responded that its

---

61 *Poetical Works of Charles Churchill,* p. 399.

62 *Wilkes–Churchill,* pp. 91–92.

63 BL Add. MSS 30865B, fol. 30.

64 Ibid., fols 33–34; Alex Potts, *Flesh and the Ideal: Winckelmann and the Origins of Art History* (New Haven and London, 1994), pp. 185, 199–201, 216, 279.

65 *Wilkes Correspondence,* vol. 1, p. 230 note.

'luscious' descriptions were something that 'Nature and woman might pardon'.[66] Later he described it as 'the *apotheosis* of the fair sex', claiming that 'there [was] not in the whole poem … a single line in disparagement of the amiable part of the creation, but some hundreds in its praise'.[67] It is true that there is not the consistently blatant misogyny in *An Essay on Woman* that characterised much seventeenth-century *pornographia* (James Turner's faux Renaissance neologism, meaning literally 'marking the whore'). Fanny Murray, the famous prostitute to whom the poem is inscribed, is treated gently, her presence little more than a matter of literary convention. In an era in which the 'honest whore' was seen as an ally in the campaign against the sodomites, she was certainly spared the vitriol directed at her Restoration predecessors. Yet as in many artefacts of eighteenth-century libertinism, there is spillage from an earlier tradition. What else would explain the inclusion in the *Essay's* title page of Agamemnon's judgement, in the words of Homer's *Odyssey*, on the murderous Clytemnestra?: 'That there is nothing more dreadful and shameless than a woman.'[68] It was the kind of attitude that prompted this riposte in *An Original Essay on Woman* (1771) from the pseudonymous Mary Seymour Montague: 'The Libertine thinks all Women lascivious, because he has reduced one or two to Prostitution.'[69]

Misogyny is also evident in some of the private exchanges of the libertines. Thomas Potter was the worst offender, routinely employing degrading language about women. One of Bath's attractions, he explained to Wilkes, was its 'parcel of dancing bitches'.[70] The closest he came to complimenting a mistress was to describe one as a spirited 'little Toad', an endearment whose effect was lost when he later remarked that toads invite disgust.[71] There is similar degrading imagery in his malediction on the marriage of his friend, William Pitt, to Hester Grenville: 'All that Wit & Fire & Spirit is to be matrimonially soaked in the cold, slimy aquatick C--- of Ly. H. Gr. What can so unnatural a mixture produce? The seed of Heaven will Congeal into Frog Spawn.'[72] (The 'mixture' in fact produced the dominant politician of the late eighteenth century, William Pitt the Younger.)

Although Potter's overt and persistent misogyny was by now unusual, a tendency to depersonalise women, to push them to the margins, persisted in libertine discourse. Despite Wilkes's protestations, what it celebrated was not

---

[66]   Revd John Kidgell, *A Genuine and Succinct Narrative of a Scandalous, Obscene, and Exceedingly Profane Libel, entitled An Essay on Woman* (London, 1763), p. 9; *Wilkes Correspondence*, vol. 3, p. 116.

[67]   *Political Register,* 2 (1768): 414.

[68]   Wilkes and Potter, ed. Cash, p. 85.

[69]   Quoted in Clark, *Scandal,* p. 46.

[70]   BL Add. MSS 30867, fol. 66.

[71]   Ibid. 30880B, fols 1, 4.

[72]   Ibid. 30867, fol. 103.

women, or even womanhood, but the male heterosexual imperative. Women appear in eighteenth-century pornography and erotica not so much as objects of desire but as the privileged viewers of men's bodies, a representation presumably calculated to allay the anxiety and to buttress the masculinity of male readers.[73]

A predatory and boastful phallicism remained the dominant theme in private libertine exchanges, its timeworn trope the association of the seduction of women with the hunting of game or with military conquest (the former an interesting discursive survival given that literal participation in the hunt itself was no longer an essential marker of manhood). John Armstrong invariably employed it in praising Wilkes's sexual career.[74] And if seduction was an act of martial valour, then the penis was a weapon. 'Your long spear is, I suppose, reeking with the blood of some sweet Welch virgin', Wilkes wrote to a friend.[75] Another peripheral member of the company of rakes was praised 'as honest a parson as ever drove a seven inch Toledo red hot from his mighty Thigh'.[76] Women were accorded enjoyment in sex only to the extent that they surrendered to this quasi-military assault. The notion is expressed in one of Armstrong's many prurient enquiries to Wilkes: 'Of all things I burn to know the circumstances of your triumphal entrance into that coy Citadel which stood so long a Siege and in what raptures you lay entranced there ... It makes me shudder to think in what Exstacies [sic] you dissolved together.'[77]

The tropes of sexual intercourse as hunting, and of women's bodies as territory to be explored and conquered, are employed throughout *An Essay on Woman*, consistent with the double-entendre of that title. 'I am happy if I shall have been allowed to have *fought a good fight* in a Field where I desire that my *Valour* and *Vigour* may be most shewn', Wilkes wrote in the preface. The lines 'Together let us beat this ample field, / Try what the open, what the covert yield', are unchanged from Alexander Pope's exhortation to study God's plan, but what follows suggests a different meaning: 'The latent Tracts, the pleasing Depths explore, / And my Prick clapp'd where thousands were before'. Then in a switch of metaphor, appropriate to a new age of scientific reason, Pope's evocation of the Newtonian universe of orbiting worlds and stellar systems is transformed into the elaborately hooped and girdled female form, a challenge to the male seducer.[78]

---

[73] Harvey, 'The Majesty of the Masculine Form', pp. 193–214.

[74] BL Add. MSS 30880B, fol. 5. On eighteenth-century penis obsession, see George Rousseau, 'Priapic Passages and "Trading in Trifles": Penis and Pornography in the Eighteenth Century', in *The Eighteenth-Century Body: Art, History, Literature, Medicine*, ed. Angelica Goodden (Bern, 2002), pp. 73–93.

[75] Wilkes to Evan Lloyd, BL Add. MSS 30880B, fol. 15.

[76] John Armstrong to Wilkes, ibid., fol. 8.

[77] Ibid.

[78] Wilkes and Potter, ed. Cash, pp. 95, 99–101, 103.

Clearly, a discordance remained between the sensible and polite acknowledgement of the equal humanity of women, characterised by heterosocial conduct in a domestic setting, and a libertine world that remained intensely homosocial, in which women were essential yet peripheral. This is not to say that libertines could not be polite or even sentimental, but in order to be so they were obliged to suspend, or dissemble, their more aggressively rakish tendencies. Wilkes was able to do this with a chameleon-like facility, yet also with an unerring sense that a hint of rakishness in his persona added an acceptable piquancy to polite exchanges.[79] There was, however, a situation in which politeness and libertinism converged, one in which politeness – or a corrupted version of it – was deployed to effect seduction. This connection found its most notorious advocacy in Lord Chesterfield's letters to his son, famously condemned by Samuel Johnson for teaching 'the morals of a whore, and the manners of a dancing master'. (A later fictional equivalent was Laclos's *Les Liaisons Dangereuses*; Wilkes kept an illustrated edition in his library.) By the time that Chesterfield's letters were published in 1774, however, their fashionable prescriptions were becoming *passé*; their 'emphasis on calculation challenged the primacy of unaffected feeling'.[80] Wilkes himself was obliged to adapt to the changing ethos, or at least pay lip service to it. Yet during the preceding period in which the letters were written, there seems little question that sexual intrigue delineated a style of libertinism that Wilkes and his circle were keen to emulate. 'What two damn'd adulterers we are', Wilkes gloated to Charles Churchill, as he planned a 'deep scheme' for the seduction of Madame Carpentier, his daughter's married governess.[81] Earlier, Wilkes had followed with malicious glee the twisting course of Thomas Potter's seduction of Gertrude Warburton, the wife of Revd William Warburton. And once the scheme had been accomplished, he and Churchill joined with relish in the literary campaign to brand the injured husband a cuckold.[82]

Medmenham Monks

The homosocial character of male libertine friendships was given flamboyant expression in libertine societies. These held a dual attraction for Wilkes because they connected sexual licence with social privilege. In 1754 he joined the Sublime Society of the Beefsteaks, where he rubbed shoulders with other rakes and wits

---

[79] For instance, his letter to Mrs Reynolds, wife of the City under-sheriff, 14 November 1771, BL Add. MSS 27925, fols 3–4.

[80] Langford, *Polite and Commercial People*, p. 586.

[81] BL Add. MSS 30880B, fol. 10.

[82] *Poetical Works of Charles Churchill*, 'Duellist', p. 283, and 'Dedication to the Sermons', p. 434; 'Letter to the Electors of Aylesbury', *Wilkes Correspondence*, vol. 3, p. 79.

such as James Boswell; Charles Churchill also became a member, probably through Wilkes's sponsorship. Meeting weekly in a room above the Covent Garden Theatre – in the heart of London's red-light district – the club's ostensible raison d'être was the patriotic consumption of beef cooked on a gridiron. The president for the day sat under a canopy, above which was emblazoned in golden letters the motto 'Beef and Liberty'. As an initiate, Wilkes would have been obliged to kiss the bone of beef that had been consumed at dinner. (As with other libertine societies, the club's ceremonies mimicked religious ones; the initiation ceremony was presided over by a 'bishop' wearing a mitre.) The carnal interests of the members notoriously extended beyond feasting on beef. The singing of bawdy catches was the principal after-dinner entertainment. Wilkes was still a member of the Beefsteaks in the 1780s, by which time, with the passage of generations, it had become an object of contempt for young men of 'rebellious instincts', who saw it as stuffy and insular.[83]

Unlike the Beefsteaks, the libertine society known as the Medmenham Monks retained its notoriety, partly because it was clandestine and ephemeral, and hence the object of lurid speculation. In the summer of 1763, tantalising rumours began to appear in the press about this mysterious assembly, which for some time had been gathering on the banks of the Thames at Medmenham Abbey in Buckinghamshire.[84] Wilkes, in the monkish guise of 'John of Aylesbury', was one of its more enthusiastic members, visiting the abbey on at least twenty occasions and serving as the society's librarian. He was also commissioned to purchase suitable silverware for the abbey, including silver cups in the shape of a woman's breast, for which, predictably, he 'forgot' to pay.[85] Wilkes later recalled Medmenham's setting in these lyrical terms: 'Beautiful hanging woods, soft meadows, a chrystal [sic] stream, and a grove of venerable old elms near the house, with the retiredness of the mansion itself, made it as sweet a retreat, as the most poetical imagination could create.'[86] The society's reputation, though,

---

[83]   BL Add. MSS 30891, 'A List of the Original Members of the Sublime Society of the Beef Steaks, instituted 6th December 1735 and their successors', fol. 3; Walter Arnold, *The Life and Death of the Sublime Society of Beefsteaks* (London, 1871), pp. xi–xix, 4–15; [James Boswell] *Boswell's London Journal, 1762–1763*, ed. Frederick A. Pottle (New York, London, Toronto, 1950), pp. 51–52; Brown, p. 66; Langford, *Polite and Commercial People*, p. 576. Clubs and societies have received much attention because, following Jürgen Habermas, they are seen as part of the institutional fabric of a public sphere that stood apart from the state and offered criticism of it. It needs to be emphasised, though, that libertine clubs typically sought to maintain privacy about their activities, and that some of them (for example, the Society of Dilettanti) were elite operations, whose members played or would play leading roles in the state.

[84]   *Public Advertiser,* 25 May 1763.

[85]   Sir Francis Dashwood, *The Dashwoods of West Wycombe* (London, 1987), p. 39.

[86]   *Wilkes Correspondence,* vol. 3, pp. 60–61.

belied this vision of pastoral innocence. Its members liked to refer to themselves as the 'Society of St Francis' or the 'Knights of St Francis' in tribute to the club's founder and host, Sir Francis Dashwood, but the names also suggested the kinds of satirical inversions in which the 'monks' apparently took great delight. The original Franciscans were dedicated to poverty, abstinence, and chastity; their namesakes at Medmenham to luxury, self-indulgence, and fornication. Dashwood clearly recognised a kindred spirit in Wilkes, and sought him as a guest at his Lincolnshire estate at Nocton as well as at Medmenham. Wilkes reciprocated Dashwood's evident regard for him. Writing to express his regret for missing a chapter meeting at the abbey, Wilkes conjured an image of Medmenham's host in a manner both friendly and familiar: 'I already see your sides shaking with laughter and see you filling your nostrils with snuff; I already hear you solving riddles in your accustomed way; everyone shows their approval with applause.'[87]

Such glimpses of Medmenham are rare, and the paucity of genuine information about the society has invited fanciful speculation, some of which, through repetition, has attained a spurious authority in the secondary literature. Modern accounts of otherwise impeccable scholarship still refer to the society as a 'Hell-Fire Club' (even *the* 'Hell-Fire Club') – a term that was not applied to it until 1776, after the society had fallen into abeyance – and envisage the monks engaging in the Black Mass. In a complex genealogy of evidence, the notion of devil worship has become detached from its main originating source, the expanded edition of Charles Johnstone's novel, *Chrysal*. That story includes the uproarious tale of John Wilkes terrifying the abbey worshippers by releasing in their midst a baboon in the guise of the Prince of Darkness, wringing from Lord Sandwich the confession that he sinned 'only from vanity of being in fashion'. The fictional anecdote illustrates how quickly Medmenham came to signify aristocratic cravenness, but it would not now be cited as an authentic, first-hand account.[88]

Like so much else about it, the society's origins are shrouded in mystery. The first clear reference to the 'Franciscans' at Medmenham is contained in a letter from John Armstrong to Wilkes, dated 20 December 1760, in which Armstrong refers to the society as a 'new order'.[89] Entries in the abbey's 'cellar book', in which imbibing guests, using their monkish pseudonyms, were obliged to record their consumption of claret and port, confirm that the frolics at Medmenham

---

[87]   Dashwood to Wilkes, 9 January 1761, BL Add. MSS 30867, fol. 167; Dashwood, p. 35.

[88]   *Morning Post*, 22 August 1776; *Chrysal; or the Adventures of a Guinea*, 7th edn, 4 vols (London, 1771), vol. 3, pp. 239–43. On how Johnstone's story fixed in the public mind the relationship between Wilkes and Sandwich, see John Brewer, *A Sentimental Murder: Love and Madness in the Eighteenth Century* (New York, 2004), pp. 110–11.

[89]   BL Add. MSS 30867, fol. 165.

were well under way by 1760.[90] In some accounts, though, the establishment of the secret brotherhood is dated as early as the 1740s, with the original meetings purportedly taking place in the George and Vulture Inn in London or the rural estates of the society's members, notably Dashwood's at West Wycombe. By extending the lifespan of the society backwards, its cast of possible members expands to include such notables as Frederick, Prince of Wales, who supposedly hosted the club at Cliveden, his country home, before his death in 1751. Because eighteenth-century Hanoverian heirs were magnets for political dissidents, Frederick's alleged patronage of the fraternity invites the hypothesis that the society was busily engaged in covert opposition to George II.[91] These claims, however, smack of conspiracy theories, unsupported by any credible evidence. Though the society would eventually be riven by politics, there is little reason to question Wilkes's claim that it strove to be apolitical. 'Party had not the least concern', he insisted, 'the brotherhood … were us'd to sacrifice … to mirth, to friendship, and to love, never to fortune, nor ambition.'[92]

Nor is there any basis for believing that the 'Knights of St Francis' existed in a meaningful way until after Dashwood leased Medmenham Abbey in 1750 and transformed it into a site where he and his friends could indulge their rakish appetites in an Arcadian milieu. There were, though, precursors for the Medmenham fraternity, the Society of Dilettanti in particular, which shaped the rituals of its members. Dashwood himself was an enthusiast for libertine societies, and what we know about Medmenham certainly carries his distinctive stamp. His image – owing in part to the ridicule that Wilkes heaped on him after relations between them soured – is that of a comic *buffo* figure, an eighteenth-century version of Sir John Falstaff. Dashwood himself tried to conceal his sophistication behind the hearty exterior of the rustic squire. He was, said Horace Walpole, 'a man who loved to know, and who cultivated a roughness of speech, [and] affected to know no more than what he had learned from an unadorned understanding'. Even his fabled sexual energy lent itself to bucolic simile: by reputation, he 'had the staying power of a stallion and the impetuosity of a bull'.[93]

As Walpole implied, Dashwood's desire to avoid the appearance of affectation was in itself something of an affectation. He was in fact a person of cultivated, cosmopolitan tastes. In 1724, at the age of sixteen, he inherited a considerable estate from his father, which furnished him with the means to indulge his love of travel in Europe and Asia Minor. Beneath his bluster, Dashwood was becoming a leading member of Britain's cognoscenti, with a sophisticated (albeit eccentric)

90   Dashwood, pp. 36–37, with photograph of a page from the cellar book.
91   The most engagingly fanciful account of the club's origins is Ashe, pp. 112–18.
92   [Almon] *History of Late Minority*, Wilkes's marginalia, p. 409.
93   Walpole, *Memoirs of George II*, vol. 2, pp. 117–18; Dashwood, p. 18.

appreciation for Europe's, and especially Italy's, artistic legacy.[94] Dashwood's sociability and his love of art and debauchery found consummate expression in two societies in which he was a leading light: the Divan Club and the Society of Dilettanti. The former flourished briefly in the 1740s; its membership was limited to those, like Dashwood and Lord Sandwich (its founder), who had ventured to the Ottoman Empire. In the Divan Club, Dashwood could indulge his proclivity for dressing up in exotic garb. In one portrait, Dashwood, as 'Il Faquir Dashwood Pasha', is resplendent in a blue cloak trimmed with ermine and a jewelled turban. A clue to one of the purposes of the club is the fact that one of its standing toasts was to 'the Harem'. The harem undoubtedly included Fanny Murray who, for the benefit of the club, was painted wearing oriental costume, with her left breast exposed.[95]

The Society of Dilettanti was founded in 1732 by Dashwood and some likeminded friends, supposedly on board a ship off Genoa. Only those who had travelled in Italy were eligible for membership, but the society was even more exclusive than that restriction would imply: most of the Dilettanti were young aristocrats and many of them, like Dashwood, would go on to occupy important positions in public life. Members included Lord Sandwich and Lord Temple; Wilkes was never invited to join, even after he became technically eligible by visiting Italy in 1765. The character and purposes of the Society of Dilettanti were richly displayed in the portraits of its members by George Knapton. The paintings, all commissioned in the 1740s, were displayed in the Westminster tavern where the society held its meetings. They depict the Dilettanti in a variety of guises and poses suggestive of the many facets of libertine culture: its debt to the cultural and political legacy of classical republicanism, its celebration of wine and women, and its tendency to religious heterodoxy. Knapton's portrait of Dashwood, completed in 1742, is especially revealing. It presents him as a tonsured monk, SAN FRANCESCO DE WYCOMBO, raising a wine glass, inscribed MATRI SANCTORUM, to a statue of Venus, thereby associating the Virgin Mary (mother of the saints) with the Roman sex goddess. Dashwood obviously relished the conceit. There is an earlier depiction of him as a friar, and a later portrait, completed by William Hogarth in the 1750s, elaborated Knapton's. It shows Dashwood in monk's habit, surrounded by 'sybaritic accoutrements' and gazing adoringly at a miniature naked Venus. The leering

---

[94]   Dashwood, pp. 18–19; Betty Kemp, *Sir Francis Dashwood: An Eighteenth-Century Independent* (London and New York, 1967), pp. 91–101.

[95]   Dashwood, pp. 22–23, 89; N.A.M. Rodger, *The Insatiable Earl: A Life of John Montagu, 4th Earl of Sandwich* (New York and London, 1993), pp. 7, 118; January the 20th [1744] 'Al Koran': Minute book of the Divan Society, SAN/V/113, Sandwich Manuscripts, National Maritime Museum, Greenwich.

face of Lord Sandwich can be seen in 'St Francis's' halo (Fig. 3.1). The jest would be continued at Medmenham, where Dashwood, the 'abbot', would be styled 'Francis of Wycombe'. At Medmenham also, as we shall see in the next chapter, the eroticisation of the cult of the Virgin appears to have been at the heart of the ceremonial parody.[96]

No society, not even the Medmenham monks, joined together more richly the Bacchanalian and Apollonian dimensions of the libertine enterprise than the Dilettanti. According to the hostile account of Horace Walpole, the 'real qualification' for membership was 'being drunk'; the fact that the society's papers were kept in a box called 'Bacchus's Tomb' lent some support to his slur. But the Dilettanti kept their wits about them sufficiently to support important ventures in classical archaeology and scholarship. The society sponsored the expeditions of James Stuart and Nicholas Revett to Greece and Asia Minor and funded the publication of the superbly illustrated volumes that presented their discoveries. Later, in 1786, the Dilettanti would publish Richard Payne Knight's *Discourse on the Worship of Priapus,* a treatise inspired by Sir William Hamilton's discovery of an ancient priapic cult still flourishing at Isernia, near Naples. Payne Knight argued that the worship of Priapus, a deity of generative powers, was a central component of ancient religion. Early Christians had attacked the cult, while inadvertently appropriating some of its erotic symbols, including the cross. Hamilton's discoveries and Payne Knight's theories came too late, of course, to inspire the frolics at Medmenham, but that society's erotic parody of Christian ceremony in a sense anticipated their theories and discoveries. The Society of Dilettanti certainly knew its man when it deemed that Wilkes would be an appropriate recipient of a presentation copy of Payne Knight's book.[97]

Something of the libertine character of Medmenham, then, can be inferred from its antecedents. Dashwood's renovations of Medmenham also offer clues. The buildings of course had not had any religious function since the dissolution of the monasteries in the 1530s; by the time Dashwood took them over, they consisted of a few remnants of the original abbey and a dilapidated Elizabethan mansion. Dashwood added a cloister and a ruined tower to the latter to give it the

---

[96] Shearer West, 'Libertinism and the Ideology of Male Friendship in the Portraits of the Society of Dilettanti', *Eighteenth-Century Life,* new series, 16 (1992): 81–87; Ronald Paulson, *Hogarth: His Life, Art, and Times,* 2 vols (New Haven and London, 1971), vol. 2, p. 257; Dashwood, pp. 184, 204.

[97] West, 'Libertinism and the Ideology of Male Friendship', p. 80; Kemp, pp. 101–05; G.S. Rousseau, 'The Sorrows of Priapus: Anticlericalism, Homosocial Desire, and Richard Payne Knight', in *Sexual Underworlds of the Enlightenment,* ed. G.S. Rousseau and Roy Porter (Chapel Hill, 1988), pp. 101–53; Randolph Trumbach, *Sex and the Gender Revolution,* vol. 1: *Heterosexuality and the Third Gender in Enlightenment London* (Chicago, 1998), pp. 87–89; Lionel Cust, compiler, *History of the Society Dilettanti,* ed. Sidney Colvin (London, 1898), pp. 13, 17–19, 123.

Figure 3.1   *Sir Francis Dashwood at his Devotions*. Engraving (of Hogarth painting). Courtesy of the Lewis Walpole Library, Yale University.

appearance of a medieval monastery.[98] Purporting to be a more immediate source about the Knights of St Francis is a curious compilation of poetry in manuscript, entitled *Eros in monachium, or the Medmenham garland*.[99] Its attributions of authorship to Wilkes, Churchill, and Thomas Potter are suspect, but the poetry itself – anticlerical, bawdy, and phallocentric – is certainly of the type that, in the words of its anonymous editor, would likely have been 'deliver'd to [the] holy Fraternity'. The main source, however, for Medmenham's composition and rituals remains John Wilkes, who, for reasons that will be discussed in chapter 5, revealed selectively the arcana of the libertine culture that he sought to emulate. At first the revelations were fairly anodyne. In June 1763, he claimed in an anonymous press report to have discovered on Dashwood's West Wycombe estate a gold button inscribed with 'I.H.S. and the Sign of the Cross', which a servant explained 'was a Part of the Pontificalibus worn by his Master on certain Festivals of high Laugh at the Mysteries of -------'. But 'I am too fair a Man to disclose to the Public the *English Eleusinian* Mysteries of that renown'd convent', Wilkes added.[100]

The disclosures became more lurid and detailed as Wilkes's problems and persecutions deepened. In 1768, he provided – purportedly as a note to Charles Churchill's poem *The Candidate* – the single most detailed description of the 'Society of St Francis'.[101] Because Wilkes was by then acting vengefully, some scepticism is justified about his account's veracity. But to dismiss it entirely is unwarranted; to a large extent it is confirmed and supplemented by other pieces of evidence.[102] According to Wilkes, twelve 'gentlemen' rented the abbey, suggesting that Dashwood did not carry the expense of the venture alone. The number twelve has encouraged the notion, intriguing but unverifiable, that there was an inner circle of 'apostles' and an inferior brotherhood of more casual visitors. Besides himself and Dashwood, Wilkes mentioned by name two other 'monks': Paul Whitehead, a friend of Dashwood's who had won minor celebrity as a 'patriot' poet, and who served as the society's secretary and steward, and Sir Thomas Stapleton, a local landowner and Dashwood's second cousin. The two were representative of the society's membership, which consisted largely,

---

[98] Thomas Langley, *History and Antiquities of the Hundred of Desborough* (1797), p. 343.

[99] MS E71M1 ca. 1760 Bound, William Andrews Clark Memorial Library, University of California, Los Angeles.

[100] *St James's Chronicle*, 2–4 June 1763.

[101] *Letters between Grafton etc. and Wilkes*, pp. 34–39.

[102] The most extreme sceptic is Betty Kemp. In her biography of Dashwood, she dismisses Wilkes's account and represents Medmenham as little more than a jolly boating club (pp. 130–36). She cites Horace Walpole's testimony that the brotherhood's dress was 'more like a waterman's than a Monk's', but omits reference to his comment that 'each is to do whatever he pleases in his own cell, into which they may carry women'. *Horace Walpole's Journals of Visits to Country Seats* (Walpole Society, 1928), pp. 51–61.

but not exclusively, of local county notables and literary rakes. The identity of some other 'monks' can be gleaned from pseudonyms in the abbey's 'cellar book' and from private correspondence. 'Francis of Cookham' was Francis Duffield, the landlord of Medmenham. 'John of Magdalen' was probably John Norris, an Oxford don. 'John of Henley', a frequent attendee, was in all likelihood John Morton, a local gentleman. The identity of 'John of Checkers' can be confirmed as Dashwood's half-brother, John Dashwood-King; his plate appears over the inscription 'Medmenham Abbey' in the order's bible. 'John of Melcombe' was John Tucker, MP for Weymouth. He wrote to Dashwood in August 1764, wishing 'all possible Joy Spirit & Vigour' to 'the pious Brotherhood'. Benjamin Bates, an Aylesbury physician, claimed in his dotage to have been one of the 'monks', and, though he never raided the abbey's wine-cellar, William Stanhope, an MP for Buckinghamshire and friend of Wilkes, was probably one, too. He certainly took a close interest in the society, writing to Dashwood: '… my compliments to all your Brethren, and assure them that they may have my prayers, particularly in that part of the Litany when I pray the Lord to strengthen them that do stand'.[103]

Among the literary rakes, Wilkes's friend Charles Churchill came to the abbey at least once and seems to have been well acquainted with the society's rituals.[104] Possibly his fellow-poet Robert Lloyd participated as well. Keenly interested in Medmenham was John Hall-Stevenson, a fox-hunting squire and misogynistic literary man, who wrote a lot of bad poetry, much of it salacious in a particularly vile way. Like Churchill, he would wield his pen in Wilkes's cause, though to considerably less effect. His Yorkshire home was a gothic ruin, which he dubbed 'Crazy Castle'; there he hosted a club of likeminded friends – who included Laurence Sterne – known to posterity as the 'Demoniacs'. One of the members was nicknamed 'Panty' after Pantagruel, Rabelais's hero, suggesting that 'Crazy Castle' and Medmenham shared a common source of literary inspiration as well as a similar gothic atmosphere. Illness may have actually prevented Hall-Stevenson from ever attending a Medmenham chapter, but he was fully engaged with its sustaining joke: the inversion of Franciscan asceticism.[105]

---

[103] Cellar Book, West Wycombe Library (information provided by Dr Arthur Cash); John Tucker to Lord le Despenser, 11 August 1764, MS D.D. Dashwood (Bucks), B 11/8/2; Robert Gibbs, *A History of Aylesbury* (Aylesbury, 1885), p. 237; Stanhope quoted in Dashwood, p. 36. The names of other 'monks' are confidently asserted in the secondary literature, including that of Thomas Potter. His presence at Medmenham can be readily imagined, but there is no conclusive evidence that he ever went there.

[104] *Wilkes–Churchill*, pp. 3–4.

[105] Lodwick Hartley, 'Sterne's Eugenius as Indiscreet Author: The Literary Career of John Hall-Stevenson', *PMLA*, 86 (1971): 428–45; Arthur H. Cash, *Laurence Sterne: The Early and Middle Years* (London, 1975), pp. 181–95; Arthur H. Cash, 'Sterne, Hall, Libertinism, and a *Sentimental Journey*', *The Age of Johnson*, 12 (2000): 291–327; BL Add. MSS 30867, fol. 165.

While the esoteric culture of the Medmenham monks was similar to that of the Society of Dilettanti, there was a difference in the social composition of the two groups. Whereas the Dilettanti consisted primarily of peers and their offspring, dedicated to the patronage of the arts, the Medmenhamites, despite embodying the culture of aristocratic libertinism, could boast of only two noblemen among their ranks: Dashwood himself, who assumed the title Baron le Despenser in April 1763, and Lord Sandwich, Dashwood's libertine companion in the Divan Club and the Society of Dilettanti. The extent and character of Sandwich's involvement quickly became a matter of lurid speculation, though evidence is scanty. Dashwood invited him to a gathering at Medmenham on 19 August 1770 – the last recorded date for the society's existence – but there are some grounds for thinking that Sandwich was an active member even before Wilkes became *persona non grata* in 1763. When Wilkes was confined in the King's Bench Prison in the late 1760s, one of his mistresses encountered Sandwich at Christie's auction house, referring to him as 'the High priest of the Renowned abbey', and castigating him for leading Wilkes astray.[106]

Determining just what went on at Medmenham is even more challenging than establishing the society's membership. There are scattered references to chapter meetings taking place there in the summer, suggesting some kind of organised parody of monastic ritual, but the abbey was also freely used at other times by members and friends of Dashwood as a rural retreat or country club. Over a door, Dashwood had inscribed the words *Fay ce que voudras* ('Do What You Will'), the injunction from Rabelais's fictional Abbey of Thélème. There it was the only rule, 'because people who are free, well-born, well-bred, and easy in honest company have a natural spur and instinct which drives them to virtuous deeds; and this they call honour'.[107] What Dashwood and his friends might have seen as conditions that promoted aristocratic virtue, however, an inquisitive public suspected as being an incentive to vice. But 'Do What You Will' is a permit for abstention as well as for participation, so there is no compelling reason to believe that all members of the society felt obliged to engage in the sexual orgies of popular imagination. Some presumably availed themselves of the more innocent pleasures that Dashwood provided, including sailing and fishing along a particularly lovely stretch of the River Thames. Wilkes himself wrote lyrically about such recreations. The collection of books in the library – many bearing Wilkes's signature and the inscription 'Medmenham Abbey' – reflected eclectic tastes. They included French erotica like *Le Cabinet d'Amour et de Venus*,

---

[106] Rodger, p. 83; BL Add. MSS 30880B, fol. 51.

[107] François Rabelais, *The Histories of Gargantua and Pantagruel*, trans. John M. Cohen (Franklin Center, Pennsylvania, 1982), p. 133.

staple fare for the gentleman libertine.[108] According to one of the monks, such 'pious books' were intended 'to occasion an extraordinary ejaculation to be sent up to heaven'. Alongside the erotica, however, were Jonathan Swift's *A Tale of the Tub,* James Thompson's *Castle of Indolence;* and works by Alexander Pope, Edmund Spenser, and William Congreve.[109]

The erotic preoccupations of the Medmenhamites were most clearly evident in the abbey's grounds. As Wilkes reported:

> The garden, the grove, the orchard, the neighbouring woods, all spoke the loves and frailties of the younger monks, who seemed at least to have sinned *naturally.* You saw in one place – *Ici pama de joie des mortels de plus heureux* [Here the happiest of mortals died of joy] – in another very imperfectly – *mourut un amant sur le sein de sa dame* [a lover dies on the bosom of his lady] – in a third – *en cet endroit mille baisers de flamme furent donnés, & mille autres rendus* [here a thousand kisses of fire were given and a thousand others returned]. Against a fine old oak was *Hic Satyrium Naias victorem victa subegit* [Here the vanquished naiad subdued the conquering satyr].

At the entrance of a cave was the Venus, stopping to pull a thorn out of her foot. The statue turned from you, and just over the two nether hills of snow were these lines of Virgil,

> *Hic locus est, partes ubi se via findit in ambas:*
> *Hac iter Elyzium nobis: et laeva malorum*
> *Exercet poenas, & ad impia Tartara mittit*
> [Here is the place where the path divided into two: this on the right is our route to Heaven; but the left-hand path exacts punishment from the wicked, and sends them to a pitiless Hell.]

On the inside over a mossy couch was the following exhortation,

> *Ite, agite, o juvenes; pariter fudate medullis*
> *Omnibus inter vos; non murmura vestra columbae,*
> *Brachia non hederae, non vincant oscula conchae.*
> [Go into action, you youngsters; put everything you've got into it together, both of you; let not doves outdo your cooings, nor ivy your embraces, nor oysters your kisses.]

---

[108] The Medmenham copy, with Wilkes's signature, is now in the British Library. One newspaper report claimed that Wilkes brought back from Paris 'curious articles' for the 'valuable collection' at Medmenham. *Public Advertiser,* 25 May 1763.

[109] Dashwood, pp. 29–30.

The favourite doctrine of the Abbey is certainly not *penitence;* for in the centre of the orchard was a very grotesque figure [Priapus presumably], *and in his hand a reed stood flaming tipt with fire,* to use Milton's words, and you might trace out, PENI TENTO non PENI TENTI [a stiff penis not penitence].

On the pedestal was a whimsical representation of Trophonius's cave, from whence all creatures are said to come out melancholy. Among that strange, dismal group you might however remark a cock crowing and a Carmelite laughing. The words – *gallum gallinaceum & sacerdotem gratis* – were only legible.* (*Omne animal post coitum triste est, praeter gallum gallinaceum, et sacerdotem gratis fornicantem.* [Every animal is sad after sex, except a dunghill cock and a priest getting a free lay.])

Near the abbey was a small, neat temple erected to Cloacine [that is, Venus], with the inscription, *This chapel of ease* [that is, lavatory] *was founded in the year 1760.* Facing the entrance on the inside,

> *Aeque pauperibus prodest, locupletibus aeque,*
> *Aeque neglectum pueris, sensibusque nocebit.*
> [It is useful to rich and poor, its neglect is harmful to young and old alike.][110]

There is some clever mischief here, especially the sly implication that the older monks (Dashwood, Sandwich, and Whitehead, presumably) ignored the injunction inscribed on the statue of Venus to refrain from 'unnatural' sexual acts. Yet discounting Wilkes's malicious asides, his account rings true. His description of Medmenham corresponds with what we know about the blatant eroticism of Dashwood's gardens at West Wycombe. And even his enemies never disputed the accuracy of Wilkes's account. They condemned him as 'a false monk', who had breached the gentleman's code by revealing the secrets of a libertine society. But in so doing they confirm the essential veracity of his account. A defence of Paul Whitehead against the aspersions of Wilkes and Charles Churchill offers a convenient encapsulation of Wilkes's disclosures:

> Now all that can be drawn from [Wilkes's] publication of these ceremonies is, that a set of worthy, jolly fellows, happy disciples of *Venus* and *Bacchus,* got occasionally together, to celebrate Woman in wine; and, to give more zest to the festive meeting, they plucked every luxurious idea from the ancients, and enriched their own modern pleasures with the addition of classic luxury.[111]

---

[110] *Letters between Grafton etc. and Wilkes,* pp. 37–39.
[111] *The Poems and Miscellaneous Compositions of Paul Whitehead; with Explanatory Notes on his Writings, and his Life written by Capt. Edward Thompson* (London, 1767), p. xxxviii.

Wilkes's breach of secrecy did not extend to revealing the identities of the women who came to Medmenham. There are passing references elsewhere to the Medmenham 'nuns'. They were probably prostitutes imported from London's more fashionable brothels, which were known as 'nunneries'. (The implied notion that convents and monasteries, especially French ones, were scenes of licentiousness had a long lineage in anti-Catholic culture.) A seemingly well-informed and sympathetic account – *Nocturnal Revels* – referred to the Medmenham women as 'Ladies' who engaged in such genteel diversions as 'reading, musick, tambour-work., &c'; 'the use of fans' was allowed 'to prevent the appearance of the Ladies' blushes', and the married ones were 'admitted in masks' so as to avoid detection by their husbands or other relations. The implausible suggestion in *Nocturnal Revels* that the offspring of Medmenham's 'connexions' were 'stiled the Sons and Daughters of ST. FRANCIS, and ... appointed in due course officers and domestics in the Seminary', undermines, however, the credibility of the rest of the description. Ultimately the source is valuable, not as an objective account, but as an interesting example of the insistence that conduct at Medmenham followed 'the rules of decency and decorum', the standard apologia on behalf of the Georgian rake. More likely, as in Shearer West's account of the Society of Dilettanti, the Medmenham women were reduced to 'the outsider, the conquered, a shared experience for the men in the club'.[112]

Sex and the Public Man

Before the fellowship at Medmenham was sundered, Wilkes kept its secrets. In so doing, he was upholding the eighteenth-century gentleman's prerogative of indulging his libertinism away from the prying eyes of the public. Yet the implication of some accounts is that Wilkes had little to lose and much to gain from his exposure as a rake. A reputation for virile gallantry simply added to his lustre, they argue, because in the increasingly gendered universe of popular politics it connected with 'the model of manly patriotism', setting him apart from establishment politicians tainted with effeminacy or with complicity in 'petticoat' government. In other words, Wilkes was successfully appropriating self-centred aristocratic libertinism for larger, civic ends. Even his ugliness – which his opponents regarded as an outward and visible sign of an inward disgrace

---

[112] *Nocturnal Revels: or, the History of King's-Place, and other Modern Nunneries*, by a Monk of the Order of St Francis, 2nd edn, 2 vols (London, 1779), introduction (unpaginated); a similar, though shorter, account of Medmenham had appeared ten years earlier in *Town and Country Magazine* (1769): 122–23; West, 'Libertinism and the Ideology of Male Friendship', p. 96.

– could be construed as an asset, because a hideous appearance was traditionally associated with sexual potency.[113]

This kind of argument has definite limits, as I shall argue, but within them there is certainly some tantalising evidence to support a notion of Wilkes as a dissolute aristocrat *manqué*, presiding over the exuberant rituals of plebeian dissidence. Not least is the fact that Wilkes, himself, occasionally betrayed a mischievous delight in imagining himself as a lord of misrule. 'England is now a demo-no-cracy [*sic*] – Who is the *demon*? – Wilkes', he confided to a friend in May 1768.[114] Some of his more humble supporters picked up the cues. Neatly conflating political liberty with sexual libertinism, a drayman declared that Wilkes was 'free from cock to wig'. Wilkes's attraction for women was raunchily trumpeted in contemporary jest books alongside tributes to his political heroism. Here is an example from 1770: 'Why is Mr. Wilkes so much esteemed by the ladies. Answer. Because he goes great lengths'. Even the ubiquitous Wilkite symbol, the number '45', took on sexual connotations: in one published tale, it suggests diagrammatically the connubial behaviour of a husband and wife in Spitalfields. More substantially, Wilkes's sexual notoriety won approval from quasi-Masonic clubs of a more plebeian and urban character than the Medmenham monks – the Leeches, Bucks, and Hiccobites – who welcomed Wilkes into their ranks and threw him their support.[115]

The deployment of sexual machismo, like flaunting a reputation as a duellist, did carry risks, and for similar reasons. It was no easy task to sustain an ultra-masculine persona – in the words of Anna Clark, 'masculinity always had to be proven and performed' – and Wilkes's opponents were quick to pounce on the slightest hint of deviation. His association with the exiled French diplomat, Chevalier d'Eon, provided such an opportunity. Despite some initial suspicions of each other, by the mid-1760s Wilkes and d'Eon had become associated in the public mind as unyielding opponents of tyranny to their respective governments. Wilkes followed d'Eon's fortunes closely and sought close ties with him. By 1768 they had become personally acquainted and d'Eon dined with Wilkes while the latter was held in the King's Bench Prison. By this time, however, d'Eon was once again in the pay of the French government, and had embarked on a byzantine career as a double agent. He tantalised the Wilkites with a story about French

---

[113] Kathleen Wilson, *The Sense of the People: Politics, Culture and Imperialism in England, 1715–1785* (Cambridge and New York, 1995), pp. 219–21; John Brewer, *Party Ideology and Popular Politics at the Accession of George III* (Cambridge and New York, 1976), pp. 190–91; Anna Clark, 'The Chevalier d'Eon and Wilkes: Masculinity and Politics in the Eighteenth Century', *Eighteenth-Century Studies*, 32 (1998): 19–40.

[114] Wilkes to Jean-Baptiste Suard, 3 May 1768, Wilkes MSS 3, fol. 18.

[115] Richard Sennett, *The Fall of Public Man* (New York and London, 1992), p. 103; Daniel Gunston, ed., *Jemmy Twitcher's Jests: or Wit with the Gravy in It* (London, 1770), p. 16; Brewer, *Party Ideology*, pp. 172, 196.

bribery of members of the British royal family and nobility at the end of the Seven Years' War, and then he enraged them by refusing to provide any evidence for this potentially explosive charge. From being a man of honour, d'Eon had apparently reverted to type, that of treacherous French courtier. In 1771 that shift became entangled with gender in an astounding way. D'Eon, it was loudly (though falsely) rumoured, was not even a man at all – let alone a man of honour – but a woman in man's clothing; a sexual double agent as well as a diplomatic one. Wilkes was compromised by this report, which probably originated from d'Eon himself. Dissident voices in the Society of the Supporters of the Bill of Rights (SSBR) accused Wilkes of a squalid attempt to profit from the scandal by promoting a gambling ring on d'Eon's sex. A series of four caricatures linked Wilkes and d'Eon together in ways that suggested that they were complicit in disrupting sexual as well as social categories. One depicts their marriage, with d'Eon cast as 'Queen of the Amazons'. Another displays a procession in which satyrs pull d'Eon in a sedan chair and carry a child. But the assumption that the child was d'Eon's by Wilkes – a joke that was doing the rounds in 1771 and at least supported a notion of Wilkes's virility – was challenged by this facetious explanation: 'When the first policy was opened concerning d'Eon's gender, it was said with some mirth that Chevalier was with child by Wilkes. Since the discovery of the fraud it is now said with sober sadness that Mr. Wilkes has miscarried by Mrs. d'Eon.' The absurdity of this attempt at rhetorical emasculation probably limited any serious damage to Wilkes's masculine persona, but it showed that he was not immune to the kind of sexual scandal-mongering at which he and his supporters were themselves becoming so adept.[116]

D'Eon was a man pretending to be a woman purporting to be a man (until he returned to France, when he became simply a man pretending to be a woman). But what of the presumably more straightforward issue of women's association with the Wilkite campaign? The masculine style of Wilkes and his followers did not preclude a role for them. Indeed some of his conservative opponents tried to discredit him by claiming that they played too big a role. Women were a visible presence on the hustings and in pro-Wilkes demonstrations. On Wilkes's re-election as MP for Middlesex in 1769, for example, 'many ladies (freeholders) among the friends of freedom' took part in a celebratory procession, 'distinguished by breast knots of blue and silver' and bearing the motto 'Bill of Rights and Magna Carta'. Their presence, however, was more suggestive of time-honoured civic rituals,

---

[116]   Clark, 'Chevalier d'Eon and Wilkes', pp. 19–40; Edna Nixon, *Royal Spy: The Strange Case of the Chevalier D'Eon* (New York, 1965), pp. 141–50; Gary Kates, *Monsieur d'Eon is a Woman: A Tale of Political Intrigue and Sexual Masquerade* (New York, 1995), pp. 124–36; *Catalogue of Political and Personal Satires Preserved in the Department of Prints and Drawings in the British Museum*, vol. 5 (1771–1783), ed. M. Dorothy George (London, 1935), nos 4870–73.

which acknowledged women as a constitutive part of the unreformed political nation, than of a meaningful advance for women in reform politics. Indeed, that would remain – in its Wilkite expression, at least – a staunchly male enterprise. In much of the propaganda of the Wilkite movement, the function accorded to women matched their role in the company of rakes. They were envisaged as little more than decorative auxiliaries of manly patriotism, supporting and flattering its flamboyant male embodiments, chiefly of course Wilkes himself. Jane Blenkinsopp, a young woman from Durham and the daughter of a Wilkes supporter, was playing her part to perfection when she sent Wilkes net ruffles ('an Emblem of [her] gratitude') while he was incarcerated in King's Bench Prison. Women supposedly became enamoured with Wilkes's squint, turning it from a liability into an asset. In one story, probably apocryphal, a lady Wilkite protested to her sceptical husband that Wilkes 'squints no more than a gentleman ought to squint'.[117]

The gendering of popular politics left radical bluestockings such as Catharine Macaulay in an awkward position. By the late 1760s she had vaulted to success and fame with the publication of the early volumes of her *History of England*. In that work, she offered an erudite, and profoundly Whiggish, exposition on Stuart tyranny and the dangers of its revival, the same theme that runs through much of Wilkes's writing in the *North Briton*. A newspaper writer dubbed her 'the Guardian Angel of the Liberties of Great Britain'.[118] Macaulay was the sister of John Sawbridge, a prominent City politician, and was credited with inspiring his radicalism. After the death of her first husband in 1766, she became the close friend of Revd Thomas Wilson, and for a few years shared his house in Bath. Sawbridge and Wilson were both founding members of the SSBR, and Macaulay's energy, connections, and erudition should have won her an equal place in Wilkite counsels. But despite her overtures and generosity to the patriot champion, it never happened. Though praised in patriot circles for her manly virtues, those very qualities also rendered her an oddity, unsuited for the role of auxiliary considered appropriate for the female in the gendered world of Wilkite politics. She was, perhaps, an early casualty of a mounting anxiety in the late eighteenth century about the instability of gender categories.[119] Even Thomas Wilson, who

---

[117] Clark, *Scandal*, p. 36; Judith S. Lewis, *Sacred to Female Patriotism: Gender, Class, and Politics in Late Georgian Britain* (New York and London, 2003), pp. 129, 160; Wilson, *Sense of the People*, pp. 225–26; Jane Blenkinsopp to Wilkes, 22 January 1769, BL Add. MSS 30870, fol. 103; *Town and Country Magazine* (1769): 71.

[118] *Public Advertiser*, 4 January 1769.

[119] Bridget Hill, *The Republican Virago: The Life and Times of Catharine Macaulay, Historian* (Oxford and New York, 1992), *passim*; Wilson, *Sense of the People*, p. 226; Dror Wahrman, '*Percy*'s Prologue: From Gender Play to Gender Panic in Eighteenth-Century England', *Past and Present*, 159 (May, 1998): 113–60.

was besotted with her, regarded her as something of a miraculous freak. In 1777, he had a statue of her erected in his London church, with an adjacent inscription that included this curious judgement:

> And once in every age I could wish such a woman to appear
> As a proof that genius is not confined to sex;
> But at the same time – you will pardon me –
> We want no more than
> One Mrs. Macaulay.[120]

The press gleefully speculated on the relationship between Wilkes and Macaulay. One newspaper conjectured that he 'might even wish for an *Essay* on that celebrated *Woman*, if he was not afraid that she could never be brought to practise the Tory doctrine of *Passive Obedience* and *Non-Resistance*'. Elsewhere there were absurd rumours of their marriage. In reality, Wilkes retained a lukewarm friendship with Macaulay (they were briefly neighbours in Prince's Court, and he attended her salon), until she committed the social gaffe of deserting Wilson and marrying a man 26 years her junior. In letters to his daughter, Wilkes joined in the ridicule and vilification that were heaped on her for violating the canons of feminine virtue. 'The female historian [is] a most abandoned prostitute', he pronounced. The judgement was both contemptible and ironic given that Catharine Macaulay had lent him a large amount of money and then, at the time of his most acute financial distress, had forgiven the loan.[121]

Libertines and reformers thus joined social conservatives in placing rhetorical shackles on women like Catharine Macaulay who dared to step out of place in politics and in life. She had to contend with the attitude, expressed in the radical *London Evening Post*, that 'a woman in politics, is like a monkey in a china shop; she can do no good, and may do a great deal of mischief'.[122] At the same time, there were definite limits, as Wilkes was quite aware, on the extent to which he could himself defy social convention by an uninhibited display of rakishness. As a rake-hero, he excited the enduring tension between people's conflicting psychological desires for the security of order and the joys of mayhem [123] With his mercurial capacity for having it both ways, he embodied the dichotomy,

---

[120] Quoted in Hill, *Republican Virago*, p. 100.

[121] *Political Register*, 3 (1768): 44; Hill, *Republican Virago*, pp. 94–129; Clark, *Scandal*, pp. 49–50; Bridget Hill, 'Daughter and Mother: Some New Light on Catharine Macaulay and her Family', *British Journal for Eighteenth-Century Studies*, 22 (1999): 39; [Wilkes] *Letters to Daughter*, vol. 2, p. 165; William Graham to Wilkes, 6 October 1795, BL Add. MSS 30874, fol. 166.

[122] *London Evening Post*, 10–13 March 1770.

[123] On ambivalent responses to the rake-hero, see Harold Weber, *The Restoration Rake-Hero: Transformations in Sexual Understanding in Seventeenth-Century England* (Madison, 1986), p. 6.

occasionally gesturing as a lord of misrule without discarding the mantle of the stern guardian of public order. His *declared* role was to protect the people from the violations of a corrupt government and senate, not that of an avowed agent of social, let alone sexual, revolution. It was government conduct, he insisted, that precipitated public disorder; his own served to quell it.[124]

Sustaining an argument that Wilkes's popularity owed much to an uncomplicated approval of his rakishness also has to contend with the fact that it was his opponents, not his supporters, who were the most eager to expose his rakish conduct and persona. The public would be repeatedly told what Edward Gibbon confided to his diary: 'He [Wilkes] is a thorough profligate in principle as in practice, his life stained with every vice, and his conversation full of blasphemy and indecency. These morals he glories in – for shame is a weakness he has long since surmounted'.[125] The campaign began almost as soon as Wilkes's name became known to the outside world through his authorship of the *North Briton*. He was, sneered government-sponsored periodicals, 'what the world calls a buck and a smart', a man who 'glory'd in licentious stile'.[126] The charge was pressed visually, and to great effect, in William Hogarth's famous portrait-caricature of Wilkes, based on a sketch that the artist had made of his onetime friend during Wilkes's triumphant appearance before the Court of Common Pleas on 6 May 1763. Hogarth was unsparing in his realistic depiction of Wilkes's squint, to which he added a leering grin and the suggestion of devil's horns in the configuration of his subject's wig (Fig. 3.2). The whole image is one of sexual licentiousness, and that was how the public – which bought thousands of copies of the print and its bastardised versions – received it. Friends such as Charles Churchill were outraged at Hogarth's attack. Wilkes, himself, affected amusement, even conceding that the cartoon was a good likeness. But his supporters made no attempts to turn around the force of Hogarth's satire by cheerfully embracing its basic premise, at least not publicly. Instead, they tried (with some success) to deflect its impact by transforming Wilkes's squint from a sign of sexual depravity into an emblem of liberty, one with, at worst, only mildly risqué associations.[127]

A few months after the appearance of Hogarth's cartoon, government and its supporters were accorded an opportunity to blacken Wilkes's reputation

---

[124] *Wilkes Correspondence,* vol. 1, pp. 261–71.

[125] Edward Gibbon, *Memoirs of My Life and Writings,* ed. A.O.J. Cockshut and Stephen Constantine (Keele, 1994), p. 136.

[126] *A Collection of all the Remarkable and Personal Passages in the Briton, North Briton, and Auditor* (London, 1766), pp. 56–57.

[127] Shearer West, 'Wilkes's Squint: Synedochic Physiognomy and Political Identity in Eighteenth-Century Print Culture', *Eighteenth-Century Studies,* 33 (1999): 65–84; *Poetical Works of Charles Churchill,* p. 223; Salvator Rosa, *The Group* (London, 1763), pp. 43–44.

Figure 3.2   A corrupted version of Hogarth's famous cartoon, showing a
familiar whispering in Wilkes's ear. A. Bell, *John Wilkes Esqr.*
(1763). Etching and engraving. Courtesy of the Lewis Walpole
Library, Yale University.

further through the revelation of his complicity in the production of *An Essay on Woman*. It was, said one pamphleteer, 'the volatile, saline Effluvia of the unchaste Imagination of a prurient Debauchee'.[128] Because the poem was denounced as blasphemy, or, at least, impiety – with obscenity merely its offensive mode – its content and the uproar attending its exposure will be reserved for more detailed examination in the following chapter. But it needs to be noted that from the perspective of the anti-libertine crusaders, religious libertinism and sexual misconduct went hand in hand. Deists rejected revealed religion, insisted John Leland, their critical historian, 'because they cannot bear the restraints it lays upon their corrupt lusts and passions'.[129] Wilkes embodied the connection, claimed his opponents, and their invective reached a fever pitch as Wilkes engaged in his multiple attempts to re-enter Parliament in 1768 and 1769. One scribbler grotesquely envisaged Wilkes converting churches 'into brothels for performing the rites of obscenity and lewdness', where the daughters of his enemies would be 'sacrificed to [his] lusts'. The oft-repeated charge that Wilkes planned to debauch the wives and daughters of London citizens seems mild by comparison. Some later squibs were very specific. In one of them, 'Lucy', a violated virgin, protests to 'Cock-eyed Jack': 'Remember the King's Bench, you blink-eyed son of a b----, Can't you recollect when *honest Humphrey* [Cotes] and yourself both had me on the stair-case the night that Bingley was committed on account of the North-Briton?'[130]

As we shall see in chapter 5, Wilkes and his supporters contrived a careful strategy to counter such charges, one that went beyond the routine insistence of the paramountcy of his political virtue. There was an urgent necessity that they should do so, given that the Wilkites had themselves become party to a mounting campaign against aristocratic vice.

Gertrude Corradini and Jane Barnard

A detailed chronicle of Wilkes's many affairs would be as tedious to read as to write. Instead, two case studies are offered here that exhibit different facets of his amorous career and suggest ways in which external forces mediated carnal

---

[128] Kidgell, *Genuine and Succinct Narrative*, p. 14.

[129] Leland quoted in J.C.D. Clark, *English Society, 1660–1832: Religion, Ideology and Politics during the Ancien Regime,* rev. edn (Cambridge, 2000), p. 360. The same connection is made in J. H[utchinson], *The Religion of Satan: Or Antichrist Delineated* (London, 1736), p. 68, and William Warburton, *A View of Lord Bolingbroke's Philosophy; in Four Letters to a Friend,* 3 vols (1754–55), vol. 2, p. xxxiv.

[130] *The Battle of the Quills: or Wilkes Attacked and Defended* (1768), pp. 26–27, 29; *The Bow-Street Opera … Written on the Plan of the Beggar's Opera* (London, 1776), p. 38.

imperatives. In the first, *l'affaire Corradini,* Wilkes represented himself as a sexual connoisseur, a man of pleasure whose studied resistance to feminine wiles is nonetheless perilously compromised in pursuit of his love object. In the second, his adulterous liaison with Jane Barnard, the wife of a London merchant, he came dangerously close to being exposed in the unflattering role of sneaking lecher.

Wilkes's account of his affair with Gertrude Corradini takes up most of what survives, or what he ever completed, of his autobiography. The fact that it is written in the third person, and in a confessional mode, suggests that Wilkes ultimately intended it for publication, or at least for circulation among friends. Much of its phraseology corresponds with the public attempt to represent him as a reformed rake, and what Wilkes is offering is not a spontaneous account of a chapter in his erotic career, but a considered apologia, cast in the form of a moral drama in which his status as a public man is clearly in mind.[131] He recounts how 'the syren of pleasure seems to have lull'd him for a while in her lap, and to all appearances triumphed over the vigour of his soul', until a fortuitous combination of circumstance and will-power enabled him to recover his manhood.[132]

Wilkes first met Corradini in Paris in the spring of 1764. Until she claimed his exclusive attention, he had been indulging in a 'carnaval [sic] for Pego' there, in company with 'actresses' and others, under the watchful and prurient eye of the Paris police.[133] Corradini was a dancer, born in Bologna, and trained in Venice, where, according to Wilkes, she received 'the only education fitt for a courtesan, born with little or no wit, the art of adorning gracefully her person, and a flexibility of the limbs, worthy the wanton nymphs so celebrated of Ionia'. In Venice, she made her stage debut and became the mistress of the British consul, John Udney. Following his bankruptcy, she moved to Paris 'on the pretext of perfecting herself in dancing'. When Wilkes first saw her, he was immediately 'struck with so noble, gracefull a figure, as well as with an air of modesty, diffidence and timidity, which contrasted so admirably with the forwardness and insolence of the generality of the French females'.[134]

His pursuit began the following day. Her initial resistance and coyness only 'increas'd his ardour'. She at first refused his offers of money, but he gained a useful ally in her mother, in whose lap he dropped a few silver coins. A happy accident brought about Corradini's ultimate surrender. She had lost a silver crucifix, which she described 'very minutely'. After a morning's search, Wilkes

---

[131] Wilkes claimed, in a letter to his brother Heaton, dated 7 May 1767, to 'have very carefully drawn up my own Memoirs'. Wilkes MSS 2, fol. 15a.

[132] BL Add. MSS 30865A, fol. 6.

[133] *Wilkes–Churchill*, pp. 64, 65, 83; MSS 11359 (Journal de Police), fols 378–79, Bibliothèque Nationale, Paris. (My thanks to Dr Jane McLeod for this reference.)

[134] BL Add. MSS 30865B, fols 12–13.

found an identical crucifix and presented it to her. 'She was so struck with this mark of attention, that the same afternoon she ceased to be cruel', Wilkes recalled. 'The following weeks he pass'd in her arms, giving and receiving the most exquisite pleasures, of which our frame is capable, for Corradini was endow'd with singular perfections, *femore facili, clune agili, et manu procace* [nimble thighs, agile buttocks, and a questing hand].'[135]

The tribute to her sensual expertise is repeated as a refrain throughout Wilkes's account. 'In conversation she was childish and weak, but in bed she could not be call'd *fatui puella cunni* [a girl with a lazy cunt]. All her sensibility seem'd to have reference to one favourite spot.' As Wilkes's tribute shifts from the tactile to the aesthetic, she is elevated to an object of classical connoisseurship. ('She was a perfect Grecian figure, cast in the mould of the Florentine Venus, excepting that she was rather taller, and more flat about the breasts. Her whole form was the most perfect symmetry.') What is missing from the account is any concession to sentiment. His attitude towards Corradini as a person wavered between amusement, contempt, and irritation. Even at the outset of their affair, he claimed to have regarded her as jealous, vain, and peevish. Her sexual allure clearly outweighed any deficiencies of personality, however. Wilkes spared no expense in installing her in fashionable lodgings, which with his usual attentiveness to décor he furnished 'in the gayest taste of the Parisians'. The ménage included Corradini's mother, 'a ragged footboy' from Italy, and 'a spruce Frenchman', recommended by Wilkes, who served as a footman. Wilkes enjoyed 'soul-trilling rapture' on a nightly basis, until Corradini fell ill and he was excluded from her bed. She had become exhausted, Wilkes surmised, from the effect of their excessive lovemaking on 'the fine texture of her frame', exacerbated by the gloomy climate of autumn in Paris.[136]

When her health failed to improve, she resolved to return to Italy and pleaded with Wilkes to join her. Wilkes refused, however, citing a previous arrangement to meet Charles Churchill in Boulogne. Wilkes was at pains to make clear that he was not so enraptured with his mistress that the lure of the flesh took precedence over manly friendship. So Corradini set off without him (although with a family entourage that now included an uncle), generously supplied with money from Wilkes and with the right to draw on his account when she reached her native Bologna. The plan was that Churchill and his young mistress, Miss Carr, would eventually join Wilkes and Corradini in a Mediterranean tour. The two friends, Wilkes said, 'had fir'd their imaginations with the ideas of the blue skies of Italy, the luxuriant elegance of nature in that charming climate, and the peculiar felicity of partaking their raptures with two females, so dear to them'. The death of

---

[135] Ibid., fols 13–15.
[136] Ibid., fols 11–12, 15–17.

Churchill put paid to the project. Once Wilkes had recovered from his immediate grief, he decided to seek solace in the arms of Corradini, and after dispatching his daughter back to England, he set out from Paris on Christmas Day, 1764.[137] Dismissing warnings from a friend that an unseemly infatuation might damage his reputation, he claimed that, on the contrary, 'the world' would look on him 'not with pity, but with envy and admiration'.[138]

His journey through Italy was a heady mingling of aestheticism and sensuality, a kind of apotheosis for the man of pleasure. En route to Bologna, he took time to admire the art treasures of northern Italy. Once reunited with Corradini – 'absence seem'd only to have increased their mutual passion' – he divided his time between enjoying the company of his mistress and admiring Raphael's St Cecilia in an adjacent church. Corradini's own resemblance to the 'gracefull Madonna of the Italians', and her religious superstitions, lent piquancy to their lovemaking. Wilkes recalled with amusement how she would draw a silk curtain in front of a crude daubing of the Virgin Mary while the two were engaged in their amours, a scruple all the more droll given that there were no curtains to the bed or windows.[139]

The idyll in Bologna was short-lived. Wilkes was determined to take Corradini with him to Naples, where he planned to work on a History of England and his proposed edition of the poetry of Charles Churchill. Corradini, in return, demanded a settlement of £2,000 (she had read in the press that Wilkes had been left a substantial legacy) and insisted that her brother as well as her mother should live with them. Wilkes patiently explained that English protocols required such settlements only after lengthy cohabitation or the 'surrender of virgin charms', neither of which applied in this case. He did agree, though, to support Corradini's mother and servants, but refused to have her brother live with them. The deal struck, the party made a leisurely progress southwards, via Florence and Rome, where Johann Winckelmann obligingly engaged the attention of Corradini's mother while Wilkes and Corradini had sex in an adjacent apartment. Once they reached Naples, Wilkes rented a country house with a commanding view of the city, the bay, and the Isle of Capri. He purchased furniture, presumably intending a lengthy stay. He even prepared rooms for a planned visit by Winckelmann in the autumn. The moral drama, however, was about to reach its denouement.[140]

Discovering that she was pregnant, Corradini renewed her claim for £2,000 and insisted that she had to return to Bologna to place herself in the care of a

[137] Ibid., fols 18–23.
[138] BL Add. MSS 30868, fol. 164.
[139] BL Add. MSS 30865B, fols 22–24.
[140] Ibid., fols 27–44; 'John Wilkes in Italy', *Notes and Queries*, 4th Series, 4 (1869): 530.

trusted male midwife. When Wilkes balked at the plan, Corradini and her mother, in company with an uncle who had recently reappeared in Naples, absconded with some silver candlesticks, salt-shakers, and spoons. In a letter left on a table, Corradini demanded that Wilkes submit to her terms. It was a situation rife with humiliation for him, all the more so as garbled accounts of his mistress's defection soon began appearing in the London newspapers. James Boswell, clumsily trying to offer sympathy, imagined Wilkes as a 'forlorn swain' weeping in solitude for his lost love, though he could scarcely credit the reports that Corradini had robbed him. For a while, Wilkes wavered; he even sent Corradini £200 for herself and her future child. But, 'at last the enchantment broke, and the charm was dissolv'd. Mr Wilkes burst the silken chains of Corradini, when he was thought to be the most enthralled'. What restored him to a proper sense of manhood was news from England. The Grenville ministry, which had persecuted Wilkes and driven him into exile, had fallen, and Wilkes determined to draw closer to his native shore to 'prove that he had not deserted, nor despair'd of his country'. Taking care to avoid Bologna – lest 'the dear enchantress shou'd again draw him within her powerfull circle, and melt down all his manhood to the god of love' – he took passage on a tiny boat bound for Marseilles, leaving Naples on 27 June 1765. He was fortunate in his ship companion, one Major Ridley, who listened with 'manly tenderness' as Wilkes divulged 'the frailties and weaknesses of his nature, too susceptible of the soft impressions of love'. After disembarking, Wilkes made his way to Geneva, where a bracing visit to Voltaire put the seal on his recovery. 'In his happy society Mr Wilkes pass'd some weeks, and the laugh of Voltaire banished all the serious ideas the Englishman nourish'd of love and the fair Italian.'[141]

Like his affair with Corradini, Wilkes's liaison with Jane Barnard was potentially damaging to Wilkes's reputation, but for different reasons. In the former, he risked exposure as an effeminised, lovesick dupe of a manipulative siren; in the latter, as the cold-hearted seducer of another man's wife. The seduction of the 'cit's' young bride by a dashing gallant was a well-established trope, richly explored in Restoration comedy. In the same vein, a contemporary parody of Dryden's *Alexander's Feast* imagined Wilkes surrounded by London aldermen whom he had cuckolded. This was an image, however, from which Wilkes, for several reasons, now wished to dissociate himself. The social climate was changing; in polite circles, contempt for cuckolded husbands was being displaced by sympathy, and adulterous designs were increasingly condemned. Wilkes, moreover, had made pious avowals of reformation, offering a refurbished reputation that he was anxious to protect, especially after he became London's first citizen as lord

---

[141] BL Add. MSS 30865B, fols 44–56; *Public Advertiser*, 16 July 1765; *Boswell, Italy*, pp. 94, 105.

mayor in 1774. But it was during his mayoralty that his adulterous union with Jane Barnard nearly became a public scandal.[142]

Jane Barnard was the second wife of John Barnard of Berkeley Square, a wealthy placeholder and the son of a famously patriotic lord mayor. He had many attributes of the stage cuckold. Much older than Jane, he was both a valetudinarian and a miser; he had reportedly scooped up the candle ends at his father's funeral, and he stated in his will that he wished to be buried 'in the most inexpensive manner possible'.[143] In her letters to Wilkes, Jane Barnard complained about her husband's parsimony, typified by 'insipid' suppers of bread, cheese, and water. She also hinted at his sexual inadequacies – 'King Log' she called him – while coyly praising Wilkes's virility.[144] Yet Barnard had been a longstanding friend and supporter of Wilkes. He was solicitous when Wilkes was ill from the wound inflicted in the duel with Samuel Martin, and when Wilkes returned from exile, Barnard overcame his habitual stinginess to donate generously to his cause, without, he said, seeking or expecting any political advantage.[145] Latterly, he had been intending to leave Wilkes a handsome legacy, which would add a meaningful, and, for Wilkes, painful twist to the consequences of his betrayal.

Barnard learned of his wife's adultery in a manner more reminiscent of melodrama than of a comedy of manners. Late one night, Jane Barnard, in a state of 'violent agitation, and after a flood of tears', confessed to her husband 'that Mr. W. had frequently lain with her, both before and after her marriage'. What prompted this revelation, she said, were visitations by the ghost of her recently deceased stepdaughter. The ghost told her that she was in 'a place of torments' for her wickedness in running off to Paris with her music master. Her stepmother would suffer a similar fate, she warned, unless she admitted her infidelity and stopped the injustice of John Barnard leaving his fortune to a man 'who had so cruelly injured him'.[146]

When confronted by Barnard, Wilkes strenuously denied the accusation; but the evidence, which includes Jane Barnard's highly indiscreet correspondence, speaks loudly to his complicity, and it permits the anatomy of the affair to be reconstructed in some detail. It began in the early 1760s, before the marriage of

---

[142] *W----s's Feast, or Dryden Travesty; A Mock Pindarick: Addressed to his Most Incorruptible Highness Prince Patriotism* (London, 1774); David M. Turner, *Fashioning Adultery: Gender, Sex and Civility in England, 1660–1740* (Cambridge and New York, 2002), pp. 36–37, 87–97, 113, 196.

[143] H.R. Fox Bourne, *English Merchants: Memoirs in Illustration of the Progress of British Commerce,* 2 vols. (London, 1866), vol. 1, p. 425; *City Biography* (London, 1799), pp. 80–81; Barnard's will, PROB 11 1123/588 (microfilm), National Archives.

[144] BL Add, MS 30880B, fols 51, 54.

[145] Ibid., fol. 39.

[146] Ibid., fol. 36.

Jane to John Barnard. According to her account, as reported by her husband, Wilkes 'enjoyed her first at Blackheath at Grace Ozier's' before taking her to dine at Greenwich. Nearly fifteen years later, she could still name 'the dinner, wines, and dessert'. There would be other trysts in houses of assignation on the fringe of the metropolis before Wilkes's obligation to rendezvous with the Bucks militia at Winchester 'interrupted their amours'. When the affair resumed seven years later, it did so as criminal conversation because Jane in the meantime had married John Barnard. This time the venue was King's Bench Prison where Jane Barnard became one of several women to offer Wilkes sexual solace during his confinement. ('I have my choice of all the dear girls of this country', Wilkes boasted.[147]) On her first visit, her husband and his daughter accompanied her. She claimed that Wilkes 'was then very sweet upon her, and slily [*sic*] put a billet doux into her hand, desiring her to come again'. The go-between for subsequent assignations was Revd John Horne, at this time one of Wilkes's leading political supporters. Acting as Wilkes's 'pimp-general' (in Barnard's bitter term), he was evidently an agent of Wilkes's libertinism, not, as he would later become, one of its loudest critics. Jane Barnard needed little persuasion, however. 'I am in great hopes of seeing you very soon,' she wrote to Wilkes, 'as the Reverend gentleman [Horne] would not admit of any refusall.' Soon she was addressing Wilkes's penis in true libertine fashion (though she eschewed the conventional metaphors of sword and dagger): 'Pray my compliments to little Pomp and ask him how he likes his new name ... I have a thousand things to say to his Majesty.' Later she addressed 'a few words to little squib ... he has acquitted himself so well ... he may be assured of being put into Commission the first opportunity'. She also deployed the trope of the female body as territory, in this instance, apparently, to assert her right to resist 'conquest' and recover some measure of autonomy:

> If I should sally out once more and climb that dreadfull precipice again you will find me much alterd for the Better at least I think and feel so, you will now see me sole Misstress of my little Princepality and that I will no longer suffer a Petty Usurper to invade and take all power from me indeed I will allow you to have been Reigning sovereign for ... nine past. But like many others you have wanton'd in Power you have laid waste and allmost Conquer'd etc etc my Territories. But as I have now been blessd with that sweet Right for this month past you will find – if you shoud chuse to dispute the Regal dignity with me – I say you will not find it a small undertaking to wrest the reins from me.[148]

---

147 Wilkes MSS 3, fol. 18.
148 BL Add. MSS 30880B, fols 36–37, 46, 49, 52, 57.

Running counter, however, to this expression of sexual egalitarianism is a palpable anxiety about retaining Wilkes's interest and esteem. Often using her husband as a source, she tried to engage Wilkes with gossip about corruption and sexual scandal in high places. She claimed to be an active partisan and recruiter in his cause. 'Every servant that enters my house becomes a Wilkite after the first week, all though they were your greatest Enemies before', she wrote. In the manner of the political groupie, there was a slippage in her mind between Wilkes's status as a patriot hero and his sexual allure. He was at the same time 'King David' and 'my sweetest of all Lovers'. Some of his lustre rubbed off on his associates. Humphrey Cotes she thought 'very handsome'; Sir Joseph Mawbey was 'a good looking man'. By contrast, she reviled his political enemies. Colonel Henry Luttrell, 'the Pretender to the County of Middlesex', was both 'a monster' and a 'pigmy'; she knew his father well, she said, and it was impossible that such a being as Luttrell 'coud [sic] spring from his loins'. Confronting Luttrell at an exhibition at Christie's, she 'showd [sic] him by the most expressive glances what [she] thought of him'. At the same event she also encountered 'the old Satyr', Lord Sandwich. She warmed to the theme that Wilkes was the artless dupe of such roués before acknowledging and retreating from its irony:

> He saw I despised him from my very soul. [I] spoke particularly in your praise said what a pity it was that such old goats should be suffered to corrupt the morals of young men of spirit that if your mind was defiled it was owing to Lord Sandwich that I was sure you were good at heart as woud been [sic] seen by your future conduct. Perhaps this was going a little to [sic] far to tell you the truth I doubt you a little in the Primrose Path and I would not have you quit it yet is not this a little selfish but you have made me so.[149]

The affair continued to flicker after Wilkes's release from prison. Meeting by chance at a cabinet-maker's in St Paul's Church Yard, the two went to the Barnard home in Berkeley Square, where Wilkes was, she said, 'exceedingly rude'. In the only extant reference to Wilkes using force in a sexual encounter, he allegedly 'threw her on the sopha ... and enjoyed her on the spot'. After three or four subsequent liaisons, her vulnerability now painfully evident, the affair ended; she thought 'he was disgusted with her'.[150]

There matters rested until her extraordinary confession, with Wilkes and John Barnard continuing to enjoy in the meantime at least the appearance of friendship. Once Barnard learnt of the deception, he achieved a kind of frenzied eloquence (his syntax buckling under the weight of his fury) in charging Wilkes with the basest ingratitude:

---

[149]   Ibid., fols 51–52, 55.
[150]   Ibid., fols 36–37.

The first connection you had with her [that is, before Barnard's marriage to her] ... I could have erased from my mind, as I am not implacable ... but the wanton and deliberate cruelty with which you began it again; not only by practising on my unsuspicious temper, but by sending your emissary [Horne] twice to persuade her to come to the King's bench, after your lust had been long sated seven years had elapsed, and there were neither the charms of novelty or youth to excite you, can only be thus accounted for, that the Villany [*sic*] of lying with the beloved Wife of the sincerest, the most affectionate and disinterested friend you had in the world ... added a new relish to a decayed appetite, and which being a superlative genius, you still found a way to quicken when you repeated the injury in the very house of your benefactor.

When Barnard referred to Wilkes's 'wanton and deliberate cruelty', it was cruelty to himself, not to Jane Barnard, to which he was alluding. Alert, however, to any issues pertaining to his wallet, he expressed sympathy for his wife in one matter: Wilkes's 'extreme baseness' in refusing to provide her with a monetary settlement, despite having promised to do so, when she was his mistress before her marriage. Though such a transaction would have come dangerously close to defining his wife as a whore, in Barnard's moral universe, apparently, the commercial propriety of paying for services rendered was a paramount value. Or perhaps he thought that her conduct defined her as a whore anyway and that, as such, she should have received fitting compensation.[151]

Persistent to the last in his denial of the affair, Wilkes never addressed the issue of a settlement in his exchanges with Barnard. These were by letter until the two finally agreed on the time and venue for a face-to-face meeting. Both showed considerable reluctance to meet on the other's home ground, before Wilkes acceded to Barnard's insistence that the interview take place in Berkeley Square. Once there, Barnard laid out the accusation in full detail and proposed to fetch his wife downstairs to confute Wilkes's denials. Wilkes's 'changing countenance' at this suggestion, followed by his 'strange and abrupt' departure from the house, Barnard took as the conclusive proof of his guilt.[152]

Barnard had already ruled out a duel as means of achieving 'satisfaction'. 'From my Age and great infirmities Honor does not require me to demand it ... for alas! you may now almost blow me down with your breath', he wrote. He did, however, have a pecuniary weapon at his disposal, and after the interview with Wilkes he wasted no time in unleashing it. Reminding Wilkes of a conversation in which Wilkes had said 'if any friend was to leave [him] £5,000 it would make him perfectly easily', Barnard revealed that, in response to this hint, he had

---

[151] Ibid., fol. 39.
[152] Ibid.

changed his will to leave Wilkes a legacy of £8,000. Following his daughter's death, he had amended it again to leave Wilkes an additional bequest of his collection of prints and books of sculpture, valued at £2,000. Wilkes, through his casual philandering, had thrown away a golden opportunity to achieve the financial ease he had long sought. The cost of his enjoyments was 'too dear', Barnard taunted, 'even though heightened with the exquisite Zest of their being with the Wife of a Bosom Friend'.[153]

Wilkes's response to Barnard's initial accusation was to assume the pose of martyrdom that had served him well in past political battles. 'Conscious innocence Mr. W. has always found the firmest shield against the envenomed shafts of malice and falsehood', he wrote. Following the interview in Berkeley Square, he identified Jane Barnard herself as the source of the malevolence. In a blatant appeal to the transcendent bond of male friendship, he attributed her story to 'the sickly and disturbed imagination of a female mind'. When he subsequently found out about the legacy, he implied a more calculating motive: Jane Barnard was greedily seeking to prevent a portion of her husband's fortune being left to Wilkes because that would have diminished her own legacy. To discredit her, Wilkes seized in particular on her claim that she was visited by a ghost. For the self-consciously enlightened, a belief in ghosts represented the nadir of credulity. Their alleged appearance was now associated with criminal manipulation as a result of the 'Cock Lane Ghost' affair of the early 1760s. In this cause célèbre, an innocent man, on the basis of evidence collected from a ghost, endured accusations of murdering his deceased wife's sister until the perpetrators of the hoax were themselves brought to justice.[154]

Barnard responded deftly, and with some understanding of psychology, to Wilkes's counter-charges and innuendoes. 'It is a known fact,' he wrote, 'that Persons in great affliction, brought very weak by fasting, and impressed with a deep sense of some concealed guilt, have imagined they saw sights, and heard voices, which in reality they did not; and have made voluntary confessions to crimes to their own destruction.' To the insinuation that she was prompted by greed, not guilt, Barnard countered that, on the contrary, she had sufficient awareness to know that her revelation would deprive her of the 'affluent fortune' she would otherwise have enjoyed; all she could reasonably look forward to now was a tiny annuity 'to keep her from want'.[155]

After returning without comment the gift of a hare (inscribed by Wilkes, 'from an old friend'), Barnard sent a final letter to Wilkes, in which he casually

---

[153] Ibid., fols 30, 39–40. Barnard left most of his prints and paintings to a friend in the Stamp Office. PROB 11 1123/588, National Archives.

[154] BL Add. MSS 30880B, fols 32, 38, 41; *Poetical Works of Charles Churchill*, pp. 483–85.

[155] BL Add MS 30880B, fols 39–40.

informed him that he had acquainted a friend, a nobleman, with the whole story. The friend in turn reported that he already knew of Wilkes's earlier affair with Jane. Alarmed that the scandal was spreading, Wilkes angrily invoked the honour principle. By virtue of his refusal to duel, he wrote, Barnard 'may freely and with impunity take any excursions into the boundless fields of indecency, illiberality, and scurrility'.[156]

This outburst was presumably intended as a parting shot, but nearly a year later, still grieving for his lost inheritance and thwarted in two attempts to achieve financial independence through election as Chamberlain of London, Wilkes made a last, desperate attempt at reconciliation. He persuaded a mutual acquaintance, Samuel Petrie (a former rake companion and stock jobber) to write to Barnard, pleading Wilkes's case. Wilkes virtually dictated the contents of the letter: 'It should contain a few strictures on the innocence of your friend, the various proofs he [Barnard] must recollect of insanity in the Lady, your regret at knowing the interruption of so long a friendship on so unjust a suspicion, and your wishes for a reconciliation.' Petrie dutifully sent the letter, but it had no effect. Later, a sad postscript to the affair would be recorded dispassionately in Wilkes's hand: 'It is said that Mrs Barnard left Mr. Barnard's house in Berkeley Square without his knowledge about three weeks before her death, which happened at Mr Garrett's on Barnes Common in March 1777.'[157]

---

[156] Ibid., fols 42–44.
[157] Wilkes to Samuel Petrie, 21 September 1776, Wilkes MSS 3, fol. 43; BL Add. MSS 30880B, fol. 44.

Chapter 4

Religion

The Character of a Deist

When James Boswell reproached John Wilkes for being 'a very Whig and a very libertine', it was his friend's religious, not sexual, delinquency that he had principally in mind. Boswell, after all, was himself a sexual libertine of a more compulsive tendency than Wilkes, yet he was also, in Wilkes's phrase, 'a primitive Christian' who trembled at the thought of the Scottish Kirk and was once on the brink of converting to Catholicism. Boswell subscribed to the Tory shibboleth that religious infidelity was at the root of whiggery. His mentor, Samuel Johnson, had declared that 'the first Whig was the Devil', interpreted by Boswell as meaning that 'the Devil was impatient of insubordination'.[1] The association of Whigs with religious heterodoxy had been standard polemical fare in the early eighteenth century: Jonathan Swift had claimed that 'in every hundred of professed *Atheists, Deists,* and *Socinians* in the Kingdom, ninety-nine at least, are staunch, thorow-paced Whigs'.[2] Because the conduct and attitudes of men like Wilkes lent some credence to it, the charge would be periodically revived, even into the nineteenth century.[3] When Wilkes erupted into the public consciousness, however, his alleged irreligion was scarcely an issue between political parties. William Warburton, very much the worldly Whig cleric, gave more forcible expression to Boswell's amiable strictures on Wilkes's contagious impiety. In 1765, Warburton wrote: 'I have long thought him [Wilkes] under a diabolical possession; but now a *legion* has got possession of the mob'.[4]

---

[1]   *Boswell, Italy,* p. 73; Peter Martin, *A Life of James Boswell* (London and New Haven, 2000), pp. 66–69; James Boswell, *Life of Johnson,* ed. R.W. Chapman, World Classics edition (Oxford, 1980), p. 973.

[2]   Quoted in Roger D. Lund, 'Guilt by Association: The Atheist Cabal and the Rise of the Public Sphere in Augustan England', *Albion,* 34 (2002): 399.

[3]   James J. Sack, *From Jacobite to Conservative: Reaction and Orthodoxy in Britain, c. 1760–1832* (Cambridge and New York, 1993), pp. 42–43.

[4]   [William Warburton] *Letters from the Reverend Dr. Warburton, Bishop of Gloucester, to the Hon. Charles Yorke, from 1752 to 1770* (London, 1812), p. 89. On Warburton's Whiggism and his fear of a High Church revival, see ibid., 14 March 1761, pp. 40–41.

Wilkes made little effort to defend himself from the charge of impiety, once quipping that religion sounded as ridiculous in his mouth as liberty did in Samuel Johnson's. Blasphemy was a different matter. He strongly denied that serious accusation. In private he occasionally toyed with the notion that he possessed a kind of diabolical influence over his followers, but such concessions to the more extreme charges of his enemies were exceptional, driven perhaps by euphoria at his popularity. More typical was this comment, in 1776, in a letter to his daughter: 'I remain ... sound in the faith, and will keep to my good orthodox mother, the Church of England, to the last moment of – its legal establishment.' While the mischievous caveat certainly qualifies his avowed attachment to Anglicanism, it does not altogether undo it; rather it speaks to his consistent view that the denominations of Protestant dissent should be placed on a practically equal footing with the Anglican Church. Part of the Church of England's appeal, he explained to Boswell, was its moderate location between Scottish Presbyterianism and Roman Catholicism: 'Your kirk is an ill-natured, censorious, persecuting prude, and always at war with the flaunting prostitute of Babylon. The church of England is a modest, decent matron, who compassionates you both.'[5]

To be 'sound in the faith' was for Wilkes an expression of institutional allegiance, not an avowal of Christian faith itself. In response to a sermon on Faith, Hope, and Charity, he declared that of the 'three, sweet sisters, the eldest ... I know little of; but the other two good girls are my favourites, and I wish them always to dwell with me'. The Methodists, who set out with evangelical fervour to instil orthodox Christian faith in the masses, raised Wilkes's ire. Nearly two hundred years before E.P. Thompson launched his coruscating assault on Methodism for promoting a 'chiliasm of despair' among the emergent working class, Wilkes had essayed a similar attack. 'It is extraordinary that the heresy of methodism has infected almost all the seafaring people here [Brighton], and has made them cowards as well as simpletons', he wrote. (John Wesley, the Methodist leader, in turn had a loathing for John Wilkes. Perhaps the two men came to recognise that they were competing for similar constituencies, and that their methods – the generation of popular excitement followed by industrious organisation to perpetuate support – were as similar in technique as they were divergent in goals.) Unseemly piety in the great was equally bothersome to Wilkes: Empress Maria Theresa of Austria he referred to as the 'apostolic bitch'.[6]

It is difficult to discern in Wilkes's belief any components of orthodox Christianity as espoused by his 'mother church'. In discussion with Boswell in

---

[5]   Boswell, *Life of Johnson*, pp. 895–96; [Wilkes] *Letters to Daughter*, vol. 2, p. 19; Wilkes to Boswell, March 5 [1779], Boswell Collection, C3092.

[6]   [Wilkes] *Letters to Daughter*, vol. 2, pp. 19, 98; E.P. Thompson, *The Making of the English Working Class*, rev. edn (London, 1980), pp. 385–440; *Wilkes–Churchill*, p. 71.

1765, he dismissed speculation about an afterlife as lacking any empirical basis. 'Never think on futurity, as not data enough', he instructed his friend. Intimations of mortality would later cause him to modify his views a little. William Rough, his first biographer and the husband of Harriet Arnold, defended Wilkes from the charge of atheism, claiming that 'there were not only sentiments of piety, there was in his mind a *tincture* of superstition'. The lawyer, Charles Butler, who came to know him in the 1770s, thought it evident that Wilkes feared what might await him after death. By now Wilkes himself claimed 'never to neglect the inward warnings of futurity'.[7] Yet this change of attitude did not extend to an acceptance of the Christian belief in bodily resurrection, which in 1766 he had declared to be 'absurd', stating that he cared 'no more to be raised in the same body than in the same coat, waistcoat, and breeches'. In a letter to Jean-Baptiste Suard, a close Parisian friend, he was equally scathing about belief in the incarnation of Christ, while also scoffing at the story of Adam and Eve:

1. How cou'd omnipresence be squeezed into a manger?
2. How cou'd omniscience be ignorant of his A.B.C?
3. How cou'd omnicompetence not have where to lay his head?
4. How came him to have but one son, and no daughter?
5. How came only one ram and one ewe to people such a farm?
6. How came you and I to believe such trash?[8]

Such views were genuinely shocking to James Boswell, who made energetic attempts to put his friend on the path to doctrinal orthodoxy, once arranging for him to receive instruction on the Athanasian Creed from a Catholic acquaintance, John Needham. To tease Boswell, Wilkes feigned interest in discussing such 'knotty points', and apparently met Needham in Naples, but the latter's efforts at persuasion were predictably unavailing.[9]

While rejecting the main elements of Christian doctrine, Wilkes nonetheless conscientiously attended orthodox religious service, where they were declaimed in sermon and liturgy. On this count he had one over on Samuel Johnson, whom he would criticise for refusing 'rudely to join in the public worship of the Deity, whom we all adore'.[10] Wilkes's attitude was consistent with a prevailing eighteenth-century sense that allegiance to formal public worship was both

---

[7] *Boswell, Italy*, p. 58; [Wilkes] *Letters to Daughter*, vol. 1, p. 181; [Charles Butler] *Reminiscences of Charles Butler, Esq. of Lincoln's Inn*, 2 vols (London, 1822), vol. 1, p. 73; Charles Chevenix Trench, *Portrait of a Patriot: A Biography of John Wilkes* (Edinburgh and London, 1962), p. 360.

[8] *Boswell, Italy*, pp. 290–91; Wilkes to Suard, 20 June 1769, Wilkes MSS 3, fol. 23.

[9] Wilkes to Boswell, 27 April 1765, Boswell Collection, C3088; Boswell: Verses to Wilkes, ibid., M287.

[10] Wilkes to Boswell, 1 October [1785], Boswell Collection, C3095.

manly and polite, in a way that over-emotional and private religiosity was not. (Methodist ministers – purveyors of emotional religion – were often depicted in prints as unmanly.)[11] When Wilkes assumed the status of local squire in Aylesbury, he became a highly visible and active member of the local church, attending service twice on Sundays and taking the sacraments regularly.[12] He was also the church's benefactor, donating a pair of doors and supervising the construction of a gallery. His generosity as a local patron was accompanied by a manifest sense of entitlement to the prerogatives appropriate to his station. In 1756, an official of the prebend of Aylesbury, with the agreement of the churchwardens and parishioners, gave him permission to extend his family pew in order to accommodate his wife and other family members, a renovation that required the displacement of some socially humble pew holders – a carpenter, a glazier, and a perukemaker. He guarded his extended pew jealously, even after Mary Wilkes's departure; he was unwilling to give it up when absent from Aylesbury, even to friends.[13]

In 1759, by now mainly resident in the capital, Wilkes accepted the demanding responsibility of churchwarden of St Margaret's, Westminster, where his friend Revd Thomas Wilson was at that time the minister. Wilkes's performance in that office perhaps defined the limits of his dedication to his mother church: less than conscientious in performing his duties, he received neither the usual vote of thanks nor the customary nomination for re-election at the end of his year's term. His commitment to religious observance, however, remained unwavering, whatever his travails. In 1764, David Hume observed that Wilkes was 'a most regular, & devout, and edifying, and pious Attendant' at the Anglican chapel in Paris, and with appropriate allowances for the facetiousness of Hume's display of admiration, his comment was substantially accurate. Later in life, while resident on the Isle of Wight, Wilkes would often take the boat trip to Portsmouth to worship in the garrison chapel there, and he was reportedly severe on the island's governor for not emulating his example.[14]

---

[11]   Jeremy Gregory, '*Homo Religiosus*: Masculinity and Religion in the Long Eighteenth Century', in *English Masculinities, 1660–1800*, ed. Tim Hitchcock and Michèle Cohen (London and New York, 1999), pp. 85–110; G.J. Barker-Benfield, *The Culture of Sensibility: Sex and Society in Eighteenth-Century Britain* (Chicago, 1992) p. 77.

[12]   *Wilkes Correspondence*, vol. 1, p. 20; Bleackley, *Wilkes*, pp. 18–19.

[13]   Faculty Book, 1735–1785, D/A/X/9, and Parish Records (Aylesbury), PR. 11/5/1.Q, Buckinghamshire Record Office; Robert Gibbs, *A History of Aylesbury* (Aylesbury, 1884) pp. 23–24; Wilkes to John Dell, 30 October 1759, Wilkes MSS 6, fol. 55.

[14]   [Thomas Wilson] *The Diaries of Thomas Wilson D.D., 1731–37 and 1750* (London, 1964), p. 15; *A Catalogue of Westminster Records: Vestry of St Margaret's and St John*, ed. John Edward Smith (London, 1900), p. 196; *The Letters of David Hume*, ed., J.Y.T. Greig, 2 vols (Oxford, 1932), vol. 1, p. 444; *The World*, 28 July 1789.

Such conduct in itself can hardly be accepted as evidence of authentic religious piety; at worst it smacks of hypocrisy, more charitably of an anxious claim to social recognition and respectability. His injunctions to Polly, encouraging her to be a good churchwoman, have a similar ring to them. Fittingly, towards the end of his life, Wilkes and his daughter, when in London, attended Grosvenor Chapel in Mayfair, the epitome of the fashionable Anglican establishment, where they would have heard sermons denouncing the vulgar enthusiasms of Wesleyanism. Yet it would be misleading to characterise Wilkes's attachment to the church as nothing more than an outward show. He had a genuine appreciation for the finer points of liturgical style and choral music, and a good sermon could claim his critical attention.[15] His self-identification as a loyal son of the church went beyond dilettantism, however. He remained convinced that his religious position was an entirely legitimate one to uphold within the church. It was not merely that the margins of orthodoxy could be stretched to accommodate it; those who adhered to a traditional, Trinitarian creed – which in Wilkes's view was 'direct *polytheism*'[16] – were the ones in error, the dupes of full-blown superstition and its sinister corollary, priestcraft. In other words, Wilkes was a deist.

Eighteenth-century deists were not uniform in their beliefs; Samuel Clarke, a liberal theologian who opposed them, distinguished four separate deist positions, with varying attitudes towards the actions of God in the world and the question of life after death. Wilkes is best defined as occupying the minimalist position. Deism's common ground, which he occupied, was belief in God as creator, full-blown scepticism about Christ's divinity, and rejection of biblical revelation. By disposition anticlerical, deists had a particular animus towards the Old Testament, 'which was seen as a repulsive blend of ritual and superstition, the story of a people led astray by tales of wonders, imposed upon by tricksters, in the name of a cruel and savage Deity whose own behaviour frequently dropped below that of normal decent human beings'. Wilkes believed that the Old Testament Jews lacked politesse: 'they had no true notions of delicacy, or even decorum'; 'their allusions to ... the fair sex, very justly shock our manners'. The 1720s and 1730s had witnessed the so-called 'deistic controversy' within the Church, which ended in an ostensible triumph for orthodoxy. But deism did not go away; arguably it became more diffuse, opening the way for yet more extreme expressions of scepticism and unbelief.[17]

---

[15] *Wilkes Correspondence*, vol. 2, pp. 23, 130; vol. 4, p. 82; Ann Callender, ed., *Godly Mayfair* (London, 1980), p. 6; Chevenix Trench, pp. 336, 360.

[16] *Wilkes Speeches*, p. 332.

[17] Gordon Rupp, *Religion in England, 1688–1791* (Oxford and New York, 1986), pp. 259–61, 276–77; Wilkes's review of a reprint of Robert Lowth's Oxford lectures, published in 1763 as *De Sacra Poesi Hebraeorium*, Wilkes MSS 3, Item 2; Roy Porter, *The Creation of the Modern World: The Untold Story of the British Enlightenment* (New York and London, 2000) p. 98.

How did Wilkes become a deist? How did his deism find expression as libertine activity? How did the exposure of such activity, and his response to that exposure, resonate in the public forum? What were the connections between Wilkes's deism and his staunch advocacy of religious toleration, one of the more consistent strands in his otherwise mercurial career? Answers to these questions add an important dimension of understanding to Wilkes the private man and public figure, as well as throwing light on the character of religious debate at a time when the established Church was taking on a renewed commitment to religious orthodoxy.

A plausible explanation of Wilkes's religious attitudes might be that they were formed in rebellious reaction to parental piety, especially that of his mother. Yet while Sarah Wilkes periodically chastised her son for immoral conduct, she never, apparently, had occasion to reproach him on issues of religious belief or observance. The probable reason is that his movement towards deism, though a radical shift, was foreshadowed, perhaps even enabled, by her own religious liberalism. Sarah Wilkes remained a Presbyterian, unlike Wilkes's father, who switched allegiance to the Church of England, but like a growing number of her coreligionists she was neither a Calvinist nor an orthodox Trinitarian.[18]

With respect to doctrine, Sarah Wilkes shared the position of her friend, Thomas Newman, assistant at the Carter Lane Meeting House in Blackfriars from 1718 to 1746 and its pastor until 1758. Newman was an Arian (following the teaching of the fourth-century theologian Arius), meaning that while accepting the divinity of Christ, he saw him as subordinate to God the Father, a theological position that stopped well short of deism but contradicted Trinitarian theology, which in the view of a sympathetic historian of the chapel had become 'an idle burden'. Newman was described as having 'a zealous concern for practical religion; a diffuse benevolence, which led him to abhor bigotry; and an ardent attachment to civil and religious liberty'.[19]

From Sarah Wilkes's perspective, Matthew Leeson was an ideal tutor for her son John because Leeson too was an Arian. In fact, Leeson had been obliged to quit his orthodox Presbyterian congregation in Thame because of his avowal of that doctrine; in John Wilkes's words, 'because he did not hold the received opinion of the trinity, original sin, redemption, &c.'. In Holland, Wilkes began to find his tutor tiresome company. His objection was not that Leeson attacked

[18]   On the schism among the Presbyterians, see Michael R. Watts, *The Dissenters*, vol. 1: *From the Reformation to the French Revolution* (Oxford, 1978), pp. 464–71.

[19]   Newman to Sarah Wilkes, 16 March 1767, Wilkes MSS 2, fol. 11. Henry Ierson, *History of an English Presbyterian Church: A Discourse Delivered at the Chapel in the Carter Lane, October 13, 1861* (London, 1861), pp. 28–29; Walter Wilson, *The History and Antiquities of Dissenting Houses in London, Westminster and Southwark*, 4 vols (London, 1808–14), vol. 2, pp. 108, 159.

'the faith of the zealot' – Wilkes shared his teacher's scepticism – but that Leeson was so fussily 'fond of every paradox and heresy'. 'He was continually poaching in the dull volumes of the *Frates Poloni* for some new heresy to broach', Wilkes complained. According to Alexander Carlyle, a fellow student at Leiden, Leeson's 'Chief Object seem'd to be to make Wilkes an Arian also, and Teas'd him so much about it that he [Wilkes] was Oblig'd to Declare, that he Did Not Believe the Bible at all'.[20] In his attitude to Leeson, we can detect the germ of Wilkes's enduring resistance to the larger issues of propositional debate. Satire and mockery were the critical instruments of the deism he came to embrace, not anxious theological enquiry of a sort that was unbecoming to an aspiring man of taste.

It was perhaps in reaction to Leeson's pedantry that Wilkes struck up his friendship with Andrew Baxter. The Scottish philosopher had by this time achieved some recognition for his *Enquiry into the Nature of the Human Soul* (1733) and *Matho* (1740), a philosophical dialogue directed to 'young Persons' in which one of the interlocutors (Matho) is himself an adolescent. These works expounded Baxter's principle that because all matter is inert, life and movement require the action of an immaterial force – a philosophical position that won him the nickname 'Immateriality Baxter'.[21] For Baxter, the principle was a profoundly religious one: God is the immaterial spirit in nature, performing 'immediately all that is done in the material universe'. 'The end of knowledge … is … to adore the power and the wisdom of the Deity'.[22] Though a communicant member of the Anglican Church, Baxter refused to take religious orders, and he was impatient with clergymen who acted like lawyers in expounding revealed religion. 'It would be more effectual, if they put on the character of a Deist; and show the necessity of a Revelation, from the principle of Reason', he wrote to Wilkes.[23]

Baxter's strictures against quibbling clergymen were not directed specifically at Matthew Leeson, whom he respected, but they did comport with Wilkes's irritation with his tutor. Baxter's personality, as well as his philosophy, was evidently more appealing than Leeson's. According to Carlyle, although Baxter 'was a profound Philosopher and a hard Student, he was at the same time a Man of the World, and of such pleasing Conversation as attracted the Young'. One of his bon mots was: 'When Bishop Berkeley said there was no matter, 'twas no matter what he said' – hardly thigh-slapping stuff, but it must have been a refreshing

---

[20] BL Add. MSS 30865A, fols 7–8; Alexander Carlyle, *Anecdotes and Characters of the Times*, ed. James Kinsley (London, 1973), p. 87.

[21] For Baxter's religious philosophy, see John Hunt, *Religious Thought in England*, 3 vols (London, 1870–73), vol. 2, pp. 145–46.

[22] *A Letter from Mr. Baxter, Author of an Enquiry into the Nature of the Human Soul, and of Matho, to John Wilkes Esq.* (1753), pp. 7, 10.

[23] BL Add. MSS 30867, fol. 13.

change from Leeson's ponderousness.[24] Baxter made strenuous efforts to make Wilkes his protégé, and to a large extent he succeeded. Shortly after their first meeting, he set about writing a new philosophical dialogue (*Histor*), inspired by their discussions in the Capuchins' Gardens at Spa, in which Wilkes – under a fictional name – was to be the principal interlocutor. Wilkes reciprocated by giving Baxter a set of the complete works of Spinoza, in recognition perhaps that Baxter's credo bore some resemblance to the pantheism of the Dutch philosopher. Later he gave him a collection of writings in defence of Samuel Clarke.[25]

Baxter's impression on Wilkes proved to be an enduring one. Perhaps part of the appeal of Baxter's philosophy was that it provided intellectual support for Wilkes's progress as a libertine, because it implied that God's purpose is fulfilled when individuals obey nature's divine impulse, the 'immaterial' force that animates inert matter. It was a philosophy, moreover, that – partly through Baxter's own example – could be reconciled with a deist version of Christianity. Wilkes's beliefs were shaped early and so decisively that in maturity he eschewed further theological discussion, much to James Boswell's frustration. After the two of them had traipsed up Mount Vesuvius (an experience presumably calculated to provoke contemplation of the religious immensities), Boswell taxed his friend on the issues of fate and free will, only to be told 'Let 'em alone'. 'Talked to Baxter of soul; two quarto volumes and never since', Wilkes cryptically explained.[26] His comment was not a rejection of Baxter's influence; on the contrary, the implication is that it was so persuasive that it pre-empted further metaphysical enquiry.

Baxter's influence almost certainly exceeded that of Paul Henri d'Holbach. D'Holbach's subsequent fame as a leading apostle of philosophical atheism naturally invites speculation that he encouraged Wilkes along the path of religious infidelity. One can easily imagine the lively intellectual exchanges between the two friends, inspired by their mutual love of classical authors, while taking, in d'Holbach's words, 'their delightful evening walks at Leyden'.[27] Yet d'Holbach was still a pious Catholic while at university, and even after he embraced a radically secular philosophy he retained his formal allegiance to the Catholic Church.

The primary influence might actually have been from Wilkes to d'Holbach, rather than the other way around. Already familiar with the proponents of natural religion, such as Samuel Clarke, Wilkes imbibed the writings of English

---

[24] Carlyle, p. 87; Bleackley, *Wilkes*, p. 11.

[25] Baxter to Wilkes, 23 June 1745, 3 October 1745, and 10 May 1746, BL Add. MSS 30867, fols 8, 9, and 13.

[26] *Boswell, Italy*, p. 58.

[27] BL Add. MSS 30867, fol. 14.

deists during the same period that he was adhering to the conventionalities of religious worship in Aylesbury. His library included the works of Henry St John, Viscount Bolingbroke; Anthony Ashley Cooper, third Earl of Shaftesbury; Thomas Gordon; and William Wollaston, whose *Religion of Nature Delineated* drew on the science of Isaac Newton to define God as First Cause or Prime Mover. Such books did not merely adorn his shelves; Wilkes had a depth of reading in theological controversy.[28] Wilkes acquainted d'Holbach with deist writings, including those of Thomas Gordon, whose work contained a powerful indictment of priestcraft, the most derogatory term in the deist's lexicon; in 1767, d'Holbach translated one of Gordon's tracts into French.[29] Through such a route, Wilkes arguably made a contribution to the celebrated *philosophe* crusade, *écrasez l'infâme,* though, in Wilkes's mind, *l'infâme* was not religious establishments per se, but the superstition, intolerance, and persecution associated with them. As Roy Porter has pointed out, 'Enlightenment in Britain took place within, rather than against, Protestantism'.[30]

Deist anticlericalism was an extension of deist theology. By challenging the orthodox conception of Christ's divinity and sacrifice, deists cleared away theological obstruction to their assault on priestcraft, which, in their view, derived its sway from a false distinction between clergy and laity, and was perpetuated by its practitioners through the manipulation of superstition and mystery. Priestcraft, in the influential view of Lord Shaftesbury, was an offence not only against reason, but also against gentlemanly politeness, the active expression of Christian benevolence and sociability.[31] The connection between superstition and clerical arrogance was most emphatically drawn in the writings of Thomas Gordon, whose *Creed of an Independent Whig* (1720) scoffed at 'the mystery of the blessed Trinity' and offered an unflattering depiction of its priestly advocates. Yet Gordon, like Shaftesbury, still accepted the need for 'a regimen in the church, and its government by bishops'. The national church that Gordon envisaged, however, was to be entirely Erastian in its subordination to the virtuous interests of the secular community and to the authority of the civil magistracy. He thus

---

[28] *Sale Catalogues of Libraries of Eminent Persons,* gen. ed. A.N.L. Munby, vol. 8, *Politicians,* ed. Seamus Deane (London, 1973), pp. 91–117; *Wilkes Speeches,* p. 318; J.C.D. Clark, *English Society, 1660–1832: Religion, Ideology, and Politics during the Ancien Regime,* rev. edn (Cambridge and New York, 2000), pp. 367, 409.

[29] Margaret C. Jacob, *The Radical Enlightenment: Pantheists, Freemasons and Republicans* (London, 1981), pp. 175, 263; J.A.I. Champion, *The Pillars of Priestcraft Shaken: The Church of England and its Enemies* (Cambridge and New York, 1992), p. 175, note 14.

[30] Porter, *Creation of the Modern World,* p. 99.

[31] Lawrence E. Klein, *Shaftesbury and the Culture of Politeness: Moral Discourse and Cultural Politics in Early Eighteenth-Century England* (Cambridge and New York, 1994), ch. 8.

recast as Whig doctrine the classical notion of civil religion, whose end was civic virtue, not the maintenance of Christian dogma and creedal orthodoxy.[32]

One can find definite echoes of Shaftesbury and Gordon's position in Wilkes's conduct and public advocacy. As a self-appointed doyen of patriotic virtue, he claimed to exemplify *'the life of God in the soul of man'*.[33] By contrast, 'priests of all religions', he asserted in Parliament, '[were] generally ... too fond of power; ambitious, grasping at wealth, honours, and preferment, luxurious, indolent, intolerant'.[34] Yet he was always careful to pay his respects to the Church as an institution. When he became Lord Mayor of London he invited the Archbishop of Canterbury, Frederick Cornwallis, and five other bishops to dine with him at the Mansion House.[35] Wilkes was also quick to lavish praise on churchmen who took positions that he could construe, however fancifully, as according with his own. In 1753, he addressed a sonnet to the then Archbishop of Canterbury, Thomas Herring, praising him for keeping 'the Sacred vessel of Religion ... Secure from Superstition's dangerous tide', a typically Low Church refrain.[36] At the time Herring had declared himself, albeit ineffectually, in favour of amending the Church of England's binding statement of doctrine, the Thirty-nine Articles, so that nonconformists might be brought within the national church.[37] In 1777 Wilkes saluted Robert Lowth, the new Bishop of London, calling him 'a gentleman ... of solid piety ... the soundest learning, and of exquisite, classical taste'. Lowth had long been free of any suspicion of heterodoxy, but, like Herring, he had supported unfettered religious enquiry and a revision of the Thirty-nine Articles. More relevantly, perhaps, he had also engaged in a dispute with William Warburton, Wilkes's bitter enemy.[38] Wilkes also tried to lend legitimacy to his religious position by connecting it to that of leading latitudinarian churchmen of the previous generation such as Benjamin Hoadly, Lowth's patron. In doing so, he was appealing to a tradition that was rich in historical associations with mainstream Whiggism and which retained resonance despite, or perhaps because of, the revival of High-Churchmanship in the latter decades of the eighteenth

---

[32] Thomas Gordon, *A Cordial for Low Spirits: Being a Collection of Curious Tracts*, ed. Richard Baron, 3rd edn, 3 vols (London, 1763), vol. 2, pp. 49–50, 237.

[33] Wilkes to Jean-Baptiste Suard, 5 August [1769], Chauncey Brewster Tinker Manuscripts, General Collection, Beinecke Rare Book and Manuscript Library, Yale University.

[34] *Wilkes Speeches*, p. 331.

[35] Bleackley, *Wilkes*, p. 289.

[36] Wilkes MSS 5, fol. 29.

[37] Richard Burgess Barlow, *Citizenship and Conscience: A Study in the Theory and Practice of Religious Toleration in England during the Eighteenth Century* (Philadelphia, 1962), pp. 114–15.

[38] *Wilkes Speeches*, pp. 144–45; Betty Kemp, *Sir Francis Dashwood: An Eighteenth-Century Independent* (London and New York, 1967) pp. 137–38; Scott Mandelbrote, 'Lowth, Robert (1710–1787)', *ODNB*.

century.[39] In theological terms, however, he was engaged in a dubious exercise. There were important distinctions between deists and latitudinarians. The latter's attachment to 'natural religion', though central to their definition, was a qualified one. Unlike the deists, they upheld that 'the hope and promise of salvation through Christ rested upon revelations and mysteries that had no place in the realm of natural knowledge'.[40] Yet the distinctions between latitudinarianism and deism tended to collapse inside the polarities of religious and political debate. The pressure came from both ends of the spectrum. Whereas Wilkes sought to consecrate his libertinism by associating it with a mainstream tradition, religious conservatives sought to defame latitudinarianism by characterising it as a halfway house on the road to full-blown infidelity.

Some of Wilkes's friendships with the lesser clergy supported the worst fears of his opponents. Those clergy who enjoyed his favour usually embraced his libertine anticlericalism, in defiance of their profession. There were exceptions, such as Revd John Stephens, who rebuked Wilkes for putting a quotation from a heathen poet, Virgil, on a tablet in the Aylesbury churchyard in memory of Wilkes's gardener, John Smart. The inscription read: *Illum etiam lauri illum etiam flevere myricae* ('even the laurel and the myrtle wept for him'). Wilkes, though, drawing on his authority as a classical scholar, persuaded Stephens that the inscription was acceptable in a sacred space because Virgil, in his Fourth Eclogue, was believed to have prophesied the coming of Christ.[41] Charles Churchill required no such instruction in the merits of paganism. The recipient of a classical education at Westminster School and St John's College, Cambridge, Churchill became notorious as a blasphemer and clergy-baiter. According to one report, he 'has been heard [to] utter very impious expressions, such as "d--n--g the blessed Virgin, and her glorious Son, swearing, that he would eat his dinner of such a Lamb leg, if it was the Lamb of G--"'. Churchill had a low opinion of most of his fellow clerics, dubbing them 'ye old Scripture pumping Divines – ye mercenary precept-mongers – ye Retailers of Revelation'.[42] When another renegade priest, Revd John Horne, sought in 1766 to replace the recently deceased Churchill as Wilkes's friend and political ally, he knew precisely the approach to take:

---

[39] John Gascoigne, 'Anglican Latitudinarianism and Political Radicalism in the Late Eighteenth Century', *History*, 71 (1986): 23–28.

[40] Roger L. Emerson, 'Latitudinarianism and the English Deists', in *Deism, Masonry, and the Enlightenment: Essays Honoring Alfred Owen Aldridge*, ed. J.A. Leo Lemay (Newark, NJ, 1987), p. 30.

[41] *Boswell, Italy*, 59.

[42] *A Letter to the Right Honourable The Earl of T[empl]e: Or, the Case of J[ohn] W[ilke]s, Esquire* (London, 1770), p. 24; *Wilkes–Churchill*, p. 5. Churchill left the church ministry in January 1763 (about two years after he achieved fame as a poet) through resignation, not – as his enemies alleged – through 'unfrocking'. Brown, pp. 83–85.

> You are entering into a Correspondence with a *Parson*, and I am a little apprehensive lest that title should disgust you: But give me Leave to assure you I am not ordained a Hypocrite.
>
> It is true I have suffered the infectious Hand of a Bishop to be waved over me: whose Imposition, like the Sop given to Judas, is only a Signal for the Devil to enter ... But I hope I have escaped the contagion: And if I have not, if you should at any time discover the black Spot under the Tongue, assist me kindly to conquer the prejudices of Education and Profession.[43]

The religious attitudes of the likes of Wilkes and Churchill were reinforced, encouraged, and expressed in libertine societies, which throughout the eighteenth century served as a covert associational network for the more audacious expressions of deism. As such, they had long been objects of suspicion from High-Churchmen, who saw them as the disseminators of pure atheism.[44] Such societies included the Beefsteak Club, where virtuoso deist performances occasionally leavened the usual diet of beef and bawdiness. Inspired by fictitious reports of the death of the Earl of Effingham, Wilkes delivered one in February 1782. In his *jeu d'esprit*, he recounted the tale of his fellow club member's adventures in Elysium before his miraculous return to the land of the living. Purporting facetiously to challenge 'the rubbish of modern infidelity', Wilkes lamented that 'some perverse skepticks have dared to controvert the noble Earl's death and resurrection'. Wilkes proceeded to direct his mockery at two familiar deist targets: the theology of the Trinity, as expressed in the Athanasian Creed, and the barbarity of the Old Testament. Meeting St Athanasius in the underworld, Effingham 'laughing full in his face roared out, Riddle-me, riddle-me, ree/Here is not 3 but 1, here is not 1 but 3'. Later, he spots Abraham on his way to sacrifice Isaac and informs the young man that 'he kept very dangerous company ... advising him to swear the peace against the old man, if he ever attempted to draw his knife upon him again, or to bind him neck and heels, like a calf'. He then reprimands Samuel for hewing Agag to pieces in Gilgal. 'Such cruelty he said was only becoming a priest.'[45]

Earlier, a jovial deism similarly infused the activities of the Medmenham monks. As we saw in the previous chapter, religious mockery was connected to sexual titillation – it gave 'zest' to the proceedings, to employ Whitehead's euphemism – but I would argue that it also carried some deeper, quasi-legitimate (as opposed to merely transgressive) meanings. Wilkes, deploying the rhetorical

---

[43]   BL Add. MSS 30869, fol. 4.

[44]   Lund, 'Guilt by Association', pp. 391–421.

[45]   [John Wilkes] 'Remarks of [Thomas Howard] the Earl of Effingham on a late excursion to Elyzium. Read in the presence of Lord Effingham in the Beefstake [*sic*] Society in Covent Garden, Feb. 9, 1782', BL Add. MSS 30890.

device of disclosing secrets while purporting to conceal them, offered some intriguing clues:

> Among other amusements they [the monks] had sometimes a mock celebration of the more ridiculous orders of the *church of Rome,* of the Franciscans in particular ... No profane eye has dared to penetrate into the English Eleusinian mysteries of the chapter room, where the monks assembled on all solemn occasions, the most secret rites were performed, and *libations poured* forth in much pomp to the BONA DEA [the good goddess].[46]

Churchill later alluded to Dashwood's role as Prior: '[Dashwood] shall pour, from a Communion Cup, / Libations to the Goddess without eyes.'[47] The monks' choice of Roman deity is highly suggestive. *Bona Dea,* the 'goddess without eyes', presided over both virginity and fertility. Her symbol was the snake. In ancient Rome, the ceremonial worship of *Bona Dea* was supposed to be secret, and confined to women; it was even forbidden to utter the word 'wine' in her presence. In antiquity, apparently, as well as in the eighteenth century, nothing incited the (male) libertine imagination more than a predominantly female religious ceremony, especially one that emphasised sobriety and chastity as embodied by vestal virgins and nuns. The Roman satirist Juvenal gave feverish expression to the male fantasy that nymphomania lurked beneath the pieties of the *Bona Dea* cult, and he envisioned the inversion of the *Bona Dea* ceremony into an exclusively male preserve in which the goddess is propitiated with 'the stomach of a porker and a huge bowl of wine' and 'none but males may approach her altar'.[48]

Here, one can reasonably speculate, was an inviting script for Wilkes and his fellow monks. (Wilkes's library contained four editions of Juvenal's works, one of them annotated by him.[49]) What gave the joke an added dimension were the obvious parallels between the pagan cult of *Bona Dea* and the Christian cult of the Virgin Mary, whose designation as *Mater Omnium Sanctorum* recurs satirically both in the iconography of the Society of Dilettanti and the Society of St Francis. Not surprisingly, *Bona Dea* had been assimilated for Christian purposes by the early Roman church.[50] The ceremony at Medmenham, then, involved a conflation between the mock worship of *Bona Dea* and that of the Virgin Mary. What gave

---

[46] *Letters between Grafton etc. and Wilkes,* pp. 35–36.

[47] *Poetical Works of Charles Churchill,* p. 369.

[48] Juvenal, *Satires* II and IV, in *Juvenal and Persius: Loeb Classical Library,* with translation by G.G. Ramsay (Cambridge, MA, 1961), pp. 25, 109.

[49] *Sale Catalogues of Libraries of Eminent Persons,* vol. 8, pp. 109, 110, 114.

[50] Marina Warner, *Alone of All Her Sex: The Myth and the Cult of the Virgin Mary* (London and New York, 1976), p. 282.

it some added satirical zest was that the real Franciscans had played a crucial part in shaping the Christian ideal of both the Virgin and the Nativity. Wilkes conscientiously examined the pre-Reformation history of Medmenham and established that in the thirteenth century the abbey had been dedicated to the Virgin Mary. There was a book about her life in the Medmenham library.[51]

Against a charge that the mock-religious ceremonies at Medmenham were nothing more than a blasphemous incitement to vice, Wilkes and Dashwood would no doubt have responded that, on the contrary, the monks were engaging in a legitimate exercise in Protestant iconoclasm – namely a satirical foray against what the more austere English reformers had long regarded as one of the most repugnant, scripturally invalid, and frivolous aspects of Catholic worship: the cult of the Virgin. Her shrines, like that at Walsingham and the Lady Chapel at Ely, had been despoiled at an early phase of England's break with Rome. The attack was continued on the doctrinal front, so that by the eighteenth century, even those elements of her veneration that were based on scripture – the Annunciation, the Incarnation, and the Nativity – were subject to withering scepticism.[52] The fact that the Anglican Book of Common Prayer retained nearly all of the Marian festivals, and was replete with references to the Blessed Virgin, was no doubt an incentive rather than a deterrent to Wilkes and his friends.

It would, however, be overstating the case to insist that Wilkes and his fellow rakes were driven by an earnest desire to advance the Protestant Reformation beyond its settling point in the established Church. It was more a matter of the anticlerical traditions of English deism legitimating a context for activities that were unabashedly playful. As Charles Johnstone put it: 'The great *butt*, against which men of pleasure play off all their wit is Religion.'[53] Yet the rakes' play was deep play, with loud cultural resonance. For some observers, this went even beyond the noises of jocular deism. Randolph Trumbach boldly refers to a priapic 'religion of libertinism' at Medmenham, which stood 'in contradistinction to orthodox Christianity'.[54] A letter to Wilkes by John Armstrong, a voyeuristic observer of Medmenham, gives credence to this notion. After a blast at Methodism

---

[31]   Wilkes's notes on the monastery's history are pasted on the Folio Bible, West Wycombe Library.

[52]   Warner, pp. 295–96; *A Letter to the Right Honourable the Earl of T[empl]e,* p. 24 ; Roger D. Lund, 'Irony as Subversion: Thomas Woolston and the Crime of Wit', and Ronald Paulson, 'Henry Fielding and the Problem of Deism', in *The Margins of Orthodoxy: Heterodox Writing and Cultural Response, 1660–1750,* ed. Roger D. Lund (Cambridge and New York, 1995), pp. 170–94, 240–70.

[53]   *Chrysal,* vol. 3, p. 232.

[54]   'Erotic Fantasy and Male Libertinism in Enlightenment England', in *The Invention of Pornography: Obscenity and the Origins of Modernity 1500–1800,* ed. Lynn Hunt (New York, 1993), p. 254.

– which in Enlightenment mentality competed with Catholicism as a synecdoche for religious superstition – Armstrong offered his view of the religious significance of the Society of St Francis, wrapped inside some typically prurient speculation about the sexual conduct of the 'monks':

> I honour this new order of Franciscans ... you have found a good jolly [?] road to Heaven – the best and most inviting of any I have yet heard of ... And tho' you may sometimes be obliged to force your way thro' strait and narrow passes never the worse for that. Well but I hope you don't shave all – nothing below the Chin – at least I hope the sisters are excused from any ceremony of this kind ... I like the description of your situation much – such a Retreat in such Company I should think sufficient to correct the most hardened and obstinate Atheist and soften his mind to receive impressions of the universal Religion – the Religion of Nature which I believe is better delineated by your holy Order than by any metaphysical philosopher that ever wrote a dry unreadable Quarto.[55]

Armstrong's reference to the monks' espousal of 'the universal Religion – the Religion of Nature' is fairly acute. Wilkes, Dashwood, and company were not, however, seeking to oppose Christianity in their rituals. Rather, for them, an eroticised Christianity was itself a religion of nature from which a fanatical attachment to chastity, represented by the cult of the Virgin, was a regrettable departure. Outside Medmenham, both Wilkes and Dashwood gave testimony to their Christian credentials. While a Medmenham monk, Wilkes remained a pillar of the Anglican community. Dashwood enjoyed friendly contact with leading churchmen, such as Robert Lowth, who shared his literary and artistic enthusiasms, if not his deist views. In 1763, as an expression of piety and aesthetic taste, Dashwood repaired and refurbished in Italian style the church on his estate at West Wycombe. Later, in collaboration with Benjamin Franklin, he proposed an abridgement to the Anglican Book of Common Prayer along deist lines, in which the reading from the Old Testament was to be removed, along with the Nicene and Athanasian creeds. Because 'there is but one God,' Dashwood argued, 'the addressing him in Parts or Persons is omitted in the liturgy as unnecessary.' In 1774, Dashwood attended the opening of Theophilus Lindsey's Essex Street Chapel in London, which housed the first enduring Unitarian congregation in England, and subscribed 'handsomely' towards paying the chapel's expenses.[56]

---

[55]   BL Add. MSS 30867, fol. 165.
[56]   Kemp, pp. 14–15, 137–57, 168–83; *The Papers of Benjamin Franklin*, ed. Leonard W. Labaree, W.B. Willcox *et al.*, 30 vols (New Haven, 1959–) vol. 20, pp. 343–52; vol. 21, pp. 195–96.

After Wilkes and Dashwood were estranged, Wilkes scoffed at Dashwood's claims to religious piety. His propaganda succeeded to the extent that some accounts continue to depict Dashwood's religious displays as an elaborate cover for depraved conduct, or even as evidence of his Satanism.[57] Such arguments are untenable, however; there is little basis for questioning the sincerity of Dashwood's motives. His religious attitudes, in fact, comported with Wilkes's own, which was one of the reasons for their friendly collaboration in the first place.

'Jokes on Christianity'

Medmenham illustrated how deism found expression as a group activity. The production of the most infamous piece of eighteenth-century deist and anticlerical literature, *An Essay on Woman,* was similarly the product of collaboration, in this instance between John Wilkes and his fellow rake Thomas Potter, both writing with the confident expectation of a receptive response from within their libertine circle. Possibly they composed it to be read aloud at Medmenham.[58] The extent of their respective contributions became a matter of intense speculation once the existence of the *Essay* was revealed, and the debate continues; my (tentative) case for Wilkes as the principal author is made in the Appendix.

Wilkes and Potter began their composition of the *Essay on Woman* in the mid-1750s. The work is a parody of Alexander Pope's *An Essay on Man* (1734) in which Pope's poem is transformed into a scabrous celebration of nature's erotic imperatives. More precisely, Wilkes and Potter were parodying a specific edition of *An Essay on Man,* which had rambling annotations by Revd William Warburton that exceeded in length the poem itself. This context offers a clue that Pope was only an accidental victim of the authors' mockery. The *Essay on Man,* with its injunction to glorify God by studying nature's plan, carries, after all, what could be construed as a deist message, despite the fact that Pope was a Roman Catholic with a declared hostility to the deists. Wilkes actually admired Pope, once calling him 'our English Homer'.[59]

When Wilkes, in 1763, prepared *An Essay on Woman* for the printing press, he appended three shorter parodies composed around the same time: 'The

---

[57]   Audrey Williamson, *Wilkes: 'A Friend to Liberty'* (London, 1974), p. 35.

[58]   The basis of this speculation is that, because that Wilkes arranged for twelve copies of the *Essay* to be printed, it seems likely that he intended them for the twelve 'apostles' of the Medmenham brotherhood. The most authoritative support for the notion is in [Wilkes] *Letters to Daughter,* vol. 1, pp. 48–49.

[59]   Thomas Edwards reproved Wilkes for calling Pope 'our English Homer', saying that title should rather be applied to John Milton. Edwards to Wilkes, 26 December 1748, MSS Bodl. 1011.

Universal Prayer, *cunno opt. min.* [to the best smallest cunt]'; 'The Dying Lover to his Prick'; and 'Veni Creator, or, the Maid's Prayer'. The first two were also parodies of poems by Pope edited by Warburton, 'The Dying Lover to his Prick' being a travesty of 'The Dying Christian to his Soul'. The 'Maid's Prayer' is the anomaly, being a parody of a well-known hymn. Wilkes himself conceded that the *Essay* was a 'juvenile performance',[60] and the modern reader, bombarded with its obscenities, can be forgiven for a certain relief that only 94 lines survive from the 1304 in the original manuscript. The poem, in many ways, is a throwback to the obscene poetry of the Restoration period. It borrows words like 'swive' (for fuck) and 'pego' (for penis) from the vocabulary employed by Lord Rochester and other literary rakes (and by Chaucer before them) – usage that had become anachronistic by the mid-eighteenth century. Restoration and Augustan wits had also dabbled in pornographic 'imitations', both of classical writers and of contemporary English poets, such as John Dryden. Pope had been subject to parody in his lifetime and, though he never acknowledged it, he had actually written a risqué one himself – an 'imitation' of a verse translation of the First Psalm. Despite generic antecedents for *An Essay on Woman*, however, it is in many respects *sui generis*. Earlier parodies were usually only fragments; what makes the *Essay* unusual is its length and the closeness of the parody to the original text. Out of the 47 surviving couplets, 45 match precisely the rhyme scheme of *An Essay on Man*. *An Essay on Woman* was something of a tour de force, then, but it was its content, not its form, that would gain it notoriety.[61]

Wilkes acknowledged that he was making lewd 'jokes on Christianity' in the *Essay*.[62] The pattern was established in the frontispiece (Wilkes's composition exclusively), which features an erect penis with a Greek inscription translatable as 'the Saviour of the World'. The jest extends to the liturgy: the Nicene Creed's reference to God's creation as 'all that is, seen and unseen' is applied in the *Essay* to the exposed and concealed parts of a woman's body. The most daring jibes at Christian orthodoxy are in the three shorter parodies, especially the 'Veni Creator; or, the Maid's Prayer', which associates the Holy Trinity with the male genitalia.[63]

Although the *Essay on Woman* poked fun at aspects of Christianity, its real spite, in the tradition of deist anticlericalism, was directed at churchmen. In the frontispiece and the prefatory 'advertisement', Archbishop George Stone, primate of the Church of Ireland, was lampooned as a sodomite. There is also an

---

[60] Wilkes to Heaton Wilkes, 22 April 1767, Wilkes MSS 2, fol. 14.
[61] Wilkes and Potter, ed. Cash, pp. 30–33. It comes as no surprise to find copies of bawdy poetry attributed to Lord Rochester among Wilkes's papers: BL Add. MSS 30880B, fol. 13.
[62] Wilkes to Humphrey Cotes, 20 January 1764, BL Add. MSS 30868, fol. 25.
[63] Wilkes and Potter, ed. Cash, pp. 85, 127, 131 note 37.

obscure reference to sodomitical tendencies on the part of Lancelot Blackburn, a long deceased Archbishop of York, who was rumoured to have kept a seraglio.[64] The most sustained attack in the *Essay*, though, was directed at Revd William Warburton, to whom most of the commentary and notes attached to the *Essay* and the 'Universal Prayer' were attributed;[65] he was clearly the principal butt of the parody. The long-windedness and pomposity of Warburton's annotations were a broad and inviting target for ridicule. Part of the fun was to render his tortuous theological arguments into justifications for sexual excess and gluttony, the latter being the deadly sin to which the eighteenth-century Anglican clergy were notoriously susceptible. The following note is typical:

> Philosophers agree that the two great duties Nature has enjoined all her children, *are to preserve the Individual, and to propagate the Species.* We ought therefore to be studious that our daily food be such as will not only please our Palate at the time, but will afterwards turn to good account, and perhaps more to the Gratification of the Woman than the Man. This shews that it is not only lawful but expedient for Clergymen to eat Crawfish, Soup, Lampreys, &c. not to indulge their own inordinate appetites, but as Provocatives to the *fuller discharge* of what is due to the dear Partners of our Beds, according to the Modus of Benevolence prescribed by St. Paul.
>
> DR. WARBURTON[66]

There was malicious irony here. Warburton was reputed to be impotent, which provided Wilkes with a pretext for some wicked speculation – presented in the Essay's 'design' as erudite enquiry – about the condition of *Cunno Warburtoniano* [Mrs Warburton's cunt] and the alleged '*vacuum*' between her husband's legs.[67]

Who was Dr Warburton, and just what was it about him that provoked such a venomous attack? He was an ecclesiastical lawyer, theologian, biblical scholar, and man of letters. At the time Wilkes and Potter contrived their parody, he held appointments as Dean of Gloucester Cathedral and as one of the king's chaplains. As his enemies never tired of pointing out, he entertained great hopes of continued advancement in the church, and his ambitions would be

---

[64] Ibid., pp. 85, 89, 113; Horace Walpole, *Memoirs of King George II*, ed. John Brooke, 3 vols (New Haven, 1985) vol. 1, pp. 60–61.

[65] Other notes were attributed to *Roger Cunerus* and *Vigerus Mutoniatus*, clearly made-up names. 'Burman', the name attached to several prurient notes, was probably inspired by Pieter Burmann the elder, a well-known Dutch classicist. Burmann had died shortly before Wilkes went to study in Holland, but his reputation for arid scholarship outlived him. BL Add. MSS 30867, fol. 13.

[66] Wilkes and Potter, ed. Cash, p. 97.

[67] Ibid., p. 93.

fulfilled in 1759, with his elevation, at the age of sixty-one, to the Bishopric of Gloucester. He was known as a prodigious and eclectic reader; Samuel Johnson once deflected a compliment from King George II about the breadth of his own reading by responding that, compared to Warburton, he had read little. Warburton liked to represent himself as an enlightened, even tolerant, intellectual with an appreciation for John Locke and a taste for ribald authors such as Rabelais and Laurence Sterne. He was far from being a dogmatic High Churchman; some of his defences of orthodoxy were so eccentric that he was sometimes criticised for conceding too much ground to infidelity. His reputation, though, was not that of a genial and broad-minded scholar like Lowth or Herring; it was rather that of a prickly and highly engaged controversialist, quick to deploy savage and personal attacks against his critics. The historian Edward Gibbon once called him 'the Dictator and tyrant of the World of Litterature'.[68]

In the 1740s, Warburton appointed himself as the scourge of the 'pestilent Herd of libertine Scriblers [*sic*] with which the Island is overrun',[69] by which he meant deist writers of the kind with whom Wilkes identified; his vehemence was perhaps a defensive response to the fact that his own commitment to Trinitarian orthodoxy was more than a trifle suspect. Warburton had once regarded Alexander Pope as a religious subversive, but in a curious volte-face he befriended the poet before his death, wrote a vindication of *An Essay on Man,* and published a posthumous edition of his works in 1751. 'Mr. Pope's *Essay on Man* is a real vindication of Providence against *Libertines* and *Atheists*', he argued, a case that he tried to reinforce in his annotations to the poem.[70] What lent irony and controversy to his deployment of *An Essay on Man* against religious libertinism was the fact that Pope had originally dedicated his poem to Henry St John, Viscount Bolingbroke, a notorious freethinker whose collected works, published posthumously in 1753, Warburton excoriated. Wilkes and Potter followed these paper wars with great attention,[71] and *An Essay on Woman* was their idiosyncratic contribution to them. From their perspective, Warburton had committed a major offence by his heavy-handed attempt to represent Pope, an icon of neo-classicism, as a pillar of religious orthodoxy.

---

[68]   B.W. Young, 'Warburton, William (1698–1779)', *ODNB*; Arthur H. Cash, *Laurence Sterne: The Later Years* (London and New York, 1986), p. 5. Warburton did not mellow with age: in 1766, Thomas Secker, the Archbishop of Canterbury, reproved him for his 'controversial severity' towards a fellow divine: BL Add. MSS 42560, fol. 147.

[69]   William Warburton, 'Remarks on Several Occasional Reflections', part 2, in *The Works of the Right Reverend William Warburton, Lord Bishop of Gloucester,* 7 vols (London, 1788–94), vol. 6, p. 536.

[70]   *A View of Lord Bolingbroke's Philosophy; in Four Letters to a Friend,* 3 vols (London, 1754–55), vol. 1, p. 80.

[71]   Potter to Wilkes, 10 October 1754, BL Add. MSS 30867, fol. 101.

The hostility of Wilkes and Potter had a personal edge to it. On the impressive list of adversaries that Warburton had managed to acquire during his long and contentious career was Thomas Potter's father, John, who as Archbishop of Canterbury had taken exception to one of Warburton's more eccentric works of Old Testament scholarship, *The Divine Legation of Moses*. The list also included Wilkes's friend, Thomas Edwards. When Warburton overreached his literary talents by publishing a highly flawed edition of Shakespeare, Edwards wittily took him to task in a widely circulated essay. Warburton's response was typically *ad hominem*; he accused Edwards of not being a gentleman.[72] The rituals of eighteenth-century politeness often reconciled literary skirmishes of this kind; they did not in themselves preclude the possibility of cordial relations between Wilkes and Warburton. Before launching his own full-scale literary assault in the *Essay*, Wilkes had actually paid courtesy calls on Warburton in London, but Warburton's ill-health prevented him from receiving the visits. The two did meet once, though evidently it was not a happy encounter. 'The Diabolic Monster [Wilkes] ... I have ever carefully avoided, since I had the ill fortune to have his Face obtruded on me', Warburton later remarked.[73] In Potter's case, the appearance of cordial relations that he maintained with Warburton was a cloak for dark designs, that involved not just *An Essay on Woman*, but a literal essay on a particular woman, Warburton's wife, Gertrude. Potter kept Wilkes informed of the progress of his intrigue, which he characterised as retribution for Warburton's literary offences.[74] Nine months later, Gertrude gave birth to her only child. When *An Essay on Woman* became a public scandal in the next decade, Wilkes and his friends rubbed salt in the Bishop of Gloucester's wounds by supporting the rumour that Potter was the boy's true father.[75]

Wars of Religion and Reputation

On 18 June 1768, Wilkes was sentenced in the Court of King's Bench to a prison term of twelve months for 'obscene and impious libel' for publishing *An Essay on Woman*. The original 'Information', prepared by Solicitor-General Sir Fletcher Norton, had charged him with seeking 'to introduce and diffuse ... a general debauchery and depravity of manners and a total contempt of

---

[72] [Thomas Edwards] *A Supplement to Mr. Warburton's Edition of Shakespear. Being the Canons of Criticism ... By another Gentleman of Lincoln's Inn* [n.d.]; Leslie Stephen, 'Warburton, William,' DNB archive, *ODNB*.

[73] BL Add. MSS 30867, fol. 56; Warburton to Lord Sandwich, 3 November 1763, SAN V/14, Sandwich Papers.

[74] BL Add. MSS 30867, fol. 101, and Add. MSS 30880B, fol. 3.

[75] Wilkes and Potter, ed. Cash, pp. 23–25.

Religion Modesty and virtue'.[76] In passing sentence, Mr Justice Yates – as Wilkes 'Affected Ease and Indifference by picking his Teeth and talking to those near him' – expounded further on the gravity of the offence:

> By such productions the very foundations of all human gov[ernmen]t are most effectually undermined … Religion whose precepts and terrors overawe the conscience are the ground on which every humans [sic] gov[ernmen]t places its first hopes. Of all weapons employed against religion Burlesque and ridicule are most fatal. Against the serious arguments of the atheist and the Deist the believer is armed. But never was there … a purer system of morality than that which this poem traduces. It is disgusting to every virtuous ear.[77]

The judge's pragmatic insistence that Christian religion must be defended as a constraint on human depravity was conventional enough. But it was delivered in the context of a renewed attempt, following the accession of George III, to assert the authority of the confessional state against the tendencies of Enlightenment thought. Partly mandated by the new king's desire to 'attack the irreligious',[78] the enterprise entailed an intensified commitment by the Anglican hierarchy to Providentialism and Trinitarianism as the basis for effective monarchical government. It was presided over by Thomas Secker, Archbishop of Canterbury from 1758 to 1768, who, though an ex-dissenter with a connection to the Old Corps Whigs, was a stickler for the prerogatives of the church.[79] The extent to which to the doctrinal aspects of this campaign enjoyed elite backing is open to question,[80] but the emphasis on Christian subordination appealed to both laity and churchmen concerned about what they saw as the lower orders' alarming lack of deference to religious authority. An early victim of the reassertion of orthodoxy was Peter Annet, an elderly deist who in 1762 was convicted of blasphemy and sentenced to a year's hard labour and time in the pillory. There was nothing especially remarkable about Annet's beliefs; probably his mistake was to promulgate them in the Robin Hood Society, a London debating club frequented by artisans.[81]

---

[76] BL Add. MSS 57733, fols 2–3.

[77] *The Correspondence of King George the Third from 1760 to December 1783*, ed. Sir John Fortescue, 6 vols (London, 1927–28), vol. 2, p. 30; BL Add. MSS 35887, fol. 121.

[78] *Letters from George III to Lord Bute, 1756–1766*, ed. Romney Sedgwick (London, 1939), p. 166.

[79] Clark, *English Society*, pp. 256–84; Sack, *Jacobite to Conservative*, pp. 75–79; Nigel Aston, 'Horne and Heterodoxy: The Defence of Anglican Beliefs in the Late Enlightenment', *English Historical Review*, 108 (1993): 895–919; Robert Glynn Ingram, 'Nation, Empire, and Church: Thomas Secker, Anglican Identity, and Public Life in Georgian Britain, 1700–1770' (PhD diss., University of Virginia, 2002), pp. 224–82.

[80] Sack, *Jacobite to Conservative*, p. 63.

[81] *Public Advertiser*, 22 December 1762; Francis Gentleman, *The History of the Robinhood Society* (London, 1764), p. 152.

The religious climate that prompted the prosecution of Annet also suffused the prosecution of Wilkes. But in Wilkes's case, the desire to root out irreligion was tangled with other motives, including vengeance. Wilkes was probably correct that 'if the North Briton had never appeared, the Essay on Woman would never have been called into question'.[82] This challenge to the moral authority of George Grenville's ministry was heightened by the manner in which it had acquired the *Essay* in the first instance and by the character of those involved in orchestrating Wilkes's prosecution. The whole episode was something of an object lesson in the hazards of invoking piety in support of power and privilege. 'A WHIG' had warned in June 1763 that he would 'take care to convince the World, that the principal Men of the reigning Party are no greater *Saints* than Mr. Wilkes'.[83] Subsequently, the vices and foibles of those who had launched the attack on Wilkes over *An Essay on Woman* were systematically exposed in pamphlets, poetry, and the press.

Gossip about Wilkes's authorship of the parody was already circulating by September 1762, when Arthur Murphy, a government pensioner, wrote that 'he [Wilkes] has displayed a curious felicity in converting the whole essay on man into a bawdy poem'.[84] Such rumours were probably behind the early attempts to tarnish Wilkes's political writings on the grounds of his infidelity. 'Canst thou persuade oneself that an Enemy to a *Saviour*, can be a Friend to Mankind?' asked one pro-government scribe.[85] The first public disclosure of the *Essay*'s existence came in the form of a curious advertisement in the *Public Advertiser* on 10 May 1763, which announced the *Essay*'s impending publication and attributed its authorship to Philip Carteret Webb, the Treasury Solicitor. Wilkes himself was responsible for this piece of mischief. He was fearful that the manuscript of the *Essay* was among papers seized by government messengers who, at the end of April, had raided his house in search of evidence to implicate him as the author of *North Briton* no. 45. Webb was the organiser of the raid and hence the target of Wilkes's pre-emptive strike. Wilkes had reason to be concerned, but because he had not yet printed any portion of the *Essay* – except for the obscene title page, which government agents discovered in the house of one his printers – the ministry was obliged to bide its time. Wilkes's boldness would soon give it an opportunity to renew its legal assault. As we saw in chapter 2, Wilkes was encouraged by his initial vindication in the *North Briton* case to set up a print shop in the parlour of his house in Great George Street. Among his ventures

---

[82]   Wilkes quoted in [Almon] *History of the Late Minority*, p. 208. See also, Epigram on a Late Affair, *St James's Chronicle*, 8–10 December 1763.

[83]   *Public Advertiser*, 16 June 1763.

[84]   *Auditor*, 9 September 1762, quoted in *A Collection of all the Remarkable and Personal Passages in the Briton, North Briton and Auditor* (London, 1766), p. 57.

[85]   ISRAEL LOYAL, *St James's Chronicle*, 12–14 May 1763.

was an edition of the *Essay*, limited to twelve copies intended solely for private distribution, hence not, in Wilkes's view, a 'publication'. Because Wilkes gave priority to other projects, however, only a small portion of the *Essay* and notes was ever printed, together with the ancillary verses.[86]

The story of how this extract came into the hands of government, and the uses to which it was put, combined high farce and low intrigue.[87] While Wilkes was away in Paris, Samuel Jennings, a new printer at the Great George Street establishment, used a discarded proof sheet of the *Essay*, containing corrections in Wilkes's hand, to wrap some butter for his lunch. Later that day, Jennings joined company with a fellow printer, Thomas Farmer, who began reading the verse on the lunch wrapping: 'Then in the scale of various pricks, 'tis plain, / Godlike erect, BUTE stands the foremost man.' From Farmer, this potentially incendiary material found its way into the hands of William Faden, a Scottish printer eager to secure a government place. In turn, Faden passed it on to his friend, Revd John Kidgell, a fashionable clergyman, who himself had achieved literary notoriety as the author of a salacious novel, *The Card*. Kidgell made a copy of the proof fragment and gave it to his patron, the Earl of March, a lord of the bedchamber to George III and one of the most notorious rakes of his generation. March in turn presented it to the secretaries of state, Lord Halifax and Lord Egremont, who had been frustrated in their earlier attempt to prosecute Wilkes for *North Briton* no. 45. They urged Philip Carteret Webb to secure a fuller version of the 'abominable work'. Webb eagerly obliged, employing bribery to acquire it from Michael Curry, Wilkes's chief printer, who had conveniently printed an extra copy for himself. Curry resisted Webb's blandishments for a while, but he capitulated when his employer, having just returned from Paris in late September, cast some aspersions on his 'private Character'.

The ministry now had in its hands material with which to make a case against Wilkes in the House of Lords, but its agents were determined to leave nothing to chance. Webb and Kidgell rehearsed potential witnesses,[88] and kept Curry in hiding

---

[86]   Wilkes and Potter, ed. Cash, pp. 56–58; Bleackley, *Wilkes,* pp. 115–18.

[87]   This account is assembled from testimonies that often conflict, and from witnesses who changed their stories over time. Webb kept and transcribed a variety of pertinent material: Guildhall MS 214/1, fols 68–86, 151–80; MS 214/2, fols 105–138. There are also valuable documents in BL Add. MSS 22131, fols 171–219, 239–56, and Add. MSS 22132, fols 130–32, 217–27. With appropriate allowances for special pleading, the following are also useful: John Kidgell, *A Genuine and Succinct Narrative of a Scandalous, Obscene, and Exceedingly Profane Libel, entitled An Essay on Woman* (London, 1763); and Thomas Farmer, *The Plain Truth* (1763). Curry's final version of the affair is an affidavit that he swore on 3 August 1768, reprinted in *Wilkes Correspondence,* vol. 1, pp. 152–63.

[88]   Guildhall MS 214/4, fols 102–08. This is a document in Kidgell's distinctively spidery hand, entitled 'Mr. Kidgell's Queries for the examination of witnesses'. It includes questions to be put to Curry, Faden, Jennings, Kidgell himself, and others.

for four days before he was due to testify, fearful that Wilkes's friends would seek to have him arrested for felony.[89] Kidgell meanwhile was taking a large step beyond legality. When the government decided, for purposes of evidence, to produce its own printed version of the *Essay*, Kidgell took the opportunity to make it appear more offensive than it actually was by appending a forgery, possibly the line 'Thrice blessed Glorious Trinity', to Wilkes's joke against Trinitarianism in the final verse of *Veni Creator*: 'Immortal Honour, endless Fame, / Almighty Pego! to thy Name; / And equal Adoration be / Paid to the neighb'ring Pair with Thee.'[90]

While Kidgell and Webb were preparing the evidence, the senior members of the ministry were deciding what legal avenue to follow in pursuit of their quarry. Their number now included Lord Sandwich, Wilkes's libertine companion at Medmenham and the Beefsteak Club, who joined the ministry as First Lord of the Admiralty on 23 April 1763, before being promoted to Secretary of State on 9 September, following Egremont's death. The zeal with which Sandwich embraced his mission, which included mobilising government informers to spy on Wilkes,[91] is sometimes attributed to personal malice. Among the papers seized from Wilkes's house in the April raid, and which Sandwich undoubtedly perused, were mock instructions to Sandwich following his appointment as ambassador to Spain in November 1762. Intended for delivery at the Beefsteak Club, the piece jokingly implies that Sandwich's martial valour was limited to sexual conquests.[92] Yet its tenor is consistent with the familiarities of libertine friendship; it is unlikely that Sandwich would have been offended by it. As late as Wilkes's return from Paris on 26 September, Sandwich was still trying to induce his fellow rake to abandon the opposition.[93] Only after Wilkes rebuffed him did Sandwich, the consummately loyal government servant, move against him. Religious scruple can be safely discounted as any part of his motive.

Sandwich worked closely with Lord Chancellor Northington to find the most effective means of bringing Wilkes to account. Consideration was given to condemning the *Essay* in the House of Lords as blasphemy, a move that would have opened the way for Wilkes's prosecution under the provisions of the Blasphemy Act of 1697, which was directed specifically against apostates who denied the truth of Christianity and the doctrine of the

---

[89]   Guildhall MS 214/1, fol. 157.

[90]   Arthur H. Cash, 'A Goldberg Variation', *The Age of Johnson*, 13 (2002): 250–51.

[91]   BL Add. MSS 57810, fols 59, 64–68.

[92]   Guildhall MS 214/1, fols 195–99. In the event, Sandwich never went to Spain, so the *jeu d'esprit* was probably never delivered.

[93]   BL Add. MSS 32951, fol. 220. Sandwich had earlier tried to persuade Wilkes, unsuccessfully, to make common cause with the ministry in the highly political affairs of the East India Company. Sandwich to Wilkes, 8 March 1763, Guildhall MS 214/3, fol. 87; Wilkes to Sandwich, 9 March 1763, SAN V/ 14, fol. 75, Sandwich Papers.

Trinity.[94] The Lord Chancellor was not persuaded, however, of the wisdom of launching such a charge against Wilkes. He agreed, though, that the matter could be pursued on the basis of a complaint from William Warburton that his privilege had been breached because Wilkes had attributed most of the notes in the *Essay* to him. Sandwich wasted no time in seeking Warburton's co-operation, which was readily obtained as the bishop recoiled from the 'heap of diabolic lewdness and blasphemy' to which his name had been put. Warburton, Sandwich reported, was eager to 'take any part ... that shall be judged proper by the King's administration ... and seems much pleased with the scheme in general'. For his part, Sandwich was ready to do battle with what he described as 'that spirit of licentiousness which has ... manifested itself in this country'.[95]

The scheme was put into effect on the day of the opening of Parliament, 15 November 1763.[96] While Wilkes was being condemned in the House of Commons for *North Briton* no. 45, the case against him for libelling a bishop was launched in the House of Lords. Sandwich took on the role of prosecutor. With uncharacteristic modesty, he declared that the paper he held in his hand 'was so infamous, so full of filthy language as well as the most horrid blasphemys [*sic*], that he was ashamed to read the whole of it to their Lordships'. Instead he read substantial extracts, including parts that Wilkes had not ascribed to Warburton's authorship. Then Warburton himself spoke, gratuitously denying authorship of the notes to the *Essay*. 'The blackest fiends in hell would not keep company with Wilkes', he went on, 'and then begged Satan's pardon for comparing them together'. The day's business continued with Sandwich examining, 'with great Spirit and ability', the printers brought in to testify to Wilkes's culpability. Although, on Lord Mansfield's advice, the Lords stopped short of declaring Wilkes the author of the *Essay* until he could be heard in his own defence, they did pass a resolution that it was 'a most scandalous, obscene and impious libel, a gross profanation of many parts of the Holy Scriptures, and a most wicked and blasphemous attempt to ridicule and vilify the person of our Blessed Saviour'.[97]

---

[94] A copy of the statute is contained in the materials gathered by Philip Carteret Webb in preparing the case against Wilkes: Guildhall MS 214/2, fols 165–66.

[95] *A Selection from Unpublished Papers of the Right Reverend William Warburton, D.D., Late Lord Bishop of Gloucester*, ed. Francis Kilvert (London, 1841), p. 225; Sandwich to George Grenville, BL Add. MSS 57810, fol. 55; Sandwich quoted in Philip Lawson, *George Grenville: A Political Life* (Oxford and New York, 1984), p. 170.

[96] Warburton was under the impression that only two or three ministers knew of the scheme. In fact most of the cabinet was kept informed: Guildhall MS 214/1, fols 214, 218. George Grenville, the prime minister, was certainly in the know: ibid., fol. 163.

[97] Lord Bath to Elizabeth Montagu, 17 November 1763, MO4452, Elizabeth (Robinson) Montagu Papers, Huntington Library; Horace Walpole, *Memoirs of the Reign of King George the Third*, ed. G.F. Russell Barker, 4 vols (London, 1894), vol. 1, p. 247; *Correspondence of King George the Third*, vol. 1, pp. 248–49; *Journals of the House of Lords*, 30: 415.

The enduring images that stand out from these events and their sequel highlight the apparent cynicism, malice, and duplicity of Wilkes's persecutors: 'the good' Lord Lyttleton being raucously shouted down by his fellow peers when he begged Lord Sandwich to desist from reading the *Essay*; Baron le Despenser remarking to his neighbour, while Sandwich was in full flow, that he had never heard the devil preach before; Warburton fulminating against Wilkes 'with the violence of a St Dominic'; the audience at a performance of the *Beggar's Opera* alertly identifying Sandwich with Macheath's false friend Jemmy Twitcher and fixing that nickname on him for posterity. Apocryphal stories quickly circulated to support the notion of swift retribution for Wilkes's persecutors; Sandwich, it was falsely alleged, was drummed out of the Beefsteak Club for his dastardly treatment of a fellow member. This gloss on events, however, inverts their short-term effect. Sandwich was personally unscathed by them; for a while, he enjoyed an enhanced status within the administration; and he even took a perverse enjoyment in his new nickname. Wilkes, by contrast, experienced despair for the first time in his adult life. When he learnt of the proceedings in the House of Lords he was 'thunderstruck'. His usual optimism temporarily vanished, and he was in a virtually suicidal state of mind when he engaged in his near-fatal duel with Samuel Martin.[98]

The source of his alarm was two-fold: he realised immediately that his political fortunes had undergone a dramatic reversal, but beyond that he was genuinely affronted to be labelled as a blasphemer. As he recovered his equilibrium, he launched a sustained campaign to remove this blemish on his reputation. Without ever denying authorship of the *Essay*, he insisted that it was never intended for publication. He held the House of Lords responsible for the public knowledge of its existence: 'I own I was rather put to the blush by THEIR PUBLISHING to the world what they pretended was found, perhaps put, among the things stolen from me.' In so doing, they, not he, had committed the 'public insult on order and decency'.[99] His campaign was unavailing as a legal defence, however. At his trial *in absentia* at the Court of King's Bench, in February 1764, Lord Mansfield, the presiding judge, forbade Wilkes's counsel from challenging the notion that merely arranging for a paper to be printed constituted publication. When Wilkes surrendered to the same court in April 1768, his anger at this judgement had mellowed – at least for public consumption – into sorrow for the complicity of the jurors. Still insisting that he had printed only twelve copies of the poem 'for the

---

[98]   Wilkes and Potter, ed. Cash, pp. 62–66; Walpole, *Memoirs of George III*, vol. 1, p. 247; N.A.M. Rodger, *The Insatiable Earl: A Life of John Montagu, 4th Earl of Sandwich, 1718–1792* (New York and London), pp. 103–05; [Almon] *History of the Late Minority*, p. 234.

[99]   *Letters between Grafton etc. and Wilkes*, p. 112; 'Letter to the Electors of Aylesbury', *Wilkes Correspondence*, vol. 3, p. 114.

sake of merry laughing friends', he expressed the hope that 'God would forgive that jury who upon their oaths had found him guilty of publishing, what ... was never out of his custody'.[100] By this time, Wilkes had glossed the imbroglio of the *Essay* as an attack on the liberty of private conscience. It was an artful strategy because, by the 1760s, only a few diehard Tories, such as John Shebbeare, were prepared to challenge publicly this irreducible Whig principle, which had William Warburton as one of its defenders.[101] 'In my own closet, I had a right to examine, and even to try by the keen edge of ridicule, any opinions I pleased', Wilkes insisted. Those who violated that right were acting like Stuart despots, 'for a Stuart only could make the refinement in tyranny, of ransacking and robbing the recesses of closets and studies, in order to convert private amusements into state crimes'.[102] As well as rallying his supporters, Wilkes's polemic induced a defensive tone even among some of his opponents. In sentencing Wilkes, Justice Yates acknowledged as a mitigating circumstance the fact that Wilkes's parody had not been intended for publication in the usual sense, only for the entertainment for a few of Wilkes's friends, adding the feeble reproach that 'those Friends for whose use it was designed are little obliged to you'.[103]

Because blasphemy was construed in law as a public act, Wilkes could claim that, *ipso facto*, he had not engaged in it. But his public defence went further. He maintained that the actual content of the *Essay* was not in any sense blasphemous. It was merely 'ludicrous', or 'laughable', 'a treatise against the spleen, or the *taedium vitae*'.[104] His arguments came close to those of Lord Shaftesbury, who had defended 'raillery as a servant of reason'.[105] Wilkes and his supporter deployed classical pedantry to refute the claim that the Greek phrase adorning the phallus on the frontispiece was a reference to Christ; its proper translation, they disingenuously argued, was actually 'Preserver of the World', an inscription whose antiquity long preceded Christ's birth.[106] Other parts of the *Essay* were within an acceptable tradition of liberal theology, Wilkes insisted, especially his satirical strictures on the Holy Trinity. He equated these with the religious scruples

---

[100] BL Add. MSS 32989, fols 363–64.

[101] [John Shebbeare] *The History of the Excellence and Decline of the Constitution, Religion, Laws, Manners and Genius of the Sumatrans*, 2 vols (London, 1760), vol. 1, p. 254; Barlow, p. 52.

[102] 'Letter to the Electors of Aylesbury', *Wilkes Correspondence*, vol. 3, pp. 113–14.

[103] BL Add. MSS 35887, fol. 121.

[104] *Letters between Grafton etc. and Wilkes*, p. 112.

[105] Klein, p. 168.

[106] *A Letter to J. Kidgell, Containing a Full Answer to his Narrative* (London, 1763), p. 20. This pamphlet is usually credited to John Almon, but it shows evidence of Wilkes's influence. See also a letter from J.G. *Philo Veritas, London Evening Post*, 29 November–1 December 1763, in which the writer claims that his ten-year-old son had pointed out to him the ancient origins of the Greek inscription.

of John Tillotson, the latitudinarian Archbishop of Canterbury of the previous century.[107] (It was an audacious comparison: Tillotson had a well-known horror of 'filthy talk and lewd practices';[108] he would hardly have endorsed Wilkes's association of the Trinity with the male genitalia.)

Wilkes clung to the fact that he was never formally charged with, or convicted of, blasphemy as a crime, only with the common law offence of 'obscene and impious libel'. Wilkes always had a keen eye for legal technicalities that he could exploit for his benefit, but in his mind the distinction between blasphemy and impiety was of a different order; it was fundamental. When a Parliamentary clerk inadvertently wrote the word 'blasphemy' in the Commons minutes, in reference to his conviction,[109] Wilkes came from prison to the bar of the House on 27 January 1769, to demand that the offensive word be expunged 'as a reparation of [his] injured honour'. His request prompted a lively debate (characterised by the Speaker as 'disorderly'), suggesting that much was at stake in how the issue was to be resolved. John Glynn, Wilkes's principal legal adviser, insisted that 'there was no intention to blaspheme God', adding, cleverly, that if blasphemy could have been proven, then Wilkes would have been prosecuted under the Blasphemy Act. William Beckford, Lord Mayor of London, chipped in that 'blasphemy is impiety, but impiety is not blasphemy'. Government supporters, by contrast, were anxious that the odium of blasphemy should remain firmly attached to Wilkes. William Blackstone, the eminent jurist, argued that morality trumped legal nicety. 'I think the crime is direct blasphemy', he said. 'It was a vicious act, with a vicious intention'.[110] In the end, the necessity for accuracy prevailed, and the references to blasphemy were expunged. Wilkes's family had been waiting expectantly for the outcome and received it with delight. 'I have just receiv'd the agreeable as possible account that all is favourable for my dear Papa in the House of Commons', Polly Wilkes wrote to her paternal grandmother.[111]

While Wilkes was defending himself from the imputation of blasphemy, he and his supporters were going on the offensive against those who had conspired to bring about his downfall. He launched a suit for perjury against Philip Carteret Webb. And he complained bitterly about the government's suborning of his employees with public money, a grave offence in a hierarchical society where so much hinged on mutual confidence between master and servant. In the context

---

[107] 'Letters to the Electors of Aylesbury', *Wilkes Correspondence*, vol. 3, p. 113.

[108] David M. Turner, *Fashioning Adultery: Gender, Sex and Civility in England, 1660–1740* (Cambridge and New York, 2002), p. 25.

[109] John Hatsell, the clerk in question, wrote a fulsome apology to Wilkes for his error: BL Add. MSS 30870, fols 105–06.

[110] Parliamentary Diary of Henry Cavendish, British Library, Egerton MSS 216, fols 229–38.

[111] Wilkes MSS 2, fol. 58.

of religious controversy, the most inviting targets for Wilkite anathemas were a trio of especially fragile guardians of religious orthodoxy and public morality: Kidgell, Warburton, and Sandwich. The three were often linked together, as in this newspaper squib, to expose the hollowness of 'court reformation':

> That Jemmy Twitcher should his Comrade peach,
> And against Vice, like Parson Tartuffe, preach;
> That rev'rend K[idgell] should for Conscience Sake,
> Bawdy and Blasphemy so public make,
> And to our Wives and Daughters plainly tell,
> What even Wilkes himself would fain conceal;
> That G[loucester]'s mitred Prelate should be made,
> The Tool wherewith to drive so foul a Trade;
> Turns Virtue and Religion into Farce,
> And makes Court Reformation shew her A[rse].[112]

The transgressions of Kidgell – who was rhetorically effeminised by Wilkes as 'the neat, prim, smirking chaplain' – were manifold. Wilkes publicly accused him of forging 'the most vile blasphemies' in the government's copy of the *Essay*, a charge that Wilkes's supporters could not repeat without betraying knowledge of the original parody.[113] Kidgell compounded his offence by composing a pamphlet that affected shock and horror at the *Essay*, thus revealing much of its content to the public. As one scatological wit pointed out, 'It might have lain a harmless T[urd] / If not by thy vile Nose thus stirr'd'.[114] Even Philip Carteret Webb was appalled at what Kidgell had done, fearing that it might endanger subsequent court proceedings against Wilkes.[115] The widely held assumption was that the parson had written the pamphlet simply to make money, that it was, in the language of the time, a 'catch-penny' publication. The corollary was that 'curiosity to read obscenity and blasphemy', not piety, prompted people to buy it.[116] Hence it was Kidgell, not Wilkes, who was spreading blasphemy and corrupting public morals. The newspapers were filled with satirical accounts of 'ladies of fashion' and married women, hitherto respectable, brought to a frenzy

---

[112] *St James's Chronicle*, 17–20 December 1763. See also EXTEMPORE, ibid., 1–3 December 1763.

[113] 'Letter to the Electors of Aylesbury', *Wilkes Correspondence*, vol. 3, pp. 114–15. In letters to Lord March, Kidgell implies strongly that he was involved in some underhand business. Guildhall MS 214/3, fols 5–6, 39–42.

[114] *St James's Chronicle*, 17–20 December 1763.

[115] BL Add. MSS 22132, fol. 240. Kidgell claimed that his narrative was undertaken with the 'approbation, direction and corrections of the Earl of Sandwich': Kidgell to Richard Phelps, 23 December 1763, SAN V/14, No. 73, Sandwich Papers.

[116] *Letter to J. Kidgell*, p. 6; TIM SIX-PENCE, *St James's Chronicle*, 8–10 December 1763.

of unseemly speculation by the clergyman's revelations.[117] Kidgell himself had few public supporters, and his reputation was shattered beyond recovery when he absconded to the continent with the proceeds of a turnpike fund.[118]

Kidgell, as Horace Walpole observed, suffered 'the fate of inferior tools, abandoned by his masters'.[119] Warburton, a superior tool, was altogether more resilient. Yet there was a strain of hypocrisy in Warburton that compromised his credentials as the defender of religion and morality. For example, while excoriating the libertines, he defended a friend who had constructed an obscene epigram, inspired by John 13:23, alleging that Jesus was homosexual. Warburton's grounds were that his friend did 'not know, that in polished times, and in courtly places, men are accustomed to hide their disbeliefs of, or indifference for Religion, by a scrupulous decency of expression, in what relates to it'.[120] Logically, the same kind of sophisticated defence could have been extended to *An Essay on Woman*, suggesting that it was the jokes at his expense not the parody's blasphemy that Warburton found so offensive. Two months after Warburton attacked Wilkes in the House of Lords, Charles Churchill unleashed a widely read riposte. His poem *The Duellist* excoriated Warburton for pride ('[He] was so proud, that should he meet / The Twelve Apostles in the street, / He'd turn his nose up at them all, / And shove his Saviour from the wall'); for using the church for social advancement ('But he himself was thereto drawn / By some faint omens of the Lawn, / And on the truly Christian plan / To make himself a Gentleman'); and, above all, for his hypocrisy ('He drank with drunkards, liv'd with Sinners, / Herded with Infidels for dinners, / With such an Emphasis and Grace / Blasphem'd, that POTTER kept not pace').[121] In response, Warburton could only to rant in private against Wilkes, the 'desperate cutthroat outlaw', and his diabolical allies.[122]

Even more than Warburton, Sandwich was an inviting target for accusations of blasphemy and hypocrisy. William Burke undoubtedly had him in mind when he made the acerbic comment in the House of Commons that 'Mr. Wilkes's writings have been laughed at over the bottle, and criminated the morning after'.[123] It

---

[117] 'We hear that two Ladies of Fashion, after reading ... Kidgell's Account of the Essay on Woman, offered Ten Guineas for a single Copy of it. – Such is the Curiosity excited by the Publication' reported the *St James's Chronicle*, 26–29 November 1763. See also BETTY BUSY, ibid., 1–3 December 1763.

[118] Adrian Hamilton, *The Infamous Essay on Woman; or John Wilkes Seated between Vice and Virtue* (London, 1972), p. 157.

[119] Walpole, *Memoirs of George III*, vol. 1, p. 249.

[120] Warburton to Thomas Warton, 12 April 1770, BL Add. MSS 42560, fol. 224.

[121] *The Poetical Works of Charles Churchill*, ed. Douglas Grant (Oxford, 1956), pp. 280–82.

[122] *Letters from Warburton to Yorke*, p. 89.

[123] British Library, Egerton MSS 216, fol. 232.

was by Sandwich's example that Wilkes was 'harden'd to blaspheme', claimed one press poet.[124] Sandwich's blasphemy in the Beefsteak Club was notorious.[125] It was even alleged that he had expressed his approval of the *Essay* there seven years before he denounced it in the House of Lords.[126] 'A perfect Connoisseur in Statesmanship', he was, insisted the Wilkites, motivated by sordid ambition, especially by his desire to secure election as lord high steward of Cambridge University.[127] Admittedly, there was much that was factitious in the Wilkite attack; despite appearances, there was never personal rancour between Wilkes and Sandwich.[128] Yet this does not diminish the importance of rhetorical constructions about Sandwich in diverting the charge of religious transgression from Wilkes by locating its appearance in one of his chief oppressors. According to a hostile essayist, Sandwich exemplified 'the character of an atheist', the charge often levied against Wilkes himself. Anecdotes, likely apocryphal, were repeated to support the accusation, most famously the one about Sandwich dressing a baboon in canonicals and claiming that the animal was his personal chaplain, fully competent to say grace at dinner.[129] Such conduct exposed him as 'an overgrown libertine [who] … has no more soul than a windmill', a person who 'acts by mere compulsion'. He is revealed as unmanly, because 'he is no more master of his deeds, than of his being'. Hence Charles Johnstone's story about him being scared by a baboon at the Medmenham rituals was rendered that much more plausible.[130]

These attempts to impugn Wilkes's opponents did not, predictably, deter the ministerial attacks on him. As he set out to recover his political fortunes by seeking election to Parliament in 1768, government scribes continued to brand him a demonic as well as a demotic agent. The newspapers were full of reminders of his blasphemy and warnings that his election would have dire consequences for public morals and religious allegiance.[131] The campaign spilled over into the streets: during the first Middlesex election, a group of his opponents carried a banner with the inscription, 'No Blasphemer'.[132] For their part, the Wilkites trotted out the language of the libertine Whig tradition, charging that their champion

---

[124] A.B., *St James's Chronicle*, 13–15 December 1763.

[125] *Public Advertiser*, 27 March 1764.

[126] *St James's Chronicle*, 17–19 November 1763. The charge was denied by AN OLD MEMBER OF THE SOCIETY, ibid., 19–22 November 1763.

[127] *Poetical Works of Charles Churchill*, p. 358.

[128] *Walpole Correspondence*, vol. 10, p. 179; Butler, vol. 1, pp. 75–76.

[129] *Bingley's Journal*, 16 February 1771.

[130] Ibid., 22 September 1770.

[131] Much of this material, and Wilkite rebuttals to it, were reprinted in *The Battle of the Quills: or, Wilkes Attacked and Defended* (1768).

[132] *St James's Chronicle*, 26–29 March 1769.

was the object of persecution 'by the votaries of despotism, and superstition'.[133] In a novel twist of language, a *North Briton Extraordinary* (of 13 November 1770) argued that the government's acts of tyranny constituted 'blasphemy against god and king'. Wilkes, by contrast, was 'a firm Christian' because he was 'religious to his word' and 'True to dame Honour'.[134]

What the impact of this competing propaganda had on popular attitudes is difficult to assess, but there is little evidence that Wilkes's reputation as a blasphemer in any way damaged his electoral successes. Indeed – in ways that confirmed the worst fears of conservative churchmen – some of his plebeian supporters seemed less inclined to deny his blasphemy than to echo it. Following his election for Middlesex, a parody of the Anglican liturgy was published; it included the 'Wilksonian creed', in which Wilkes was substituted for Jesus Christ.[135] It was widely circulated and went through several editions, becoming something of a collector's item; versions appeared in the American colonies, and it was still being 'sold and sung in the streets in 1770'.[136] This kind of irreverence suggests that Wilkes – while consistently avowing the right to privacy of the gentleman libertine – in effect served as a bridge between the religious heterodoxy of early Whiggism and its instantiation in the flamboyant, popular deism of the 1790s and early nineteenth century.[137] Under Wilkes's influence, the poor apprentice 'openly ridicules the religion of his country at the *Robinhood*', complained one pamphleteer. In December 1776 the members of another London debating club, the Society of Free Debate, discussed the following question: 'Whether the Athanasian Creed can be defended on the Principles of Reason and Revelation?' The question was determined in the negative before the society moved on to discuss the urgent problem of how best to resolve Wilkes's chronic indebtedness.[138] The authority of church and state, especially when buttressed by the conservative tendencies of evangelical religion, would prove sufficiently resilient to contain such popular, Wilkes-inspired heterodoxy, but insufficiently powerful to suppress it.

---

133 *Battle of the Quills,* p. 60.

134 *The Works of John Hall-Stevenson, Esq.,* 3 vols (London, 1795), vol. 2, p. 9.

135 *Britannia's Intercession for the Happy Deliverance of John Wilkes, Esq.* (n.d.).

136 John Brewer, *Party Ideology and Popular Politics at the Accession of George III* (Cambridge and New York, 1976), p. 173.

137 On connections between Tom Paine and Whigs of the early Enlightenment, see Roy Porter, 'The Enlightenment in England', in *The Enlightenment in National Context,* ed. Roy Porter and Mikulás Teich (Cambridge and New York, 1981), p. 16.

138 [Joseph Cradock] *The Life of John Wilkes, Esq. in the Manner of Plutarch* (London, 1773), p. 26; *Gazetteer,* 27 December 1776.

'Unlimited Toleration'

On 10 March 1779 Wilkes stood in the House of Commons to urge that dissenting ministers and schoolmasters be relieved from the burden of subscribing to the doctrinal portion of the Thirty-nine Articles. The old aspersions still dogged him in the wake of his appeal. He was 'the *pure essayist* on woman', the *Morning Post* reminded its readers. And more to the point, he had acquired his taste for blasphemy in a dissenting academy.[139] In the House, the sight of Wilkes as an advocate for religious reform prompted occasional laughter, but he was generally listened to with respect, because he spoke with eloquence and from conviction.[140] His speech was the culmination of a consistent support for religious toleration. He had long identified himself within a Low Church tradition that, though not defined by heterodoxy, would have enabled its expression through an emphasis on tolerance over conformity, the unity of the Protestant community over the prerogatives of the Church establishment, and the priority of free religious enquiry over an officially enforced orthodoxy. His approval of the Act of Toleration of 1689, a cornerstone of Whiggism, was qualified by the concerns of the enlightened deist: 'It has proved a firm bulwark against the fury of bigots ... though a philosophical mind must object to the unjust shackles which tyranny has forged of all subscriptions, creeds, tests, and oaths.'[141]

His attitudes were forged early. As a child, Wilkes was surrounded by reminders of religious intolerance. He would have observed daily the magnificent dome of St Paul's cathedral, which dominated the view to the south from St John's Gate, a few steps from his house; yet the history of St John's Square itself resonated with the strife that attended the construction of the Anglican ascendancy, which the cathedral so powerfully symbolised. The Wilkes family home and the Anglican Church next to it were actually built on the rubble of a medieval priory. During the Glorious Revolution, an anti-Catholic mob had been set to attack the priory before being dispersed by the Horse Guards. In 1710, a crowd rioted in the square in support of the High Church incendiary Dr Henry Sacheverell, targeting dissenters and Low Churchmen.[142]

Wilkes's parents exemplified the alliance between Low Church Anglicanism and nonconformity, which had so infuriated Sacheverell. After his shift to

---

[139] 18 March 1779.

[140] Different assessments of Wilkes's performance, which correspond in substance, can be found in the *Morning Post*, 11 March 1779, and the *Morning Chronicle*, 11 March 1779.

[141] 'Introduction to the History of England from the Revolution to the Accession of the Brunswick Line', in [Wilkes] *Letters to Daughter*, vol. 4, p. 256.

[142] William J. Pinks, *History of Clerkenwell*, 2nd edn (London, 1882), pp. 310, 324–25.

the Church of England, Israel Wilkes remained an active supporter of the (Presbyterian) Carter Lane Meeting House, in 1748 contributing two guineas to a fund 'for necessary repairs' to the building. He also attended a Presbyterian church in Highgate, arriving there in his coach-and-six. For her part, Sarah Wilkes frequently worshipped in Anglican churches. Such ecumenicalism had its pitfalls. In April 1750 she went to a Sunday service at Bow Church, where a woman refused her request for a seat. Sarah wrote anonymously to the woman to condemn her snobbery and to lecture her about Christian responsibility. She enjoyed a more hospitable atmosphere in Walbrooke Church, when Revd Thomas Wilson was minister there. Like her, Wilson favoured the union of all Protestants, and although he was an opponent of deism, he became a loyal supporter of her son's political causes. Sarah Wilkes evidently warmed to his sermons, taking extensive notes on one that blasted sodomites.[143]

John Wilkes assimilated, at a young age, his parents' commitment to Protestant unity. Writing to his father he described an encounter that had taken place when he was returning to school in Aylesbury. In the coach, he fell into an argument with 'a bigoted uncharitable old woman', who displayed a particular 'spite and malignity' towards dissenters. To the diversion of the other passengers, Wilkes 'had the pleasure of making [her] look ridiculous'.[144] Once married, Wilkes emulated the example of his father by joining Mary Wilkes in worship at the Carter Lane Chapel when he was resident in London. Polly, their daughter, was baptised there. Wilkes sometimes balked at the religiosity of the household in Red Lion Court. 'I hate your d-----d Gospel Gossips', he once exclaimed to some pious friends of his mother-in-law. Yet he claimed to have 'frequented sectarian meetings' even after his marriage ended.[145]

Wilkes's identification with the continental Enlightenment reinforced attitudes derived from his familial experience. As a student at Leiden, Wilkes would have heard sophisticated arguments in support of religious toleration and freedom of religious enquiry. He was there during the culmination of the so-called Strinstra Affair, when the relative merits of 'forbearance' and untrammelled toleration were fully debated, with Leiden faculty prominent among the discussants.[146] Later he followed closely the case of Jean Calas, a French Protestant accused of

---

[143] Register of Baptisms etc., Carter Lane Meeting House, Blackfriars, microfilm no. RG4/4231, Family Record Centre, London; *Gentleman's Magazine*, 68 (1798): 126; Sarah Wilkes to ?, 22 April 1750, Wilkes MSS 1, fol. 25; ibid., 2, fol. 105.

[144] Wilkes to his father, 22 January 1744, General Manuscript Collection: Wilkes, Columbia University.

[145] Bleackley, *Wilkes*, p. 19; Sharp Ms 28, Durham Cathedral Chapter Library; *The Life and Times of Frederick Reynolds*, 2 vols (London, 1826), vol. 1, p. 21.

[146] Joris Van Eijnatten, *Mutua Christianorum Tolerantia: Irenicism and Toleration in the Netherlands: The Strinstra Affair, 1740–1745* (Florence, 1998), *passim*.

killing his son to prevent him from embracing Catholicism, a bogus charge that led to Calas's torture and execution in March 1762. The case became a cause célèbre for the self-consciously enlightened: Voltaire and others campaigned to clear the name of Calas and his family and to condemn the religious bigotry that had brought about his death. In France, Wilkes befriended Elie de Beaumont, the advocate who had worked on behalf of Calas and written a widely applauded memoir of the case. When Beaumont visited England, Wilkes urged his friends to welcome this 'gentleman of genius and merit' and recommended his election to the Royal Society.[147]

There were no religious martyrdoms in Britain to match that of Jean Calas, but in the 1760s there was growing alarm in dissenting circles that the church was becoming 'a bloated and arrogant instrument of state control'.[148] Dissenters were becoming increasingly dissatisfied with the Act of Toleration, shifting their emphasis from the disabilities that it had removed to those that it still retained. From being loyal pillars of the Hanoverian state under the first two Georges, the dissenters were becoming some of its harshest critics. As such, their leaders followed the fortunes of John Wilkes closely, although they disagreed as to whether he was an asset or a liability to their cause. Certainly, Wilkes's defence of freedom of enquiry struck a chord among a group for whom dissent now carried its own rationale: among most dissenters, 'freedom of thought' was now the assumed basis of free moral agency, having shed the connotation of moral relativism that had made 'freethinking' repugnant to an earlier generation.[149] Hence many nonconformists, most prestigiously Joseph Priestley, gave enthusiastic backing to Wilkes during the Middlesex election controversy, lending support to Samuel Johnson's judgement that he was favoured 'by the sectaries, the natural fomenters of sedition, and confederates of the rabble, of whose religion little now remains but hatred of establishments'.[150]

For many leading dissenters, though, Wilkes's deism was not a point in his favour. They shared the view of orthodox churchmen in seeing deists 'as mere libertines, determined to throw over every moral and political restraint'.[151]

---

[147] *Wilkes–Churchill*, pp. 90–91; Wilkes to Thomas Birch, 10 September 1764, BL Add. MSS 4321, fol. 267; Wilkes to Temple, 9 September 1764, *Grenville Papers*, vol. 2, p. 437.

[148] James E. Bradley, *Religion, Revolution, and English Radicalism: Nonconformity in Eighteenth-Century Politics and Society* (Cambridge and New York, 1990), p. 418.

[149] Russell E. Richey, 'The Origins of British Radicalism: The Changing Rationale for Dissent', *Eighteenth-Century Studies*, 7 (1974): 179–92; Peter N. Miller, '"Freethinking" and "Freedom of Thought" in Eighteenth-Century Britain', *Historical Journal*, 36 (1993): 599–617.

[150] Joseph Priestley, *A View of the Principles and Conduct of the Protestant Dissenters with Respect to the Civil and Ecclesiastical Constitution of England* (1769); *Wilkes Correspondence*, vol. 5, p. 251; Samuel Johnson, *Political Writings*, ed. Donald J. Greene (New Haven and London, 1977), p. 344.

[151] Clark, *English Society*, p. 359.

The leading rational dissenter James Burgh – who urged marital fidelity and condemned illicit sex in any form – balked at supporting such a dissolute character as Wilkes, though he felt obliged to uphold the cause of electors' rights that Wilkes's expulsion by Parliament raised.[152] Richard Price, Burgh's Arian friend, who had a 'puritanical abhorrence of all forms of dissipation', was left in a similarly uncomfortable position. Like Wilkes, Price espoused freedom of conscience, enquiry, and worship. But there the resemblance ended. Price believed that 'every man's will, if perfectly free from restraint, would carry him invariably to rectitude and virtue'. It was an optimistic view, directly contrary to the defence of a priestly establishment as the essential instrument to restrain an inevitable tendency to human depravity. Its key was the operation of reason, which served to prevent an individual's moral capacity from being overpowered by instinctive desires. Wilkes's libertinism, justified as a response to the 'reasonable' imperatives of nature, clearly undermined Price's case. Hence, while supporting Wilkes's political causes, Price resorted to some strong language in condemning him as a person. 'He [Wilkes] was a man he could trample under his foot', he said.[153] Interestingly, Sarah Wilkes, Price's fellow Arian, gave the most passionately eloquent expression to Price's moral doctrine, while tempering it with a mother's belief in the possibility of her son's redemption. 'O! my dear son,' she wrote (after he had been discovered *in flagrante delicto* with a prostitute in her neighbourhood), 'do not sacrifice temporal and eternal felicity to any criminal indulgences; but let that … gift reason regulate and subdue inordinate passions, which will be the noblest triumph and reward you with inexpressible satisfaction and tranquillity.'[154]

John Wilkes blithely disregarded his mother's counsel as well as the notion that he was in any way at odds with the leaders of dissent. He publicly praised Richard Price and Joseph Priestley as 'wise and virtuous citizens' who brought 'honour to the age', and linked their plight to that of leading anti-Trinitarian and Low Church Anglicans of the previous generation – those 'good and exemplary men' William Whiston, Samuel Clarke, and Benjamin Hoadly. All were victims, Wilkes insisted, of the archaic survival of religious tests.[155]

By the time that Wilkes re-entered the House of Common as MP for Middlesex in December 1774, there had already been a number of Parliamentary attempts to eliminate or relax the requirement for such tests. There were distinct but

---

[152] Carla H. Hay, *James Burgh: Spokesman for Reform in Hanoverian England* (Washington, D.C., 1979), pp. 36, 73–74.

[153] D.O. Thomas, *The Honest Mind: The Thought and Work of Richard Price* (Oxford, 1977), pp. 7, 170, 172; Thomas Somerville, *My Own Life and Times* (Edinburgh, 1861), p. 146.

[154] 23 October 1771, Wilkes MSS 2, fol. 95.

[155] *Wilkes Speeches*, pp. 332–33.

connected campaigns. The first came from a small group of Anglican clergymen who objected to tests per se and had a special objection to subscribing to the Thirty-nine Articles, which had Trinitarianism at their doctrinal core. Their case was made in the Feathers Tavern Petition, which was rejected twice by the House of Commons, in February 1772 and May 1774. It was in the wake of this rejection that Theophilus Lindsey defected from the church to establish the Unitarian Chapel in Essex Street, London. A second campaign took the form of bills, in 1772 and 1773, to relieve dissenting clergy and schoolmasters from subscription to the doctrinal part of the Thirty-nine Articles. They passed through the House of Commons before being rejected in the House of Lords, although the margin of defeat of the second bill was sufficiently narrow to encourage a third attempt.[156]

The debates on these questions revived much of the rhetoric of former party divisions over ecclesiastical polity. When on 19 May 1772 a bishop invoked the traditional Tory spectre of the 'Church in danger', William Pitt, the Earl of Chatham, a supporter of the dissenters' relief bill, responded with a furious display of Whig anticlericalism.[157] His outburst came a time when some other ecclesiastical controversies were raising the temperature of religious debate. Thomas Nowell's sermon before the House of Commons that year on 30 January, the anniversary of Charles I's execution in 1649, was so aggressively Tory in tone – Nowell compared George III's enemies with Charles's – that the traditional thanks of the House were expunged from the *Journal*. Soon after, there was a bitter division over the inflammatory issue as to whether the Church could revive long-dormant claims to property in lay hands.[158]

Sensing an apparent renewal of party strife, Wilkes wasted no time in jumping into the politico-religious fray. His first speech on his return to the Commons deplored the observance of the day of Charles I's execution as one of fasting and prayer, proposing instead that it be a day of festival to celebrate the removal of an odious tyrant. His subsequent speeches supporting Parliamentary reform and condemning the government's American policy were not overtly religious in content, but they certainly echoed the refrains of the rational dissenters, with their insistence on civil liberty as the corollary of religious liberty. He would have to wait until 10 March 1779, however, for a further opportunity to promote the cause of religious toleration more directly. His speech on behalf of relief for dissenting ministers and schoolmasters was nothing if not audacious. Carefully

---

[156] G.M. Ditchfield, 'The Subscription Issue in British Parliamentary Politics, 1772–79', *Parliamentary History*, 7, part 1 (1988): 45–80.

[157] Ibid., p. 54; Clark, *English Society*, pp. 412.

[158] Robert Hole, *Pulpits, Politics and Public Order in England, 1760–1832* (Cambridge and New York, 1989), p. 52; Ditchfield, 'Subscription Issue', p. 47.

distinguishing deism from atheism, he pronounced that the former had become 'almost the religion of Europe', and that its inroads were actually greater in the established church than in dissenting ones. He opposed subscription, not simply as a violation of religious liberty, but because it meant endorsing the 'absurdity' of the doctrinal parts of the Thirty-nine Articles, especially their orthodox insistence on Trinitarianism. To insist on subscription, he said, showed a 'total want of Christian charity ... indecency ... foolish prejudice, and even insolence'.[159]

Wilkes took his argument a step further on 20 April when he spoke against the attempt to amend the relief bill by allowing exemption from subscription only to those who, as Christians and Protestants, accepted a declaration that the Old and New Testaments contained the 'revealed will of God'. The amendment was not one to which a deist, who rejected biblical revelation and found the Old Testament repugnant, could conscientiously agree. Wilkes referred to recent biblical scholarship, some of it by Anglican clergy, to cast doubt on 'the purity of the sacred text'. But he also opposed the declaration on the broader ground that it implied denial of toleration to those avowedly outside the limits of Christian faith. 'I contend for the most general and unlimited toleration ... to take in all sects and all religions', he said. He parted company with the pre-eminent apostle of toleration, John Locke, in declaring that he would not 'persecute even the Atheist'. And he offered a vision of a national church existing harmoniously alongside the visible expression of other religious faiths, each protected, not persecuted, by the civil authorities:

> I would support the sublime dome of St. Paul's, but I would not destroy a beautiful *Pantheon.* I wish to see rising in the neighbourhood of a Christian cathedral, near its gothic towers, the minaret of a Turkish mosque, a Chinese pagoda, and Jewish synagogue; with a temple of the sun, if any Persians could be found to inhabit this island, and worship in this gloomy climate the God of their idolatry.[160]

(The image had been evolving in Wilkes's mind for some time: a month earlier, in expounding his views on toleration to James Harris MP, he said that 'he wished to see a Mosque on one side of [St] Pauls, and a synagogue on the other'.[161]) Wilkes's attack on the proposed declaration claimed much of the public's attention to the issue, though it failed to dissuade MPs from passing the relief bill with the amendment attached. Although the rational dissenters shared his distaste for the declaration, his advocacy probably alarmed other nonconformists,

---

[159] *Wilkes Speeches,* pp. 316–21.
[160] Ibid., pp. 326–43.
[161] Quoted in Thomas, *Wilkes,* p. 185.

especially those with doctrinally orthodox views, who were simply seeking a modest improvement in their status. When the body of London dissenting ministers formally thanked Wilkes for 'his generous and active zeal in support of religious liberty', it was likely in spite of, not because of, its fulsome mode of expression.[162]

The ultimate test of Wilkes's support for religious toleration was his attitude to Roman Catholicism. From John Milton onwards, Protestant advocates for the free exercise of religion had typically sought to exclude Roman Catholics from its putative benefits. The reasons for this exclusion were deeply embedded in Protestant historiography and mythology, namely that Catholics were intent on destroying Protestantism and that they constituted an *imperium in imperio*, whose primary allegiance was to the Pope and the Catholic states. In the early eighteenth century, these fears took on a new dimension because of the various Jacobite attempts to restore the Catholic Stuarts to the British throne.[163] Wilkes's particular brand of Whig politics was shaped in this context, and his popular support in London retained some distinct odours of anti-Catholic xenophobia. Wilkes, himself, as we have seen, engaged at Medmenham in an elite version of anti-Catholicism, justified in the mind of the deist by the Old Church's incorrigible attachment to the twin evils of priestcraft and superstition. Later, in Naples, he claimed to have exposed as a priestly cheat the biannual 'miracle' of the liquefaction of the blood of St Januarius. Throughout his six-month sojourn in Italy, in fact, he self-consciously took on the mantle of the English Protestant gentleman, appalled, not only by Catholic superstition, but by its cultural corollaries: unmanliness and a wretched attachment to unnatural vice.[164]

Yet there were also limits to Wilkes's clichéd objections to Catholicism that prevented them from breaching his commitment to full religious toleration. Just as he praised some Anglican churchmen, he also acknowledged genuine piety among those in Catholic orders. On his return from Italy, he stayed at the monastery of Grande Chartreuse, near Grenoble, where not only was he impressed by the romantic gloom of the setting but also 'edified ... greatly' by 'the pious conversation of the good fathers'.[165] His reaction suggests that one must be careful not to overstate self-consciously enlightened objections to Catholicism when perceived as a spiritual as distinct from an ecclesiastical force. As we have seen, Wilkes's *philosophe* friend Baron d'Holbach retained his formal allegiance to the Catholic Church even as he made his shift to philosophical atheism.

---

[162] Ditchfield, 'Subscription Issue', p. 63 and note 148.
[163] Colin Haydon, *Anti-Catholicism in Eighteenth-Century England, c. 1714–80: A Political and Social Study* (Manchester, 1993), pp. 1–163.
[164] *Wilkes Correspondence*, vol. 2, pp. 162–65; BL Add. MSS 30865B, fols 39–43.
[165] *Wilkes Correspondence*, vol. 2, p. 182.

As Wilkes entered London civic life as an alderman after his return from continental exile, he showed a reluctance to associate himself with the anti-Catholic populism of many of his supporters. In the summer of 1774, the passage of the Quebec Bill – which gave a privileged status to the Catholic Church in the former French colony of Canada – was inflaming opinion in the capital. Frederick Bull, the Lord Mayor and one of Wilkes's closest political allies, used his legal powers to close two Catholic churches in London, in order 'to stop the progress of Popery', as he put it. Wilkes, however, withdrew from the Common Council meeting that drew up a petition against the Act and he was absent from the delegation that presented it to the king.[166] There was press speculation that he had abandoned the '*good cause*'.[167] But once in Parliament, Wilkes sought to redeem himself, railing against the Quebec Act for establishing 'French tyranny and the Romish religion in their most abhorred extent' in Canada.[168]

Although Wilkes was belatedly aligning himself with popular opinion in London, he could also have legitimately claimed that any appearance of ambiguity was illusory, that there was no inconsistency in condemning the Act as an affront to the constitution and to Protestant interests in North America, while distancing oneself from the irrationally heated response to it. Over the issue of limited relief for his own country's Catholic subjects, Wilkes showed no equivocation. He declared himself in support of the first Catholic Relief Act, which went into law in the summer of 1778 after passing without opposition through both Houses. The bill's sponsor was Sir George Savile, a country gentleman, who like Wilkes had opposed the Quebec Act in Parliament; it had the support of the ministry, which was keen to reward and encourage Catholic loyalty during the American War of Independence. In return for taking a new oath of allegiance to the crown, English Catholics were now accorded the legal right to own land, while the threat of severe punishments for Catholic priests and schoolmasters was lifted.[169] In Parliament, Wilkes applauded the Act because it meant that Catholics were no longer 'in the power of every infamous informer' – probably an allusion to William Payne, a London constable and notorious anti-Catholic zealot, who had brought a number of indictments against Catholic priests, schoolmasters, and laymen – and Wilkes alone protested when anti-Catholic tumults in Edinburgh and Glasgow persuaded the government to defer the passage of an equivalent relief bill for Scotland. While supporting relief, he also expressed regret that Catholics had not been accorded full civil rights and unobstructed freedom of worship. Their cause was that 'of religious liberty,

---

166 Thomas, *Wilkes*, pp. 164–65.
167 'O', *Middlesex Journal*, 16–18 June 1774.
168 Quoted in Haydon, p. 197.
169 Ibid., pp. 204–05.

and the rights of private conscience, no less than the cause of all Protestant dissenters'. His motives were 'without suspicion', Wilkes insisted, 'for no man, who ever continued so long at Rome and Italy, was ever less suspected of being tainted with the errors of Popery'.[170]

Wilkes's defensiveness on the issue was understandable. Anyone advocating the least measure of tolerance for Catholics was likely to be branded 'a Papist in disguise'.[171] And not all such attitudes were crudely populist in origin; many 'enlightened' dissenters, with the notable exception of Joseph Priestley, shared them. Wilkes himself had the charge of popery levelled against him when he played an active part in suppressing the Gordon Riots, the outbreak of anti-Catholic violence that in June 1780 erupted in London and, less severely, in the provinces. The trigger for the disturbances was the presentation to Parliament on 2 June of a mammoth petition from the Protestant Association, which had been organised on a nationwide basis to demand repeal of the Relief Act. As Lord George Gordon, the association's London president, seconded by Frederick Bull, urged acceptance of the petition, a large and menacing crowd surged around the Houses of Parliament; it came, Wilkes said later, 'like the Evil Spirits in Milton'.[172] (Ironically, a party of these marchers had earlier filed off to cheer outside Wilkes's house in Great George Street.) Guards dispersed the mob, but that night two Catholic chapels attached to foreign embassies were burnt. After a brief lull, looting and burning resumed on a more terrifying scale and continued for several days, reaching a climax on 7 June ('Black Wednesday'), with heavy loss of life among the rioters. Although the crowd's targets soon moved beyond the residences and businesses of rich Catholics to encompass Newgate Prison, the Bank of England, and the homes of unpopular authority figures, there is little doubt that fear and hatred of Catholicism was the animating cause of the violence, not simply an excuse for class-driven mayhem. The two residences of Lord Mansfield were attacked, for example, because he was alleged to be a friend to Catholics, perhaps even a closet Papist himself.[173]

Wilkes had initially balked at the prospect of regular troops being deployed to suppress the riots without authorisation from the civilian authorities. Nor did he oppose a motion by London's Common Council on 8 June to petition for repeal of the Relief Act for the purpose of 'quieting the minds of the people'. But by that time the inertia of most of his fellow aldermen, including the Lord Mayor, was impelling him to action. Rather than opposing the Royal Proclamation of 7 June

---

[170] *Wilkes Speeches*, pp. 317, 336.

[171] Haydon, pp. 182–85.

[172] *Public Advertiser*, 22 June 1780.

[173] Haydon, pp. 213–44; Christopher Hibbert, *King Mob: The Story of Lord George Gordon and the London Riots of 1780* (London and Cleveland, 1958), pp. 45–145.

that authorised the use of military force, he helped to raise a band of volunteers that would make the army's continuing presence in the capital unnecessary. Perhaps he glimpsed in such action a chance to reclaim popularity lost by his support for Catholic relief. Certainly one of his correspondents was thinking in those terms. 'If you can get rid of the military,' he wrote, 'and establish an inward force to defend the City from riots by making the Train'd Bands as formidable as they were in Chas I's time, you may claim a civic crown and live to be the most popular Man in the Kingdom.' In effect, though, if not in intention, the voluntary associations proved to be a supplement to the army, not a substitute for it. Wilkes himself fought alongside regular troops in defence of the Bank of England, winning commendations for his courage and skill from army officers present at the affray. He was equally energetic in his civic capacity. Throughout the riots and their aftermath, he tirelessly exercised his authority as alderman and magistrate: issuing arrest warrants, interrogating suspects, and dispatching them to prison pending trial. One of those he committed was William Moore, the author of some rabidly anti-Catholic publications, which alleged that the government was riddled with papists and their friends; one publication referred to 'the *Romish* complexion of *Pious* the *third* our *Protestant* king'.[174]

Wilkes's support for Catholic relief, and his willingness to defend it in the face of violent opposition, brought him into some unusual alliances. One of them was with another eloquent advocate of religious toleration, Edmund Burke, the leading spokesman for the Rockingham Whigs, an aristocratic party with whom Wilkes had for some time been at odds. Even government ministers were now singing Wilkes's praises; he was '*the* heroic Justice', wrote Lord Clarendon, Chancellor of the Duchy of Lancaster.[175] Meanwhile, Wilkes's relationship with erstwhile friends deteriorated in a climate of mutual recrimination. He was not in a conciliatory mood when, on 19 June, he spoke in the House of Commons against the City petition to repeal the Catholic Relief Act. His old friend, Frederick Bull, was his main target. Wilkes accused him of pusillanimity in the face of the riots; of being continually at Gordon's side on the day the riots began; and of allowing the constables in his ward to sport the blue cockade, the adopted symbol of the Protestant Association. Wilkes, in turn, was obliged to withstand charges of base ingratitude to Bull, who had been Wilkes's patron as well as his friend.[176]

Denunciations of Wilkes spilled over from Parliament to the press and the hustings. He was, claimed one newspaper scribe, a '*Renegado* Christian ... worse

---

[174] Journal of Common Council, 68: fols 66–67, Corporation of London Record Office; *Gazetteer*, 7 June 1780; *Public Advertiser*, 13 June 1780; BL Add. MSS 30866, fols 240–41; J. Wilson to Wilkes, BL Add. MSS 30872, fol. 196; Haydon, *Anti-Catholicism*, pp. 226–27.

[175] Clarendon quoted in Thomas, *Wilkes*, p. 188.

[176] *Public Advertiser*, 22 June 1780; Thomas, *Wilkes*, p. 189.

than either Turk or Infidel', with a dangerous 'zeal for Popery'. Others pointed to the irony of Wilkes, the erstwhile political firebrand, asserting himself as the guardian of public order and committing William Moore to trial for the same kinds of criminal libel for which he had himself been convicted. His apostasy was driven by a corrupt desire for a government place, some alleged, a charge that was not intended as an alternative to that of crypto-Catholicism, but as the natural corollary of it.[177] At the midsummer gathering of the London livery, Wilkes was shouted down with cries of 'No Popish Chamberlain', in reference to the lucrative City position he had assumed the previous year.[178] Two months later, he was again on the defensive at a meeting of the Middlesex electors.[179] One must, however, resist overstating the extent to which Wilkes lost support in London; the radical camp was shaken by the Gordon Riots, but not irrevocably divided by it.[180] Wilkes's grasp on the chamberlainship was never seriously challenged, and he was re-elected for his Middlesex seat without significant opposition. At the same time, his reputation as a friend of the Catholics damaged his popularity in a way that his reputation as a blasphemer had not – an interesting comment on popular religious attitudes in the capital. There is no indication that Wilkes ever regretted his stance over Catholic relief: he was clearly intent on being identified as an enlightened, cosmopolitan, tolerant deist, with all the elitist connotations of that combination, even as a chorus of the *vox populi*, which he had once declared to be an infallible guide, was urging him in another direction altogether. Wilkes had discovered that being an emblem of liberty actually brought with it a threat of constraint to his personal freedom.[181]

There was a postscript. Eleven years after the Gordon Riots, anti-Catholic violence erupted in France, as part of the revolutionary assault on the old order. Wilkes's attitude remained constant, albeit now confined to the private sphere. The French mob, in its 'barbarous absurdity', was 'condescending to copy the canaille of this country', he wrote to his daughter. He was even-handedly scathing about the concurrent excesses of 'Church and King' loyalists in England, especially the 'savage, cruel, and persecuting spirit of the mechanics at Birmingham' who in July 1791 destroyed the house of Joseph Priestley. Government must 'exert itself

---

[177] *Gazetteer*, 24 June 1780; 'A Detester of Apostasy', ibid., 30 June 1780; 'Q. in the Corner', *Morning Post*, 22 June 1780.

[178] *Public Advertiser*, 26 June 1780.

[179] *London Evening Post*, 12–14 September 1780.

[180] Nicholas Rogers, 'Crowd and People in the Gordon Riots', in *The Transformation of Political Culture: England and Germany in the Late Eighteenth Century*, ed. Eckhart Helmuth (London and Oxford, 1990), pp. 39–55.

[181] Raymond Postgate, *That Devil Wilkes* (London and New York, 1930), p. 206; Richard Sennett, *The Fall of Public Man* (New York and London, 1992) p. 104.

in the punishment of so vile and wicked a crew', he declared, consistent with
his long-held view that the protection of religious freedoms, not their negation,
was government's primary religious duty.[182]

---

[182]   [Wilkes] *Letters to Daughter,* vol. 4, pp. 58, 88.

Chapter 5

Class

The Trouble with Friends

In June 1767 John Wilkes, weary of exile, grumbled about the indifference of the British aristocracy to his plight. 'The great expect you shou'd bear all, and never utter a whisper of complaint', he wrote.[1] He had expressed such sentiments before. On 17 February 1764 he declared: 'I am too proud ever to ask a pardon, or even to receive favour from any of the great (however great) whom I hate and despise.'[2] But this outburst, born of frustration, was not yet a settled conviction. What was different and significant about the comment in June 1767 was that around the time he made it, Wilkes was starting to look for political succour from a different quarter: the plebeian citizens of the metropolis. The implications of this shift merit careful examination, but there is an important question that needs to be addressed first. Why, in light of his persecutions, had Wilkes remained attached for so long to the belief that it was from the ranks of 'the great' that he would find his principal friends and benefactors? After all, what transpired in Parliament on 15 November 1763, as described in the previous chapter, had the finality of a ritualised ejection from an exclusive Mayfair club. Only Lord Temple offered token resistance as his fellow peers rounded on his client for the offence of the *Essay on Woman*.[3] That episode was followed by Wilkes's expulsion from Parliament, his convictions for sedition and impiety, and his outlawry. One can scarcely conceive of a more thoroughgoing expulsion from elite society.

The basic reason for Wilkes's lingering regard for aristocracy is that he had invested so much in his social and political ambitions that he was slow to relinquish them. Even as he was reviled as a blasphemer or championed as a lord of misrule, he hankered for a more conventional place in the social hierarchy. For a long time he remained trapped in a set of false assumptions. The first was that it was his declared foes, not himself, who were out of step with the mainstream of

---

[1]   Wilkes to William Fitzherbert, 24 June 1767, Fitzherbert Papers, 0239M/F 8260, Derbyshire Record Office.

[2]   *Wilkes Correspondence*, vol. 2, pp. 56–57.

[3]   Thomas, *Wilkes*, p. 42.

aristocratic opinion. In this category, he placed Lord Mansfield – 'my personal enemy', Wilkes called him – who, Wilkes said, insisted in presiding over his trials in the Court of King's Bench in order to indulge both a private grudge and lingering Jacobite loyalties.[4] In fact, Old Corps Whigs had a lot of sympathy and praise for Mansfield's handling of what the Duke of Newcastle called 'this ticklish affair of Wilkes' and were quite prepared to tell him so.[5]

Second, Wilkes found it hard to accept that his sexual and religious libertinism, of the sort described in the two previous chapters, had gone from being a social asset to a liability once it was no longer safely cloistered in the private realm; he assumed that he retained stable friendships with highborn acquaintances at a time when such relationships could no longer bear the weight of his notoriety.

Third, Wilkes was slow to recognise that there was a lack of correspondence between his notions of friendship and those of the aristocrats with whom he presumed an easy familiarity. The misperception was understandable: the term friendship and its cognates had malleable meanings in the eighteenth century. They could signify an affective and enduring relationship on a heroic scale, modelled on the love of Achilles for Patroclus. Such 'sacred ties', to use Charles Churchill's expression, elided the distinction between public and private and, in theory, transcended political faction. They were, in effect, a patriotic virtue, basic to social cohesion: 'betrayal of friendship was equated with betrayal of country'. Yet friendship could also mean something more pragmatic and less stable: a mere acquaintanceship or a political alliance, devoid of emotional content.[6] When Lord Rockingham, who assumed leadership of the Old Corps Whigs in 1765, said that 'he loved [Wilkes] as a friend', it was not like Achilles talking about Patroclus, or Baron d'Holbach talking about Wilkes, or Churchill and Wilkes talking about each other. Rockingham was referring to the lesser category of friendship as a preface to narrowing the extent of any obligation that he owed to Wilkes.[7]

There was a class-driven dynamic behind these distinctions. Among the Whig aristocrats, Wilkes's sprightly wit and polemical skills were widely acknowledged; that did not, however, guarantee his unqualified acceptance into full social intimacy, the higher order of friendship. His insistence on the essential

---

[4]   'Letters to the Electors of Aylesbury', *Wilkes Correspondence,* vol. 3, p. 109; Wilkes to Humphrey Cotes, 20 January 1764, BL Add. MSS 30868, fol. 24.

[5]   Newcastle to Rockingham, 10 June 1768, BL Add. MSS 32990, fols 191–93, and Newcastle to Mansfield, 10 June 1768, ibid., fol. 190.

[6]   George E. Haggerty, *Men in Love: Masculinity and Sexuality in the Eighteenth Century* (New York, 1999), p. 11; *The Poetical Works of Charles Churchill,* ed. Douglas Grant (Oxford, 1956) p. 213; Shearer West, 'Libertinism and the Ideology of Male Friendship in the Portraits of the Society of Dilettanti', *Eighteenth-Century Life,* new series, 16 (1992): 97; Charles Wentworth Dilke, *The Papers of a Critic,* 2 vols (London, 1875), vol. 2, pp. 239–60.

[7]   Lauchlin Macleane to Wilkes, 4 January 1766, BL Add. MSS 30869, fol. 6.

equality of gentlemen, expressed at the time of his duel with Lord Talbot, ran up against the harsh realities of social convention. Aristocratic friendships were deemed inviolable and often survived political division (as, for example, in the case of Lord Mansfield's friendship with Lord Rockingham[8]), but their privileges and comforts were fully extended only to those who recognised each other as equals. Those of more humble birth, like Wilkes, could linger indefinitely on the fringes of the charmed circle of aristocracy, even as they deluded themselves that they stood within it.

Libertine friendships of the sort discussed in chapter 3 had their own complex character. Arguably, despite the vows of comradeship, they were inherently volatile, unless supported by other ties, because the centrifugal tendencies of self-gratification often proved stronger than the integrative tendencies of the shared libertine experience. William Rough, with Wilkes's libertine friendships specifically in mind, compared them to waves beating on the beach: 'their course is the same, but it is a course of jostle and opposition.'[9]

Such friendships, unstable in themselves, could scarcely withstand the intrusion of politics. The collapse of Wilkes's association with Sandwich is a case in point. What is noteworthy is that the two men continued to have kind words for each other in private, despite their rancorous public exchanges, a circumstance that probably sustained Wilkes's lingering belief that the mysterious bonds of aristocratic fraternity somehow confounded vulgar assumptions of acrimony.[10] Wilkes enjoyed a more genuine friendship with Sir Francis Dashwood, which is why the two men at first resisted the consequences of Dashwood's appointment, in May 1762, as Chancellor of the Exchequer in Lord Bute's government. Dashwood wrote to Wilkes about his elevation in his jocular and self-disparaging fashion, and Wilkes continued to be a regular guest at Medmenham through the summer and autumn of 1762.[11] Dashwood had no hesitation in recommending Wilkes as his successor to command the Bucks militia, praising his deputy 'as a man of spirit, good sense and civil deportment; who has shown resolution and industry'.[12]

Wilkes's attacks on Bute in the *North Briton* eventually took their toll, however. According to Wilkes, Dashwood began to avoid his company at Medmenham

---

[8]   W.M. Elofson, *The Rockingham Connection and the Second Founding of the Whig Party, 1768–1773* (Montreal and Kingston, 1996), pp. 109, 120–21.

[9]   [Wilkes] *Letters to Daughter*, vol. 1, p. 18. Rough's comment finds implicit support in George Haggerty's rejection of the libertine model as an appropriate paradigm for authentic male–male friendships in the eighteenth century: Haggerty, p. 10.

[10]   *Walpole Correspondence*, vol. 10, p. 179; *Reminiscences of Charles Butler, Esq. of Lincoln's Inn*, 2 vols (London, 1822), vol. 1, pp. 75–76.

[11]   BL Add. MSS 30867, fol. 176; British Library, Egerton MSS 2136, fol. 49.

[12]   *Wilkes Correspondence*, vol. 1, p. 39.

because of them. Wilkes claimed to be surprised at Dashwood's attitude, insisting that the *North Briton* respected pre-existing friendships: 'No private tie had been broke, no connection dissolv'd, nor any attack begun, where there was a friendly intercourse.'[13] Dashwood was certainly spared the vitriol directed at his ministerial colleagues, and Wilkes's well-known quip that Dashwood went 'from puzzling all his life at tavern bills' to administering the country's finances appeared in print only after the connection between the two men had been irrevocably sundered.[14] Yet despite Wilkes's protestations, he made some snide references to Dashwood in the *North Briton.*[15] Elsewhere, Wilkes scoffed (anonymously) at Dashwood's claims to religious piety. His renovated church at West Wycombe was an expensive folly, Wilkes charged; its famous golden orb on the steeple was 'for the celebration, not of devotional, but of convivial rites'.[16] By the summer of 1763, the growing antagonism between Wilkes and Dashwood had spilled over into the public arena. At a Quarter Sessions dinner in Aylesbury on 14 July 1763, Dashwood successfully proposed a loyal address to the throne in support of the Peace of Paris. Wilkes's protests were unavailing. After this public clash, he was definitely not welcome at Medmenham, and he never went there again.[17]

The loss of his friendship with Dashwood, regrettable though it was, did nothing to puncture Wilkes's belief that he was still in good odour with the Whig grandees, whose cause, he argued, apostates such as Dashwood had abandoned. More serious was the defection of William Pitt. In the aftermath of Wilkes's incarceration in the Tower of London, he had remained ominously silent. The Duke of Newcastle later commented with acuteness that 'he [Pitt] always had a backwardness, in what relates to Wilkes; except, it carries … some constitutional point'.[18] Pitt's attitude was gradually revealed in the Commons debates of November 1763. On the 15th, breaking his long silence, he drew a distinction between Wilkes as an individual and the constitutional and legal issues that he had brought to the political foreground; but his criticisms of Wilkes were so muted that one observer thought he seemed 'tacitly to favour him'. (Charles Townshend was less cautious, saying that he held his old Leiden acquaintance 'in abhorrence'.)[19]

---

[13] [Almon] *History of the Late Minority,* Wilkes's marginalia, pp. 407–409.

[14] The comment appeared as a footnote in a later edition of *The Fall of Mortimer* (*Wilkes Correspondence,* vol. 1, p. 75), not in the first edition published in March 1763.

[15] 'Have we not at the head of our finances, the *experienced,* the *eloquent,* the *able* Sir Francis Dashwood?' *North Briton,* 37, 12 February 1763.

[16] *St James's Chronicle,* 2–4 June 1763.

[17] *Grenville Papers,* vol. 2, pp. 76–77.

[18] BL Add. MSS 32954, fol. 123.

[19] Jeremy Black, *Pitt the Elder* (Cambridge and New York, 1992), p. 247; Bleackley, *Wilkes,* p. 129.

But on the 23rd, while vainly resisting the government's attempt to eliminate the protection of Parliamentary privilege for seditious libel, Pitt's rhetoric escalated dramatically. With 'affected piety', according to one hostile witness,[20] he rashly anticipated the judgment of the courts by branding Wilkes as 'an impious criminal, that sets at defiance his God, his King, and his country'.[21] For Wilkes, Pitt's venom smarted as much as the shot from Samuel Martin's pistol, and its effects were longer lasting. It was especially galling that libertine performances, which had helped to secure him a foothold in elite society, should now be flung back at him as a reason for his ejection from it. Yet Wilkes waited for three years before responding, reluctant to come to terms with the fact that his charismatic patron had rejected him with extreme malice.[22]

During his continental exile, Wilkes also resisted any notion that his plight was one of social ostracism. One of his initial concerns was that, irrespective of the reasons for his presence in the French capital, he should find favour with English grandees who happened to reside there or be passing through. Any gesture of condescension from one of their number was received with almost pathetic gratitude.[23] He fretted in particular about eliciting a stamp of social approval from Lord Hertford, the ambassador, and his son, Lord Beauchamp. 'As a private Nobleman, I should be Ambitious to merit and most fortunate to Obtain, his Friendship, as well as Lord Beauchamp's, from their Sterling Sense, great Intrinsic Worth, and what Sets off the Whole, their Amiable manners', Wilkes explained (his usual mastery of syntax temporarily deserting him). He would meet with a mixed response to his unflagging social ambition. To his delight and surprise, Hertford returned an early visit by Wilkes, but later, in June 1764 – after Wilkes had been tried *in absentia* for his offences – he offended Wilkes's amour-propre by neglecting to invite him to a dinner in honour of the king's birthday, held at the British Embassy and attended by seventy English guests 'of the first rank'. Wilkes consoled himself that the dinner must have been a 'dull' affair, with tedious conversation, followed by long hours spent playing the detestable card game of faro.[24]

Despite Hertford's snub, Wilkes was far from being a social outcast in Paris. He resumed his friendship there with a kindred spirit, Laurence Sterne, the libertine

---

[20] *An Enquiry into the Conduct of a Late Right Honourable Commoner*, 3rd impression (London, 1766), p. 24.

[21] Pitt quoted in Thomas, *Wilkes*, p. 44.

[22] Wilkes made no mention of Pitt in his 'Letter to the Electors of Aylesbury', *Wilkes Correspondence*, vol. 3, pp. 85–121, written in October 1764.

[23] Such as the Duke of Richmond. BL Add. MSS 30868, fols 207–08.

[24] BL Add. MSS 30867, fol. 249; Robin Eagles, *Francophilia in English Society, 1748–1815* (Basingstoke and New York, 2000), p. 72; *Wilkes Correspondence*, vol. 3, pp. 124–27.

clergyman, who was still revelling in the success of his novel *Tristram Shandy*, of which six of the eventual nine volumes had by then been published. In March 1764 Wilkes helped promote a typically eccentric sermon that Sterne delivered at the ambassador's chapel; a couple of weeks later, Wilkes reported, the two friends amused themselves in the company of 'two, lively, young, handsome actresses' at the home of Wilkes's landlord. Wilkes also found congenial company of a different kind at the salon of Baron d'Holbach, where he was lionised by the attendant *philosophes* for his bold stand in favour of liberty. Equally gratifying for Wilkes was his reception from some members of the French aristocracy, notably the rakish Louis François de Brancas, Comte de Lauraguais. Here would begin his enduring attachment to the French nobility, continued vicariously through his daughter Polly.[25]

The plaudits and pleasures of what he called 'this frivolous, giddy nation' made life in exile tolerable, while enhancing the cosmopolitan gloss to his social pretensions. But they did nothing to advance his cause at home. Here a larger danger than being reviled was being forgotten. To rectify that, he promised to 'feed the papers from time to time with gall and vinegar against the [Grenville] administration'.[26] His missives, though, had little impact in a political world preoccupied with other matters, including the emerging crisis with the American colonies. And when the issue of general warrants came before Parliament, the champions of liberty followed Pitt's lead in dissociating themselves from the person who had forced it into the public arena.[27] Wilkes was obliged to recognise that even the sainted Lord Temple had a political agenda that scarcely took his own into account. In May 1765 Temple was reconciled with his brother, Prime Minister George Grenville; later there were rumours that he was making overtures to Wilkes's enemies, Lord Sandwich and Lord Halifax. 'I see that every thing is offer'd up to the shrine of Stowe', Wilkes reflected bitterly.[28] In gloomy moments he imagined himself as 'an exile for life', supported less by aristocratic friends than by an aristocratic stoicism. When he arrived in Naples in the spring of 1765, the London press was confidently predicting that he would settle there permanently.[29]

The collapse of the Grenville government in June 1765 gave him grounds for hope, however. News of the event pried him from the arms of Corradini and

---

[25]   Arthur H. Cash, *Laurence Sterne: The Later Years* (London and New York, 1986) pp. 180–82; Bleackley, *Wilkes*, pp. 155–58.

[26]   Wilkes to Polly Wilkes, 3 March 1766, BL Add. MSS 30879, fol. 91; Wilkes to Cotes, 20 January 1764, BL Add. MSS 30868, fol. 25.

[27]   Thomas, *Wilkes*, pp. 50–56.

[28]   Wilkes to William Fitzherbert, 6 July 1766, Fitzherbert Papers, 0239M/F8255.

[29]   BL Add. MSS 30868, fol. 40; *St James's Chronicle*, 23–25 April 1765.

drew him back towards his mother country to await a favourable political tide. From Paris, he anxiously sought news about the incoming ministers. Fearful that Lord Bute was 'the breath of their nostrils', he threatened to 'lash them with scorpion rods' if they proved to be his enemy.[30] Yet the ministry's composition was ostensibly favourable. Headed by the 35-year-old Lord Rockingham, it included many of the Old Corps Whigs' younger adherents, including those who had previously expressed sympathy for Wilkes and his cause. The Duke of Grafton was a Secretary of State; George Onslow sat on the Treasury Board; and William Fitzherbert, a denizen of the Beefsteak Club, was a member of the Board of Trade. William Dowdeswell, a former Tory recently recruited to the party, was appointed Chancellor of the Exchequer; he had known Wilkes as a fellow student at Leiden and he retained an indulgent view of his friend's character in the wake of the *Essay on Woman* scandal.[31]

The Rockingham Whigs had not yet developed the conception of party that Edmund Burke would famously celebrate, in which the private friendship of public-spirited aristocrats constituted a basis for principled political conduct. Yet Wilkes had some basis for believing that he was in good standing with a Whig faction appreciative of his previous labours in the cause of liberty. Its agents sought to entice him into the Rockingham camp by pointing out the fickleness of other potential benefactors.[32] George Onslow, following his appointment to the Treasury, wrote him a fawning letter in which he praised Wilkes's 'amazing abilities', evidenced in his notes on Churchill's poems, which he had seen in manuscript form. Onslow singled out the satirical assault on the 'sc[oundre]l' William Warburton, thus all but declaring himself a partisan in Wilkes's cause in the *Essay on Woman* affair. But Onslow, while comprehensively avowing himself Wilkes's friend 'as a public and as a private man', was ominously silent on the crucial issue of how the ministry intended to serve its exiled ally.[33] On this point, Wilkes was emphatic: 'I ought at the entrance into power of the present gentlemen to have had a pardon under the great seal without my asking for it, and to have been indemify'd, as far as it cou'd be, for two years sufferings, and the cruel anxiety of near four.'[34] He went further in conversation with Richard

---

[30] BL Add. MSS 30868, fol. 201.

[31] Peter D.G. Thomas, *George III: King and Politicians, 1760–1770* (Manchester, 2002) p. 120; F.P. Lock, *Edmund Burke,* vol. 1 (*1730–1784*) (Oxford and New York, 1998), p. 280 note 70. Wilkes chose to ignore the fact that the administration included holdovers from the previous régime, including Charles Yorke and Lord Northington.

[32] Lauchlin Macleane to Wilkes, 4 January 1766, BL Add. MSS 30869, fols 6–7.

[33] *Wilkes Correspondence,* vol. 5, pp. 240–42. Humphrey Cotes had shown Onslow copies of the notes on Churchill's poems in manuscript form.

[34] Wilkes to Fitzherbert, 4 December 1765, Wilkes MSS 1, fol. 91a.

Burke, grandiosely invoking a principle of party solidarity to suggest that the Rockingham Whigs should not have accepted office without first having brought him back into the political fold.[35] Meanwhile he pressed what in his mind were practical solutions for redress. They included the revival of his request for the ambassadorship to Constantinople. As he explained to his brother Heaton, the posting would sustain him pending a general election, when he would be restored to the House of Commons and able to return to England with 'honour and dignity'. He also envisaged himself as governor of Jamaica, with his friend Lauchlin Macleane as his deputy.[36]

As various intermediaries tried to explain to Wilkes, it was impossible for the Rockingham Whigs to accede to his requests. Even had they been inclined to do so, the ministers would have run up against the implacable opposition of the king. As William Fitzherbert pointed out, a pardon – the essential first step in Wilkes's political rehabilitation – was a public act. Rockingham himself was not prepared to put the issue to the test, though he indicated that he was 'willing to do almost anything for [Wilkes] from his private Pocket, and to avow it to the K. or to any person'. Although the Rockinghamite legatees of Old Corps Whiggery were famously alert to encroachments of royal prerogative, their allegiance to the crown proved greater than to the person who had assailed it with 'personal invectives'.[37] In this respect they were closer to the mandarins of the party, such as the Duke of Newcastle, than Wilkes was prepared to recognise. The most that the ministry could do for Wilkes was to laud his political principles, avow friendly intentions, and offer him a pension of £1,000 a year to be paid out of the salaries of government ministers. Wilkes immediately recognised that he was being induced to stay away, not encouraged to return. He haughtily rejected the proffered pension as 'precarious, eleemosynary, and clandestine'. Financial necessity soon prevailed over honour, and though he later denied it, Wilkes took the ministers' money, but without giving up his larger claims. These he pressed in person when he made a secret visit to London in May 1766 in defiance of his outlawry. In addition to a pardon, he demanded a financial settlement that was open, honourable and secure, namely £5,000 in cash and an annual sinecure of £1,500 on the Irish civil list. Rockingham refused to treat with him in person, leaving that vexing task to a group of his junior colleagues. Parrying Wilkes's demands, they pacified him with vague assurances of future relief and enhanced

---

[35]   Richard Burke to Fitzherbert, Paris, 8 December 1765, Fitzherbert Papers, 02389M/ F8248.

[36]   Wilkes MSS 1, fols 88, 91a.

[37]   Fitzherbert to Wilkes, 3 January 1766, BL Add. MSS 30869, fol. 2; Edmund Burke to Richard Burke, *ante* 14 January 1766, *Burke Correspondence*, vol. 1, p. 231; Lauchlin Macleane to Wilkes, 4 January 1766, BL Add. MSS 30879, fol. 6.

financial support. Wilfully blind to the fact that he was being fobbed off, Wilkes seized on some friendly comments by Edmund Burke, then Lord Rockingham's private secretary, to convince himself that plans were afoot to restore him to the political fold. On his return to Paris, he wrote to Burke, avowing himself 'your fellow labourer' and expressing confidence that he would shortly be returning to England as a free citizen; Burke was non-committal in response.[38]

Shortly after Wilkes's return to Paris, the Rockinghams were dismissed. Wilkes's disappointment was short lived, however, because the new ministry had the Duke of Grafton as first lord of the treasury.[39] (At first, Wilkes's joy was not diminished by the fact that William Pitt, now ennobled as the Earl of Chatham, was the administration's nominal head.) Grafton was one of the 'spirited, young nobles' in whom the authors of the *North Briton* had invested such high hopes. Along with other Whig cadets, he had apparently shown his colours by seeking access to Wilkes during his imprisonment in the Tower of London. According to Grafton's later account, however, his gesture was wrongly construed as a ringing endorsement of the prisoner's conduct. Rather it was prompted by the need to ascertain 'the fact' of Wilkes's 'very oppressive and unjustifiable confinement' and 'to hear from [Wilkes] himself his own story and defence'. He had balked at standing bail for the prisoner, despite Wilkes's personal plea for support from liberty's 'great protector'. 'I must ... have trod very warily on ground that seemed to come any ways under the denomination of an insult on the Crown', Grafton explained. But Wilkes and Churchill were blind to Grafton's caution. Churchill continued to praise him in his poetry and left him a ring in his will.[40] Wilkes was convinced that with Grafton in high office, he would finally have redress. When, after three months, he had heard nothing but silence, he decided to press matters with another secret visit to England, having been assured, he said, by Grafton's brother that the duke was 'extremely desirous' to do him justice.[41]

On his arrival in London, Wilkes contacted Grafton through William Fitzherbert and then directly through a letter, dated 1 November, in which he asked Grafton – whom he praised for his 'noble manner of thinking' – to intercede with George III to secure him a pardon.[42] According to Grafton's loftily vague recollection, he showed the letter to the king, who offered no comment, and then to Chatham, who 'remarked on the awkwardness of the business, with which it was so difficult

---

[38] Paul Langford, *The First Rockingham Administration, 1765–1766* (London, 1973), pp. 218–19; Thomas, *Wilkes*, pp. 63–64.

[39] Thomas, *Wilkes*, p. 64.

[40] *Autobiography and Political Correspondence of Augustus Henry, Third Duke of Grafton*, ed. William R. Anson (London, 1898), pp. 190–92; Wilkes to Grafton, 3 May 1763, BL Add. MSS 30867, fol. 205; *Poetical Works of Charles Churchill*, pp. xx, 414, 553.

[41] Wilkes to Temple, 1 February 1767, BL Add. MSS 42085, fol. 3.

[42] Ibid. 30869, fol. 79.

to meddle', before advising Grafton to ignore Wilkes's request. Soon afterwards, Grafton explained, 'from the hurry of weighty business, the concerns of Mr. Wilkes engaged but little the attention of Ministry, or indeed of the Court'. In answer to entreaties from Wilkes's friends that he should intercede for a pardon, Grafton 'constantly replied' that he thought himself 'not yet equal to the business' and that 'the weight of Lord Chatham's name could alone effect it'.[43]

Grafton's dismissive attitude infuriated Wilkes. Returning to Paris, he made sure that his letter of 1 November was published in the London press,[44] and he set about composing a pamphlet, *A Letter to His Grace, the Duke of Grafton*, which would appear in several widely read versions over the coming months. It was a curious document in the literature of emergent radicalism. In it, Wilkes laid claim to the status of political martyr with a compelling account of his persecutions. He did not, however, challenge the personal nature of elite politics, but rather his exclusion from them, appealing for public sympathy over what he characterised as violations of the canons of private friendship.

He related that in response to his enquiry via Fitzherbert, he was told, '*Mr. Wilkes must write to Lord Chatham*', and that he received the same verbal message in reply to his letter of 1 November, with this addition: '*I* [Grafton] *do nothing without Lord Chatham*'. Wilkes affected more sorrow than anger towards the duke. Declaring that 'every principle of honour, both public and private' forbade him from asking a favour from the man who had traduced him, he expressed 'astonishment' that Grafton, 'a nobleman of parts and discernment', should, for his part, retain his 'infatuation' with Chatham.[45]

Wilkes's insistence that he had been given grounds for regarding Grafton as 'his real and sincere friend' launched a furious partisan inquiry into the nature of their connection. The dispute intensified when Grafton became the head of the ministry that presided over the renewal of Wilkes's persecutions in 1768. For his part, Grafton acknowledged only a slight acquaintanceship, protesting that he had never spent time alone with Wilkes, a disclaimer that was probably true but which Grafton's detractors vigorously disputed.[46] 'The conversation of Mr. Wilkes was … your delight, his intimacy was your pride', insisted one Wilkite scribe. Another creatively attributed Grafton's betrayal of friendship to his Stuart ancestry. *Junius* joined the argument on Wilkes's side. His first letter to the press blasted Grafton for his treatment of Wilkes. 'Other Men have been abandoned by their Friends; Mr. Wilkes alone is oppressed by them', *Junius* wrote, while

---

[43]   *Autobiography of Duke of Grafton*, p. 193.

[44]   *St James's Chronicle*, 2 December 1766.

[45]   *A Letter to His Grace, The Duke of Grafton, First Commissioner of His Majesty's Treasury* (1767), pp. 4–5.

[46]   Ibid., p. 3; *Autobiography of Duke of Grafton*, p. 189.

accusing Grafton of pursuing Wilkes 'to destruction'. In a subsequent letter, he reminded Grafton that 'you have continued your connexion with Mr. Wilkes long after he had been convicted of those crimes, which you have long since taken pains to represent in the blackest colours of blasphemy and treason'. He added a harsh reflection on Grafton's character: 'For my own part, my Lord, I am proud to affirm, that, if I had been weak enough to form such a friendship, I would never have been base enough to betray it.'[47]

Wilkes let others continue the attack on Grafton. In his own open letter to that nobleman, his principal target was Chatham. He lambasted his former patron for violating the canons of friendship:

> I believe that the flinty heart of *Lord Chatham* has known the sweets of private friendship, and the fine feelings of humanity, as little as even Lord Mansfield. They are both form'd to be admir'd not belov'd. A proud, insolent, overbearing, ambitious man is always full of the ideas of his own importance, and vainly imagines himself superior to the equality necessary among real friends, in all the moments of true enjoyment. Friendship is too pure a pleasure for a mind canker'd with ambition, or the lust of power and grandeur … I have had as warm and express declarations of regard as cou'd be made by this marble-hearted friend, and *Mr. Pitt* had no doubt his views in even feeding me with flattery from time to time; on occasions too where candour and indulgence were all I cou'd claim.

Wilkes went on to charge Chatham with egregious hypocrisy for condemning him as a blasphemer:

> He may remember the compliments he paid me on two certain poems in the year 1754. If I were to take the declarations made by himself and the late *Mr Potter à la lettre*, they were more charm'd with those verses after the ninety ninth reading than after the first …
> I will now submit … if there was not something peculiarly base and perfidious in *Mr. Pitt's* calling me a *blasphemer of my God* for those very verses, at a time when I was absent, and dangerously ill from an affair of honour. The charge too he knew was false, for the whole ridicule of those two pieces was confined to certain mysteries, which formerly the *unplac'd and unpension'd Mr. Pitt* did not think himself oblig'd even to affect to believe.[48]

In attacking Chatham, Wilkes was taking a small step towards embracing the kind of popular, metropolitan support that 'the great commoner' himself had

---

[47] *A First Letter to the Duke of Grafton* (London, 1770), p. 9; ANTI-BRIBE DENTATUS, *Bingley's Journal*, 29 December 1770; *The Letters of Junius*, ed. John Cannon (Oxford, 1978), pp. 60–61, 455.

[48] *Letter to His Grace, the Duke of Grafton*, pp. 8–10.

enjoyed before his baffling decision to accept a peerage tarnished his credentials as a patriot. ('He should be prouder to be an alderman than a peer', Pitt had told the Commons in 1758.[49]) Wilkes relished reports that his 'firmness' in refusing to knuckle under to Chatham was applauded in the City.[50] Perhaps a seed had been sown for his emergence as a London politician. Yet Wilkes's intention at this stage was not to distance himself from the Whig grandees. For a while, he tried to convince himself that the letter to Grafton had actually enhanced his reputation with the 'staunch whigs', including Lord Rockingham and his friends.[51] The fact that they continued to give him money probably supported this misapprehension.

Wilkes miscalculated in thinking that the effect of the *Letter to … Grafton* would work towards the political isolation of Chatham rather than his own. Those loyal to both Grafton and Chatham were dismayed by its contents. They included George Onslow, who now withdrew his financial support for Wilkes and spent much of the rest of his life trying to live down his embarrassment at their former friendship. His alarm at the mob activity inspired by Wilkes's return to public life in 1768 surpassed that of his uncle, the Duke of Newcastle. Possibly in an attempt at redemption, Onslow would introduce the motion in April 1769 that deprived Wilkes of his seat as the elected member for Middlesex and installed Luttrell in his place.[52]

Wilkes had better grounds for thinking that Lord Temple would approve of his denunciation of Chatham, because Temple had recently had a dramatic falling-out with his brother-in-law, which from Wilkes's perspective partly compensated for Temple's earlier reconciliation with his brother, George Grenville. But although Temple reportedly approved of Wilkes's refusal to approach Chatham for a pardon, he was dismayed by Wilkes's public attack on Chatham in the *Letter to … Grafton*. In May 1767, relations between Temple and Wilkes took a further turn for the worse when Wilkes published the long letter that he had written to Temple in the wake of the Talbot duel in which he mocked his opponent while congratulating himself on his own courage and coolness.[53] Its publication caused a minor sensation; as a result Talbot was 'consigned to eternal ridicule', according

---

[49] Pitt quoted in Paul Langford, *Public Life and the Propertied Englishman, 1689–1798* (Oxford and New York, 1991), p. 516.

[50] Wilkes MSS 1, fol. 97.

[51] Wilkes to William Fitzherbert, 24 July 1767, Fitzherbert Papers, 0239M/F8260.

[52] Heaton Wilkes to Wilkes, 11 May 1767, BL Add. MSS 30869, fol. 121; Onslow to Newcastle, 27 April 1768, BL Add. MSS 32989, fols 396–97; *Letters of Junius*, pp. 603–04; Thomas, *Wilkes*, pp. 101–02.

[53] The letter was first published in *St James's Chronicle*, 14–17 May 1767, and was widely reprinted after that.

to one observer.[54] Outraged by the letter, Talbot rather perversely demanded immediate satisfaction from its recipient, the physically frail Temple, and only swift intervention by their fellow peers prevented a sword fight. Provoking conflict between members of the peerage proved to be a counterproductive tactic for garnering their support. Heaton Wilkes reckoned that the letter's publication caused 'a great deal of Harm' to John's connection with Temple, who, much embarrassed by the whole affair, increasingly distanced himself from his troublesome client.[55] In the weeks and months that followed, Heaton sent progressively ominous accounts of Temple's state of mind. In July he was reportedly 'Spiritless & Discontented', determined 'to wash [his] hands of all pecuniary Transactions' with John. By September, Heaton was dismissing Temple as just another 'Scoundrell Lord'. In October, Temple was saying things about Wilkes that his brother could 'neither forget, not forgive'.[56]

His support from former friends and patrons dissipating, Wilkes for the first time began to take a serious interest in mobilising public support in London. In 1763, he had inspired exuberant displays of popular feeling in the capital, beginning with his dramatic appearances before the Court of Common Pleas in May and culminating on 3 December, when a crowd prevented the burning of *North Briton* no. 45 by the public hangman, a riot implicitly endorsed by London's Common Council.[57] But Wilkes, at the time, seemed largely indifferent to the benefits of such activity, except to the extent that it enhanced his standing with the dwindling band of hot-blooded Whig politicos, for whom mob activity was an acceptable ancillary to Parliamentary opposition. At the outset of his exile, he had expressed contempt for 'the fickleness of the people' and vowed never to trust his 'security and indemnity to them'. As late as May 1767, he described 'the public' as 'too corrupt, too selfish, too unfeeling' to relieve and vindicate him; that could only come from 'some private advantages' he still enjoyed.[58] Yet even as he wrote this, he had already started exploring the daring scheme of offering himself as a Parliamentary candidate for the City of London in the 1768 general election. He pursued the project in the face of gloomy assessments of his prospects from City politicians like Arthur Beardmore, who was concerned that Wilkes would make himself a 'contemptible figure'.[59] Heaton Wilkes was even

[54]   N. William Wraxall, *Historical Memoirs of My Own Time*, ed. Richard Askham (London, 1904), p. 269.

[55]   BL Add. MSS 30869, fol. 125.

[56]   Ibid., fols 140, 155, 164.

[57]   Thomas, *Wilkes*, pp. 31–32, 45.

[58]   Wilkes to Cotes, 20 January 1764, BL Add. MSS 30868, fol. 25; Wilkes to Temple, 11 May 1767, BL Add. MSS 42085, fol. 21.

[59]   BL Add. MSS 30869, fol. 148.

more discouraging. He supported his brother's desire to re-enter Parliament as a way of contesting his outlawry, but the plan for the City was 'Moon Shine'. 'Can you Flatter yourself with an absent Patriot being able to satisfy Fellows (who are longing for their Septennial Ale ...) with a recital of past Deeds[?]', he asked.[60] John insisted, however, that the prospect of his candidature was 'relish'd' in the City and that 'several independent merchants take it up warmly'. He began to identify with patriot heroes such as Admiral Edward Vernon, the hammer of Spain at the beginning the War of the Austrian Succession, who in 1741 had parlayed his enormous popularity into electoral success.[61]

There was at the same time a characteristically flippant opportunism about Wilkes's decision, consistent with his enduring belief that the greatest chapter in the book of life was 'the chapter of accidents'. He explained to the sceptical Heaton: 'The making the experiment will cost nothing, and the success wou'd retrieve my affairs.' It might force the ministry into coming to terms, because they dreaded 'a confusion in the capital'.[62] But Wilkes's decision to engage in the volatile world of London politics acquired a momentum that took him beyond his initial goals and along some unfamiliar paths. Popular attitudes in the capital and its civic institutions tended to be not only anti-ministerial, but anti-aristocratic as well, hence the dismay at Pitt's acceptance of a peerage. They involved an enduring suspicion of the cronyism of the Whig grandees, even those in opposition; until the mid-1750s, this social and political truculence often expressed itself as Tory allegiance. So as Wilkes engaged with the world of London politics, he would be obliged to conceal his private attachments to the beau monde under some robustly anti-aristocratic rhetoric. Meanwhile the extra-Parliamentary movement over which he presided adopted the symbols – in which 'true blue' was prominent – of its populist, Tory ancestry, even as its polemic recalled the belligerent language of seventeenth-century radical Whiggism. Contemporaries marvelled at Tory, High Church 'mobbers' who had now become 'absolutely Staunch for Wilkes and Liberty'.[63]

---

[60] Ibid., fols 140, 152.

[61] Wilkes MSS 2, fol. 29; BL Add. MSS 30869, fol. 154; Kathleen Wilson, *The Sense of the People: Politics, Culture and Imperialism in England, 1715–1785* (Cambridge and New York, 1995) pp. 150–51.

[62] BL Add. MSS 30868, fol. 201; Wilkes to Heaton Wilkes, 7 September 1767, Wilkes MSS 2, fol. 29.

[63] Linda Colley, 'Eighteenth-Century English Radicalism before Wilkes', *Transactions of the Royal Historical Society*, 5th Series, 31 (1981): 1–19; Wilson, *Sense of the People*, pp. 214–18; *Dialogue Between the Two Giants at Guildhall, Humbly Addressed to John Wilkes* (London, 1768), p. 5.

'Damned Aristocracy'

John Wilkes's career in London politics was formally launched on 10 March 1768, when he was admitted as a liveried freeman of the Worshipful Company of Joiners.[64] A few days later, he addressed his fellow liverymen – the electors of the City of London – in whose hands he had chosen to place his destiny: 'I stand here, Gentlemen, a private Man, unconnected with the Great, and unsupported by any Party. I have no Support but you: I wish no other Support: I can have none more certain, none more honourable.'[65] His private sentiments at the time were rather less flattering towards his would-be constituents. On 18 March, he wrote archly to Jean-Baptiste Suard: 'This ought to be a short letter … because it will be a dull one of course, dated from the city regions. I am now in the midst of my brother Joiners, Carpenters, soap-boilers, distillers, &c, &c and we are polling away at a great rate … It wou'd amuse you to see such a sett of voters.'[66] Wilkes's disdain for the City electors was compounded by the fact that he was languishing at the foot of the poll and remained there throughout the electoral contest. Ten days later his attitude had changed dramatically, because by then, amid scenes of popular jubilation, he had secured election for Middlesex. He wrote in triumph to Suard:

> I am now the first commoner in England, representing the first county. My friends lost me the city, but I have gain'd the county, and will now keep it for life.
>
> I, out-law'd, exil'd, and proscrib'd, am return'd member of Parliament for this first County. All is finish'd to-day. What a spirited nation is this! How infinite are my obligations to them![67]

Wilkes understood with a clarity that eluded his opponents and even some of his allies that the Middlesex freeholders had granted him an unparalleled opportunity to confront the existing political order, a situation unaffected by his subsequent imprisonment. His confidence was enhanced when John Glynn, his lawyer and chief adviser, was returned in a by-election as his fellow Middlesex MP. Wilkes had now moved well beyond merely seeking a bargaining chip with which to deal with government. In March 1770 he declared: 'I am determined never to have any connection with this *court,* nor with any minister'; but that resolution

---

[64] William Purdie Treloar, *Wilkes and the City* (London, 1917) p. 63.

[65] *St James's Chronicle,* 15–17 March 1768.

[66] Wilkes MSS 4, fol. 13.

[67] 29 March 1768, John Wild Autograph Collection, vol. 38, fol. 106, Princeton University Library. Wilkes's characterisation of Middlesex as 'the first county' matched contemporary opinion. Langford, *Public Life,* p. 188.

had long been in effect. In November 1768, he rejected an offer from the Duke of Grafton, delivered through intermediaries, that the ministry would secure his release from prison and leave him in peace if he made 'some small submission' to the king and withdrew his planned petition to the House of Commons for the redress of his grievances.[68] Rumours of attempted bribery followed (Fig. 5.1). While the problem of how to deal with his petition was preoccupying the House, he taunted the ministry by publishing an inflammatory preface to a letter from Lord Weymouth, a Secretary of State, to the Lambeth magistrates, which contended that the government had plotted the 'horrid massacre' of Wilkes supporters in St George's Fields on 10 May 1768. That provocation led in fairly short order to his expulsion from the House of Commons.[69] But Parliament's decision in April 1769 to ignore the reiterated verdicts of the Middlesex voters and declare Henry Luttrell as MP for the county only stiffened his resolve. 'I look upon the violence of the House of Commons in favour of Luttrell as one of the luckiest circumstances of my life', he wrote.[70]

He was now comparing himself to Oliver Cromwell, spurning the necessity of kow-towing to the peerage. 'I will make my men, and give them importance', he declared, echoing Cromwell's celebrated egalitarianism.[71] His attitude derived from a reassessment of where power in the nation ultimately resided:

> I have the public more and more my friends, but the aristocracy hate me, and with reason. I stand upon the foundation of the people, whom I shew their strength upon every occasion. I have great and essential points to carry from them, and they are content to give me the lead for that purpose. All the independent people I have; the nobility, and the overgrown gentry, who hope to be ennobled, are against me, almost to a man, but in a government like our's, and a nation of merchants and traders, the people have the greatest weight.[72]

He applied a similar class analysis to City politics when, from prison, he successfully sought election as alderman for the ward of Farringdon Without. A Wilkite broadside reassured the voters that he would have no truck with those City aldermen, such as Thomas Harley, who were tied to the court interest: 'Though an Alderman, he will still consider himself as your Brother Freeman; and

---

[68] Thomas, *Wilkes,* pp. 87–91; Wilkes to Jean-Baptiste Suard, 2 March 1770, Wilkes MSS 3, fol. 30.

[69] Thomas, *Wilkes,* pp. 92–99.

[70] Wilkes to Jean-Baptiste Suard, 20 June 1769, Wilkes MSS 3, fol. 23.

[71] Ibid.

[72] Wilkes to Jean-Baptiste Suard, 28 August 1768, John Wild Autograph Collection, vol. 38, fol. 107, Princeton University Library.

Figure 5.1 *The Political Coal Heavers* (1769). The Duke of Grafton, seated, addresses John Wilkes: 'Would you be quiet, Mr. W— I could help you to a little Scotch Cole'. Wilkes, shaking an empty purse, replies, 'I had rather be frozen to Death than purchase warmth by my Country's Ruin'. Etching. By permission of the Guildhall Library, London.

tho' a Member of your UPPER HOUSE, he will scorn to conduct himself as a CITY LORD. He abhors the Idea of an ARISTOCRACY.' After his release from prison, he reported proudly on his first ward meeting: 'The applause was prodigious. I have not yet been at any place of public diversion, nor visited a single lord'.[73]

Wilkes's publicly militant disenchantment with the nobility converged in a potent mixture with a heightened resentment of aristocratic power and privilege. Some of the most powerful expressions of grievance were delivered by Alderman William Beckford, a fabulously wealthy sugar planter and London MP, who was for many years William Pitt's henchman in the City of London. In 1761, while stressing the importance of 'the middling people', Beckford launched the following salvo in the House of Commons: 'The scum is as mean as the dregs, and as to your nobility, about 200 men of quality, what are they to the body of the nation? Why, Sir, they are subalterns ... They receive more from the public than they pay to it.'[74] Such attitudes found renewed expression on the eve of the general election of 1768. John Almon's *Political Register,* which persistently sought to link the cause of Wilkes with larger issues of political reform, echoed Beckford's class antagonism:

> The power of the *grandees* is ... become more formidable than ever. Their numbers, their privileges, their court emoluments, their *influence* in *elections,* their weight in the law, the army, the navy, the church, and the public offices, are all to an unexampled degree increased ... *Lords* are naturally drawn to join with the court against the interests of the people ... What is the value of the ridiculous privileges of a few great men, generally speaking the scum of the people, to the inestimable liberties of twelve millions of subjects.[75]

Wilkes's supporters credited him with disturbing this lordly complacency in some unprecedented ways. One proclaimed: 'Though pension'd peers grow frantic at the name, / Thy cause, and Liberty's, are still the same.'[76] Yet no one was predicting the imminent demise of aristocracy. Indeed, while John Almon articulated the depth of hostility towards the grandees, he also conceded their growing strength in a way that, stripped of its hostile tone, is generally supported in modern scholarship.[77] The belligerence of Wilkes's own rhetoric is also in

---

[73] 'To the Worthy Inhabitants of the Ward of FARRINGDON WITHOUT'. City Elections, 1768–96 [A Broadside Collection], An. 5.4. No. 15, page 7, Guildhall Library; Wilkes to Jean-Baptiste Suard, 1 May 1770, Wilkes MSS 3, fol. 34.

[74]   Quoted in Ian R. Christie, *Wilkes, Wyvill and Reform: The Parliamentary Reform Movement in British Politics, 1760–1785* (London and New York, 1962), p. 9.

[75] Quoted in ibid., p. 20.

[76] *English Liberty,* p. vii.

[77] For instance, Colley, 'Eighteenth-Century English Radicalism before Wilkes', p. 18.

some ways deceptive. Despite the bombast, his innovative, yet circumscribed, goal was to constitute himself and his followers as an independent force – the civilian equivalent of Cromwell's regiment of horse – who could treat with aristocratic factions on a basis of equality, no longer as humble subalterns of lordly authority, thus challenging what Kathleen Wilson aptly calls 'the culture of patrician entitlement'.[78] Wilkes's comments, in the wake of the Duke of Grafton's resignation as prime minister at the end of January 1770, need to be understood in that context:

> His [Grafton's] retreat has spirited our political hounds, and the scent of the Middlesex election is strong in their nostrils. At present the Rockingham, Grenville, and Shelburne packs are united, and hunt well, but I doubt their success, nor indeed do I wish it on their terms, for I foresee a damned aristocracy, which Wilkes must at all events destroy, or he will be annihilated. But mark ... the political events of this summer, and you will find what a firm support I have in the people, and how truly I follow *their* interests.[79]

The word 'damned' in 'damned aristocracy' was meant as an epithet, not as a predictor of the aristocracy's imminent political demise. What is more remarkable about Wilkes's comments is that he now saw as inimical to his interests the kind of unity among the aristocratic leaders of the Whig opposition he had once so strenuously promoted in the pages of the *North Briton*. The irony was that such unity now appeared possible precisely because of his exclusion from Parliament. That the rights of electors had been violated in the case of Middlesex was a proposition that all members of the opposition could support, whatever their differences over questions of fundamental political reform. They had given voice to their newfound sense of unity at a dinner held on 9 May 1769 at London's Thatched House Tavern, attended by 72 MPs. One of the toasts was: 'May all personal, party, and national distinctions be lost in the publick good!'[80] In the months that followed, opposition leaders organised scores of petitions to the crown from boroughs and counties across the kingdom, protesting the violation of the Middlesex electors' rights. The content of these petitions reflected the different agendas of their promoters, but their cumulative effect was to enhance, at least temporarily, a sense of unity among the Parliamentary opposition in ways that aroused Wilkes's suspicion.[81]

---

[78] *Sense of the People*, p. 231.

[79] Wilkes to Jean-Baptiste Suard, 2 March 1770, Wilkes MSS 3, fol. 30.

[80] John Brooke, *The Chatham Administration, 1766–1768* (London and New York, 1956), p. 225.

[81] On the petitioning campaign, see Lucy S. Sutherland, *The City of London and the Opposition to Government, 1768–1774: A Study in the Rise of Metropolitan Radicalism* (London, 1959), pp. 25–33, and George Rudé, *Wilkes and Liberty: A Social Study of 1763 to 1774* (Oxford, 1962), pp. 105–48.

Wilkes was justified, however, in his doubts that such unity could be sustained among the opposition parties; they quickly reverted to their squabbling habits.[82] A fractured Parliamentary opposition meant that Wilkes and his supporters could continue to dominate public attention. In September 1770, Edmund Burke gloomily reported to Lord Rockingham that the ministers 'respect and fear that wretched Knot beyond anything that you can readily imagine, and far more than any part or than all the other parts of the opposition'.[83] It had not been Wilkes's original intention to dissociate himself entirely from the individual 'packs' of opposition, such as the Rockinghams. But nor was he prepared to make special efforts to retain connections with the 'damned aristocracy' if it meant compromising his hard-won support in the capital. He understood full well that opposition leaders entered a political snake-pit when they sought popularity in the City. What was hard-won there could be easily lost, as even Lord Chatham discovered, and Wilkes was determined not to be tainted by association.

Any possibility that Wilkes might revive his association with the Grenvilles was probably doomed from the outset. Shortly after his return from exile, Wilkes had sought a meeting with Temple, but Temple avoided any face-to-face dealings with Wilkes until he visited him in King's Bench Prison at the end of April 1768. Temple still expressed some sympathy for his former client: 'he thought his persecutions had been great, & tho' his faults were enormous, he had suffered abundantly'; he even provided him with a freehold estate in Middlesex so that he could qualify for election there; but his reference to Wilkes's 'profligate or exploded Character' did not augur well for any recovery of friendship.[84] That in any event was precluded by the fact that Temple was now firmly in the same political camp as his brother George Grenville, whose animus towards Wilkes had not mellowed with the years. Grenville was appalled by the mob activity that followed Wilkes's imprisonment, and he applauded the then Lord Mayor, Thomas Harley, for personally apprehending rioters. Later he surprised the House of Commons by opposing Wilkes's expulsion from Parliament, but his grounds for doing so were pragmatic and scarcely flattering to Wilkes, whose character he roundly condemned. Wilkes was so affronted when he saw a printed version of Grenville's speech that he responded anonymously with a rancorous pamphlet of his own in which he expounded on the theme of Grenville's 'low cunning'. It was a blast, Wilkes explained to Jean-Baptiste Suard, 'against an odious fellow'.

---

[82]   John Brewer, *Party Ideology and Popular Politics at the Accession of George III* (Cambridge and New York, 1976) p. 60.

[83]   *Burke Correspondence*, vol. 2, p. 157.

[84]   Temple to Wilkes, 28 April 1768, *Grenville Papers*, vol. 4, p. 279; James West to Newcastle, 24 April 1768, BL Add. MSS 32989, fol. 377; Bleackley, *Wilkes*, p. 189.

The *Gentleman's Magazine* said that the tract expressed 'a degree of malignity not common even in party disputes'. Its publication was especially vexing for Temple because it contained personal information presumably obtained at a time when he and Wilkes were intimate. Not surprisingly, Temple had pleaded with Wilkes not to publish; after Wilkes went ahead and did so, there was scarcely any contact between the two men ever again.[85]

The prospects for reciprocal support between Wilkes and the Rockingham faction – which had ambitions to raise its profile in metropolitan politics – were brighter and longer lasting, partly because there was no legacy of bad blood to overcome. For the time being, Wilkes continued to regard Edmund Burke, the emerging luminary of his party, as a friend. And when Wilkes was assessing his chances of becoming a City MP, he had sought the counsel of another loyal follower of Rockingham, Sir William Baker, a prominent London merchant. Wilkes was apparently undismayed when the Rockinghams supported William Beauchamp Proctor – a man variously described as an independent and as a courtier – against John Glynn in the Middlesex by-election of July 1768. When in June 1770 the London livery chose two Rockingham supporters (one of them Sir William Baker's son) as London's sheriffs, Wilkes declared: 'Every thing goes on according to my most sanguine wishes.' He likewise applauded the livery's choice of the Rockinghamite Barlow Trecothick to succeed the recently deceased William Beckford as Lord Mayor.[86] Such tactical alliances, however, papered over some evident differences. As Burke promoted the Yorkshire petition in October 1769, he expressed concern that some 'cast a stain of prophaneness upon our Conduct, from our supposed Patronage of Wilkes'. He later mused that a party like his own, which courted 'the sober, large-acred part of the Nation', was ill equipped to capture and retain support in the metropolis. Sheriff William Baker shared his pessimism. Meanwhile, Trecothick's brief mayoralty was foundering, in part over his reluctance to resist the operations of naval press gangs in the City – a clumsy and much-resented intrusion of state authority opposed by popular politicians like Alderman John Wilkes – during the crisis with Spain over the Falkland Islands.[87]

---

85   Thomas, *Wilkes*, pp. 84, 97; *Burke Correspondence*, vol. 2, p. 117; [John Wilkes] *A Letter to the Right Honourable George Grenville, occasioned by … the Speech he made in the House of Commons on the Motion for Expelling Mr. Wilkes* (London, 1769), p. 14; Wilkes to Suard, 18 November 1769, Wilkes MSS 3, fol. 25; *Gentleman's Magazine* (1769): 599.

86   Wilkes to Heaton Wilkes, 28 September 1767, Wilkes MSS 2, fol. 32; Wilkes to Polly Wilkes, 26 June 1770, and 29 June 1776, BL Add. MSS 30879, fols 153 and 156.

87   *Burke Correspondence*, vol. 2, pp. 96, 174–75; Baker to W. Talbot, 13 September 1770, William Baker MSS, C9/1, Hertfordshire Record Office, Hertford; John Norris, *Shelburne and Reform* (London and New York, 1963), p. 77; Elofson, pp. 106–07.

Behind these squabbles was a profound ideological divide, vented in Burke's *Thoughts on the Cause of the Present Discontents* and in the radical response to his prescriptions. First published in April 1770, Burke's tract urged a Whig reunion led by the Rockinghams to counter what he identified as the pernicious influence of the court. His paeans to the Whig nobility, and his refusal to countenance Parliamentary reform and greater control of MPs by their constituents – measures supported by the City radicals – brought a stinging rebuke from Catharine Macaulay, who claimed to see 'the corrupt principles of self-interest' behind Burke's advocacy. Her critique of the aristocracy was one of the most forceful between the age of Oliver Cromwell and that of Thomas Paine. Still supporting Rockinghamite candidates in the City's midsummer elections, Wilkes was slow to recognise the exchange between Burke and Macaulay as a defining moment in the emergence of radical politics. But Macaulay's language and prescriptions, along with those of the reformer James Burgh, would become his own. In his Parliamentary speech of 21 March 1776 in favour of thoroughgoing political reform, Wilkes declared: 'The disfranchising of the mean, venal, and dependent boroughs would be laying the axe to the root of corruption and treasury influence, as well as *aristocratical tyranny*.'[88]

Subsequently, on some specific issues, such as opposition to the government's American policy and enlightened support for Catholic relief, Wilkes would co-operate with the Rockinghams and their most illustrious recruit, Charles James Fox. And he applauded when Lord Rockingham replaced Lord North as prime minister in 1782. But there was a legacy of suspicion, which should have made it no surprise, regardless of the indignation of Foxite Whigs, when Wilkes attacked the Fox–North coalition of 1783 and then threw his support to the government of William Pitt the Younger, one personally backed by George III, which replaced it. Pitt's nominal support for Parliamentary reform was reassuring to Wilkes. But more importantly, Wilkes's objections to the ambitions of Whig aristocracy now overshadowed any fears of monarchical tyranny. Polly Wilkes's attitudes mirrored his own. From Paris in 1789, she anxiously followed the course of the Regency Crisis, desperately hoping that the king would recover his sanity in time to avert a Whig coup d'état.[89]

---

[88]   Elofson, pp. 103–04; Catharine Macaulay, *Observations on a Pamphlet, Entitled Thoughts on the Cause of the Present Discontents* (1770); *Wilkes Speeches*, p. 68.

[89]   John Sainsbury, *Disaffected Patriots: London Supporters of Revolutionary America, 1769–1782* (Kingston and Montreal, 1987), pp. 144–61; Wilkes to Rockingham, 2 April 1782, BL Add. MSS 30872, fol. 190; Polly Wilkes to Wilkes, 7 January 1789, Wilkes Letters, Add. 8781/1, Cambridge University Library. For a persuasive analysis of the continuities of Wilkes's political conduct from the early 1770s onwards, see Thomas, *Wilkes*, ch. 11.

Although, over the long haul, it was Wilkes's shifting relationship with the Rockingham and Foxite Whigs that best charted his career from Whig acolyte to City radical to Pittite monarchist, in the hectic period from 1769 to 1772 it was his dealings with the Shelburne 'pack' that riveted public attention. Lord Shelburne, who carried a reputation for duplicity, had entered public life as a follower of Bute, but he switched his allegiance to Chatham and followed his leader into opposition when Chatham finally resigned his government post in October 1768. The reform-minded Shelburne was ambitious to rekindle the kind of support that Chatham had once enjoyed in London. Part of that effort involved refurbishing the tarnished image of Chatham himself, who according to a Wilkite writer had long since 'dwindled into a titled lunatic'. By the summer of 1769 Chatham had returned to an active political role, even re-establishing cordial links with his brothers-in-law, George Grenville and Lord Temple. In November, his profile was boosted by the election of his ally, William Beckford, to a second term as Lord Mayor of London. Beckford's prestige was so great that even Wilkes was obliged to defer to it. It reached a peak in May 1770 when the story circulated that, after presenting a City Remonstrance to George III, which according to Wilkes exceeded 'in boldness all compositions', Beckford had rebuked the king. His untimely death a few weeks later was a major blow to Chatham's fragile recovery of popularity.[90]

Chatham's Parliamentary speeches remained trenchantly populist – in November he referred to 'the monied interest of the city' as 'bloodworms of the constitution' and expressed his preference for 'the middling citizens, who preferred law and liberty to loans and contracts' – but his rhetoric no longer had the effect that it formerly did during his glory days as 'the great commoner'. His 'patriotic rage' at the City radicals for resisting naval impressment did not help matters. In December, Wilkes or one of his allies pronounced Chatham's political obituary: 'The constant City phrase of him is, *The funeral Sir, is gone by.*' He had lost his popularity, Catharine Macaulay concluded, 'by his Inconsistencies, & Fondness for a Title'.[91]

The same suspicion of aristocracy ultimately blighted the prospects of Lord Shelburne, but not before he had made some headway in courting support in London. Unlike Chatham, he remained behind the scenes, preferring to operate through more visible lieutenants. These included James Townsend and John Sawbridge (the brother of Catharine Macaulay); both were landowners and radical MPs who in the summer of 1769 won election to the City's aldermanic bench and also as London's sheriffs. They had already shown their support

---

[90] Norris, pp. 64–77; Sutherland, pp. 1–15; RHADAMANTHUS, *Political Register*, 2 (1768): 393; Thomas, *Wilkes*, pp. 116–17; Wilkes MSS 3, fol. 30

[91] *London Evening Post*, 27–29 November 1770; *Controversial Letters*, p. 221; Macaulay quoted in Sainsbury, *Disaffected Patriots*, p. 44.

for Wilkes by nominating him for re-election for Middlesex in February 1769. Shelburne was also on friendly terms with Revd John Horne, who had sought out Wilkes in Paris and was energetic in organising his electoral campaigns. The association of the Shelburne group with Wilkes found its most important institutional expression in the Society of the Supporters of the Bill of Rights (SSBR), established on 25 February 1769. There, Sawbridge, Townsend and Horne joined a heterogeneous group of reform-minded gentlemen, merchants, and lawyers, united in their determination, according to Horne's public advertisement, 'to support Mr Wilkes and his cause, as far as it is a public cause'. The caveat was important: after a few months of fruitful harmony, the society began to fracture because of what Horne later charged was Wilkes's desire to 'change a generous *public Society* into a Sponge to be squeezed only into his pocket'. Wilkes was no longer worthy of public approbation, said Horne, because he sought to 'intice them [the public] to an idolatrous worship of himself'.[92]

As we shall see in the next chapter, Horne drew up a comprehensive indictment of Wilkes's alleged financial delinquencies. But Wilkes pointed to a different reason for division among the radicals, blaming it squarely on the attempt of Shelburne and his toadies to manipulate City politics for sinister, aristocratic purposes. The fact that Shelburne's nickname was 'Malagrida', after a Portuguese Jesuit executed in 1761 for plotting the death of his king, suggests that Wilkes's principal target was already an object of suspicion. When *Junius* urged Wilkes to make common cause with the Shelburne party and support Sawbridge in London's mayoralty election of 1771, he met with this response: 'He [Sawbridge] is become the absolute dupe of Malagrida's gang ... I should fear the Mansion House would be besieged and taken by the banditty of the Shelburnes.'[93] Wilkes was equally severe on James Townsend for waiting on the support of 'some great men' – notably Lord Chatham – before taking a stand with other London magistrates during the 'printers' case' in the spring of 1771. Shelburne's pleas to Chatham that Townsend be permitted to align himself with the radical printers only served to underscore Townsend's lack of independence, while giving Wilkes a chance to vaunt his own. 'The *prudent* Mr. Townsend may wait the consent of great men', he declared. 'I will, on a national call, follow instantly the line of my duty, regardless of their applause or censure. Public spirit and virtue are seldom in the company of his Lordship or his Grace.'[94] The bad blood between

---

[92]   Norris, pp. 56, 58; Thomas, *Wilkes*, pp. 98–99, 111–12; *Controversial Letters*, pp. 83, 182.

[93]   *Letters of Junius*, p. 415. The division of the City radicals in the 1771 mayoral election led to the ministerial candidate, William Nash, becoming mayor. Wilkes and Sawbridge were later reconciled and, in 1775, Wilkes supported Sawbridge's candidature to be his successor as Lord Mayor.

[94]   Norris, p. 77; *Letters of Junius*, p. 427 note 6.

Wilkes and Townsend spilt over to the streets the following year. After the Court of Aldermen chose Townsend as Lord Mayor over Wilkes, who had polled the most livery votes, an angry Wilkite mob attacked the Guildhall during the Lord Mayor's inaugural ball.[95]

The Wilkite attack on the nobility is perhaps best construed as an investment in the future of radical politics. According to John Brewer: 'In these years [1768 to 1770] were planted the seeds of a political sensibility that was to flower in the 1780s and 1790s, manifesting itself in strains of thought that were both anti-aristocratic and reformist.'[96] But in the short term, Wilkes's attack arguably strengthened the hand of aristocratic government, because he was as concerned about dividing the aristocratic leaders of the Parliamentary opposition as he was about confronting the administration. We need to remind ourselves that when Wilkes inveighed against the 'damned aristocracy', it was these leaders that he was talking about. His determination to prevent their union played into the hands of the new prime minister, Lord North, who was able to exploit opposition divisions to restore the kind of stability at the centre of political life that had proved so elusive in the 1760s, a stability that until 1782 survived even the stresses of the American War of Independence. The Parliamentary elections of 1774 – which brought Wilkes back to the House of Commons – partially realised the potential for a radical politics, independent of the patronage of grandees, yet North's government was scarcely discomfited, in part because the elections reaffirmed the gulf between the Wilkites and the mainstream opposition parties.[97]

Vicious Lords, Annoying Aldermen, and an Injured Queen

At the same time as the political conduct of aristocrats was subject to increasing scrutiny, their private vices were also engaging public attention in an unprecedented way. No longer was it just notorious individuals such as Lord Sandwich who provoked moral indictment: it was becoming something of a standard assumption, expressed in pamphlets and periodicals, that adultery and other forms of misconduct had become endemic among the well-born denizens of fashionable society, setting them apart from lesser mortals in an invidious way and giving a moral twist to the notion of a 'damned aristocracy' (Fig. 5.2).

---

[95] Thomas, *Wilkes*, p. 148.

[96] Brewer, *Party Ideology*, pp. 179–80.

[97] The extent of Wilkite success in the 1774 elections is a classic 'glass half empty/half full' scenario. See respectively, Ian R. Christie, 'The Wilkites and the General Election of 1774', in his *Myth and Reality in Late Eighteenth-Century British Politics and Other Papers* (London and Berkeley, 1970), pp. 244–60, and Wilson, *Sense of the People*, pp. 228–30.

Figure 5.2   'The Great in one eternal Round, / Of Folly and Excess are found ...'. *High Life in the Evening, or Quality Dinner Hour* (1769). Artist unknown. Etching and engraving. Courtesy of the Lewis Walpole Library, Yale University.

As we have already seen, adultery offended the emerging canons of sentiment; at the same time, it was increasingly defined as an aristocratic vice. It is difficult to ascertain if indeed there was a socially differentiated loosening of moral standards, but certainly from the late 1760s onwards there was a higher level of inquisitiveness about, and a reduced public tolerance of, lapses in conduct in upper-class circles that might previously have gone unnoticed. Fuelling the public appetite for scandal were some high-profile divorce cases, their salacious details providing much of the content for new gossip journals like the *Town and Country Magazine*. One such case in 1770 was particularly compelling because it brought the breath of scandal uncomfortably close to the royal family. The offender was the Duke of Cumberland, the king's brother, who was charged with criminal conversation with Henrietta, the wife of the Earl of Grosvenor. At the trial, the attorney for the aggrieved husband argued that 'the very great quality of the defendant' must be held against him as a deterrent to all aristocratic adulterers. The jury responded by awarding the plaintiff the astounding sum of £10,000 in damages. The Wilkite press seized this opportunity to lambaste the nobility for its degeneracy. Wilkes himself followed the trial, and Cumberland's subsequent amours, with salacious interest.[98]

The exposure of aristocratic vice – which sought to extend categories of failed manhood beyond the familiar ones of sodomy and sexual impotence – did not merely run parallel to the assault on aristocratic politics; it became an essential component of it. For one thing, it challenged the right of aristocracy to impose its moral authority on the lower orders: 'Let us hear no more of the vices of the poor and mean, while we have such barefaced and numerous adulteries, whoredom, drunkenness, luxury, gaming, and perfect contempt of God in his moral government among ... statesmen and Arthur's noble gamblers', declared a writer for the *Middlesex Journal*.[99] The attack went further: moral degeneracy fostered corruption and incompetence, thereby undermining aristocracy's presumptive right to govern. For this reason, Wilkes's advocates eagerly engaged in the campaign, despite their champion's own well-publicised indulgences in the pleasures of the flesh. A principal target was his 'friend' turned nemesis, the Duke of Grafton, First Lord of the Treasury from August 1766 to February 1770 and Prime Minister for most of that period. Even before he attained office, Grafton had acquired a reputation as a womaniser and gambler. He attended the Newmarket races regularly, often forsaking Parliamentary business to do so.

---

[98] *First Letter to the Duke of Grafton*, p. 8; *The Devil Divorced: or the Diabo-Whore* (London, 1782), p. 1; Donna T. Andrew, '"Adultery à-la-Mode": Privilege, the Law and Attitudes to Adultery 1770–1809', *History*, 82 (1997): 5–9; BRUTUS, *North Briton*, 172, 14 July 1770; Wilkes to Mrs Reynolds, 14 November 1771, BL Add. MSS 27925, fol. 3.

[99] 'Andrew Marvel', *Middlesex Journal*, 9–11 January 1770.

Horace Walpole, a friend, noted Grafton's belief 'that the world can be postponed to a whore and a horse-race'. Without any apparent sense of contradiction, he also called Grafton 'one of the best bred men alive'.[100]

For a long time Grafton's fashionable vices caused scarcely a ripple of attention, and while the duke was still thought to be Wilkes's friend, the Wilkite press was silent about them. But everything changed in the wake of an incident that occurred when the political world was reeling from Wilkes's dramatic re-entry into national life. On the night of 16 April 1768 Grafton attended the opera at the King's Theatre in the Haymarket, accompanied by his mistress, the demi-rep Nancy Parsons. Also present in the audience were the king and queen as well as Grafton's wife, from whom he had been separated for four years. Grafton was roundly criticised for his arrogant disregard for public decency. 'It is not the private indulgence, but the public insult of which I complain', explained *Junius*. 'The name of Miss Parsons would hardly have been known, if [Grafton] … had not led her in triumph through the Opera House, even in the presence of the Queen.' In the eyes of Thomas Whateley, a member of the Grenville faction, Grafton's indiscretion transgressed even the expansive code of aristocratic libertinism. 'Libertine men are as much offended as prudish women,' Whateley wrote, 'and *it is impossible he* [Grafton] *should think of remaining Minister who thus defied all decency,* is almost the general conclusion.'[101]

Not satisfied with calling Grafton to account for his social offence, the Wilkite press continued a vitriolic attack on his character and fitness to govern. He was accused by one pamphleteer of behaving with 'all the unguarded folly of boyish effeminacy' in his 'doting fondness' for Nancy Parsons, who was unkindly described as 'an antiquated Figure-dancer, remarkable only for the sickened features of stale beauty, the artificial vivacity of hackneyed prostitution, and the infatuated adoration of a filly keeper'.[102] Grafton's distraction was so great, claimed another, that he had lost all sense of paternal affection, refusing to see a dying child.[103] Charges of public malfeasance accompanied those of domestic vice. Parsons, it was widely alleged, not only lured Grafton away from government business, but also accepted bribes – which she invested in public stocks – to influence the distribution of places and pensions. Similar charges

---

[100] Walpole quoted in Lawrence Stone, *Broken Lives: Separation and Divorce in England, 1660–1857* (Oxford and New York, 1993), pp. 140, 141.

[101] Horace Bleackley, *Ladies Fair and Frail: Sketches of the Demi-Monde during the Eighteenth Century* (London, 1909), p. 101; *Letters of Junius,* pp. 78–79; Whateley to George Grenville, 22 April 1768, *Grenville Papers,* vol. 4, pp. 275–77.

[102] *First Letter to the Duke of Grafton,* p. 6. For a kinder view of Nancy Parsons, which stresses her religious piety and fidelity as a mistress, see Bleackley, *Ladies Fair and Frail,* pp. 101–45.

[103] RHADAMANTHUS, *Political Register,* 2 (1768): 393–94.

would soon be aimed at other women of the demi-monde, including Martha Ray, the mistress of Lord Sandwich, accused of being a go-between in the sale of Admiralty offices.[104] Inevitably, Grafton's misconduct was connected to his Stuart ancestry: he was descended in a bastard line from Charles II, which apparently explained both his 'swarthy face' and his willingness to 'sell his country for a bribe' (though he apparently matched his royal ancestor only in vice, not in wit). This same attack pointed to Grafton as typifying the depravity of the peerage in general: 'Gods! What a motley group of fools, / Jockeys and gamblers, slaves and tools, / Our noble Senate house contains!'[105]

A moral campaign that focused on vice in high society had complex implications for Wilkes. At one level, it helped to distract from charges of his own delinquency by shifting attention to the hypocrisy of his high-born oppressors. 'Is [Grafton] the man who dares to talk of Mr. Wilkes's morals?' asked *Junius* pointedly. But the charge of hypocrisy could cut both ways, which presented Wilkes and his supporters with the tricky problem of representing the conduct of debauched grandees as meaningfully distinct from his own. Wilkite spokesmen did not shy away from the task, though their frequently baffling arguments underscored its difficulty. One contended that Grafton's 'pleasures, suited to his inferior capacity[,] were not of so refined a nature' as Wilkes's, so that 'he [Grafton] was guilty of as great a crime with less temptation'. The same writer was on more secure ground when he lambasted Grafton for his love of gambling and his association with the louche crowd at the Newmarket races. Grafton was often referred to as 'a jockey' in the radical press, a term that neatly associated a disreputable love of the turf with womanising and a propensity for devious and fraudulent conduct.[106] As we have seen, Wilkes genuinely despised gambling, calling the habitués of horse races 'the vilest vermin'.[107]

There was, of course, a special difficulty in dissociating Wilkes's conduct from those of his aristocratic boon companions. One approach was to represent their vices as so egregiously decadent that, by comparison, Wilkes appeared as something of an ingénu. We have already noted one example of this: Wilkes's innuendo that Lord Sandwich and Baron le Despenser engaged in 'unnatural' sex acts with women at Medmenham. In the latter's case, this was enlarged by

---

[104] *North Briton*, 68, 1 October 1768; Bleackley, *Ladies Fair and Frail*, p. 112; Anna Clark, *Scandal: The Sexual Politics of the British Constitution* (Princeton, 2004), p. 40.

[105] ODE to LORD CHATHAM, *Bingley's Journal*, 29 December 1770.

[106] *Letters of Junius*, p. 75; *A fair Comparison between* Mr. WILKES, *and the* D--- *of* G-----n, *Middlesex Journal*, 29–31 August 1769. On the eighteenth-century meanings of jockey, see Nicholas Rogers, 'Pigott's Private Eye: Radicalism and Sexual Scandal in Eighteenth-Century England', *Journal of the Canadian Historical Association*, new series, 4 (1993): 254.

[107] [Wilkes] *Letters to Daughter*, vol. 2, p. 20.

John Hall-Stevenson – a self-appointed Wilkite propagandist – into a grotesquely scurrilous charge of incest with his mother, his sisters, and an aunt (with a sexual liaison with a male cousin thrown in for good measure). In Sandwich's, it supported the rumour that one of his 'foul faults' was buggery.[108] Wilkes, prompted by Sandwich's treachery in the *Essay on Woman* affair, had previously made a less specific allusion to Sandwich's 'abandoned and profligate' conduct, his 'loose and barefaced' attitude to women, and the 'variety of his vices'. These charges prefaced a cutting appraisal of Sandwich's qualities as a public official: 'slow, tedious, and dull'. By the late 1760s, with Sandwich back in office as joint postmaster-general alongside Baron le Despenser, the charges against him had escalated to arson and the drugging of women in order to rape them. Such a man, marvelled one pamphleteer, 'who had suborned a servant [Curry] to the robbery of his master [Wilkes] … was now entrusted with the circulating property, and private correspondence of the whole nation'.[109]

The charge against Sandwich of drug-induced rape was strikingly similar to the one levelled against Luttrell, the government's ill-advised choice to replace Wilkes as MP for Middlesex. Luttrell, the son of a peer, was not only a well-known rake, but also an unredeemed one, without any mitigating marks of sentiment of the sort occasionally attributed to Wilkes. Newspapers and pamphlets excoriated Luttrell's character and conduct, focusing especially on his sexual assault of one Arabella Bolton some 15 years previously. The indictment was horrifying in the extreme. Luttrell had allegedly wheedled his way into the confidence of Miss Bolton's family and servants before drugging her to the point of unconsciousness so that he could have his way with her. She was left pregnant and infected with a venereal disease. Meanness compounded the viciousness of his conduct: Luttrell had at first planned to have the child of this encounter placed in the Foundling Hospital and raised at the public expense.[110]

There was nothing in Wilkes's career to match this kind of villainy, his advocates assured their readers. 'Man of pleasure, as he may have been,' said one, 'he never did, so far as I have ever heard, invade, either by force or by fraud, the honour of any maid or matron: so that even his pleasures have been regulated by the

---

[108]   *The Works of John-Hall Stevenson, Esq.*, 3 vols (London, 1795), vol. 3, pp. 269–73; *Wilkes and Liberty: or, The Universal Prayer* (London, 1764), p. 15.

[109]   *Wilkes Correspondence*, vol. 1, p. 230–31; John Brewer, *A Sentimental Murder: Love and Madness in the Eighteenth Century* (New York, 2004), p. 109; *First Letter to the Duke of Grafton*, pp. 24–25.

[110]   Lewis Namier and John Brooke, *The History of Parliament: The House of Commons, 1745–1790*, 3 vols (London and New York, 1964) vol. 3, p. 65; *Wilkes's Jest Book; or the Merry Patriot* (1770) pp. 51–52; *The Memoirs of Miss Arabella Bolton. Containing a Genuine Account of Her Seduction, and the Barbarous Treatment she Afterwards Received from the Honourable Colonel L------l* (London, 1770).

strictest maxims of honour.'[111] Putting Wilkes's career as a man of pleasure in the past tense alluded to another strand of Wilkite strategy after his return from exile: going beyond the routine emphasis on the paramountcy of his political virtues, his propagandists insisted that his sexual libertinism, despite reports and rumours to the contrary, was now a thing of the past. Henceforth he would no longer be lost 'in the primrose path of pleasure': all his energies would be devoted to the cause of the public. Declared one jingle: 'The foes of Wilkes affirm with scorn, / A greater rake was never born: / "True," say his friends, "but now 'tis plain / He's a new man, and born again."' Wilkes himself tried to lend believability to the notion of his reformation. In response to a newspaper enquiry, Wilkes acknowledged his membership of the Medmenham monks, but claimed that he had now repented such 'sallies and indiscretions' and that he was entitled to be judged 'by what he now is, as a private as well as a public man'. He invoked Horace: *Nec lusisse pudet, sed non incidere ludum* (Nor is it shameful to have had fun, but it is shameful not to cut off one's sport). Later, in 1771, during the course of his virulent exchanges with John Horne, he went further, discarding Horace's dictum and avowing that 'I hope to redeem and bury in oblivion every past folly by great and virtuous actions, by real services to my country'.[112]

The strategy's obvious purpose was to credit Wilkes with a double measure of manliness. He had exhibited both heterosexual virility – an appealing quality for some of his plebeian supporters, as we saw in chapter 3 – but also, supposedly, the self-mastery to put aside the follies of youth in the interest of the public, something that the incorrigible Lord Sandwich, unconstrained by religious scruple beyond the crassest kind of superstition, was incapable of doing. Wilkes's commitment to moral reform even in the short term was highly questionable, however. His adulterous affair with Jane Barnard was a clear violation of it. And a few months after his pious riposte to Horne, Wilkes was seen entering the house of Mrs Gardiner, a well-known courtesan. Recently elected Sheriff of London, he had arrived at her door in his official chariot, thus compounding licentiousness with indiscretion, the same offence as the Duke of Grafton's. Wilkes's action prompted a stinging rebuke from his mother, who happened to live in Mrs Gardiner's neighbourhood. Claiming that a crowd had hissed as he entered the courtesan's house, Sarah Wilkes lambasted her son for his 'Insult upon Public decency' and predicted that it would 'sink *a great Patriot* into Contempt'.[113]

---

[111] *A Letter to the Right Hon. Thomas Harley, Esq; Lord Mayor of the City of London. By an Alderman of London*, 4th edn (London, 1768), p. 18. This defence preceded Wilkes's possible rape of Jane Barnard in 1770.

[112] *Political Register*, 3 (1768): 42–43, 269; *Controversial Letters*, p. 29.

[113] 23 October 1771, Wilkes MSS 2, fol. 95.

What is intriguing about Sarah Wilkes's censure is that she pitched it in class terms. 'Many of the Midling [*sic*] Class of People (thank Heaven) revere Virtue, and see vice countenanced by a Magistrate with *double* abhorrence, whose duty it is to suppress it', she wrote.[114] She was not a lone voice: it was becoming almost a cliché that special virtue, political as well as domestic, adhered to the middle ranks of society, though few gave expression to the idea with such eloquence as Wilkes's mother. Celebrations of middle-class virtue were routinely juxtaposed with laments about the 'Dissipation and Luxury' of the 'upper Parts' of society, suggesting that the attack on aristocratic vice was, at its core, a middle-class campaign.[115]

To what extent was Wilkes reclaimed to the values associated with his social origins in the manner that Sarah Wilkes so powerfully urged? There is some superficial evidence to suggest that Wilkes was prepared to put aside aspects of aristocratic libertinage. Apart from lapses like the one that incurred his mother's wrath, gallantry in the boudoir was not something that he now generally wished to flaunt, even within his libertine circle. Following his return from exile he also refused the opportunity to repeat his displays of gallantry on the duelling ground, turning down a public challenge from Lauchlin Macleane, a former friend turned bitter enemy.[116] More positively, after his release from prison, he was a willing drudge when it came to City business, prompting Horace Walpole to speculate that the 'dignity' of his civic role had 'dulled him into prudence'.[117] Wilkes joined his fellow aldermen in issuing annual injunctions against 'Vice, Prophaneness and Immorality', and he served regularly as a magistrate in the Guildhall, committing (and sometimes discharging) women arrested for soliciting.[118] When he became Lord Mayor, he presided over trials at the Old Bailey, pronouncing sentence on murderers, rapists, and embezzlers.[119] In his

---

[114]   Ibid.

[115]   BRUTUS, *North Briton*, 172 , 14 July 1770; *A Cautionary Address to the Electors of England: Being a Touchstone between the Constituents and Candidates* (London, 1768), p. 7. Dror Wahrman, *Imagining the Middle Class: The Political Representation of Class in Britain, c. 1780–1840* (Cambridge and New York, 1995) is a compelling account of the emergence of a 'middle-class idiom', driven by political argument rather than socioeconomic change. Despite the persuasiveness of Wahrman's argument, I question his chronology. What strikes him as novel in the 1790s had ample precedent in preceding decades.

[116]   James N.M. MacLean, *Reward is Secondary: The Life of a Political Adventurer and an Inquiry into the Mystery of 'Junius'* (London, 1963), pp. 258–74.

[117]   Thomas, *Wilkes*, p. 119.

[118]   *Gazetteer*, 18 April 1776; Guildhall Justice Room Minutes, GJR/M6, 26 January 1778, and Repertories of the Aldermanic Bench, vol. 181, fol. 9, Corporation of London Record Office.

[119]   *The Whole Proceedings on the King's Commission of the Peace, Oyer and Terminer, and Gaol-Delivery for the City of London; and also the Gaol-Delivery for the County of Middlesex; Held at Justice Hall in the Old Bailey*. Sessions, November 1774–October 1775, pp. 47–582.

own ward of Farringdon Without, he sought to confiscate the licences of public houses that accommodated prostitutes, an action that prompted some satirical doggerel in *Bingley's Journal,* which expressed compassion for those Wilkes was seeking to persecute: 'Tho' draggled-tail'd, weary, and wet to the skin, / Not a sinner to serve them one spoonful of gin; / For he vows, since HE found it so dang'rous a trade, / No *Essay on Woman* by you shall be made.'[120] Even those on the fringes of his circle of rakes enjoyed no support from Wilkes if their sexual conduct was openly transgressive. In 1772, one of Wilkes's political allies, Robert Morris, first secretary of the SSBR, abducted a twelve-year-old heiress and took her to the continent. Facing legal proceedings for his offence, he appealed to Wilkes for help, but received the cold shoulder instead.[121]

Yet such evidence scarcely compels us to see Wilkes as even a partial convert to what could be meaningfully described as middle-class moral values. He had long taken the patrician's dim view of plebeian indulgence in the same vices that, as a gentleman, he felt entitled to enjoy himself. Lust after all was a 'noble passion'. His central criticism of upper-class rakes such as Sandwich was that they had breached the aristocratic honour principle, whereas middle-class reformers saw the honour principle itself as subversive of morality. (One of Wilkes's supporters made the same criticism of Grafton, accusing him of dismissing honour as a mere 'bagatelle'.)[122] And although he was a conscientious magistrate, Wilkes was not keen to associate with his aldermanic colleagues or to identify with their values. Interestingly, Wilkes seems to have had a less fraught relationship with London's Common Councilmen, who were usually from a more humble social station than the aldermen, and perhaps more receptive to Wilkes's gentlemanly (as distinct from lordly) condescension. His devoted followers included such men as Luke Stavely, a linen draper and councilman for Bread Street, and John Piper, a packer and councilman for Queenhithe, described in one squib as 'Deputy Piper / Jack Wilkes's A--e wiper'.[123] These individuals were unlikely to annoy Wilkes by turning up in social contexts where they were unwanted, unlike the aldermen who in 1773 vexed Wilkes by making an appearance in his favourite resort of Brighthelmstone. 'There is very little company here,' he grumbled to Polly, 'and that sunk so low as London Aldermen, Kennet, Oliver, &c. In one

---

[120] *Bingley's Journal,* 5 January 1770. William Bingley, the paper's founder and editor, was an erstwhile Wilkes supporter who suffered hardship, including imprisonment, in his cause.

[121] *Diaries of Robert Morris,* pp. 28–32; Peter D.G. Thomas, '"Bill of Rights Morris": A Welsh Wilkite Radical and Rogue – Robert Morris (1743–1793)', in *Hanoverian Britain and Empire: Essays in Memory of Philip Lawson,* ed. Stephen Taylor, Richard Connors, and Clyve Jones (Woodbridge, 1998), pp. 279–80.

[122] *Boswell, Italy,* p. 59; *Harlequin Premier: A Farce, As It is Acted Daily* (1769), p. 22.

[123] Sainsbury, *Disaffected Patriots,* pp. 65, 92, 109, 132, 186, 187; *Public Advertiser,* 15 July 1773.

part of the town you see "London Porter sold here". The next door might be "London Aldermen seen here".'[124]

When Wilkes was obliged to mingle with the aldermen, he made little effort to conceal his contempt, even for his political allies. Edmund Burke noticed his conduct at a Lord Mayor's dinner in 1773:

> His petulance and Levity are something beyond what is credible. I sat near him and he was ridiculing and abusing his adherents without any management, and in the hearing of several people. I hinted to him jestingly that his friends, by being such, were too respectable not to be treated with a little Decorum. O, says he, I never laugh at my *friends,* but these are only my *followers.*[125]

Another observer marvelled at his ability to lead 'fat-headed Turtle-eating Aldermen by the Nose'.[126] When Wilkes became Lord Mayor in 1774, a cartoon of him with his fellow aldermen supported his self-conceit. It flatters him as an elegant, patrician figure, surrounded by his civic colleagues, who with one handsome exception – probably Sir Watkin Lewes – are in various stages of decrepitude, deformity, and obesity (Fig. 5.3). The image of hanging paunches was an obvious reference to the notorious aldermanic sin of gluttony, a condition popularly associated with sexual incapacity and cuckoldry. Wilkes was constantly referring to the gluttony of aldermen and it inspired a number of his recorded jokes.[127] As we have seen, during the Gordon Riots Wilkes's denigration of the anti-Catholic aldermen took on a more serious dimension, escalating to the charge of bigotry. They were, he said, 'gloomy, barbarous, ignorant Wretches'.[128] The outburst was undoubtedly triggered by the special circumstances of the times, but it exposed an attitude that had long been in the making.

Wilkes's disdain for his fellow aldermen indicated that he retained aristocratic attitudes, even as he embraced anti-aristocratic politics. Incidents of social ostracism after his return to England, gleefully reported by enemies like George Grenville, did nothing to undermine his sense of social entitlement, but they did

---

[124] BL Add. MSS 30879, fol. 214.

[125] *Burke Correspondence,* vol. 2, p. 483.

[126] *The Letters of Charles Burney,* vol. 1 (1751–1784), ed. Alvaro Ribeiro (Oxford, 1991), p. 238 note 20.

[127] Anti-Hopkins song, City Elections, 1768–96 [A Broadside Collection], An. 5.4. No. 15, page 28, Guildhall Library; *European Magazine,* 33 (1798): 225–28. At least one of Wilkes's 'gluttony' jokes also took a swipe at his victim's humble social origins: 'At a Lord Mayor's dinner one afternoon he observed a certain civic dignitary, who had begun life as a bricklayer, helping himself plentifully to the cheese. "Why, Mr. Burnel," said Wilkes, "you lay it on with a trowel."' Bleackley, *Wilkes,* pp. 253–54.

[128] *Public Advertiser,* 22 June 1780.

Figure 5.3   *Court of Aldermen, with John Wilkes as Lord Mayor at the head of the table* (1774). Engraving. By permission of the Guildhall Library, London.

have an impact.[129] Perhaps as a way of pre-empting rejection, John and Polly Wilkes appointed themselves arbiters of politesse, rather than slavish imitators of it, seeking out 'the politest people among the sauvages de l'Europe'.[130] Society's most fashionable couple – Georgiana, Duchess of Devonshire, and her husband – passed the test: in John's judgement, they were 'deservedly beloved'. Sometimes younger brothers fared better than their titled siblings. After visiting the estate of Thomas Fitzmaurice, Wilkes compared him favourably to his older brother, Lord Shelburne: 'The conversation runs in much superior strain', he reported to Polly.[131] Not content with asserting the essential equality of all gentlemen, Wilkes also came round emphatically to the view, so strongly advocated by his late friend Charles Churchill, that high birth without merit was worthless. He scolded James Boswell for taking excessive pride in his noble ancestors. 'You are rich enough in personal worth, without borrowing from your family', he told him.[132]

It was Boswell, though, who in 1776 stage-managed his friend's famous dinner meeting with Samuel Johnson – someone accustomed to condemning Wilkes's personal and political vices – thus providing Wilkes with the opportunity for a virtuoso display of politesse. Engaging Johnson in witty repartee, displaying classical learning lightly carried, and exercising with flamboyance the gentleman's prerogative of serving the roast, Wilkes set out to elicit his old adversary's approval. It came eventually, albeit in grudging form: 'Jack has a great variety of talk, Jack is a scholar, and Jack has the manners of a gentleman', Johnson said (without ever conceding that Wilkes actually *was* a gentleman).[133] George III, another apparently implacable enemy, was rather more generous. After Wilkes, in his capacity as London's first magistrate, had presented a City petition condemning the government's American policy, the king remarked, according to Horace Walpole, that 'he had never seen so well-bred a Lord Mayor'.[134]

Wilkes's social ambitions continued to run higher than occasional nods of approval from the likes of Samuel Johnson or even George III. He inhabited an imagined space among the French nobility, who were exempted from his increasingly egalitarian views, and who had never rejected him like their English confrères. 'In his real politics he was an aristocrat,' observed Charles Butler, 'and [he] would much rather have been a favoured courtier at Versailles, than the most

---

[129]   Grenville to Whateley, 13 April 1768, *Grenville Papers,* vol. 4, p. 267.
[130]   Wilkes to Jean-Baptiste Suard, 14 December 1774, Special Manuscript Collection: Halsband, Columbia University Library.
[131]   [Wilkes] *Letters to Daughter,* vol. 2, p. 7; BL Add. MSS 30879, fols 187–88.
[132]   1 October 1785, Boswell Collection, C3095.
[133]   James Boswell, *Life of Johnson,* ed. R.W. Chapman, introduced by Pat Rogers (Oxford, 1980) pp. 767–76, 862.
[134]   Horace Walpole quoted in Sainsbury, *Disaffected Patriots,* p. 84.

commanding orator in St. Stephen's chapel.'[135] As Wilkes plotted his demotic career after his release from King's Bench Prison, he was also preoccupied with Europe's most glittering social event: the marriage of the French dauphin to an Austrian princess, Marie Antoinette. He begged Polly to send him details of the wedding and its accompanying celebrations. 'Is the Dauphiness happy in France, and are the French as much pleased with her as the first week?' he enquired. Later he followed with pride his daughter's apparently effortless passages through French high society during her lengthy visits there.[136] ('She has great social graces, with a politesse which is very noble and always in its place', reported Madame La Vallière, Duchesse de Chastillon, an old family friend.[137]) When the French Revolution appeared to be degenerating – at least as viewed from across the Channel – into a bloody conflict between patricians and their plebeian rivals, the sympathies of the Wilkes's were with the former. Polly fussed over the correct protocol in approaching exiled French bluebloods.[138] In August 1793 John wrote to her: '*Il est vrai que le diable est dechainé, et regne actuellement dans le beau pays de France*', a pronouncement with uncanny parallels to the earlier charge, directed against himself, that he enjoyed a diabolical influence over England's sans-culottes.[139] He rejoiced over the murder of Marat and looked forward to a similar fate for 'the monster Robespierre'.[140] Polly's contribution to the royal cause was to translate into French the paragraph in Edmund Burke's *Reflections on the Revolution in France* that lamented, in famously evocative and sentimental language, the brutal treatment of Marie Antoinette at the hands of the Paris mob. (When the queen, before her execution, was shown the passage, 'she Burst into a Flood of Tears'.[141])

There was a profound irony in all this. As Edmund Burke and Polly Wilkes upheld Marie Antoinette as the epitome of regal virtue, she was being exposed by the French *libelles* as the embodiment of regal vice. Nymphomania, incest, lesbianism, and complicity in the Diamond Necklace affair were just some of the charges levelled against her. Such vilification was a key element in the attack on France's old regime, the queen's bodily transgressions emblematic of decadence

---

[135] Butler, vol. 1, pp. 73–74. Wilkes's yearnings for the French court were not entirely secret. He was occasionally reproved for them in the anti-Wilkite press. SOLOMON SMOAKY, *Public Ledger*, 11 December 1771.

[136] BL Add. MSS 30879, fols 144–45, 146–47, 150; [Wilkes] *Letters to Daughter*, vol. 3, pp. 38–39.

[137] BL Add. MSS 30872, fol. 244.

[138] Mary (Polly) Wilkes to Mrs Maria Cosway, n.d., Misc. MSS, Lewis Walpole Library, Farmington.

[139] [Wilkes] *Letters to Daughter*, vol. 4, p. 157.

[140] Ibid., pp. 153–54, 182.

[141] *Burke Correspondence*, vol. 6, p. 204.

within the larger body politic. Arguably, this exposure of courtly vice was simply a devastating extension of the politics of sexual defamation deployed by John Wilkes against Lord Bute and the Princess Dowager, or by Wilkite propagandists against the Duke of Grafton. Charles Pigott, an English radical of the 1790s, certainly thought so. As he assailed the sexual decadence of the British aristocracy, thereby challenging its presumptive right to govern, and transcribed for an English readership the libels against Marie Antoinette, Pigott assumed that he was operating in a tradition that Wilkes had previously established. In September 1792, Pigott was arrested for toasting the French Republic and for referring to George III as a 'German hog butcher'. From confinement, he appealed to Wilkes as a fellow-sufferer in the cause of liberty to intercede on his behalf by securing bail for him. His language had a distinctly Wilkes-like ring: 'I never uttered a word that I cannot justify, nor that all the refinements of malice or sophistry can torture into Sedition or treason.' Wilkes ignored his radical legatee, who was obliged to spend a month in jail until a grand jury tossed out the indictment against him. Pigott would have had no way of knowing that the French court, whose vices he denounced with such venom, was for Wilkes the untainted exemplar of the refined, aristocratic values to which he still secretly clung.[142]

---

[142] Lynn Hunt, *The Family Romance of the French Revolution* (London and Berkeley, 1992); Rogers, 'Pigott's Private Eye', pp. 247–63; Pigott to Wilkes, Compter Prison, BL Add. MSS 30876, fol. 9.

Chapter 6

Money

The Debtor as Patriot Hero

In September 1781 'Toby', a pseudonymous correspondent, addressed Wilkes as follows:

> It was with no small concern that I lately heard of the serious apprehensions you begin to entertain for your character as a Gentleman, and the singularity of your situation in the house of Commons – by getting out of debt.
>
> The Circumstance is awkward enough, no doubt, for a man of fashion, a Legislator, and a Patriot; and were not your other claims so numerous, and well founded, might justly give you some alarm.[1]

The letter refers to the fact that Wilkes, having been elected Chamberlain of London two years previously, had finally achieved something approaching financial solvency. What is intriguing is the suggestion, albeit a facetious one, that Wilkes's release from chronic indebtedness might compromise his status not only as a gentleman and a man of fashion – that was a predictable canard – but also as a patriot.

On the face of it, Wilkes's financial career would appear to have been not just a personal embarrassment, but an unmitigated public liability as well, a condition creating deep scepticism about the purity of his political motives. What his supporters construed as blows in favour of liberty his enemies were able to represent as being driven by squalid pecuniary self-interest. At the height of the Middlesex election controversy, a hostile commentator delivered this oft-repeated judgement: '[T]he only Use [Wilkes] made of his Seat in P[arliamen]t, had been to contract Debts with Impunity; and rob his Creditors and Tradesmen of their Due.'[2]

Wilkes's situation was manifestly different from that of more humble debtors victimised by economic circumstances beyond their control, and it is important

---

[1] BL Add. MSS 30872, fol. 214. 'Toby' was an ironic and apparently independent observer of City politics. See *Gazetteer*, 26 June 1777.

[2] *A Vindication of the D[uke] of G[rafton]* (London, 1769), p. 30.

to understand the vulnerabilities of such individuals in order to appreciate that distinction. As the trading system developed in scale and complexity, without a compensatory increase in circulating currency, the extension of credit came to assume a central function in economic life. A consequence was to increase the usual perils of commerce, especially when general trading conditions deteriorated in times of war or in the wake of financial panic. Few involved in commerce, except for financial capitalists with large monetary reserves, lived without the fear of insolvency. Some were confronted with the prospect or reality of bankruptcy, which in the eighteenth century was never a voluntary act, but a legal process initiated by creditors. The horrors of that condition could be real enough, yet in a grim sense, bankrupts were the privileged victims of commercial failure. The bankruptcy law applied only to those defined as 'traders' with debts of at least £100. Most retailers and artisans stood outside its provisions. For them, the spectre that lurked over economic failure was debtors' prison, notwithstanding the fact that only a minority of debtors was actually confined, and of those some were imprisoned voluntarily through 'friendly actions' as a way of warding off their creditors. Imprisonment for debt rose steadily in the latter half of the eighteenth century, reflecting the rapid increase in business failures, especially after the mid-1760s. In 1750, the King's Bench Prison received 615 debtors; by 1770, the year that John Wilkes was released from the institution, the number had grown to 1,098.[3]

Almost any contemporary discussion of the debtor's plight drew a distinction between the honest and prudent businessman, overwhelmed by adverse economic circumstances, and the spendthrift who sought to evade his creditors.[4] And while there was considerable public sympathy for those in the former category,

---

[3]   On the operation and contemporary perceptions of the credit system, see the following, all by Julian Hoppit: *Risk and Failure in English Business, 1700–1800* (Cambridge and New York, 1987); 'Attitudes to Credit in Britain, 1680–1790', *Historical Journal*, 33 (1990): 305–22; and 'The Use and Abuse of Credit in Eighteenth-Century England', in *Business Life and Public Policy: Essays in Honour of D.C. Coleman*, ed. Neil McKendrick and R.B. Outhwaite (Cambridge and New York, 1986), pp. 64–78. On the process of imprisonment for debt, see Joanna Innes, 'The King's Bench Prison in the Later Eighteenth Century: Law, Authority and Order in a London Debtors' Prison', in *An Ungovernable People: The English and their Law in the Seventeenth and Eighteenth Centuries*, ed. John Brewer and John Styles (London and New Brunswick, 1980), pp. 250–61. On the growth in numbers of those imprisoned for debt, see Margot C. Finn, *The Character of Credit: Personal Debt in English Culture, 1740–1914* (Cambridge and New York, 2003), pp. 114–15.

[4]   For example, James Stephen, *Considerations on Imprisonment for Debt* (London, 1770), p. 18; [Thomas Delamayne], *The Rise and Practice of Imprisonment for Debt in Personal Actions Examined* (London, 1772), pp. v–vi; *Thoughts of a Citizen of London on the Conduct of Dr. Dodd in his Life and Death* (London, 1777), p. 29. See also A LIVERYMAN, *Morning Chronicle*, 23 February 1776, where the distinction is applied specifically to Wilkes.

the rakish Wilkes seemed to fit more squarely into the latter. Libertinism itself carried connotations of reckless consumption, as well as of sexual and religious delinquency. Wilkes was readily depicted as a financially irresponsible drone, the bane of the industrious tradesman trapped in a client economy – in other words, as an 'abuser' of credit rather than a legitimate user of it. He boasted that he had 'never done any thing unbecoming a man of honour', but honouring debts to tradesmen was not part of the code to which he claimed allegiance. When rumours of his financial difficulty circulated in 1758, Wilkes dismissed them as 'things [that] hurt merchants, not Gentlemen', and he followed the lead of Sir William Stanhope, his neighbour and fellow Medmenham monk, in laughing them off.[5] His attitude implicated him in yet another transgression of the vicious aristocrat. The definition of 'a Lord', pronounced a radical writer, is 'one who is above paying his debts, or regarding his promises'.[6]

The preceding chapters have already suggested some of the reasons why Wilkes's expenditures habitually exceeded his income: his desire for expensive and lavishly furnished accommodations; his determination to secure a seat in the House of Commons; his insistence on giving Polly the best of everything, including a costly education; and his generosity to a succession of mistresses, including Gertrude Corradini. Even his brand of religious worship did not come cheaply: renting a pew in Grosvenor Chapel would have cost him £15 a year.[7] His extravagance meant that he was continually taking on new debts before he had paid off existing ones. For example, while embarking on re-election for Aylesbury in 1761, he was still encumbered with expenses from the previous campaign. With typical bravura, he had assured his brother Heaton in September 1760 that 'I now see an end to all our difficulties', but his 'solution' was in fact compounding them; to meet obligations, he was borrowing capital from moneylenders to be paid back in the form of annuities.[8] Increasingly, he resorted to the simple expedient of refusing to pay tradesmen, using Parliamentary privilege as his protection.[9] When Wilkes fled England on Christmas Day 1763, he was already deeply in debt, and his decision to remain in continental exile was probably dictated as much by the fear of debtors' prison in England as it was by the desire to avoid judicial punishment for his transgressions.

In Paris, Wilkes made occasional genuflections in the direction of financial prudence. 'I cou'd live here as well as I wish for one half of what it wou'd cost me in London,' he wrote at the outset of his exile, 'and when Miss W. was of an age

---

5   *Wilkes Correspondence,* vol. 2, p. 36; Wilkes MSS 6, fol. 42.
6   *Bingley's Journal,* 24 November 1770.
7   Ann Callender, ed., *Godly Mayfair* (London, 1980), p. 1.
8   Wilkes MSS 1, fol. 37.
9   GENEROSUS, *Public Advertiser,* 10 June 1763.

to marry, return to England not a farthing in debt, which at present oppresses my spirits. I am grown prudent, and will be œconomical to a great degree.' Shortly afterwards, he left the 'very expensive' Hotel de Saxe and moved with Polly to more modest accommodation on the rue St Nicaise. But such economies were few and far between, fitful gestures in a continuing saga of extravagance that inevitably increased both his indebtedness and his reputation for profligacy. According to Heaton, even John's 'sincere Friends' feared that 'his Talk about getting less and less expensive [was] only talk'. His creditors in England, meanwhile, were clamouring for repayment, ignoring Wilkes's insistence that many of their claims were bogus. Bateman, the landlord of Will's Coffee House, took matters into his own hands, seizing Wilkes's silver plate as security against £320 of debt. (Mary Wilkes was more patient when John fell into arrears with his annuity payments.)[10]

Bad luck and bad timing compounded Wilkes's self-inflicted problems. To pre-empt his creditors and secure desperately needed funds, Wilkes in early 1764 authorised the sale of nearly all of his English properties, including the Prebendal estate and his cherished library.[11] In August, in anticipation of his outlawry, he suggested that his agent, Humphrey Cotes, dispose of all his remaining assets and remit the proceeds to him in France.[12] Liquidation of capital did not have the expected result, however. Cotes had encouraged Wilkes to expect an income of £500 a year from the sale of the Aylesbury property, but instead he received virtually nothing. Clearly Wilkes was unlucky in his choice of agent (a wine merchant with a drinking problem). In January 1765 Cotes told Wilkes: '[I]t is absolutely impossible for me to make you any remittances as … I am in the utmost distress myself.' As he later admitted, Cotes had been putting Wilkes's money into his own account in a futile attempt to ward off bankruptcy. When Cotes actually did go bankrupt in early 1767, the assets that Wilkes had entrusted to him were lost. Wilkes's outlawry meant that another possible source of funds was closed off: as an outlaw, he was not able to pursue the legal action he had initiated against Lord Halifax for unlawful arrest. In fact, Wilkes believed that he had been outlawed precisely for that reason. In the one suit settled before his outlawry, Wilkes was granted £1,000 in damages from Robert Wood, an under-

---

[10] Wilkes to Humphrey Cotes, 20 January 1764, and 17 February 1764, BL Add. MSS 30868, fols 24, 40; Heaton Wilkes to Wilkes, 2 April 1767, BL Add. MSS 30869, fol. 109; William Jacomb to Wilkes, 3 January 1767, Add MSS 30869, fol. 93.

[11] Wilkes to Cotes, 17 February 1764, BL Add MSS 30869, fol. 40.

[12] Ibid., fol. 110. Cotes acted slowly, if at all, on that particular request, but in 1767 all of Wilkes's remaining properties in Buckinghamshire and Bedfordshire were sold (Thomas Life to Wilkes, 28 April 1768, BL Add. MSS 30869, fols 117–18). Wilkes retained a couple of small estates in other counties from which he was still collecting rents after his return to England. BL Add. MSS 30873, fol. 32, and BL Add. MSS 30874, fol. 177.

secretary to Lord Egremont, but Cotes pocketed the money, sending Wilkes just twenty guineas of it.[13]

Wilkes did have one asset always at his disposal – his pen – which after Charles Churchill's death he pledged to put to profitable use. His principal projects were an edition of Churchill's poetry and a multi-volume History of England. The image of writer-in-exile was one that appealed to Wilkes. In April 1765, he wrote from Naples: 'I am in the bosom of philosophy and Corradini, calm and pensive, giving myself entirely to the two works.' His ambitions were high; his history would match 'the dignity of Livy', the historian of the Roman Republic; but in fact his literary efforts were desultory. A few notes on Churchill's poems appeared in the press, but never the proposed edition. And despite signing a contract with John Almon for publication of the history – for which he received a small advance – he only ever completed the introduction. In the latter part of his exile, virtually his only income was the donations from the Rockingham Whigs – which at first he had haughtily spurned – and gifts from sympathetic visitors such as the banker Thomas Walpole.[14] But such handouts could not keep pace with his escalating indebtedness, and in December 1767 he was obliged to flee Paris in order to avoid the seizure of his property and possible arrest. His departure with Polly from their apartment was so precipitous that they abandoned nearly all their moveable possessions, including Polly's angora cat, which was found 'howling and dying' by one of Wilkes's agents.[15] Wilkes also left behind a host of highly disgruntled French creditors – among them a wine-merchant, a tailor, a harpsichord-maker, and a watchmaker – some of whom, with a kind of futile tenacity, were still pressing their claims in the late 1770s.[16] Soon a story was doing the rounds that before leaving Paris, Wilkes had moved beyond financial irresponsibility and engaged in deliberate fraud. The allegation was that he obtained £1,000 worth of jewels for inspection and then pawned them, fleeing the French capital the following day.[17]

With such rumours circulating, Wilkes in 1768 appealed for political support from the voters of London and Middlesex. As discussed in chapter 5, these constituencies were famous for their traditions of popular opposition to central government, which explains their courtship by Wilkes, but they also consisted

---

[13] Cotes to Wilkes, 7 January 1765, BL Add. MSS 30869, fol. 8; Thomas, *Wilkes*, pp. 58–67.

[14] Wilkes to James Boswell, 27 April 1765, Boswell Collection, C3088; Wilkes to George Colman, 25 March 1765, Osborn Shelves fc 76, vol. 2, letter 101, Osborn Collection; Thomas, *Wilkes*, pp. 59, 63, 67–68.

[15] BL Add. MSS 30870, fol. 19.

[16] BL Add. MSS 30869, fol. 176; BL Add. MSS 30870, fols 4, 10; BL Add. MSS 30871, fol. 141; BL Add MSS 30872, fol. 161. Perhaps Wilkes's election as chamberlain revived the hopes of his French creditors.

[17] Thomas, *Wilkes*, p. 69.

of the very people who one might assume would have been most disturbed by his financial improprieties. On the face of it, someone whom Benjamin Franklin, conflating moral worth with financial standing, dismissed as 'of bad personal character, not worth a farthing', was an unlikely candidate for favour in a commercial community. Typical was the judgement of an anti-Wilkite scribe who denounced Wilkes as unconscionably seeking 'to establish a Confidence among a People, from most of whom, for very substantial Reasons, he would find it difficult to procure the Loan of a single shilling'. One pamphleteer was prepared to forgive Wilkes his love of pleasure, but claimed 'that far heavier things are alleged against him, namely, that he is ... *careless* of other people's property, no matter how *it* or the *evidence of it* come into his hands'.[18] Certainly, in throwing in his lot with Fortuna, Wilkes had left many hostages to that fickle goddess, which his opponents persistently tried to exploit. They rejoiced to hear of his 'pecuniary difficulties', Heaton reported, and John himself was concerned that publicity about his parlous economic state might wreck his electoral chances.[19] Ominously, his enemies not only condemned him for his financial delinquency; they also implied its connection to other aspects of inappropriate conduct. Stealing his anti-Gallican thunder, they pointedly alleged an addiction to French whores and French wines – grave charges against a self-proclaimed patriot.[20]

Yet such allegations did not sway 'the "middling" type of tradesman, merchant and manufacturer' who supported Wilkes's successive bids to become MP for Middlesex.[21] Nor did they deter the rate-paying freemen in the ward of Farringdon Without, a comparable socioeconomic group, who brought Wilkes into London's civic life as their alderman. As we have seen, the London liverymen moved more cautiously to his support, rebuffing his hastily organised attempt to win election as a City MP following his return from Paris in 1768; but within a few years he was their choice as Sheriff and then Lord Mayor of London. Only when Wilkes sought the office of Chamberlain of London, under circumstances to be discussed below, did his chosen constituency temporarily abandon him.

What made Wilkes's electoral successes all the more remarkable was the fact that the critical bombardment against him was joined by some of his erstwhile supporters, most notably Revd John Horne, who could wield a pen with as much

---

[18]   *The Papers of Benjamin Franklin*, ed. Leonard W. Labaree, W.B. Willcox *et al.*, 30 vols (New Haven, 1959–) vol. 15, pp. 98–99; T.G., *Public Advertiser*, 8 November 1771; *Essays on Patriotism and the Character and Conduct of Some Late Famous Pretenders to that Virtue Particularly of the Present Popular Gentleman* (London, 1768), p. 53.

[19]   Heaton Wilkes to Wilkes, 2 April 1767, BL Add. MSS 30869, fol. 109; Wilkes to Heaton Wilkes, 25 December 1767, Wilkes MSS 2, fol. 95.

[20]   TULLIUS, *Public Ledger*, 2 October 1771.

[21]   This characterisation of Wilkes's support is from George Rudé, *Wilkes and Liberty: A Social Study of 1763 to 1774* (Oxford, 1962), p. 89.

polemical force as Wilkes himself. One of the things at issue was Wilkes's use of money raised by the Society of the Supporters of the Bill of Rights (SSBR). From the beginning, Horne regarded the SSBR in a different light from his former ally. Acknowledging that Wilkes had aroused important public causes, Horne and his allies judged the society's principal task as protecting these from 'the just abhorrence of Mr. Wilkes as a private man' by discreetly paying off his creditors. They resented Wilkes's attempt to intercept subscriptions intended for the payment of his just debts so that he could continue his career of extravagance. Horne's indictment was contained in a public exchange of letters with Wilkes and his supporters, in the course of which Horne laid out a full catalogue of Wilkes's financial misconduct. These would be repeated as a litany of accusation throughout Wilkes's subsequent political career. The least effective complaints were those levelled at Wilkes's domestic extravagances; as we saw in chapter 1, they ran up against sentimental approval of Wilkes's dedication to family life, with Polly at his side. But there were some graver charges that were not so readily disposed of. According to Horne, Wilkes bilked honest tradesmen in London and Paris, engaging in 'fraudulent pretence' to obtain goods even after his release from the King's Bench Prison in 1770. He reportedly evaded repayment of money owed to one Isaac Fernandes Silva – who had purchased debt that Wilkes had taken on when he sought election for Aylesbury – by destroying the bonds when they were presented to him. He also allegedly diverted regimental funds to his own use while he was the colonel of the Buckinghamshire militia, and robbed innocent orphans by embezzling money from the Aylesbury branch of the Foundling Hospital during his tenure as its treasurer and director.[22]

Not unexpectedly, Wilkes and his supporters responded energetically to most of these charges (appealing to a popular prejudice against Jewish moneylenders in combating the complaint of Silva).[23] Yet some of them were supported by disturbing pieces of evidence. As early as 1763, a clothier insisted that Wilkes had not paid for some militia uniforms, claiming that Wilkes brushed him off with the remark that he should 'think it a favour' that Wilkes had employed him.[24] Heaton Wilkes reported, without comment, that a merchant had supplied coals to the Aylesbury Foundling Hospital without receiving payment, even though the hospital's accounts showed that John had received the money to pay him.[25] Other of Horne's charges remained unanswered, including the one that Wilkes justified

---

[22] *Controversial Letters*, pp. 58–67; Bleackley, *Wilkes*, pp. 264–65.

[23] TRUTH, *Gazetteer*, 9 August 1771. On the hostility to Jewish moneylenders, see Hoppit, 'Attitudes to Credit', pp. 313–34.

[24] Henry Allnutt to Francis Dashwood, 21 January 1763 and 10 July 1763, MS D.D. Dashwood (Bucks), B 8/1/8–9, Bodleian Library.

[25] BL Add. MSS 30869, fols 98–99.

his financial delinquency by airily remarking that 'those who do pay make amends for those who do not; and that tradesmen always charge accordingly'.[26] Despite the apparent weight of Horne's indictment, however, it was Wilkes who survived the fracas with his support largely intact, going on to further electoral triumphs.

Those of the 'middling sort' not only supported Wilkes with their votes, they also lent him support in the clubs and associations that were becoming such an important part of the informal institutional fabric of commercial and civic life. Wilkes certainly had traits of personality that made him eminently clubbable. He was unremittingly affable and gregarious, and, as we saw in chapter 3, his strutting masculinity had much appeal for the denizens of all-male societies. Yet there was discordance between Wilkes's casual attitude to money matters and an emerging commercial sensibility that the network of associations was helping to foster. The clubs of London and the provinces – at least those with membership drawn predominantly from the 'middling sort' – characteristically blended a boozy conviviality with the more serious functions of mutual economic support. Membership in them could extend an individual's range of commercial contacts and customers and thereby help to free him from the snares of aristocratic clientage. At the same time, clubs offered direct assistance; pooled resources could be made available to protect financially distressed members against foreclosure by creditors, thus serving to lift somewhat the spectres of bankruptcy and debtors' prison.[27]

In addition to practical help, many clubs also furnished an institutional framework for the reinforcement of a set of values that, once internalised, offered the prospect of greater certitude in commercial transactions. According to John Brewer, '[m]any of the clubs were, in effect, vehicles for the promotion of a morality and outlook conducive to successful trading'. Prudence, reliability, moderation, and probity – all things that promoted creditworthiness and defused the destructive potential of the credit system – were some of the ethical components of this emerging commercial sensibility, one which mediated the delicate intersection of social conscience and self-interest. Not all associations, of course, were equally involved in this process. But it seems, nonetheless, to have been a fairly general one, extending to organisations, such as the Freemasons, that diverged from the cosmopolitanism and enlightened freethinking of their continental confrères in favour of a different ethos, one that associated commercial propriety with religious orthodoxy and reverence for King and Country.[28]

---

26 *Controversial Letters*, p. 183.

27 John Brewer, 'Commercialization and Politics', in *The Birth of a Consumer Society: The Commercialization of Eighteenth-Century England*, ed. Neil McKendrick *et al.* (Bloomington, 1982), pp. 217–30.

28 Ibid., p. 223; John Money, 'The Masonic Moment; Or, Ritual, Replica, and Credit: John Wilkes, the Macaroni Parson, and the Making of the Middle-Class Mind', *Journal of British Studies*, 32 (1993): 358–95.

Wilkes, though an enthusiastic clubman, was scarcely in sympathy with the sensibility that many clubs were now displaying, which perhaps explains why he was selective in his membership of them. But he did join the Freemasons while in prison in 1769, as well as a handful of quasi-Masonic orders. One can reasonably speculate that he was attracted more by the libertine associations of such organisations than their newfound emphasis on commercial responsibility. The Freemasons, for example, had a tradition of deism, although their character was changing. As befitted a boisterous patriot, Wilkes also seized the opportunity to parade his contrived Francophobia by accepting the presidency of the Antigallicans, a group dedicated to promoting British manufactures at the expense of French ones. But he was clearly most at home in socially privileged organisations like the Beefsteaks, where the emphasis remained squarely on hedonistic pleasure and racy conversation.[29]

To some of the values promoted by less privileged societies, Wilkes and his inner circle showed not simply indifference, but studied resistance. Infusing much of the poetry of his soul-mate Charles Churchill – who perhaps more than anyone gave coherent philosophical expression to Wilkes's own sensibilities – was a profound sense that 'where COMMERCE proudly rears her throne', values were subverted as they were redefined. Churchill's particular target was 'prudence', by some reckoning a central bourgeois quality. He saw it as having lost its classical association with 'godlike wisdom', becoming instead 'the stalking-horse of vice, and folly's screen'. In his view, prudence bore no connection to altruism and every connection to self-interest: 'PRUDENCE, almighty PRUDENCE gives thee all. / Keep up appearances; there lies the test, / the world will give thee credit for the rest.' Wilkes himself, as his mother periodically scolded him, could not be charged with prudence; and when he set out on his abortive mission to produce his annotated edition of his late friend's poetry, he picked out with particular approval the lines: 'Might the whole world be plac'd within my span, / I would not be *that* THING, *that* PRUDENT MAN.'[30]

However, Wilkes's obvious distaste for some of the values that clubs and associations were upholding in no way discouraged them from offering him apparently unqualified backing. They supported him with resolutions and

---

[29]   A.M. Broadley, *Brother John Wilkes, MP: Alderman, Chamberlain, and Lord Mayor of London, as Freemason, 'Buck', 'Leech' and 'Beefsteak'* (Weymouth, 1914); Brewer, 'Commercialization and Politics', p. 233; Wilkes to Jean-Baptiste Suard, 13 April 1770 and 27 April 1770, Wilkes MSS, 3, fols 32, 33.

[30]   'The Ghost', line 521, 'Night', lines 298–300, 310–12, 343–44, in *The Poetical Works of Charles Churchill*, ed. Douglas Grant (Oxford, 1956) pp. 59, 60, 119; *Wilkes Correspondence*, vol. 3, p. 12. On the centrality of prudence to a developing commercial ethos, see Jerry Z. Muller, *Adam Smith in his Time and Ours: Designing the Decent Society* (New York, 1993), pp. 97, 165–66.

presents and above all with generous subscriptions of money. The SSBR was only the apex of a network of organisations that furnished cash for his political campaigns and for the alleviation of his personal insolvency. In April 1770, at the expiry of Wilkes's two-year prison term, there was an emergency collection to clear his debts, thus depriving any malicious creditors of the opportunity to keep him jail.[31] On top of the £7,404 already disbursed by the SSBR on Wilkes's behalf, the society scrambled to find the money to pay remaining debts and fines totalling nearly £10,000; it fell some ways short, but its efforts were sufficient to enable Wilkes to recover his freedom.[32]

There is much here that requires explanation. Why would businessmen and tradesmen expend hard-earned money, as well as cast their votes, in support of a man whose attitudes and conduct were of a kind that was widely recognised as causing commercial difficulties for them? The inquiry should start with a couple of provisos. It is entirely possible that beneath the surface of popular enthusiasm for Wilkes, there were many who harboured profound misgivings about his financial delinquencies. After all, even in his bailiwick of the City of London, support for Wilkes among the 'middling sort', though impressive, was never total, a circumstance inadequately explained by ministerial interference in local politics. And when he sought the position of Chamberlain of London, the fact of his indebtedness provided a clear focus for successful opposition to his candidacy. There is also evidence that many people supported Wilkes because of the public issues that he raised, while maintaining a tacit objection to aspects of his private conduct.[33] There is no reason to assume that such tactical support was confined to political elites. There were those of the 'middling sort' who were capable of distinguishing between what they perceived as Wilkes's frequently repellent conduct and the Wilkite agenda, which offered a prospect of independence from oligarchic politics.

Yet even after such allowances are conceded, the enthusiasm of Wilkes's core supporters, so unqualified that it verged on idolatry, still has to be accounted for. There was an affinity between Wilkes and his followers that could only have proceeded from a clear mutuality of outlook and a predisposition to accept Wilkes's interpretation of events. Wilkes's engagingly libertine and anti-establishment persona, described in the previous chapters, is part of the

---

[31] Brewer, 'Commercialization and Politics', pp. 233–35; *Middlesex Journal*, 15–17 June 1769; *Independent Chronicle*, 13–16 April 1770.

[32] Thomas, *Wilkes*, pp. 113–15.

[33] For examples of this kind of pragmatic support, see J.A.W. Gunn, *Beyond Liberty and Property: The Process of Self-Recognition in Eighteenth-Century Political Thought* (Kingston and Montreal, 1983), p. 207; John Sainsbury, *Disaffected Patriots: London Supporters of Revolutionary America, 1769–1782* (Kingston and Montreal, 1987) p. 18.

explanation. But something was also owed to his success in representing himself as a patriot-hero, as defined by classical criteria and imagery. This undertaking sought the inversion and transcendence of the conventional relationship between creditor and debtor. Wilkes, the incorrigible debtor, now became the nation's creditor when he returned in 1768 like a patriot-hero of ancient Rome – an image that he consciously embraced – to enjoy the public's favour. The public, his propagandists argued, was in debt to him for his bold and patriotic stand against the government's illegal deployment of general warrants and seizure of papers. 'Consider how much you are indebted to Mr. Wilkes', declared a broadside addressed to the citizens of the ward of Farringdon Without. 'Think how much to him we owe', London's livery was told as Wilkes sought its support in the 1768 Parliamentary elections.[34] The gifts that flooded into the King's Bench Prison from all parts of the empire during his incarceration there were the tangible expression of such gratitude. There were some interesting literary precedents for the lionisation of Wilkes: sixteenth-century stories, addressed to London citizens, conferred hero status on local worthies who conducted themselves with the valour of ancient Romans, and on merchants who spent like gentlemen.[35]

Wilkes filled his self-prescribed role with skill and conviction, marking out a well-defined and, for many, reassuring image in a bustling commercial metropolis of increasingly confused identities. Instead of the equivocal values of commerce, he offered the time-honoured ones of civic humanism. His knowledge of classical literature and history stood him in good stead as he identified himself with the patriotic opponents of corruption and tyranny in classical Greece and Rome, and their spiritual descendants in English history. He dubbed himself, in Roman style, the 'tribune of the people'.[36] His patrons and supporters endorsed these conceits. He was variously lauded as Cato, the Spartan Leonidas, and the 'English Brutus'. In 1772, as a reward for his resolution in the 'printer's case', the Common Council of London presented him with a silver cup depicting the death of the tyrant Caesar in the Capitol.[37] Wilkes carefully cultivated the image of warrior-citizen, an ideal of civic humanism, in ways that appealed to contemporary patriotism. His exploits on the field of honour were important in this context. It was when

---

[34] William Purdie Treloar, *Wilkes and the City* (London, 1917), p. 46; AN ENGLISHMAN, 'To the Worthy and Independent Inhabitants of the Ward of Farringdon Without', and a jingle, 'Wilkes and the Livery: To the Voters for the City of London', City Elections, 1768–96 [A Broadside Collection], An. 5.4. no. 15, pages 6, 24.

[35] Laura Stevenson O'Connell, 'The Elizabethan Bourgeois Hero-Tale', in *After the Reformation: Essays in Honour of J.H. Hexter*, ed. Barbara C. Malament (Manchester, 1980), pp. 269–75.

[36] Wilkes MSS 3, fol. 26

[37] *Grenville Papers*, vol. 2, p. 3; A SON OF FREEDOM, *Middlesex Journal*, 2–5 September 1769; BL Add. MSS 30871, fol. 180; [Wilkes] *Letters to Daughter*, vol. 1, p. 121; Judith Banister, '"In the Cause of Liberty": A Cup and Cover in the Mansion House', *Country Life*, 170 (1981): 1671–72.

confronting the prospect of death from a duelling pistol that Wilkes exhibited 'self-control' in its classical definition, as distinct from its emerging sense as prudence in commercial transactions.

Wilkes's martial ardour merged with his reputation as a resolute defender of Britain's imperial interests, which especially among London's trading community were regarded as the basis for enduring commercial prosperity. As we saw in chapter 2, his first significant intervention in political life was to denounce the peace settlement that ended the Seven Years' War as a despicable and unpatriotic 'sell-out' to the country's imperial competitors, France and Spain. Later, he would condemn government for ripping up the fabric of empire by driving well-intentioned and patriotic Americans to independence through a wilful disregard for their liberties.[38] His well-defined position on imperial issues positioned him to inherit the mantle of popularity enjoyed by heroes such as Admiral Vernon and William Pitt.[39] Crucially, Wilkes's robust attachment to the assumed basis of commercial prosperity served to deflect attention from his lack of attachment to commercial propriety. He endorsed what in time would become a hackneyed theme: that great empires are built and sustained by men of heroic vision, not by the eighteenth-century equivalent of men in grey business suits prudently fussing over account books.

Wilkes's credentials as a patriot were far from being universally accepted, however, and Samuel Johnson was not the only person to scoff at them. The appeal to antiquity encountered considerable scepticism. One critic lampooned Wilkes's attempt to portray himself as a classical patriot beyond the petty claims of commercial propriety. In a facetious panegyric of Wilkes 'in the manner of Plutarch', the writer asked with heavy irony:

> Would it not have been deemed as the height of absurdity that a *Cicero* or a *Maecenas* should have stopped to have regulated a Grocer's bill, when the welfare of millions depended on their public counsels? – *Pericles* one of the most admired heroes of antiquity, when his accounts were confused, and could not well be given up, not only destroyed the Notes (if I may so express it) but to drown the remembrance, involved his country in the Peloponnesian war.[40]

---

[38]   Sainsbury, *Disaffected Patriots,* pp. 31–33, 82, 129.

[39]   On the legacy of popularity to which Wilkes laid claim, see Kathleen Wilson, 'Empire, Trade and Popular Politics in Mid-Hanoverian Britain: The Case of Admiral Vernon', *Past and Present,* 121 (November 1988), pp. 74–109; Nicholas Rogers, *Whigs and Cities: Popular Politics in the Age of Walpole and Pitt* (Oxford, 1989), pp. 87–129; Marie Peters, *Pitt and Popularity: The Patriot Minister and London Opinion during the Seven Years' War* (Oxford and New York, 1980), *passim.*

[40]   [Joseph Cradock] *The Life of John Wilkes, Esq., in the Manner of Plutarch* (London, 1773), pp. 20–21.

Clearly, classical analogy did not always work in Wilkes's favour. Ministerial writers employed the appeal to Rome to expose demagogic subverters of public order. The *Auditor* called Wilkes 'Colonel Cataline' after the bankrupt rabble-rouser of the late Roman republic.[41] Such characterisations, however, in themselves betrayed an uneasy awareness that Wilkes was not a patriot-hero shaped in an austerely Ciceronian mould (unlike, say, William Pitt or George Washington), but rather one who enjoyed an uncanny intimacy with his followers. Wilkes himself gave a distinctive popular twist to the precepts of civic humanism by his aspersions against 'the damned aristocracy', examined in the previous chapter, and by his denial that wealth was a sufficient precondition for disinterested public service.[42] His views struck a chord. In 1769, a ministerial apologist sought to denigrate a petition on Wilkes's behalf from the citizens of Westminster on the grounds that it was 'signed by BASE-BORN booksellers and BASE-BORN people ... low mechanics not fit to enter the gates of his Majesty's palace'. In vigorous response, John Almon reassigned 'credit' and 'debt' along class lines, while tactfully ignoring Wilkes's own financial delinquencies:

> Such low mechanicks as signed the Westminster petition, are the pillars of his Majesty's palace. We pay our debts when they are contracted; we pay our taxes when they are demanded. Can the profligate part of the Great, who value themselves upon their manors and their pedigrees, say as much? It is from the labours, the stock, the traffic of such mechanics as signed the Westminster petition, that his Majesty's revenue receives its most essential support; that revenue out of which the placeman receives his salary for betraying the right of the people, and the pensioner the wages of his iniquity.[43]

Connected with such an outlook was a sustained critique of the system of public financial funding. This campaign, which was at the rhetorical core of eighteenth-century expressions of civic humanism, perhaps more than anything else served to fuse Wilkes's political agenda with the economic anxieties of his followers. Beginning with its institutionalised inception in the form of a managed national debt, government borrowing had been vehemently attacked as a poisonous source of political and moral corruption. The Bank of England, which managed the debt, was routinely described as 'a fountain of evil'.[44] Ignoring the reality that such

---

[41] Quoted in *A Collection of all the Remarkable and Personal Passages in the Briton, North Briton, and Auditor* (London, 1766), p. 57.

[42] Paul Langford, *Public Life and the Propertied Englishman, 1689–1798* (Oxford and New York, 1991), p. 233.

[43] [John Almon] *Memoirs of a Late Eminent Bookseller* (London, 1790), pp. 56–57.

[44] *London Evening Post*, 2–4 January 1776.

deficit financing funded popular wars of imperial expansion, the critique insisted that the public debt, with all the evils of speculation and stockjobbery that it brought in its train, was inimical not only to the traditional values and interests of landed society but also to the benign operation of commerce itself.[45] Elements of the argument were probably misconceived. For much of the century, failures of public credit, including the South Sea Bubble (1720), had only a marginal impact on the operations of normal commerce; and conversely some financial panics, such as that of 1772, were confined to the private sector.[46] But such are the retrospective judgements of economic historians; contemporary perceptions were a different matter. And the arguments against the national finance system retained a distinct resonance for hard-pressed tradesmen in the 1760s and 1770s, for whom government borrowing spelled high taxes and diminished circulating currency. In newspapers, pamphlets, and on political platforms, connections were established between public and private debt in ways that tended to shift responsibility for indebtedness from the individual to the state. 'Burdened as we are with taxes,' wrote one newspaper correspondent in 1769, 'we have seen fresh ones raised, and every scheme pursued that could destroy the very means of complying with them; our manufactures and trade.'[47]

Wilkes's own situation was scarcely comparable with that of the 'poor mechanic' and 'declining merchant' who were the objects of the writer's sympathetic concern. Yet he was linked to them as a fellow victim of the system of government financing because of the political corruption that it supposedly engendered. In the *North Briton* no. 42 he had attacked the wastefulness and favouritism involved in the allocation of public loans. For this and other temerities, so the Wilkites alleged, he was hounded by the venal agents of the

---

[45]   Shelley Burtt, *Virtue Transformed: Political Argument in England, 1688–1740* (Cambridge and New York, 1992), pp. 100–103; J.G.A. Pocock, *The Machiavellian Moment: Florentine Political Thought and the Atlantic Republican Tradition* (Princeton, 1975), pp. 447–48.

[46]   Julian Hoppit, 'Financial Crises in Eighteenth-Century England', *Economic History Review,* 2nd Series, 39 (1986), pp. 39–58.

[47]   A CITIZEN OF LONDON, *Middlesex Journal,* 16–18 May 1769. See also 'Andrew Marvel', ibid., 9–11 January 1769, and HUE AND CRY, ibid., 30 September–3 October 1769, which blamed high taxes for giving a competitive advantage to French traders. The debate over public debt intensified antagonism between the 'moneyed interest', those rich merchants and financiers who, as fund-holders, benefited from the system, and the middling and lower orders, which saw themselves as its victims. The divide was not an absolute one because some members of the 'middling sort' purchased government and allied stocks. Amateur investors even had their own guidebook, Thomas Mortimer's *Every Man his own Broker,* which went through numerous editions from the middle of the eighteenth century. The book vehemently attacked stockjobbers, but despite its title Mortimer was far from being a proto-Thatcherite apostle of people's capitalism. His advice was directed to 'merchants and gentlemen', and he was scathing about humble folk who involved themselves in high finance.

system that he had sought to expose. In the petition of the Middlesex freeholders, delivered to the king on 24 May 1769, a protest about 'public loans perverted to private ministerial purposes' meaningfully preceded the central issue of complaint: Wilkes's expulsion from the House of Commons by the votes of corrupted members.[48]

The motives of the government agents who moved against Wilkes were denounced in the same terms as those of creditors acting against their victims. Following his arrest for seditious libel in 1763 on the basis of a general warrant, Wilkes had complained of the 'premeditated malice' of his persecutors. 'The only motive of the creditor,' protested one newspaper correspondent, 'may be passion, malice, or revenge.' Further, the means deployed against Wilkes in that arrest mirrored the methods deployed by creditors and bailiffs against their victims. Wilkes talked of his house being 'ransacked and plundered'; a typical complaint on behalf of debtors was that 'one's own house or apartment is not even an asylum, or refuge here, against … malevolent surprizes and insults'.[49] Such parallels suggest why Wilkes won support when, on his return to England from his French exile, he took his political stand on 'the two important questions of public liberty, respecting *General Warrants* and the *Seizure of papers*'. These violations had more than an abstract or technical connotation for those who were subject to the arbitrary whims of their creditors.[50]

The association of the Wilkite cause with the political culture of debt might have proceeded even if Wilkes himself had not been a debtor. Yet in the forging of an emotional link between himself and his supporters, the circumstance of his own indebtedness was of positive value, despite the fact that it also provided political ammunition for his enemies. Paradoxically, an understanding of this dimension of Wilkes's support must proceed from recognition of the moral incubus that attached to debt. In large part this was a corollary of the development of the ethic of creditworthiness, alluded to earlier. Insolvency entailed more than simple economic failure. It attached a stigma to its victims, which meant that a shattering blow to self-esteem usually attended the misery of bankruptcy or debtors' prison. Probably for this reason, debtors sometimes resorted to public attempts at exoneration. Rubbing salt in the wounds of debtors was a host of finger-pointing commentators only too willing to ascribe indebtedness to a

---

[48] *Annual Register* (1769), Appendix to the Chronicle, p. 199.

[49] Ibid. (1763), Appendix to the Chronicle, 139; LIBERTAS, *Middlesex Journal*, 15–17 August 1769. See also, *Middlesex Journal*, 6–8 April 1769.

[50] *Gentleman's Magazine* (1768): 124. For the account of an artisanal victim of a general warrant, see *Battle of the Quills*, pp. 50–51. Debtors were not without legal protections from their creditors, but the frequency of their complaints suggests that these were frequently violated.

deficiency in conduct or personal morality: excessive risk-taking, for example, or addiction to luxury.[51]

In such a context, the course of Wilkes's career – raised as it was from the picaresque to the realm of epic by his publicists, himself included – took on a powerful significance for the embattled debtor. By his words and actions, he displayed an insouciant disregard for rigid commercial proprieties, yet at the same time he embraced a code of values, associated with traditional patriotism, that transcended them and restored a classical, pre-commercial definition to the concept of virtue. An intimate and vicarious association with his career thus acted as an antidote to the loss of self-worth that attached to indebtedness or its prospect. Becoming a Wilkite could not, of course, relieve financial obligations, but it could lift the moral incubus that attached to insolvency as those in, or at the brink of, debt bathed in a sense of patriotic virtue generated by association with their hero. Some sense of that process can be elicited from the letters sent to Wilkes by those who had fallen on hard times. Typically the writers acknowledge a combination of youthful folly and cruel oppression as responsible for their plight, thus echoing Wilkes's own career. The letters convey a sense of yearning for release from the moral contamination of poverty and debt, and a conviction that redemption was to be found in bucolic simplicity, or more typically in attachment to the patriot cause as embodied in Wilkes himself. Humphrey Cotes expressed perfectly the transcendent appeal of patriotic virtue to the embattled debtor. After stating his desire to re-enter commerce after his bankruptcy, he added a condemnation of 'those prudential maxims of the generality of men, which serve only to conceal deeds, that will not stand the test of honour, or, to excuse the exercise of those great principles of Liberty, their little minds are incapable of comprehending'.[52]

The best-documented case is that of Charlotte Forman.[53] Possessed of an elegant and clear handwriting, she eked out a living as a translator and political essayist. By the late 1760s ill-health and the loss of family support had left her, to use her own words, in 'a situation that would stagger the constancy of a Stoic'. When

---

[51] For some suggestive comments concerning the moral burden on debtors, see Hoppit, *Risk and Failure,* pp. 161–81. For appeals to the public by debtors, see *The Extraordinary Case of William Penrice* (London, 1768), and *The Case of Anne and Isaac Scott, Bankrupts, late Merchants and Dry-salters* (London, 1768). The Scott pamphlet prompted a libel action, and a copy of it is contained in KB 1/17 part 1, Bundle Hilary 9th George III, no. 2, National Archives.

[52] Cotes to Wilkes, 16 June 1767, London, BL Add. MSS 30869, fol. 132; also letters to Wilkes from John Nesbitt, C.B. (a woman in distress), [?] Preston, Charles Churchill (the son of Wilkes's friend of the same name), and John Burnby in BL Add. MSS 30868, fols 141–42, 173, 183–84; Add. MSS 30870, fols 157–58; Add. MSS 30871, fol. 32; Add. MSS 30872, fols 149–50, 153.

[53] For a summary of available evidence on Forman, see Joel J. Gold, '"Buried Alive": Charlotte Forman in Grub Street', *Eighteenth-Century Life,* new series, 8 (1982): 28–45.

she first wrote to Wilkes in June 1768, seeking him as a patron and protector, she had already spent time in debtors' prison and was facing the prospect of recommittal. Wilkes, from jail, effected some form of relief and in return received effusive expressions of gratitude from Forman and the dedication of her literary talents to the man whom she lauded as 'the Father of his country; the English David; the beloved Patriot; the heroic champion; the Martyr of Liberty'. She drew a pointed comparison between Wilkes's conduct and that of the Earl of Hillsborough, her brother's former employer, who had denied her assistance. Addressing the earl, she asked rhetorically, 'Has Benevolence ... forsaken the gilded Mansion, to take up her abode in a Prison? Is it credible, My Lord, that a private Gentleman [that is, Wilkes], labouring under the pressure of heavy prosecutions, should display more greatness of soul than the mighty, and the affluent?' Forman repeatedly identified her own afflictions with those of her champion, even her country. 'My constitution, like that of Old England, is broke by repeated outrages', she wrote.[54]

The notion, so evident in the letters of Charlotte Forman, that the stigma of indebtedness was eradicable through immersion in the patriot cause readily slid over into the notion that financial indebtedness in a patriot was in itself a badge of honour, and one burnished by sentiment. The concept of the debtor as patriot-hero was supported by the circulation of poignant stories of courageous soldiers and sailors and their widows, rendered destitute by malicious and, by implication, unpatriotic creditors. This theme would find its dramatic apotheosis in a short play written by Maria Barrell, a debtor in the King's Bench Prison. In this melodramatic piece, the hero (Captain Heartly) is a brave soldier cruelly imprisoned and driven to his death by his villainous creditor (Teasewell), who has lascivious designs on Heartly's wife (Amelia). The marks of such melodrama had already been indicated in the perception that the Wilkites urged in favour of their hero. Deploying the language of sentiment, they maintained that their champion was 'a man of free and generous spirit', and as such did not give 'proper attention to his domestic affairs' – hence his insolvency. By contrast, the Duke of Grafton, Wilkes's *bête noire,* was 'a knave' who conducted himself 'with all the art and meanness of an experienced sharper'.[55]

The vindication of the debtor hints at ways in which the values of traditional patriotism, defined by the language of civic humanism, coexisted with an

---

[54]   Forman to Wilkes, 12 June 1768, 28 October 1769, 9 April 1770, BL Add. MSS 30870, fols 52–53, 216; Add. MSS 30871, fol. 26; Forman to Hillsborough, 19 August 1769, BL Add. MSS 30870, fol. 66.

[55]   William Stewardson, *Middlesex Journal,* 5–8 August 1769; Maria Barrell, *The Captive* (1790); *A Fair Comparison between Mr. WILKES and the D--- of G-----n, Middlesex Journal,* 29–31 August 1769.

emerging commercial ethos (later tendentiously labelled as bourgeois) that found expression in many of the clubs and associations who threw Wilkes their support. The two are customarily defined as opposed; yet each is claimed as the central mode of discourse for opposition to government in the eighteenth-century Anglo-American world.[56] The evidence presented here points to an alternative way of looking at the relationship between them. While classically derived patriotism was, indeed, in many respects at odds with 'bourgeois' sensibilities – a discordance that would surface in the contests for the post of London chamberlain – their values also operated symbiotically within the same community. Arguably the emergence of a new commercial ethos, driven by the imperatives of a credit-based economy, imposed such rigorous demands on conduct and conscience that it fostered a revival of civic humanism as means of assuaging or transcending those demands.[57] Certainly there was considerable resistance to the idea that 'œconomy' was a virtue; if it was, claimed one essayist 'none approaches so near to vice', because 'œconomists' invariably lacked 'an amiable disposition'.[58] Understandably, adherence to pre-commercial values would find its most focused expression among the impoverished Grub Street literati (including Churchill, Forman, and on occasion Wilkes himself), but clearly they were not whistling in the dark: their message received widespread endorsement.[59] And in the process,

---

[56]   Isaac Kramnick, *Republicanism and Bourgeois Radicalism: Political Ideology in Late Eighteenth-Century England and America* (Ithaca, 1990), asserts the essential 'bourgeois radicalism' of the Wilkites, including Wilkes himself. John Brewer warned against the parlour game of 'spot the bourgeoisie' ('English Radicalism in the Age of George III', in *Three British Revolutions, 1641, 1688, 1776*, ed. J.G.A. Pocock [Princeton, 1980], p. 330), yet in a concurrent publication, he concludes that Wilkite 'attitudes' were 'bourgeois', while conceding that Wilkes himself represented a special case ('The Wilkites and the Law, 1763–74: A Study of Radical Notions of Governance', *Ungovernable People,* ed. Brewer and Styles, p. 171). Kramnick's formulation can be compared with that of J.G.A. Pocock, who has traced the persistence of civic humanism as a central mode of opposition thought. See especially his *Virtue, Commerce and History: Essays on Political Thought and History, Chiefly in the Eighteenth Century* (Cambridge and New York, 1975), esp. pp. 48–49, 68–69, 114–15. Pocock does, however, acknowledge the possible appearance 'in middle-Georgian London' of 'a democratic radicalism furnishing the individual with the politics of life in a world of exchange relationships', but he warns that we should not 'fetishize the term "bourgeois" and construct a naive and crude antithesis between republican and Lockean forms of radicalism'. Ibid., p. 260.

[57]   For a different view, see John Brewer who argues that Wilkes parlayed 'a special, commercial brand of politics' that diverged from 'the classical republican framework of traditional country-party ideology'. *Party Ideology and Popular Politics at the Accession of George III* (Cambridge and New York, 1976), p. 180.

[58]   'Reflections on œconomy', *Town and Country Magazine* (1769): 120.

[59]   Another indigent hack, William Combe, commented: 'Love of gain entirely envelopes all traits of feeling and delicacy of sentiment ... I bless heaven I am not a man of merchandize', quoted in G.J. Barker-Benfield, *The Culture of Sensibility: Sex and Society in Eighteenth-Century Britain* (Chicago, 1992), p. 219.

the debtor, of whom Wilkes was the exemplar, could be redeemed from the status of pariah and elevated to that of patriot-hero.

King's Bench Debtors

Wilkes's confinement in the King's Bench Prison heightened the association between his political cause and that of the debtor. Wilkes was not, of course, himself confined for debt, but many of his fellow prisoners were, and Wilkes himself faced suits from creditors during his incarceration.[60] It was no coincidence that a spirited movement for debtors' rights should have occurred in King's Bench Prison in the wake of Wilkes's tenure there. His success in appealing to constitutional liberty in opposing the arbitrary operation of the legal system, specifically in his stand against general warrants, aroused expectations among some of his fellow inmates that imprisonment for debt could be likewise exposed as contrary to fundamental law. Some articulate and forceful spokesmen, notably James Stephen, pressed the case. A Scot with self-taught legal knowledge, Stephen was committed to King's Bench Prison for debt in August 1769. While there, Stephen drew support from a representative institution known as the 'college', which fostered within prison gates something equivalent to that sense of civic pride and independence that was so crucial to Wilkes's own success in London.[61] From prison, Stephen published a pamphlet that denounced imprisonment for debt as contrary to *Magna Carta* and as a 'tyrannic practice' sustained by the 'exorbitant profits' which accrued to 'the courts, their dependents and creatures'.[62]

Stephen and his associates employed a Wilkite combination of legal manoeuvres, appeals to the public, and direct action to press their case. In November 1770, having exhausted other legal avenues, Stephen brought himself before the judges of King's Bench on a writ of habeas corpus and demanded his release, challenging the court to demonstrate a basis in statute or common law for his continued imprisonment. The day before the hearing, Revd William F. Jackson, one of Stephen's debtor friends, wrote to Wilkes seeking his support for this initiative. There is no evidence that Wilkes responded.[63] After his legal

---

[60] *Middlesex Journal*, 22–25 April 1769.

[61] On the campaign for prisoners' rights, see Innes, 'The King's Bench prison', pp. 290–98. Printed versions of the rules of the prison college are in Guildhall MS 659.1, Guildhall Library. Biographical information on Stephen is contained in his son's *Memoirs of James Stephen*, ed. Merle M. Bevington (London, 1954), pp. 89–103.

[62] *Considerations on Imprisonment for Debt*, pp. 14, 64–65.

[63] 18 November 1770, BL Add. MSS 30871, fols 46–47. For Dublin-born Jackson's colourful and disputatious career, see *Biographical Dictionary of Modern British Radicals*, ed. Joseph O. Baylen and Norbert J. Gossman, 3 vols (Hassocks and Atlantic Highlands, 1979), vol. 1, pp. 254–59; and Lucyle Werkmeister, 'Notes for a Revised Life of William Jackson', *Notes and Queries*, 206 (1961): 43–47.

challenges proved fruitless, Stephen organised breakouts of prisoners from King's Bench, an undertaking designed less as an attempt to win freedom by force than as a symbolic protest against illegal imprisonment.[64]

There was much here, both in terms of legal argument and of tactics, that would seemingly have attracted Wilkes's sympathy. And Stephen and his associates expected his support, or at least thought that they were entitled to it. After all, as Stephen pointed out, had not Wilkes encouraged 'the Struggle for the Liberty of the lower Class of Men, and the Unfortunate'? Expectations were raised when Wilkes was elected Sheriff of London in June 1771. As a magistrate and peace officer, he was now at the centre of the legal process by which debtors were committed to prison. 'Mr. Wilkes, in the Capacity of Sheriff,' declared W.F. Jackson, 'had a glorious Opportunity to combat a Species of Despotism much more infamous than General Warrants.'[65]

Wilkes was put to the test in November 1771 when Stephen, now freed from jail, challenged a warrant, which Wilkes had signed, committing one Nicholas Grimshaw to prison for debt. In a widely reported exchange between Wilkes and Stephen in the under-sheriff's office, Stephen argued strenuously that Grimshaw's committal was illegal and contrary to *Magna Carta*. On the defensive, Wilkes suggested that 'long custom' had made imprisonment for debt 'a part of the common law'. Stephen, alluding to Wilkes's stand against general warrants and his more recent opposition to naval impressment, had a telling retort:

> Long custom made law for you. Mr. Wilkes! Has not the custom been to press seamen ever since there was a ship of war belonging to this nation? Yet did you not discharge the impressed men: Were not general warrants sanctified by long custom? Will you, of all men, plead long custom against *Magna Carta*?

The interview ended with Wilkes tamely arguing that he was obliged to act 'ministerially' and not 'magisterially', and in such a capacity was unable to pass judgment on the legality of the warrant. Redress for debtors, he suggested, would have to come from another quarter.[66]

During this episode, Wilkes the debtor-hero came perilously close to exposing feet of clay as hero to the debtors. It is not hard to understand his dilemma. Had he moved to free debtors, he would have been vulnerable to legal actions from their creditors for allowing their escape. Wilkes, though, in a lengthy

---

[64] Innes, 'The King's Bench prison', pp. 293–96.

[65] *Public Advertiser*, 25 January 1772, and 26 December 1771.

[66] *Miller's London Mercury*, 23 November 1771.

apologia to the London livery, dismissed the 'cowardly meanness of such a defence'. His principal reason for caution was to preserve confidence in the credit system, which a bold gesture in support of debtors' rights might have compromised. 'I could not think myself justified', he said, ' ... to commit a manifest injury against a great number of creditors, who were pursuing the accustomed course of actions at law for the recovery of their property.'[67] (He was on more secure patriotic ground when he had earlier agreed to challenge the privilege of immunity from imprisonment for debt enjoyed by servants of foreign diplomats.[68]) He thus tacitly supported a widespread view that there was no immediate alternative to the threat of imprisonment for debt, however loathsome the practice, as the ultimate sanction for maintaining discipline in commercial transactions.

Wilkes's attitude, though appropriate for the dignitary of a great trading city, seemed inappropriate for a man continually in debt himself, and strangely palsied from one whose courage in the face of authority had become a byword. His critics charged him with exchanging the virtues of the patriot for those of the counting house. He had acquired 'that domestic Virtue, PRUDENCE', but had abandoned 'the more disinterested Virtues of Fortitude and public Spirit', commented one newspaper essayist. 'This English Lion', lamented W.F. Jackson, 'is now metamorphosed into a passive Lamb, that frisks, wantons, or lies down as best suits the Purpose of the King's Bench Fox.'[69]

Wilkes was discomfited by the attack and the loss of popularity that it threatened, much more so than by the earlier press assault of Revd John Horne. He and his supporters scrambled desperately to refute the damaging depiction of him 'as only the Boast, the outside shell of a Patriot', and to cast doubt on the motives of his principal antagonist. They alleged (unconvincingly) that Stephen was an unreformed Jacobite who was seeking to embarrass Wilkes at the connivance of the administration.[70] In a more positive spirit, Wilkes announced himself in favour of a 'new Code of Laws respecting Debtors'; he provided few details, however, beyond a pledge to press for the more regular passage of Insolvency Acts, which periodically freed debtors from prison. Together with Frederick Bull, his fellow-sheriff, he made a point of examining conditions in London prisons where both felons and debtors were held. Wilkes and Bull also moved to protect debtors from abuses by bailiffs and creditors, and they dismissed from the sheriff's office

---

[67] *London Evening Post*, 18–21 January 1772.

[68] *Gazetteer*, 17 July 1771.

[69] A CIVILIAN, *Public Advertiser*, 13 January 1772; Jackson, ibid., 26 December 1771.

[70] A TRUE BRITON, C.P.G., *Westminster Journal*, 28 December 1771–4 January 1772; ANGLO-BRUNSIVICENSIS, *London Evening Post*, 2–4 January 1772; Wilkes, ibid., 18–21 January 1772.

some individuals who had become notorious for their maltreatment of prisoners. Such actions, though, scarcely mollified Wilkes's critics.[71]

Wilkes's contretemps with the King's Bench debtors and their allies was significant in two connected ways. It suggests that his popularity was compromised when he stepped out of the role of paternalistic gentleman, with an insouciant disregard for financial proprieties, and assumed a less familiar role as guardian of commerce. And it indicates the limitations of the Wilkite movement as a vehicle for addressing popular grievances, exemplified by imprisonment for debt, which were strongly felt by those who rallied enthusiastically to his support.

Certainly, Wilkes's own success in using the courts to challenge what he represented as illegal affronts to his own person and property offered recognised potential for a sustained assault on discriminatory laws and repressive legal process. Wilkes encouraged such activity by seeking in various ways to make the court system more open and accountable. As sheriff, he experimented with eliminating fees for admission to the public galleries of the Old Bailey, and shortly after his retirement as Lord Mayor he proposed measures to make the court's sessions papers an accurate transcription of trials. But the potential for using litigation to spearhead social reform was only partially realised, for reasons that had as much to do with Wilkes's own indifference as with the inertia and conservatism of Parliament and the courts. Wilkes himself was fitful in endorsing popular issues. An avid consumer of game, he showed no interest in opposing what 'A REFORMED WILKITE' referred to as 'the unconstitutional[,] the slavish Game Act'. And although, on retirement as sheriff, he expressed concern about capital punishment for 'inferior crimes', he later expressed support for it in all its 'severity'. On the other hand, he did take a special interest in defending the rights of printers and publishers (a crusade dear to his heart) and, as a magistrate, sought to restrain naval impressment within his jurisdiction. While sheriff, he also sought to reform the notorious 'special-jury' system. Yet activity of this kind in support of traditional liberties scarcely amounted to a coherent campaign. Wilkes's enduring belief was that the rights of 'the inferior and middling class of people' were best served through his personal vindication as a patriot champion,

---

[71] *Public Advertiser,* 21 December 1771, and 22 January 1772; *Gazetteer,* 8 November 1771; *A True and Genuine Account of the Life, Trial and Execution of James Bolland,* 2nd edn (London, 1772), p. 15. One of Wilkes's severest critics was Robert Holloway, a gentleman of Gray's Inn, who was bitter at the seizure of his 'furniture, books, papers, and every thing [he] was possessed of, under PRETENCE of debt, and the more flagrant PRETENCE of EXECUTION': Robert Holloway, *A Letter to John Wilkes, Esq; Sheriff of London and Middlesex* (London, 1771), p. vii. Holloway bombarded Wilkes with recommendations for reforming abuses in the sheriff's office, but he was clearly not satisfied with Wilkes's response. *Public Advertiser,* 13 December 1771.

not through the endorsement of an enlarged version of patriotism (of the kind that Jackson and Stephen were urging) tantamount to a programme of social reform. Wilkes's more limited agenda enjoyed a remarkable appeal; but it offered a constrained basis for the emergence of popular radicalism, and suggests one reason why the Wilkite movement – though it left an important legacy for future protest – was an evanescent one.[72]

Vice versus Virtue: The Election for Chamberlain

During Wilkes's shrievalty a focus of attention in metropolitan politics was his attitude to the treatment of debtors. In his four contests for the chamberlainship, from February 1776 to June 1778, attention returned to the question of Wilkes's own indebtedness. This issue became a central one in a lively debate among London's citizens about the qualities required in a civic leader. The office of chamberlain – election to which was determined by a vote of the London livery – was a lucrative sinecure. The holder enjoyed a variety of fees, gratuities, and the use of balances in the city chamber. Beyond that, the chamberlain exercised a general supervisory responsibility for the morals and welfare of the city's orphans and apprentices, and for guiding their path to citizenship.[73]

Wilkes made no secret of the fact that he sought the position as a way of finally discharging his debts. His lavish mayoralty of 1774–75, during which his expenditures exceeded receipts by more than £3,000, had compounded his financial woes. His income was limited to rents from his small estates, some financial entitlements as an alderman, and donations from friends and admirers. William Temple, who had once contributed to the *North Briton*, left him £300 in his will. Lord Granby sent the same amount. The most eccentric contributor was Samuel Cutler, who dubbed himself *Philo-Wilkes*, and gave and lent Wilkes money accompanied by a bombardment of gratuitous advice. Such funds permitted survival, but they never arrived in sufficient quantity to reduce the level of his insolvency. No wonder Wilkes was tormented by the inheritance lost from John Barnard. Faced with the inadequacy of funds from private sources, Wilkes and his supporters persisted in the contentious argument that the debts of the public's champion were a public responsibility and, on that basis, they sought relief in the form of an annuity from London's Common Council. Tradesmen

---

[72] Brewer, 'Wilkites and the Law', pp. 128–71; Simon Devereaux, 'The City and the Sessions Paper: "Public Justice" in London, 1770–1800', *Journal of British Studies*, 35 (1996): 484–90; A REFORMED WILKITE, *Public Ledger*, 24 June 1771; Supplement to *English Liberty*, MS 3332/2, page 159; *Memoirs of the Life of Samuel Romilly*, 2nd edn, 3 vols (London, 1840), vol. 1, p. 84.

[73] Betty R. Masters, *The Chamberlain of the City of London, 1237–1987* (London, 1988), pp. 53–71.

who wanted payment for articles ordered during Wilkes's mayoralty joined them in their importunities. Common Council, though, despite its continuing Wilkite sympathies, refused these requests; to accede to them, it concluded, would be 'a most dangerous precedent'.[74]

Wilkes, however, could point to an immediate precedent in justifying his ambitions for the chamberlainship. The retiring incumbent, Sir Stephen Theodore Janssen, was a former Lord Mayor who had ruined himself in the business of manufacturing high-quality enamelled goods, such as jewellery cases, to compete with French imports. In recognition of his patriotic enterprise, the London livery elected him as chamberlain, and he promptly used the revenue from the position to pay off his debts.[75] Wilkes (unsuccessfully) sought Janssen's endorsement for his own claim and in his campaign implied similarities in their respective situations. But he was compromised by an earlier declaration – made when he was high-mindedly disavowing any desire for a place or pension – that he would never accept the chamberlainship. Moreover, in seeking it, he had to contend with a revived pro-ministry party within the London livery who found a resilient candidate in the person of Benjamin Hopkins, a newly elected alderman.[76]

Hopkins provided a telling contrast to Wilkes in terms of political affiliation and commercial status and conduct. As an MP, he generally voted on the government side and was marked down as one of its supporters. Within the City corporation, he resisted the Wilkite attempt to address issues of national as distinct from municipal concern. In 1775, as Common Council debated the crisis over the American colonies, he interjected that 'the members of that court should confine themselves to their natural and proper spheres, that of watching the city, pavements &c. &c'.[77] He was a prominent insurance underwriter, a director of the Bank of England, and clearly a man of financial substance, with a set of attitudes to match. In his maiden speech in Parliament, he declared: 'I am not possessed of, nor do I buy, what I can't pay for.'[78] The respective advocates of Wilkes and Hopkins could scarcely deny the differences between their candidates; the issue

---

[74] Treloar, pp 142–49, 173–90; Bleackley, *Wilkes*, pp. 306–07; *Wilkes Correspondence*, vol. 5, pp. 40–41; BL Add. MSS 30872, fol. 92; Journals of Common Council, 67, fols 85, 100, Corporation of London Record Office.

[75] On Janssen, see Masters, pp. 59–60; *City Biography*, 2nd edn (London, 1800), p. 63; Linda Colley, *Britons: Forging the Nation, 1707–1837* (New Haven and London, 1992), p. 95.

[76] Wilkes to Janssen, 18 November 1775, BL Add. MSS 30871, fol. 259; *Controversial Letters*, p. 101. On Hopkins, see Masters, *Chamberlain*, pp. 60–61, and Lewis Namier and John Brooke, *The History of Parliament: The House of Commons, 1754–1790*, 3 vols (London and New York, 1964), vol. 2, pp. 639–40.

[77] *Morning Chronicle*, 22 February 1775.

[78] Quoted in Namier and Brooke, vol. 2, p. 640.

in the sequence of elections hinged on what construction should be placed on the evident contrast.

For the supporters of Hopkins, the issue was clear enough. As one of them put it, 'the question is ... whether vice and insolvency shall triumph over virtue and credit'. Hopkins, said another, had a '[c]haracter unimpeached, unsullied and respectable', while his opponent had committed 'crimes so numerous and enormous, that virtuous Sensibility shrinks at the very Review of them'.[79] Wilkes was 'a man who never exercised any branch of commerce but that of vice; a man who is a stranger to œconomy'. As such, he was disqualified from performing one of the chamberlain's principal functions: 'the preservation of the morals of the rising Generation' through the supervision of the City's orphans and apprentices. Such a responsibility, argued Hopkins's backers, required 'a man of cool temper, sound judgement, and irreproachable morals'.[80]

The supporters of Wilkes accepted that the contest was between 'virtue' and 'vice', but shifted the criteria by which these were defined, rejecting the equation of virtue with commercial propriety and creditworthiness. Their attitude suggests a continuity from an earlier period when, in the words of Shelley Burtt: 'English citizens steeped in the civic humanist ideal simply could not grant individuals enmeshed in the gilded webs of commercial enterprise the autonomy and breadth of mind necessary for civic virtue.'[81] The Wilkite position also confirmed this droll definition in 'a modern glossary': 'VICE/VIRTUE: Subjects of discourse'.[82] From the pro-Wilkes perspective, Hopkins's financial standing was not a point in his favour. Though one of his few interventions in Parliament was to condemn the practice of stockjobbery, his connection with the Bank of England positioned him at the heart of the corrupt system of public credit and marked him out as a ministerial tool. He was accused of having 'the worst of characters in a commercial city – the character of a vindictive and most malicious creditor'.[83] His alleged failure to live up to canons of virtue, as defined by classical tradition, was made very explicit. One correspondent complained that Hopkins had forgotten Cicero's injunction 'that justice is the first cardinal virtue'. The case was worse yet, rejoined another: in all likelihood, Hopkins had never heard of Cicero. Instead, his reading must be confined to works such as 'Cocker's Arithmetic, [and Thomas Mortimer's] Every Man his Own Broker',

---

[79]   A LIVERYMAN, *Gazetteer*, 24 February 1775; 'A Calm Address to the Worthy Liverymen of LONDON', City Elections, 1768–96 [Broadside Collection], An. 5.4. no. 15, page 85.

[80]   An old-fashioned citizen of Sir John Barnard's days, *Morning Chronicle*, 14 February 1776; An Impartial Citizen, *Morning Post*, 24 February 1776.

[81]   Burtt, p. 33.

[82]   *The Humours of the Times, Being a Collection of Several Curious Pieces, in Verse and Prose. By the Most Celebrated Geniuses, for Mirth, Wit, and Humour* (London, 1771), p. 211.

[83]   JUSTICE, *Gazetteer*, 24 February 1776.

which helped him to pursue his own interest at the expense of 'the weak and deluded part of creation'.[84] His financial rapacity elided into gluttony, which in turn was connected with sexual impotence, according to this song written after his election as an alderman:

> For his Worship's chief Skill lay in Stuffing and Cramming,
> And he ne'er thought of *Breeding,* save breeding a Famine;
> Which from his plump Spouse oft extracted a Frown,
> For no Belly did *He* ever raise – but his own.[85]

Wilkes, by contrast, neither gluttonous nor impotent, was praised as the embodiment of true patriotic virtue. He was a man 'whose public conduct … has been uniform, noble, and praise-worthy; whose fortune has been spent in withstanding malicious prosecutions, and opposing arbitrary ministers'. In such a circumstance his 'only fault' became almost a virtue: he had 'incurred private debts, from an unalterable attachment to the rights of Englishmen, and the laws of the land, by which the public have been hitherto benefited, and himself sorely distressed'. He, not Hopkins, his supporters claimed, was a proper model for youth, because he showed them that 'public spirit, with the love of their country, is the purest of all social virtues'.[86]

After two successive electoral victories by Hopkins in 1776, the Wilkite cause received a boost with the revelation that Hopkins had been involved in lending money to a 16-year-old baronet at a high rate of annual interest. Parliament would shortly pass the Annuity Bill proscribing practices of this kind, and the incident was seized upon to discredit Hopkins's claim that he was a proper guardian for the youth of the city, and to expose the hollowness of the commercial values that he embraced. He was denounced as 'our Christian Shylock' and 'our city extortioner'. His conduct was worse than that of 'the professed debauchee' because it was masked by the hypocritical attempt 'to give the world an opinion of good qualities in himself, by loudly exclaiming against the misconduct of others'.[87] Wilkes himself entered the fray in the midsummer Common Hall of 1777 by artfully pointing out that as a young man, 'at an age of much dissipation and little reflection', he too had been 'the victim of avarice, usury, and extortion' at the hands of men like Hopkins.[88] The commotion over Hopkins's conduct coincided with the opening in London of Richard Sheridan's play *The School for Scandal,* a

84   EXAMINER, ibid., 15 April 1777; OBSERVATOR, ibid., 2 May 1777.
85   City Elections, 1768–96 [Broadside Collection], An. 5.4. no. 15, page 28.
86   *London Evening Post,* 22–24 February 1776; REGULUS, *Gazetteer,* 12 April 1776.
87   EXAMINER, *Gazetteer,* 15 April 1777, 17 May 1777, and 20 March 1777.
88   *Gazetteer,* 25 June 1777.

satire of contemporary manners and sensibility that included a stinging attack on modern-day usurers. The play contained unflattering allusions to a principal moneylender, described as a Christian, who seemed so clearly a representation of Hopkins that the Lord Chamberlain hesitated before granting a licence to allow the play's public performance. Following its staging, Wilkes was quickly identified with the play's rake-hero, Charles Surface, a charming spendthrift who cheerfully swindled tradesmen, but whose dissipation was redeemed by a generosity of soul lacking in his moralistic detractors.[89]

Despite this fortuitous assistance to the Wilkite cause, Hopkins prevailed at the polls in 1777 and again in 1778. On the latter occasion a mere 287 liverymen polled for Wilkes, while 1,216 voted for his opponent. Wilkes was finally elected chamberlain only after Hopkins's death in November 1779 (no other candidates were involved in their mutual contests).[90] It is tempting to leap from such psephological evidence to a conclusion that, at the time of the appearance of Adam Smith's *Wealth of Nations* (published in 1776), the commercial ethos represented by Hopkins now enjoyed greater appeal among London's livery than the classically derived patriotism purveyed by Wilkes. Such a judgement, though, must be tempered by the recognition that the contests for the chamberlainship were the latest chapter in a long and bitter political struggle between ministry supporters and the forces of popular opposition for control of London's civic institutions. And at the time that they took place, the American War of Independence was generating a surge of loyalism in the metropolis and a concomitant erosion of morale among the Wilkite forces. The dissemination of war contracts among livery tradesmen might have contributed to this political shift. There is also evidence that some were irritated by Wilkes's persistent attempts, in defiance of tradition, to unseat the incumbent chamberlain after Hopkins's initial victory.[91]

Yet even when such circumstances are taken into account, it remains significant that the debate over the respective claims of Wilkes and Hopkins was expressed in a discourse over competing definitions of virtue, the one associated with classically derived patriotism, the other with commerce. The evidence suggests that, in this instance at least, attitudes loosely defined as 'bourgeois', ascribed by some historians to the Wilkites, in fact more readily applied to his pro-government opponents. For its part, Wilkes's particular brand of patriotism appeared increasingly attenuated. Already exposed as a limited instrument

---

[89] *The Dramatic Works of Richard Brinsley Sheridan*, ed. Cecil Price, 3 vols (Oxford, 1973), vol. 1, pp. 300–303; James Morwood, *The Life and Works of Richard Brinsley Sheridan* (Edinburgh, 1985), pp. 72–73; PLAIN TRUTH, *Gazetteer*, 20 May 1777.

[90] Treloar, pp. 196–99.

[91] On the impact of the American War on City politics, see Sainsbury, *Disaffected Patriots*, pp. 114–43.

for social reform during his shrievalty, it was now, from a different quarter, represented in an electoral contest as inappropriate for a commercial metropolis. Patriotism, of course, did not disappear as an emotional force in national life with the eclipse of its most vocal champion; far from it. But a bellicose patriotism would henceforth survive and prosper in harmony with commercial values and the desires of central government, not discordantly with them, as was usually the case during the heyday of the Wilkite movement. The gradual emergence of this more modern patriotism has been effectively described elsewhere;[92] but it is worth remarking that Wilkes himself, in the final ironic twist of his political career, in many respects personified the process. As chamberlain, he relished opportunities to officiate at the presentation of the freedom of the City to national heroes, from William Pitt the Younger to Admiral Nelson.[93] 'Toby', Wilkes's pseudonymous interlocutor, need not have worried. Wilkes's patriotism survived the financial ease that the chamberlainship brought him. But, disengaged from the politics of debt, it became anodyne and respectable as it fused with a groundswell of national sentiment endorsed by the political establishment.

---

[92]   For example, Linda Colley, 'The Apotheosis of George III: Loyalty, Royalty and the British Nation 1760–1820', *Past and Present*, 102 (1984): 94–129.

[93]   Treloar, pp. 204–05.

Conclusion

A Vivid Enigma

The ultimate paradox of Wilkes's career is that someone who was so paradoxical should have projected such a vivid image to his contemporaries. The problem is echoed among historians, where there is widespread acknowledgement of Wilkes's importance, but lingering uncertainty as to what it actually was. He is associated with the emergence of a middle-class sensibility and politics, while being most readily locatable within the 'bi-polar field of force' of patricians and plebs identified by E.P. Thompson. Certainly, when Thompson refers to 'the picaresque flouting of the provident bourgeois virtues', the image of Wilkes as faux-aristocratic provocateur comes readily to mind.[1] When Wilkes periodically discarded this role, it was not to step outside the polarity of patricians and plebs; rather it was to take on the mantle of stern patrician as defined by precepts of classical humanism. Wilkes's validation of 'politeness' and 'sentiment' fits less comfortably within Thompson's paradigm, but Wilkes saw them as attributes of gentlemen, not of a putative bourgeoisie.

It has not been my intention, however, to deploy Wilkes's career to contest the notion that we can make meaningful statements about a middle class in eighteenth-century Britain. If nothing else, to do so would be to close our ears to the compelling voice of Wilkes's own mother, who had a clear notion of who the 'middling-class' were and of what values they upheld. But the evidence presented in this book suggests that for much of his life Wilkes was in full retreat from his family's moral inheritance, with some exceptions, such as his genuine abhorrence of the aristocratic vice of gambling. What is intriguing is that many of those in the sociological middle shared Wilkes's resistance to the very values so often ascribed to them. In his libertine attitudes to sex, religion, and money, he offered a vicarious release from a set of ethical and religious constraints that were perhaps all the more burdensome for being internally generated as well as externally imposed. Wilkes's discomfort in the role of guardian of commercial propriety in London was palpable; and when he tried to perform it, his popularity was seriously compromised.

Generally, Wilkes avoided constraining his broad appeal – which as even George III conceded was not class-based – by targeting specific social elements,

---

[1]   E.P. Thompson, *Customs in Common* (London and New York, 1993), pp. 72, 89.

especially once he arrived at his epiphany that in 'a nation of merchants and traders, the people have the greatest weight'.[2] The term 'people', of course, was not an unproblematic one in the eighteenth century, as Wilkes's comment itself might imply. As Kathleen Wilson has pointed out, it was employed both as a code word for literate, middle-class, Protestant men – those with the loudest claim to active political citizenship – and as a euphemism for 'the mob'.[3] Wilkes took a more expansive view, however. While agreeing that 'the people' stood apart from government and had a legitimate role in overseeing its operations, he employed the term to include all adult men, irrespective of social class or levels of literacy. Unusually for most eighteenth-century political reformers – and unlike, for example, John Horne – he was an advocate of universal male suffrage, as forcefully expressed in his Parliamentary motion of 21 March 1776.[4] Wilkes's emphasis on inclusiveness extended to religious affiliation, which put him at odds with 'the people' defined as a demotic force, who in 1780 took to the streets in opposition to Catholic relief. When he did acknowledge class differences, it was in order to assert a universal right to liberty and protection, as he did most famously in his speech to the Court of Common Pleas on 6 May 1763. There was a high level of abstractedness in Wilkes's attitude to 'the people'; their actual presence was often distressing to him; and even as he offered himself as their tribune and advocate, he was refining a sense of himself as one of nature's aristocrats. His rejection by most of the incumbent English nobility might actually have advanced this process. As Alex Potts has pointed out, noble simplicity 'could ... suggest a kind of *tabula rasa* of subjectivity that was at odds with the affectations and excesses of high society, something approaching a proto-revolutionary ideal';[5] and one, it might be added, that was consistent with those precepts of artless sentiment that Wilkes upheld.

Maintaining a case that Wilkes advanced middle-class politics requires that we distinguish his immanent presence, with which this book is mainly concerned, from the pre-conditions and secondary consequences of his career. Some important scholarship has shown that the Wilkite political phenomenon was made possible by the pre-existence of a vibrant, middle-class urban culture, characterised by patterns of association and an active press, and which promoted a self conscious sense of engagement in the public sphere in ways that were already

---

[2]   Tamara Hunt, *Defining John Bull: Political Caricature and National Identity in Late Georgian England* (Aldershot, 2003), p. 39; see above, p. 190.

[3]   Kathleen Wilson, *The Sense of the People: Politics, Culture and Imperialism in England, 1715–1785* (Cambridge and New York, 1995), pp. 3–26.

[4]   *Wilkes Speeches*, pp. 54–69.

[5]   Alex Potts, *Flesh and the Ideal: Winckelmann and the Origins of Art History* (New Haven and London, 1994), p. 1.

contesting aristocratic hegemony.[6] Through his defence of his personal liberty and his corrosive attacks on his persecutors, Wilkes contributed significantly to this process, which is why he attracted support from some middle-class men who were otherwise repelled by his libertine conduct. Likewise, Wilkes's Parliamentary campaign in 1777 for a national art gallery – one independent of royal control or noble patronage – was urged in the name of 'the public' and 'the nation at large', but its most obvious potential beneficiaries were middle-class 'consumers' of culture.[7]

Many of Wilkes's contemporaries would probably have sympathised with historians grappling with Wilkes's elusiveness, the difficulty of placing him in predictable social and political categories. Yet those confronted with his actual presence usually witnessed clarity, not confusion, except in those situations when he deliberately donned a mask, either figuratively or literally. This takes us to the heart of the puzzle: he was a person of contradictory facets, but, as my book has sought to demonstrate, each was sharply etched and consistently displayed to its assigned audience. He was a devoted and sentimental father; an energetic and unsentimental lover; a dedicated student of the classics; a model for politeness; a rake 'with more wit, more fancy, more learning, more every thing than his co-mates in frantic gaiety';[8] and a man of the Enlightenment, genuinely attached to religious toleration. To his plebeian followers, he presented an image of the distressed yet cheerfully rakish gentleman – outlawed, just like Robin Hood – intrepid and unyielding in his defiance of his, and their, highborn oppressors. It was an image reinforced by strategically flamboyant appearances, trumpeted in the press throughout the country, at sites of contested political terrain throughout the capital. Its clarity can be contrasted with the confusion surrounding Wilkes's arch-rival, John Horne, whose attachment to political radicalism was paradoxically single-minded, enduring, and unimpeachable. (In 1778 he was imprisoned for his ardent defence of the American revolutionaries, and in 1794 he was tried for high treason.) Usually clothed in black, he projected a dour persona, reinforced by a reputation for humourlessness. Unlike Wilkes, he spurned the title of gentleman. 'I only call myself a *Man,* and desire no other distinction', he told *Junius.* Wilkes mischievously sought to complicate this sober image. He stopped short of revealing that Horne had pimped for him in the King's Bench Prison; that would have been self-incriminatory. But he did reveal that Horne had left for safekeeping in Paris a wardrobe of expensively fashionable

---

[6] See especially Wilson, *Sense of the People,* and Nicholas Rogers, *Whigs and Cities: Popular Politics in the Age of Walpole and Pitt* (Oxford, 1989).

[7] Jonathan G.W. Conlin, 'High Art and Low Politics: A New Perspective on John Wilkes', *Huntington Library Quarterly,* 64 (2001): 356–81.

[8] William Rough's description in [Wilkes] *Letters to Daughter,* vol. 1, p. 19.

clothes, including a suit in scarlet and gold, one in flowered silk, and a velvet *surtout*. The implication was that Horne was a closet libertine, and for a while he was obliged to share the soubriquet of the 'macaroni parson' with Revd William Dodd, a dandified clergyman who was later hanged for forgery (see Fig. 7.1). Horne himself ruefully acknowledged that his rival was more successful than he was in winning popular support. The contrast became painfully evident on the occasion of Wilkes's election as Sheriff of London: on that same night, the effigy of Horne in 'canonical habit' was burned by a Wilkite mob, his symbolic punishment for association with the despised Shelburne faction.[9]

Unlike Horne, and despite the best efforts of his enemies, Wilkes was able to represent his own libertine predilections as a public asset, or failing that, to overcome their consequences – including outlawry – in the mythic style of the rake-hero. It was a performance compelling to contemporaries, but as politics became stridently ideological in the age of the French Revolution, Wilkes had little left to offer beyond a bland and conventional patriotism. By now the details of his private life, into which he increasingly retreated, had only limited public resonance. An ageing defender of traditional liberties with a covert affection for the court of Versailles, he would scarcely have been heard above the more incisive voices of Edmund Burke, Charles James Fox, and Thomas Paine, even had he wanted to be. He saw himself as a futile voice of moderation, lamenting that 'Fox and Burke spit so much venom at each other'; and while his political sympathies were now close to Burke's, he described one of Burke's writings on the French Revolution as 'the melancholy ravings of a lunatic'.[10]

As Wilkes gradually faded from public view, he became an object of the kind of benign curiosity usually reserved for harmless eccentrics. A cartoon from the last year of his life shows him in his familiar, though now outdated, military costume, striding purposefully through the London streets on some unspecified mission. The caption describes him as a 'Friend to Liberty', though 'quondam' is inserted in front of 'friend'. The complexity of the relationship between Wilkes's pursuit of liberty and his libertinism is aptly conveyed, 'Liberty' having been visibly changed to 'Libertynism' before being changed back to 'Liberty' (Fig. 7.2). Subsequent generations were less kind to Wilkes, and certainly less amused by him. Some nineteenth-century Whig politicians – high-minded guardians of the grand narrative of English history – became almost apoplectic at the suggestion

---

[9]   *The Letters of Junius*, ed. John Cannon (Oxford, 1978) p. 255; Alexander Stephens, *Memoirs of John Horne Tooke*, 2 vols (London, 1813), vol. 1, pp. 213–14; *Controversial Letters*, p. 39; *Catalogue of Political and Personal Satires Preserved in the Department of Prints and Drawings in the British Museum*, vol. 4 (1761–1770), ed. Frederic George Stephens (London, 1883), no. 4827; George Rudé, *Wilkes and Liberty: A Social Study of 1763 to 1764* (Oxford, 1962), p. 166.

[10]   [Wilkes] *Letters to Daughter*, vol. 4, pp. 59, 72.

Figure 7.1   *The Macaroni Parson* [John Horne] (1772). Etching and engraving.
Courtesy of the Lewis Walpole Library, Yale University.

Figure 7.2   [John Wilkes] *A (QUONDAM) FRIEND TO LIBERTYNISM*. 'So
             Politic as if one Eye / upon the Other were a spy.' From Horace
             Bleackley, *Life of John Wilkes*.

that Wilkes's libertine career might actually have served to advance political and constitutional liberties.[11] To find a rare favourable judgement, we have to turn, appropriately enough, to another exiled libertine, Lord Byron. In his *Vision of Judgment* (1816), Byron conceives of Wilkes as '[a] merry, cock-eyed, curious-looking sprite / ... Dress'd in a fashion now forgotten quite', who is called upon by the Archangel Michael to propose the eternal fate of George III. With typical perversity and generosity, Wilkes votes for his old enemy's habeas corpus into heaven.[12] Not one to hold a grudge, Wilkes would have been well pleased with Byron's sympathetic flight of fancy.

---

[11]   Bleackley, *Wilkes*, pp. 404–05.
[12]   *Selected Poems of Byron*, ed. Robin Skelton (London, 1969), pp. 123–24.

Appendix

The Authorship of *An Essay on Woman*

Once the existence of *An Essay on Woman* became known, there was intense speculation as to whether it was Wilkes or Potter who had had the main hand in its composition. The debate continues, but it is not one that is likely to be resolved with certainty. Potter's tangled association with the Warburtons makes him the obvious suspect, though his seduction of Gertrude is not so much a reason for malice towards her husband as proof of it. Other evidence tilts towards Wilkes as the principal author, but it is far from conclusive. Some parts of the *Essay* were obviously written by him alone, because they were inserted after Potter died. They include the swipe at Lord Bute, who did not rise to prominence until the early 1760s. The frontispiece was certainly Wilkes's doing. It contained his facetious reference to the 'intrepid hero', Lord George Sackville, who was court-martialled for cowardice at the Battle of Minden in August 1759, a few months after Potter's death. The name of the fictitious author, 'Pego Borewell', probably alludes through a double pun to Sir Welbore Ellis, a dull, timeserving placeman (and, after 1761, Wilkes's fellow MP for Aylesbury) and to his wife's nephew Welbore Ellis Agar, whose sexual capers impressed even Casanova, and who would have been better known to Wilkes than to Potter.[1] Textual analysis has determined that 'the advertisement' (in modern parlance, the preface) was also written exclusively by Wilkes, or at least substantially amended by him, as were the three ancillary parodies.[2] This is consistent with the likelihood that the strictures against homosexuality in 'the advertisement' were Wilkes's work alone. Unlike Potter, he was one of the new generation of gentlemen libertines for whom the idea of male sodomy had become anathema.

Evidence as to who wrote the rest of the *Essay* – the poem itself and the notes – is less clear cut, and points in divergent directions. Some of it is special pleading. When Wilkes faced prosecution for the *Essay*'s publication, it was not surprising

---

[1]   Giacomo Casanova, Chevalier de Seingalt, *History of My Life*, trans. Willard R. Trask, 12 vols (Baltimore, 1997) vol. 9, pp. 322–24.

[2]   *Wilkes and Potter*, ed. Cash, pp. 150–52.

that his friends would seek to play down the level of his involvement. One pro-Wilkes pamphlet maintained that the work was a collective project, crafted by a 'society of men, mad with wine, and wanton with desire; designing, no doubt, to create a laugh among themselves'.[3] In the press, there was a concerted campaign to imply that Potter was the author, and thus to exonerate Wilkes.[4] Whether it initiated a rumour or perpetuated an existing one is difficult to judge, but the story certainly took hold. John Glynn cited the 'universal notoriety' of Potter's authorship when he prepared his defence of Wilkes before the Court of King's Bench.[5] Horace Walpole, the century's most avid and articulate gossip, was convinced. Wilkes and Potter, he wrote, 'composed this indecent patchwork in some of their bacchanalian hours', but Potter 'had the chief hand in the composition of the verses'. William Temple, writing to his friend James Boswell on the same day that Potter's authorship was insinuated in the *Public Advertiser,* had a similar opinion: 'The pamphlet was written by the late Mr. Potter … The notes are Mr. Wilkes's, but he supposes them the Bishop of Gloucester's [Warburton].'[6]

The assiduity with which the rumour of Potter's authorship was circulated does not, however, establish its veracity. Some of Wilkes's biographers have sought to advance the case for Potter through circumstantial evidence, namely that many of the personalities referred to in the poem and its notes achieved their celebrity at a time when he was already a hardened rake but Wilkes was still a callow student or a respectable newlywed. Fanny Murray certainly achieved the pinnacle of her notoriety in the 1740s, as did Margaret ('Peg') Woffington, the Irish-born actress, famous for her beauty, affability, and affairs, which included living in a *ménage-à-trois* with David Garrick and his fellow actor, Charles Macklin. A reference to Woffington's alleged sexual rapacity is included in a note that also makes one of the work's two allusions to Edward Hussey, who was rumoured to have a very large penis, a circumstance that generated hilarious gossip at the time of his marriage to the Duchess of Manchester in 1746. Murray, Woffington, and Hussey retained an iconic status in the libertine imagination, however, even after they became peripheral to the public gaze. In any event, Wilkes was not so immersed in his books in the 1740s as to be unaware of them then; as we have seen, the persona of the priggish 15-year-old schoolboy, shocked at the earthiness

---

[3]　Quoted in ibid., p. 141.

[4]　A Prudent Enemy to Immorality, Obscenity, and Profaneness, *Public Advertiser,* 30 November 1763; To the Author of a Malicious Narrative, ibid., 7 December 1763.

[5]　BL Add. MSS 30885, fol. 155.

[6]　Horace Walpole, *Memoirs of the Reign of King George the Third,* ed. G.F. Russell Barker, 4 vols (London, 1894), vol. 1, pp. 246, 248; *Boswell in Holland, 1763–64,* ed. Frederick A. Pottle (New York, London, Toronto, 1952), p. 78.

of Homer, was quickly replaced, as early as his student days in Holland, by that of the apprentice libertine.[7]

Circumstantial evidence fails to make a convincing case for Potter. That claim ultimately hinges on a particular interpretation of a portion of a letter that Potter sent to Wilkes in July 1755:

> Who your Mrs M. is with whom you rather wish me to copulate I am at a Loss to guess. I could reverse the Letter & attempt the Essay on Woman without even the hope of having a Commentator. They are a cursed race & often marr the Text. Take notice I do not mean to censure your Annotation. Thou art no marr text. But you sometimes supply a Text when without your assistance it wd be defective.[8]

The paragraph was in the same letter in which Potter related his amorous adventure with Gertrude Warburton in Devon and Cornwall. The reversal of the letter 'M' into a 'W' thus refers to Mrs Warburton, whom Potter was in the process of seducing. But there is an obvious double entendre here; the mention of 'the Essay on Woman' is confirmation that Wilkes and Potter were, or had been, collaborating in writing the parody. The subsequent reference to 'a commentator' suggests that Wilkes was providing the ancillary notes to Potter's composition, while offering some valuable proposals for the text itself; it could also simply refer, though, to Wilkes's eager participation in Potter's post-coital reflections.[9]

Any assumptions that this letter confirms Potter's principal authorship are challenged by an earlier letter of his that points, albeit indecisively, to Wilkes as playing the major role. Writing to Wilkes from Bath on 27 October 1754, Potter remarked, 'I have read your Parody for the 99th Time & have laughed as heartily as I did at the first … '. He also describes a dinner the previous day at which the guests (including William Pitt) 'read over yr Parody'. The allusion could be to one of the shorter parodies, not necessarily to the *Essay* itself, but a subsequent comment suggests otherwise. 'I have made a few verbal Amendments', Potter continued. 'The Battle of the Tweed may do very well upon the Banks of the River or wherever the Passions are interested. The rest of the World will not *feel* the Wit of it.' There is a section of a parody, then, which, in libertine style, conflates military and sexual conquest, and connects that with an allusion to

---

[7]   Wilkes and Potter, ed. Cash, pp. 144–45; John Timbs, *Clubs and Club Life in London* (London, 1908), p. 135.

[8]   BL Add. MSS 30880B, fol. 3.

[9]   Cash in Wilkes and Potter, ed. Cash, pp. 147–48, uses the letter to argue for Potter's authorship of the *Essay*. For the opposite interpretation, see Calhoun Winton, 'John Wilkes and "An Essay on Woman"', in *A Provision of Human Nature: Essays on Fielding and Others in Honor of Miriam Austin Locke,* ed. Donald Kay (Tuscaloosa, AL, 1977), p. 124.

Wilkes's failed bid to become MP for Berwick six months earlier. But there is not such a passage in the shorter parodies, or in the surviving portion of *An Essay on Woman*. Potter, in a confusing *non sequitur,* might have been alluding to another Wilkes composition entitled 'The Battle of the Tweed', but the reference could also be to a portion of the *Essay* now lost. Towards the end of the letter, Potter remarks that, if he happens to see Thomas Brewster, he will 'shew him the Parody', suggestive of an enterprise larger than the slight achievement of one of the shorter poems.[10]

After his conviction for printing and publishing *An Essay on Woman* and the ancillary pieces, Wilkes made a number of admissions that he was indeed their author.[11] These were part of a bravura display designed to expose the government's suppression of private opinion; their value as evidence must therefore be judged accordingly. Heaton Wilkes read one of them as an avowal of authorship, however, and John in response to his brother justified his admissions rather than retracting them.[12] Ultimately, though, any attempt to force an absolute judgement about principal authorship of the *Essay* obscures more than it clarifies, because it detracts from the essential point that the parody was conceived and executed as a collaboration, the literary analogue of the libertine enterprise itself, at the heart of which was mutual encouragement to unfettered erotic performance.

---

[10]   BL Add. MSS 30867, fol. 103.

[11]   Bleackley, *Wilkes*, pp. 438–40.

[12]   Heaton Wilkes to John Wilkes, 14 April 1767, BL Add MSS 30869, fol. 111; John Wilkes to Heaton Wilkes, 22 April 1767, Wilkes MSS 2, fol. 14.

Bibliography

I. Manuscripts

American Philosophical Society, Philadelphia
  Richard Henry Lee Papers
Beinecke Rare Book and Manuscript Library, Yale University
  Boswell Collection. General Collection
  Chauncey Brewster Tinker Manuscripts. General Collection
  James Marshall and Marie-Louise Osborn Collection
Bibliothèque Nationale, Paris
  MSS 11359 (Journal de Police)
Bodleian Library, Oxford
  Dashwood Papers   Ms D.D. Dashwood (Bucks)
  Thomas Edward Papers   MSS Bodl. 1011
British Library
  Add. MSS 4321   Birch Collection
  Add. MSS 12114   Samuel Butler Collection
  Add. MSS 22131–2   Papers relating to the Trial of John Wilkes
  Add. MSS 27777   Contributions to the Public Advertiser
  Add. MSS 27925   Letters of Literary men, etc.
  Add. MSS 30865-96   Wilkes Papers
  Add. MSS 32568   J. Mitford Note Books
  Add. MSS 32948–3053   Newcastle Papers
  Add. MSS 35404–887   Hardwicke Papers
  Add. MSS 39781–2   Flaxman Papers
  Add. MSS 41354–5   Martin Papers
  Add. MSS 42083–8   Grenville Papers
  Add. MSS 42560   Letters to Thomas Warton, the Younger
  Add. MSS 57733   Copy of Information against Wilkes
  Add. MSS 57810   Supplementary Grenville Papers
  Add. MSS 59680   John Jaques, The Life of John Wilkes
  Egerton MSS 216–17   Parliamentary Diary of Sir Henry Cavendish
  Egerton MSS 2136   Letters to Francis Dashwood
Volume belonging to John Wilkes with verses by him in print and manuscript.
BL Call No. 1106. ccc. 33.

Buckinghamshire Record Office, Aylesbury
  Faculty Book, 1723–1785. D/A/X/9
  Lee Papers. D/LE
Duncombe Estate Deeds. D/DU
  Parish Records, Aylesbury. PR 11/5/1. Q
Cambridge University Library
  Wilkes Letters. Add. 8781/1.
Columbia University, New York
  General Manuscript Collection: Wilkes
  Special Manuscript Collection: Halsband
Corporation of London Record Office
  Guildhall Justice Room Minute Books. GJR/M
  Journals of Common Council
  Repertories of Aldermanic Bench
Derbyshire Record Office, Matlock
  Fitzherbert Papers
Durham Cathedral Chapter Library
  Sharp MS
Family Records Centre, London
  Register of Baptisms etc., Carter Lane Meeting House, Blackfriars, Microfilm, No. RG4/4231.
Guildhall Library, London
  King's Bench Prison, Misc. Papers, 1750–1820. MS 659.1
  King versus Wilkes. Original Papers connected with the prosecution of John Wilkes. MS 214/1–4
  Wilkes material, presented by Miss Treloar. MS 2892
  Wilkes Letters. MS 14173–76
Hampshire Record Office, Winchester
  Malmesbury Manuscripts
Hertfordshire Record Office
  William Baker MSS
Huntington Library, San Marino
  Elizabeth (Robinson) Montagu Papers
Kensington and Chelsea Public Library
  Parish Records of St Mary Abbot's Church (Transcript)
  Press Cuttings
Lewis Walpole Library, Farmington, Connecticut
  Miscellaneous Manuscripts (not Horace Walpole)
London Metropolitan Archives
  Abstract of Prior Title to Hoxton Square Estate. BRA/437/4.
  Consistory Court Records. DL/C

Parish Register, St John the Baptist, Clerkenwell. Microfilm X97/244
National Archives, London
  Chatham Papers   PRO 30/8
  King's Bench Papers   KB
  Wills   PROB 11 (Microfilm)
National Maritime Museum, Greenwich
  Sandwich Manuscripts
New York Public Library
  Myers Collection
Princeton University
  John Wild Autograph Collection, vol. 38 ('Celebrated Men')
Royal Society, London
  Journal, vol. 20
William Andrews Clark Memorial Library, University of California, Los
  Angeles
  Eros in monachium, or the Medmenham garland. MS E71M1 ca. 1760 Bound.
William L. Clements Library, University of Michigan
  Wilkes MSS

II. Printed Primary Sources

Newspapers and Periodicals

Annual Register
Auditor
Bingley's Journal
Bon Ton Magazine
European Magazine
Gazetteer
Gentleman's Magazine
Independent Chronicle
London Chronicle
London Evening Post
London Magazine
Matrimonial Magazine
Middlesex Journal
Miller's London Mercury
Morning Chronicle
Morning Post
North Briton
Oxford Magazine

Political Register
Public Advertiser
Public Ledger
St James's Chronicle
Town and Country Magazine
Westminster Journal
The World

Broadside Collections

Guildhall Library, London: City Elections 1768–96
William L. Clements Library

Pamphlets and Pamphlet Collections

[Almon, John] *The History of the Late Minority, Exhibiting the Conduct, Principles, and Views of that Party, during the Years 1762, 1763, 1764, and 1765.* Third Impression, London, 1765; reprinted with some additions in 1766. (John Wilkes's copy with his extensive marginalia)

[Armstrong, John] *A Day: An Epistle to John Wilkes, of Aylesbury, Esq.* London, 1761.

B[agsho]t H[ea]th: or the Modern Duel. 1762.

The Bagshot Frolick, or the Pot-lid & the Inkhorn. 1762.

Battle of the Quills: or Wilkes Attacked and Defended. 1768.

[Baxter, Andrew] *A Letter from Mr. Baxter, Author of an Enquiry into the Nature of the Human Soul, and of Matho, to John Wilkes, Esq.* 1753.

The Bow-Street Opera ... Written on the Plan of the Beggar's Opera. London, 1776.

Britannia's Intercession for the Happy Deliverance of John Wilkes, Esq. n.d.

[Brown, John] *Thoughts on Civil Liberty, and Licentiousness and Faction.* Newcastle Upon Tyne, 1765.

The Case of Anne and Isaac Scott, Bankrupts, late Merchants and Dry-salters. London, 1768.

A Cautionary Address to the Electors of England: Being a Touchstone between the Constituents and Candidates. London, 1768.

A Collection of all the Remarkable and Personal Passages in the Briton, North Briton and Auditor. London, 1766.

[Cradock, Joseph] *The Life of John Wilkes, Esq., in the Manner of Plutarch.* London, 1773.

[Davys, Mary] *The Accomplished Rake: or the Modern Fine Gentleman.* London, 1756.

[Delamayne, Thomas] *The Rise and Practice of Imprisonment for Debt in Personal Actions Examined*. London, 1772.

The Devil Divorced: or the Diabo-Whore. London, 1782.

Dialogue Between the Two Giants at Guildhall, Humbly Addressed to John Wilkes. London, 1768.

[Edwards, Thomas] *A Supplement to Mr. Warburton's edition of Shakespear. Being the Canons of Criticism. By another Gentleman of Lincoln's Inn*, n.d.

English Liberty: being a Collection of Interesting Tracts from the Year 1762 to 1769, 2 vols, continuous pagination. London, 1769. (With manuscript supplement, Guildhall MS 3332)

An Enquiry into the Conduct of a Late Right Honourable Commoner. 3rd impression. London, 1766.

An Epistle from Col. John Lilburn in the Shades, to John Wilkes, Esq; late a Colonel in the Buckinghamshire Militia. London, n.d.

Essays on Patriotism and the Character and Conduct of Some Late Famous Pretenders to that Virtue Particularly of the Present Popular Gentleman. London, 1768.

The Fall of Mortimer. An Historical Play Dedicated to the Right Honourable John, Earl of Bute. London, 1763.

Farmer, Thomas. *The Plain Truth*, 1763.

A First Letter to the Duke of Grafton. London, 1770.

Gentleman, Francis. *History of the Robinhood Society*. London, 1764.

Gordon, Thomas. *A Cordial for Low Spirits: Being a Collection of Curious Tracts*, ed. Richard Baron, 3 vols, 3rd edition. London, 1763.

Gunston, Daniel, ed. *Jemmy Twitcher's Jests: or Wit with the Gravy in It*. London, 1770.

Harlequin Premier: A Farce, As It is Acted Daily. 1769.

Holloway, Robert. *A Letter to John Wilkes, Esq; Sheriff of London and Middlesex*. London, 1771.

The Humours of the Times, Being a Collection of Several Curious Pieces, in Verse and Prose. By the Most Celebrated Geniuses, for Mirth, Wit, and Humour. London, 1771.

H[utchinson], J. *The Religion of Satan: or Antichrist Delineated*. London, 1736.

Kidgell, Revd John. *A Genuine and Succinct Narrative of a Scandalous, Obscene, and Exceedingly Profane Libel, Entitled An Essay on Woman*. London, 1763.

A Letter to J. Kidgell, Containing a Full Answer to his Narrative. London, 1763.

A Letter to the Right Honourable Earl Temple. London, 1763.

A Letter to the Right Honourable the Earl of T[empl]e: or, the Case of J[oh]n W[ilke]s, Esquire. London, 1770?

A Letter to the Right Hon. Thomas Harley, Esq; Lord Mayor of the City of London. By an Alderman of London, 4th edition, London, 1768.

The Life and Political Writings of John Wilkes, Esq. Birmingham, 1769.

The Memoirs of Miss Arabella Bolton. Containing a Genuine Account of her Seduction, and the Barbarous Treatment she Afterwards Received from the Honourable Colonel L------l. London, 1770.

Macaulay, Catharine. *Observations on a Pamphlet, Entitled Thoughts on the Cause of the Present Discontents.* 1770.

A Mirror for the Multitude; or, Wilkes no Patriot. London, 1769.

Nocturnal Revels: or the History of King's-Place, and other Modern Nunneries, by a Monk of the Order of St Francis, 2nd edition, 2 vols. London, 1779.

[Penrice, William] *The Extraordinary Case of William Penrice.* London, 1768.

Philo-Patriae. *An Address to the Public Wherein the Conduct of Mr. Wilkes is Candidly and Impartially Considered.* London, 1768.

Poetical Excursions on the Isle of Wight. London, 1777.

Priestley, Joseph. *A View of the Principles and Conduct of the Protestant Dissenters with Respect to the Civil and Ecclesiastical Constitution of England.* London, 1769.

Rosa, Salvator. *The Group.* London, 1777.

[Shebbeare, John] *The History of the Excellence and Decline of the Constitution, Religion, Laws, Manners and Genius of the Sumatrans,* 2 vols, London, 1760.

Stephen, James. *Considerations on Imprisonment for Debt.* London, 1770.

Thoughts of a Citizen of London on the Conduct of Dr. Dodd in his Life and Death. London, 1777.

A Vindication of the D[uke] of G[rafton]. London, 1769.

[Wilkes, John] *The Controversial Letters of John Wilkes, Esq. The Rev. John Horne, and their Principal Adherents.* London, 1771.

[——] *A Letter to His Grace, The Duke of Grafton, First Commissioner of His Majesty's Treasury.* 1767.

[——] *A Letter to the Right Honourable George Grenville, occasioned by … the Speech he made in the House of Commons on the Motion for Expelling Mr. Wilkes.* London, 1769.

[——] *Observations on the Papers Relative to the Rupture with Spain, Laid Before both Houses of Parliament on Friday, Jan. 29th, 1762.*

Wilkes and Liberty: or, The Universal Prayer. London, 1764.

W----s's Feast, or Dryden Travesty; A Mock Pindarick: Addressed to his Most Incorruptible Highness Prince Patriotism. London, 1774.

Wilkes's Jest Book; or the Merry Patriot. London, 1770.

Other Primary Sources in Print

[Almon, John] *The Debates and Proceedings of the British House of Commons from 1743 to 1774,* 11 vols. London, 1766–75.

[——] *Memoirs of a Late Eminent Bookseller.* London, 1790.

[——] *The Parliamentary Register, 1774 to 1780,* 17 vols. London, 1775–80.

[Boswell, James] *Boswell's London Journal, 1762–63,* ed. Frederick A. Pottle. New York, London, Toronto: McGraw Hill, 1950.

[——] *Boswell in Holland, 1763–64,* ed. Frederick A. Pottle. New York, London, Toronto: McGraw Hill, 1952.

[——] *Boswell on the Grand Tour: Italy, Corsica, and France, 1765–1766,* ed. Frank Brady and Frederick A. Pottle. London and Toronto: William Heinemann, 1955.

Boswell, James. *Life of Johnson,* ed. R.W. Chapman, Introduction by Pat Rogers, World Classics edition. Oxford: Oxford University Press, 1980.

[Burney, Charles] *The Letters of Charles Burney,* vol. 1 (1751–1784), ed. Alvaro Ribeiro. Oxford: Clarendon, 1991.

[Burke, Edmund] *The Correspondence of Edmund Burke,* ed. Thomas W. Copeland *et al.,* 10 vols. Cambridge: Cambridge University Press; Chicago: University of Chicago Press, 1958–78.

Burrows, Sir James, ed. *Reports of Cases Argued and Adjudged in the Court of King's Bench, during the Time Lord Mansfield Presided in that Court,* 5 vols. London, 1812.

[Butler, Charles] *Reminiscences of Charles Butler, Esq. of Lincoln's Inn,* 2 vols. London, 1822.

[Byron] *Selected Poems of Byron,* ed. Robin Skelton. London: Heinemann, 1969.

Carlyle, Alexander. *Anecdotes and Characters of the Times,* ed. James Kinsley. London: Oxford University Press, 1973.

Casanova, Giacomo, Chevalier de Seingalt. *History of My Life,* trans. Willard R. Trask, 12 vols. Baltimore: Johns Hopkins University Press, 1997.

A Catalogue of Westminster Records: Vestry of St. Margaret's and St. John, ed. John Edward Smith. London: Wightman, 1900.

[Churchill, Charles] *The Poetical Works of Charles Churchill,* ed. Douglas Grant. Oxford: Clarendon Press, 1956.

City Biography, 2nd edition. London, 1800.

Copies taken from the Records of the Court of King's Bench, at Westminster. London, 1763.

[Crosby, Brass] *Memoirs of Brass Crosby, Esq. Alderman of the City of London and Lord Mayor, 1770–1771.* London, 1829.

[Franklin, Benjamin] *The Papers of Benjamin Franklin,* ed. Leonard W. Labaree, W.B. Willcox *et al.,* 30 vols. New Haven: Yale University Press, 1959– .

[George III] *The Correspondence of King George the Third from 1760 to December 1783,* ed. Sir John Fortescue, 6 vols. London: Macmillan, 1927–28.

[——] *Letters from George III to Lord Bute, 1756–1766,* ed. Romney Sedgwick. London: Macmillan, 1939.

Gibbon, Edward. *Memoirs of My Life and Writings,* ed. A.O.J. Cockshut and Stephen Constantine. Keele, Staffordshire: Keele University Press and Ryburn Publishing, 1994.

[Grafton] *Autobiography and Political Correspondence of Augustus Henry, Third Duke of Grafton,* ed. William R. Anson. London: John Murray, 1898.

The Grenville Papers: Being the Correspondence of Richard Grenville, Earl Temple, K.G., and the Right Hon. George Grenville, Their Friends and Contemporaries, ed. William J. Smith, 4 vols. London, 1852–53.

[Hall-Stevenson, John] *The Works of John Hall-Stevenson, Esq.,* 3 vols. London, 1795.

[Hume, David] *The Letters of David Hume,* ed. J.Y.T. Greig, 2 vols. Oxford: Clarendon Press, 1932.

Johnson, Samuel. *Political Writings,* ed. Donald J. Greene. New Haven and London: Yale University Press, 1977.

[Johnstone, Charles] *Chrysal; or the Adventures of a Guinea,* 7th edition, 4 vols. London, 1771.

Journals of the House of Commons.

Journals of the House of Lords.

[Junius] *The Letters of Junius,* ed. John Cannon. Oxford: Clarendon Press, and New York: Oxford University Press, 1978.

Juvenal and Persius: Loeb Classical Library, with translation by G.G. Ramsay. Cambridge, MA: Harvard University Press, 1961.

Langley, Thomas. *History and Antiquities of the Hundred of Desborough,* 1797.

[Morris, Robert] *Radical Adventurer: The Diaries of Robert Morris,* ed. J.E. Ross. Bath: Adams and Dart, 1971.

Mortimer, Thomas. *Every Man his Own Broker,* various editions.

[Pitt, William] *Correspondence of William Pitt, Earl of Chatham,* ed. William Stanhope Taylor and John Henry Pringle, 4 vols. London: John Murray, 1838–40.

Rabelais, François. *The Histories of Gargantua and Pantagruel,* trans. John M. Cohen. Franklin Center, PA: Franklin Library, 1982.

Records of the Honourable Society of Lincoln's Inn: Admissions, 2 vols. London: Lincoln's Inn, 1896.

[Reynolds, Frederick] *The Life and Times of Frederick Reynolds,* 2 vols. London: Henry Colburn, 1826.

[Rockingham] *Memoirs of the Marquis of Rockingham and his Contemporaries,* ed. George Thomas, Earl of Albemarle, 2 vols. London: Richard Bentley, 1852.

[Romilly, Samuel] *Memoirs of the Life of Samuel Romilly Written by Himself with a Selection of his Correspondence Written by his Sons,* 3 vols. 2nd edition. London: John Murray, 1840.

Sale Catalogues of Libraries of Eminent Persons, gen. ed. A.N.L. Munby, vol. 8, *Politicians,* ed. Seamus Deane. London: Mansell, Sotheby Parke, 1973.

[Sheridan, Richard] *The Dramatic Works of Richard Brinsley Sheridan,* ed. Cecil Price, 3 vols. Oxford: Clarendon Press, 1973.

[Stephen, James] *Memoirs of James Stephen, Written by Himself for the Use of his Children*, ed. Merle M. Bevington. London: Hogarth Press, 1954.

Stephens, Alexander. *Memoirs of John Horne Tooke, Interspersed with Original Documents*, 2 vols. London: 1813.

[Stevens, William Bagshaw] *The Journal of the Rev. William Bagshaw Stevens*, ed. Georgina Galbraith. Oxford: Clarendon Press, 1965.

[Suard, Jean-Baptiste] 'Lettres Inédites de Suard à Wilkes', ed. Gabriel Bono. *University of California Publications in Modern Philology*, 15 (1932).

'Two Welsh Correspondents of John Wilkes', ed. E. Alfred Jones. *Y Cymmrodor*, vol. 29.

[Walpole, Horace] *Horace Walpole's Journals of Visits to Country Seats*, ed. Paget J. Toynbee, Walpole Society, vol. 16, 1928.

——. *Memoirs of King George II*, ed. John Brooke, 3 vols. New Haven and London: Yale University Press, 1985.

——. *Memoirs of the Reign of King George the Third*, ed. G.F. Russell Barker, 4 vols. London: Lawrence and Bullen, 1894.

[——] *The Yale Edition of the Correspondence of Horace Walpole*, ed. W.S. Lewis *et al.*, 48 vols. New Haven: Yale University Press, 1937–83.

[Warburton, William] *Letters from the Reverend Dr. Warburton, Bishop of Gloucester, to the Hon. Charles Yorke, from 1752 to 1770*. London, 1812.

[——] *The Works of the Right Reverend William Warburton, Lord Bishop of Gloucester*, 7 vols. London, 1788–94.

[——] *A Selection from Unpublished Papers of the Right Reverend William Warburton, D.D., Late Lord Bishop of Gloucester*, ed. Francis Kilvert. London, 1841.

Warburton, William. *A View of Lord Bolingbroke's Philosophy; in Four Letters to a Friend*, 3 vols. London, 1754–55.

[Whitehead, Paul] *The Poems and Miscellaneous Compositions of Paul Whitehead; With Explanatory Notes on his Writings, and Life written by Capt. Edward Thompson*. London, 1767.

The Whole Proceedings on the King's Commission of the Peace, Oyer and Terminer, and Gaol-Delivery for the City of London; and also the Gaol-Delivery for the County of Middlesex; Held at Justice Hall in the Old Bailey. Sessions, November 1774–October 1775.

[Wilson, Thomas] *The Diaries of Thomas Wilson D.D., 1731–37 and 1750*, ed. C.L. S. Linnell. London: SPCK, 1964.

[Wilkes, John] *Some Bath Love Letters of John Wilkes, Esq.*, ed. Emanuel Green. Bath: George Gregory, 1918.

[——] *The Correspondence of John Wilkes and Charles Churchill*, ed. Edward H. Weatherly. New York: Columbia University Press, 1954.

[——] *The Correspondence of the Late John Wilkes with his Friends Printed from the Original Manuscripts in Which are Introduced Memoirs of his Life,* ed. John Almon, 5 vols. London: 1805.

[——] *Letters between the Duke of Grafton, the Earls of Halifax, Egremont, Chatham, Temple, and Talbot, Baron Bottetourt, Right Hon. Henry Bilson Legge, Right Hon. Sir John Cust, Bart. Mr. Charles Churchill, Monsieur Voltaire, the Abbé Winckelman, etc. etc. and John Wilkes, Esq. With Explanatory Notes.* London: 1769.

[——] *Letters from the Year 1774 to the Year 1796, of John Wilkes Esq. Addressed to his Daughter, the Late Miss Wilkes,* 4 vols. London, 1804.

[——] *Speeches of Mr. Wilkes in the House of Commons,* 3 vols, continuous pagination. London: 1786.

Wilkes, John and Thomas Potter. *An Essay on Woman: A Reconstruction of a Lost Book with a Historical Essay on the Writing, Printing, and Suppressing of this 'Blasphemous and Obscene' Work,* ed. Arthur H. Cash. New York: AMS Press, 2000.

Wollstonecraft, Mary. *A Vindication of the Rights of Woman,* 1792. London: Penguin, 1992.

Wraxall, N. William. *Historical Memoirs of My Own Time,* ed. Richard Askham. London: Kegan Paul, 1904.

III. Secondary Works Cited

Books

Andrew, Donna T. *Philanthropy and Police: London Charity in the Eighteenth Century.* Princeton, NJ: Princeton University Press, 1989.

Arnold, Walter. *The Life and Death of the Sublime Society of Beefsteaks.* London: Bradbury, Evans, 1871.

Ashe, Geoffrey. *The Hell-Fire Clubs: A History of Anti-Morality,* rev. edn. Stroud, Gloucestershire: Sutton, 2000.

Barker-Benfield, G.J. *The Culture of Sensibility: Sex and Society in Eighteenth-Century Britain.* Chicago: University of Chicago Press, 1992.

Barlow, Richard Burgess. *Citizenship and Conscience: A Study in the Theory and Practice of Religious Toleration in England during the Eighteenth Century.* Philadelphia: University of Pennsylvania Press, 1962.

Beckett, John. *The Rise and Fall of the Grenvilles: Dukes of Buckingham and Chandos, 1710 to 1921.* Manchester: Manchester University Press, 1994.

Bertelsen, Lance. *The Nonsense Club: Literature and Popular Culture, 1749–1764.* Oxford: Clarendon Press, and New York: Oxford University Press, 1986.

Biographical Dictionary of Modern British Radicals, ed. Joseph O. Baylen and Norbert J. Gossman, vol. 1 (1770–1830). Hassocks, Sussex: Harvester Press, and Atlantic Highlands, NJ: Humanities Press, 1979.

Black, Jeremy. *Pitt the Elder*. Cambridge and New York: Cambridge University Press, 1992.

Bleackley, Horace. *Ladies Fair and Frail: Sketches of the Demi-Monde during the Eighteenth Century*. London: John Lane, 1909.

——. *Life of John Wilkes*. London: John Lane, 1917.

Bradley, James E. *Religion, Revolution and English Radicalism: Nonconformity in Eighteenth-Century Politics and Society*. Cambridge and New York: Cambridge University Press, 1990.

Brewer, John. *Party Ideology and Popular Politics at the Accession of George III*. Cambridge and New York: Cambridge University Press, 1976.

——. *The Pleasures of the Imagination: English Culture in the Eighteenth Century*. London: HarperCollins, and New York: Farrar Straus and Giroux, 1997.

——. *A Sentimental Murder: Love and Madness in the Eighteenth Century*. New York: Farrar Straus and Giroux, 2004.

—— and John Styles, eds, *An Ungovernable People: The English and Their Law in the Seventeenth and Eighteenth Centuries*. London: Hutchinson, and New Brunswick, NJ: Rutgers University Press, 1980.

Broadley, A.M. *Brother John Wilkes, MP; Alderman, Chamberlain, and Lord Mayor of London, as Freemason, 'Buck', 'Leech' and 'Beefsteak'*. Weymouth, Dorset: Sherren, 1914.

Brooke, John. *The Chatham Administration, 1766–1768*. London: Macmillan, and New York: St Martin's Press, 1956.

Brown, Wallace Cable. *Charles Churchill: Poet, Rake, and Rebel*. New York: Greenwood Press, 1968 (originally published 1953).

Burtt, Shelley. *Virtue Transformed: Political Argument in England, 1688–1740*. Cambridge and New York: Cambridge University Press, 1992.

Callender, Ann, ed. *Godly Mayfair,* London: Grosvenor Chapel, 1980.

Carter, Philip. *Men and the Emergence of Polite Society, Britain, 1660–1800*. London and New York: Longman, 2001.

Cash, Arthur H. *Laurence Sterne: The Early and Middle Years*. London: Methuen, 1975.

——. *Laurence Sterne: The Later Years*. London and New York: Methuen, 1986.

Catalogue of Political and Personal Satires Preserved in the Department of Prints and Drawings in the British Museum, vol. 4 (1761–1770), ed. Frederic George Stephens, and vol. 5 (1771–1783), ed. M. Dorothy George. London: British Museum, 1883–1935.

Champion, J.A.I. *The Pillars of Priestcraft Shaken: The Church of England and Its Enemies, 1660–1730*. Cambridge and New York: Cambridge University Press, 1992.

Christie, Ian R. *Wilkes, Wyvill and Reform: The Parliamentary Reform Movement in British Politics, 1760–1785.* London: Macmillan, and New York: St Martin's Press, 1962.

Clark, Anna. *Scandal: The Sexual Politics of the British Constitution.* Princeton, NJ: Princeton University Press, 2004.

Clark, J.C.D. *English Society, 1660–1832: Religion, Ideology, and Politics during the Ancien Regime,* rev. edn, Cambridge and New York: Cambridge University Press, 2000.

Cohen, Michèle. *Fashioning Masculinity: National Identity and Language in the Eighteenth Century.* London and New York: Routledge, 1996.

Colley, Linda. *Britons: Forging the Nation, 1707–1837.* New Haven and London: Yale University Press, 1992.

Crowley, John E. *The Invention of Comfort: Sensibilities and Design in Early Modern Britain and Early America.* Baltimore: Johns Hopkins University Press, 2000.

Cust, Lionel (compiler). *History of the Society of Dilettanti,* ed. Sidney Colvin. London: Macmillan, 1898.

Dashwood, Francis. *The Dashwoods of West Wycombe.* London: Aurum Press, 1987.

Davidoff, Leonore, and Catherine Hall, *Family Fortunes: Men and Women of the English Middle Class, 1780–1850.* London: Hutchinson, and Chicago: University of Chicago Press, 1987.

Dilke, Charles Wentworth. *The Papers of a Critic.* 2 vols, London: John Murray, 1875.

Donald, Diana. *The Age of Caricature: Satirical Prints in the Reign of George III,* New Haven and London: Yale University Press, 1996.

Eagles, Robin. *Francophilia in English Society.* Basingstoke: Macmillan, and New York: St Martin's Press, 2000.

Earle, Peter. *The Making of the English Middle Class: Business, Society and Family Life in London, 1660–1730.* London: Methuen, and Berkeley: University of California Press, 1989.

Elofson, W.M. *The Rockingham Connection and the Second Founding of the Whig Party, 1768–1773.* Montreal and Kingston: McGill-Queen's University Press, 1996.

Finn, Margot C. *The Character of Credit: Personal Debt in English Culture, 1740–1914.* Cambridge and New York: Cambridge University Press, 2003.

Fletcher, Anthony. *Gender, Sex and Subordination in England, 1500–1800.* New Haven and London: Yale University Press, 1995.

Fox Bourne, H.R. *English Merchants: Memoirs in Illustration of the Progress of British Commerce,* 2 vols, London: Richard Bentley, 1866.

Gibbs, Robert. *A History of Aylesbury.* [self-published:] Aylesbury, 1884.

Gilmour, Ian. *Riot, Risings and Revolution: Governance and Violence in Eighteenth-Century England.* London: Pimlico, 1993.

Gray, Francine du Plessix. *At Home with the Marquis de Sade: A Life.* London and New York: Penguin, 1998.

Gunn, J.A.W. *Beyond Liberty and Property: The Process of Self-Recognition in Eighteenth-Century Political Thought.* Montreal and Kingston: McGill-Queen's University Press, 1983.

Haggerty, George E. *Men in Love: Masculinity and Sexuality in the Eighteenth Century.* New York: Columbia University Press, 1999.

Hamilton, Adrian. *The Infamous Essay on Woman; or John Wilkes Seated between Vice and Virtue.* London: André Deutsch, 1972.

Hanley, Hugh, *The Prebendal, Aylesbury: A History.* Aylesbury: Ginn, 1986.

Hay, Carla H. *James Burgh: Spokesman for Reform in Hanoverian England,* Washington, DC: University Press of America, 1979.

Haydon, Colin. *Anti-Catholicism in Eighteenth-Century England, c. 1714–80: A Political and Social Study.* Manchester: Manchester University Press, 1993.

Hellmuth, Eckhart, ed. *The Transformation of Political Culture: England and Germany in the Late Eighteenth Century.* London: German Historical Institute; Oxford: Oxford University Press, 1990.

Hibbert, Christopher. *King Mob: The Story of Lord George Gordon and the London Riots of 1780.* London: Longmans Green, and Cleveland: World Publishing Company, 1958.

Hill, Bridget, *The Republican Virago: The Life and Times of Catharine Macaulay, Historian.* Oxford: Clarendon Press, and New York: Oxford University Press, 1992.

Hitchcock, Tim. *English Sexualities, 1700–1800.* Basingstoke: Macmillan, and New York: St Martin's Press, 1997.

—— and Michèle Cohen, eds, *English Masculinities, 1660–1800.* London and New York: Longman, 1999.

Hole, Robert. *Pulpits, Politics and Public Order in England, 1760–1832.* Cambridge and New York: Cambridge University Press, 1989.

Hoppit, Julian. *Risk and Failure in English Business, 1700–1800.* Cambridge and New York: Cambridge University Press, 1987.

Hunt, John. *Religious Thought in England,* 3 vols. London: Strahan, 1870–73.

Hunt, Lynn. *The Family Romance of the French Revolution.* London: Routledge, and Berkeley: University of California Press, 1992.

——, ed. *The Invention of Pornography: Obscenity and the Origins of Modernity, 1500–1800.* New York: Zone Books, 1993.

Hunt, Margaret. *The Middling Sort: Commerce, Gender, and the Family in England, 1680–1780.* Berkeley: University of California Press, 1996.

Hunt, Tamara L. *Defining John Bull: Political Caricature and National Identity in Late Georgian England.* Aldershot: Ashgate, 2003.

Ierson, Henry. *History of an English Presbyterian Church: A Discourse Delivered at the Chapel in the Carter Lane, October 13, 1861*. London: Edward T. Whitfield, 1861.

John Ingamells, *National Portrait Gallery: Mid-Georgian Portraits, 1760–1790*. London: National Portrait Galley, 2004.

Ingram, Robert Glynn, 'Nation, Empire, and Church: Thomas Secker, Anglican Identity, and Public Life in Georgian Britain, 1700–1770'. PhD dissertation, University of Virginia, 2002.

Jacob, Margaret C. *The Radical Enlightenment: Pantheists, Freemasons and Republicans*. London: George Allen and Unwin, 1981.

Kates, Gary. *Monsieur d'Eon is a Woman: A Tale of Political Intrigue and Sexual Masquerade*. New York: Basic Books, 1995.

Kelly, James. *That Damn'd Thing Called Honour: Duelling in Ireland, 1570–1860*. Cork: Cork University Press, 1995.

Kemp, Betty. *Sir Francis Dashwood: An Eighteenth-Century Independent*. London: Macmillan, and New York: St Martin's Press, 1967.

Kiernan, V.G. *The Duel in European History: Honour and the Reign of Aristocracy*. Oxford: Oxford University Press, 1988.

Klein, Lawrence E. *Shaftesbury and the Culture of Politeness: Moral Discourse and Cultural Politics in Early Eighteenth-Century England*. Cambridge and New York: Cambridge University Press, 1994.

Kors, Alan Charles. *D'Holbach's Coterie: An Enlightenment in Paris*. Princeton, NJ: Princeton University Press, 1976.

Kramnick, Isaac. *Republicanism and Bourgeois Radicalism: Political Ideology in Late Eighteenth-Century England and America*. Ithaca, NY: Cornell University Press, 1990.

Kronenberger, Louis. *The Extraordinary Mr. Wilkes: His Life and Times*. London: New English Library, and Garden City, NY: Doubleday, 1974.

Langford, Paul. *The First Rockingham Administration, 1765–1766*. London: Oxford University Press, 1973.

——. *A Polite and Commercial People: England 1727–1783*. Oxford and New York: Oxford University Press, 1989.

——. *Public Life and the Propertied Englishman, 1689–1798*. Oxford: Clarendon Press, and New York: Oxford University Press, 1991

Lawson, Philip. *George Grenville: A Political Life*. Oxford: Clarendon Press, and New York: Oxford University Press, 1984.

Lewis, Judith S. *Sacred to Female Patriotism: Gender, Class, and Politics in Late Georgian Britain*. New York and London: Routledge, 2003.

Lloyd Hart, V.E. *John Wilkes and the Foundling Hospital at Aylesbury, 1759–1768*. Aylesbury: HM&M, 1979.

Lock, F.P. *Edmund Burke*, vol. 1 (1730–1784). Oxford: Clarendon Press, and New York: Oxford University Press, 1998.

Lund, Roger D. ed. *The Margins of Orthodoxy: Heterodox Writing and Cultural Response, 1660–1750*. Cambridge and New York: Cambridge University Press, 1999.

Maccubbin, Robert Purks, ed. *'Tis Nature's Fault: Unauthorized Sexuality during the Enlightenment*. Cambridge and New York: Cambridge University Press, 1987.

MacLean, James N.M. *Reward is Secondary: The Life of a Political Adventurer and an Inquiry into the Mystery of 'Junius'*. London: Hodder and Stoughton, 1963.

Maloney, William J. *George and John Armstrong of Castleton: Two Eighteenth-Century Medical Pioneers*. Edinburgh and London: E. and S. Livingstone, 1954.

Martin, Peter. *A Life of James Boswell*. London: Phoenix Press, and New Haven: Yale University Press, 2000.

Masters, Betty. *The Chamberlain of the City of London, 1237–1987*. London: Corporation of London, 1988.

Morwood, James. *The Life and Works of Richard Brinsley Sheridan*. Edinburgh: Scottish Academic Press, 1985.

Muller, Jerry Z. *Adam Smith in His Time and Ours: Designing the Decent Society*. New York: Free Press, 1993.

Namier, Lewis, and John Brooke. *The History of Parliament: The House of Commons, 1754–1790*, 3 vols. London: HMSO, and New York: Oxford University Press, for the History of Parliament Trust, 1964.

Namier, Lewis. *The Structure of Politics at the Accession of George III*, 2nd edn. London: Macmillan, and New York: St Martin's Press, 1957

Nichols, R.H. and F.A. Wray. *The History of the Foundling Hospital*. London: Oxford University Press, 1935.

Nixon, Edna. *Royal Spy: The Strange Case of the Chevalier D'Eon*. New York: Reynal, 1965.

Nobbe, George. *The North Briton: A Study in Political Propaganda*. New York: Columbia University Press, 1939.

Norris, John. *Shelburne and Reform*. London: Macmillan, and New York: St Martin's Press, 1963.

Norton, Rictor. *Mother Clap's Molly House: The Gay Subculture in England, 1700–1830*. London: GMP, 1992.

Oxford Dictionary of National Biography. Oxford: Oxford University Press, 2004.

Paulson, Ronald. *Hogarth: His Life, Art, and Times*, 2 vols, New Haven and London: Yale University Press, 1971.

Peters, Marie. *Pitt and Popularity: The Patriot Minister and London Opinion during the Seven Years' War*. Oxford: Clarendon Press, and New York: Oxford University Press, 1980.

Pinks, William J. *The History of Clerkenwell*, 2nd edn. London: Charles Herbert, 1882.

Pocock, J.G.A. *The Machiavellian Moment: Florentine Political Thought and the Atlantic Republican Tradition*. Princeton, NJ: Princeton University Press, 1975.

——. *Virtue, Commerce and History: Essays on Political Thought and History, Chiefly in the Eighteenth Century*. Cambridge and New York: Cambridge University Press, 1975.

Porter, Roy. *The Creation of the Modern World: The Untold Story of the British Enlightenment*. New York and London: Norton, 2000.

Postgate, Raymond. *That Devil Wilkes*. London: Constable, and New York: Vanguard, 1930.

Potter, Tiffany. *Honest Sins: Georgian Libertinism and the Plays and Novels of Henry Fielding*. Montreal and Kingston: McGill-Queen's University Press, 1999.

Potts, Alex. *Flesh and the Ideal: Winckelmann and the Origins of Art History*. New Haven and London: Yale University Press, 1994.

Price, Richard. *British Society, 1680–1880: Dynamism, Containment and Change*. Cambridge and New York: Cambridge University Press, 1999.

Redford, Bruce. *The Converse of the Pen: Acts of Intimacy in the Eighteenth-Century Familiar Letter*. Chicago: University of Chicago Press, 1986.

[Reynolds, Frederick] *The Life and Times of Frederick Reynolds. Written by Himself*, 2 vols, London: Henry Colburn, 1827.

Rodger, N.A.M. *The Insatiable Earl: A Life of John Montagu, 4th Earl of Sandwich, 1718–1792*. New York and London: Norton, 1993.

Rogers, Nicholas. *Whigs and Cities: Popular Politics in the Age of Walpole and Pitt*. Oxford: Clarendon Press, 1989.

Rudé, George. *Wilkes and Liberty: A Social Study of 1763 to 1774*. Oxford: Clarendon Press, 1962.

Rupp, Gordon. *Religion in England, 1688–1791*. Oxford: Clarendon Press, and New York: Oxford University Press, 1986.

Sack, James J. *From Jacobite to Conservative: Reaction and Orthodoxy in Britain, c. 1760–1832*. Cambridge and New York: Cambridge University Press, 1993.

Sainsbury, John. *Disaffected Patriots: London Supporters of Revolutionary America, 1769–1782*. Montreal and Kingston: McGill-Queen's University Press, 1987.

Sennett, Richard. *The Fall of Public Man*. New York and London: Norton, 1992.

Somerville, Thomas *My Own Life and Times*. Edinburgh, 1861.

Stone, Lawrence. *Broken Lives: Separation and Divorce in England, 1660–1857*. Oxford and New York: Oxford University Press, 1993.

Sutherland, Lucy S. *The City of London and the Opposition to Government, 1768–1774: A Study in the Rise of Metropolitan Radicalism*. London: University of London, Athlone Press, 1959.

Survey of London, gen. eds F.H.W. Sheppard *et al.* (1900– , 41 vols as of 1983), vol. 27: *Spitalfields and Mile End New Town*. London: London County Council and the Committee for the Survey of the Memorials of Greater London, 1957.

Telfer, J. Buchan. *The Strange Career of the Chevalier d'Eon de Beaumont*. London: Longmans Green, 1885.

Thomas, D.O. *The Honest Mind: The Thought and Work of Richard Price*. Oxford: Clarendon Press, 1977.

Thomas, Peter D.G. *George III: King and Politicians, 1760–1770*. Manchester, Manchester University Press, 2002.

——. *John Wilkes: A Friend to Liberty*. Oxford: Clarendon Press, and New York: Oxford University Press, 1996.

Thompson, E.P. *Customs in Common*. London: Merlin, and New York: New Press, 1993.

——. *The Making of the English Working Class*, rev. edn. London: Penguin, 1980.

Thompson, Grace E. *The Cyprian: The Life of a Covent Garden Lady*. London: Hutchinson, 1932.

Timbs, John. *Clubs and Club Life in London*. London: Chatto and Windus, 1908.

Treloar, William Purdie. *Wilkes and the City*. London: John Murray, 1917.

Trench, Charles Chevenix. *Portrait of a Patriot: A Biography of John Wilkes*. Edinburgh and London: William Blackwood, 1962.

Trumbach, Randolph. *Sex and the Gender Revolution*. vol. 1: *Heterosexuality and the Third Gender in Enlightenment London*. Chicago: University of Chicago Press, 1998.

Turner, David M. *Fashioning Adultery: Gender, Sex and Civility in England, 1660–1740*. Cambridge and New York: Cambridge University Press, 2002.

Turner, James Grantham. *Libertines and Radicals in Early Modern London: Sexuality, Politics and Literary Culture, 1630–1685*. Cambridge: Cambridge University Press, 2002.

Van Eijnatten, Joris, *Mutua Christianorum Tolerantia: Irenicism and Toleration in the Netherlands: The Strinstra Affair, 1740–1745*. Florence: Leo S. Olschki, 1998.

Vickery, Amanda. *The Gentleman's Daughter: Women's Lives in Georgian England*. New Haven and London: Yale University Press, 1998.

Wahrman, Dror. *Imagining the Middle Class: The Political Representation of Class in Britain, c. 1780–1840*. Cambridge and New York: Cambridge University Press, 1995.

Warner, Marina. *Alone of All Her Sex: the Myth and Cult of the Virgin Mary*. London: Weidenfeld and Nicolson, and New York: Knopf, 1976.

Watts, Michael R. *The Dissenters*, vol. 1: *From the Reformation to the French Revolution*. Oxford: Clarendon Press, 1978.

Weber, Harold. *The Restoration Rake-Hero: Transformations in Sexual Understanding in Seventeenth-Century England*. Madison: University of Wisconsin Press, 1986.

Western, J.R. *The English Militia in the Eighteenth Century: The Story of a Political Issue, 1660–1802*. London: Routledge and Kegan Paul, 1965.

Whiteley, William T. *Artists and their Friends in England, 1700–1799,* 2 vols. New York and London: Benjamin Blom, 1968.

Williamson, Audrey. *Wilkes: 'A Friend to Liberty'.* London: George Allen and Unwin, 1974.

Wilson, Kathleen. *The Sense of the People: Politics, Culture and Imperialism in England, 1715–1785.* Cambridge and New York: Cambridge University Press, 1995.

Wilson, Walter. *The History and Antiquities of Dissenting Houses in London, Westminster and Southwark,* 4 vols. London, 1808–1814.

Articles

Andrew, Donna T. '"Adultery à-la-Mode": Privilege, the Law and Attitudes to Adultery 1770–1809', *History,* 82 (1997).

——. 'The Code of Honour and its Critics: The Opposition to Duelling in England, 1700–1850', *Social History,* 5 (1980).

Aston, Nigel, 'Horne and Heterodoxy: The Defence of Anglican Beliefs in the Late Enlightenment', *English Historical Review,* 108 (1993).

Banister, Judith. '"In the Cause of Liberty": A Cup and Cover in the Mansion House'. *Country Life,* 170 (1981).

Beatty, Joseph M. 'Mrs. Montagu, Churchill, and Miss Cheere', *Modern Languages Notes,* 41 (1926).

Beckett, Ian. 'Wilkes and the Militia, 1759–1763', *Army Quarterly and Defence Journal,* 112 (1982).

Boucé, Paul-Gabriel. 'Chthonic and Pelagic Metaphorization in Eighteenth-Century English Erotica', in *'Tis Nature's Fault: Unauthorized Sexuality during the Enlightenment,* ed. Robert Purks Maccubbin. Cambridge and New York: Cambridge University Press, 1987.

Bredvold, Louis I. 'The Contributions of John Wilkes to the *Gazette Littéraire de l'Europe'. University of Michigan Contributions in Modern Philology,* 15 (February 1950).

Brewer, John. 'Commercialization and Politics', in *The Birth of a Consumer Society: The Commercialization of Eighteenth-Century England,* ed. Neil McKendrick *et al.* Bloomington: Indiana University Press, 1982.

——. 'English Radicalism in the Age of George III', in *Three British Revolutions, 1641, 1688, 1776,* ed. J.G.A. Pocock. Princeton, NJ: Princeton University Press, 1980.

——. 'This, That and the Other: Public, Social and Private in the Seventeenth and Eighteenth Centuries', in *Shifting the Boundaries; Transformation of the Languages of Public and Private in the Eighteenth Century,* ed. Dario Castiglione and Lesley Sharpe. Exeter: Exeter University Press, 1995.

——. 'The Wilkites and the Law: 1763–74: A Study of Radical Notions of Governance', in *An Ungovernable People: the English and their Law in the Seventeenth and Eighteenth Centuries*, ed. John Brewer and John Styles. London: Hutchinson, and New Brunswick, NJ: Rutgers University Press, 1980.

Campbell, Colin. 'Understanding Traditional and Modern Patterns of Consumption in Eighteenth-Century England: A Character-Action Approach', *Consumption and the World of Goods*, ed. John Brewer and Roy Porter. London and New York: Routledge, 1993.

Cash, Arthur H. 'Goldberg Variation', *The Age of Johnson*, 13 (2002).

——. 'Sterne, Hall, Libertinism, and a *Sentimental Journey*', *The Age of Johnson*, 12 (2000).

——. 'Wilkes, Baxter, and D'Holbach at Leiden and Utrecht: An Answer to G.S. Rousseau', *The Age of Johnson*, 7 (1996).

Christie, Ian R. 'The Wilkites and the General Election of 1774', in his *Myth and Reality in Late Eighteenth-Century British Politics and Other Papers*, London: Macmillan, and Berkeley: University of California Press, 1970.

Clark, Anna. 'The Chevalier d'Eon and Wilkes: Masculinity and Politics in the Eighteenth Century', *Eighteenth-Century Studies*, 32 (1998).

Cohen, Michèle. 'Manliness, Effeminacy and the French: Gender and the Construction of National Character in Eighteenth-Century England', in *English Masculinities 1600–1800*, ed. Tim Hitchcock and Michèle Cohen. London and New York: Longman 1999.

Colley, Linda. 'The Apotheosis of George III: Loyalty, Royalty and the British Nation, 1760–1820', *Past and Present*, 102 (1984).

——. 'Eighteenth-Century English Radicalism before Wilkes', *Transactions of the Royal Historical Society*, 5th series, 31 (1981).

Conlin, Jonathan G.W. 'High Art and Low Politics: A New Perspective on John Wilkes', *Huntington Library Quarterly*, 64 (2001).

Crompton, Louis. '"An Army of Lovers": The Sacred Band of Thebes', *History Today*, 44 (November 1994).

Dell, Alan. 'A Political Agent at Work in Eighteenth-Century Aylesbury', *Records of Buckinghamshire*, 30 (1988).

Devereaux, Simon. 'The City and the Sessions Paper: "Public Justice" in London, 1770–1800', *Journal of British Studies*, 35 (1996).

Ditchfield, G. M., 'The Subscription Issue in British Parliamentary Politics, 1772–79', *Parliamentary History*, 7, part 1 (1988).

Emerson, Roger L. 'Latitudinarianism and the English Deists', in *Deism, Masonry, and the Enlightenment: Essays Honoring Alfred Owen Aldridge*, ed. J.A. Leo Lemay. Newark: University of Delaware Press, 1987.

Foyster, Elizabeth. 'Boys will be Boys? Manhood and Aggression, 1660–1800', in *English Masculinities*, ed. Hitchcock and Cohen.

Freud, Sigmund. 'A Childhood Recollection from *Dichtung und Wahreit'*, *The Standard Edition of the Complete Psychological Works of Sigmund Freud*, ed. James Strachey, 24 vols. London: Hogarth Press, 1968 (repr.), vol. 17.

Gascoigne, John. 'Anglican Latitudinarianism and Political Radicalism in the Late Eighteenth Century', *History*, 71 (1986).

Gold, Joel J. '"Buried Alive": Charlotte Forman in Grub Street', *Eighteenth-Century Life*, new series, 8 (1982).

——. 'The Unlikely Visitor; John Wilkes in the Highlands', *Notes and Queries*, 224 (1979).

Gregory, Jeremy. '*Homo Religiosus*: Masculinity and Religion in the Long Eighteenth Century', in *English Masculinities*, ed. Hitchcock and Cohen.

Hartley, Lodwick. 'Sterne's Eugenius as Indiscreet Author: The Literary Career of John Hall-Stevenson', *PMLA*, 86 (1971).

Harvey, Karen. '"The Majesty of the Masculine Form": Multiplicity and Male Bodies in Eighteenth-Century Erotica', in *English Masculinities*, ed. Hitchcock and Cohen.

Hill, Bridget, 'Daughter and Mother: Some New Light on Catharine Macaulay and her Family', *British Journal for Eighteenth-Century Studies*, 22 (1999).

Hoppit, Julian. 'Attitudes to Credit in Britain, 1680–1790'. *Historical Journal*, 33 (1990).

——. 'Financial Crises in Eighteenth-Century England'. *Economic History Review*, 2nd Series, 39 (1986).

——. 'The Use and Abuse of Credit in Eighteenth-Century England', in *Business Life and Public Policy: Essays in Honour of D.C. Coleman*, ed. Neil McKendrick and R.B. Outhwaite. Cambridge and New York: Cambridge University Press, 1986.

Innes, Joanna. 'The King's Bench Prison in the Later Eighteenth Century: Law, Authority and Order in a London Debtors' Prison', in *An Ungovernable People*, ed. Brewer and Styles.

——. 'Politics and Morals: The Reformation of Manners Movement in Later Eighteenth-Century England', in *The Transformation of Political Culture: England and Germany in the Late Eighteenth Century*, ed. Eckhart Hellmuth. London: German Historical Institute; Oxford: Oxford University Press, 1990.

'John Wilkes in Italy'. *Notes and Queries*, 4th Series, 102 (1869).

Lund, Roger D. 'Guilt by Association: The Atheist Cabal and the Rise of the Public Sphere in Augustan England', *Albion*, 34 (2002).

——. 'Irony as Subversion: Thomas Woolston and the Crime of Wit', in *The Margins of Orthodoxy: Heterodox Writing and Cultural Response, 1660–1750*, ed. Roger D. Lund. Cambridge and New York: Cambridge University Press, 1995.

McCracken, George, 'John Wilkes, Humanist', *Philological Quarterly*, 4 (1923).

Miller, Peter N. '"Freethinking" and "Freedom of Thought" in Eighteenth-Century Britain', *Historical Journal*, 36 (1993).

Money, John. 'The Masonic Moment; Or Ritual, Replica, and Credit: John Wilkes, the Macaroni Parson, and the Making of the Middle-Class Mind', *Journal of British Studies*, 32 (1993).

O'Connell, Laura Stevenson. 'The Elizabethan Bourgeois Hero-Tale', in *After the Reformation: Essays in Honor of J.H. Hexter*, ed. Barbara C. Malament. Manchester: Manchester University Press, 1980.

Paulson, Ronald. 'Henry Fielding and the Problem of Deism', in *Margins of Orthodoxy*, ed. Lund.

Porter, Roy. 'The Enlightenment in England', in *The Enlightenment in National Context*, ed. Roy Porter and Mikulás Teich. Cambridge and New York: Cambridge University Press, 1981.

Richey, Russell E. 'The Origins of British Radicalism: The Changing Rationale for Dissent', *Eighteenth-Century Studies*, 7 (1974).

Rogers, Nicholas. 'Crowds and People in the Gordon Riots', in *Transformation of Political Culture*, ed. Hellmuth.

——. 'Pigott's Private Eye: Radicalism and Sexual Scandal in Eighteenth-Century England', *Journal of the Canadian Historical Association*, new series, 4 (1993).

Rousseau, G. S. '"In the House of Madam Vander Tasse, on the Long Bridge": A Homosocial University Club in Early Modern Europe', in Kent Gerard and Gert Hekma, eds, *The Pursuit of Sodomy: Male Homosexuality in Renaissance and Enlightenment Europe*. New York and London: Harrington Park Press, 1989.

——. 'Priapic Passages and "Trading in Trifles": Penis and Pornography in the Eighteenth Century', in *The Eighteenth-Century Body: Art, History, Literature, Medicine*, ed. Angelica Goodden. Bern: Peter Lang, 2002.

——. 'The Sorrows of Priapus: Anticlericalism, Homosocial Desire, and Richard Payne Knight', in *Sexual Underworlds of the Enlightenment*, ed. G.S. Rousseau and Roy Porter. Chapel Hill: University of North Carolina Press, 1988.

Russell, Gillian. '"Faro's Daughters": Female Gamesters, Politics, and the Discourse of Finance in 1790s Britain', *Eighteenth-Century Studies*, 33 (2000).

Russo, Elena. 'Sociability, Cartesianism, and Nostalgia in Libertine Discourse', *Eighteenth-Century Studies*, 30 (1997).

Sainsbury, John. 'Wilkes and Libertinism', *Studies in Eighteenth-Century Culture*, 26 (1998).

Schaeffer, Neil. 'Charles Churchill's Political Journalism', *Eighteenth-Century Studies*, 9 (1976).

Shields, David S. 'Anglo-American Clubs: Their Wit, Their Heterodoxy, Their Sedition', *The William and Mary Quarterly*, 3rd Series, 60 (1994).

Simpson, Antony E. 'Dandelions on the Field of Honor: Dueling, the Middle Classes, and the Law in Nineteenth-Century England', *Criminal Justice History*, 9 (1988).

Stephanson, Raymond. '"Epicœne Friendship": Understanding Male Friendship in the Early Eighteenth Century, with some Speculations about Pope', *The Eighteenth Century: Theory and Interpretations*, 38 (1997).

Statt, Daniel. 'The Case of the Mohocks: Rake Violence in Augustan London', *Social History*, 20 (1995).

Thomas, Peter D.G. '"Bill of Rights Morris": A Welsh Wilkite Radical and Rogue – Robert Morris (1743–1793)', in *Hanoverian Britain and Empire: Essays in Memory of Philip Lawson*, ed. Stephen Taylor, Richard Connors, and Clyve Jones. Woodbridge: Boydell Press, 1998.

Tosh, John. 'The Old Adam and the New Man: Emerging Themes in the History of English Masculinities, 1750–1850', in *English Masculinities*, ed. Hitchcock and Cohen.

Trumbach, Randolph. 'Sex, Gender, and Sexual Identity in Modern Culture: Male Sodomy and Female Prostitution in Enlightenment London', *Journal of the History of Sexuality*, 2 (1991).

——. 'Erotic Fantasy and Male Libertinism in Enlightenment England', in *The Invention of Pornography: Obscenity and the Origins of Modernity, 1500–1800*, ed. Lynn Hunt. New York: Zone Books, 1993.

Turner, James G. 'The Properties of Libertinism', in *'Tis Nature's Fault: Unauthorized Sexuality during the Enlightenment*, ed. Robert Purks Maccubbin. Cambridge: Cambridge University Press, 1987.

——. 'The Sexual Politics of Landscape: Images of Venus in Eighteenth-Century English Poetry and Landscape Gardening', *Studies in Eighteenth-Century Culture*, 11 (1982).

Wahrman, Dror. '*Percy's* Prologue: From Gender Play to Gender Panic in Eighteenth-Century England', *Past and Present*, 159 (May 1998).

Werkmeister, Lucyle. 'Notes for a Revised Life of William Jackson', *Notes and Queries*, 206 (1961).

West, Shearer. 'Libertinism and the Ideology of Male Friendship in the Portraits of the Society of Dilettanti', *Eighteenth-Century Life*, new series, 16 (1992).

——. 'Wilkes's Squint: Synedochic Physiognomy and Political Identity in Eighteenth-Century Print Culture', *Eighteenth-Century Studies*, 33 (1999).

Wilson, Kathleen. 'Empire, Trade and Popular Politics in Mid-Hanoverian Britain: The Case of Admiral Vernon', *Past and Present*, 121 (1988).

Winton, Calhoun. 'John Wilkes and "An Essay on Woman"', in *A Provision of Human Nature: Essays on Fielding and Others in Honor of Miriam Austin Locke*, ed. Donald Kay. Tuscaloosa: University of Alabama Press, 1977.

Index

Entries in *italics* refer to publications, paintings and foreign terms.